'TRIUMPHS OF ENGLISH'

London, College of Arms, MS Vincent 152, p. 178. Prince Ferdinand of Spain, Archduke of Austria, dining on the day of his Investiture as a Knight of the Garter. To his right sit Morley and Sir William Hussey; to his left Edward Lee and Sir Thomas Wriothesley. Reproduced by kind permission of the College of Arms.

‘TRIUMPHS OF ENGLISH’
HENRY PARKER, LORD MORLEY
Translator to the Tudor Court

New Essays in Interpretation
edited by
MARIE AXTON AND JAMES P. CARLEY

Introduction by
DAVID STARKEY

THE BRITISH LIBRARY

First published 2000 by
The British Library
96 Euston Road
London NW1 2DB

British Library Cataloguing in Publication Data
A CIP record is available from The British Library

ISBN 0 7123 4649 X

Designed by John Trevitt
Typeset by Norman Tilley Graphics, Northampton
Printed in England by Hobbs the Printers, Southampton

Jeremy Frank Maule
11 August 1952-
25 November 1998

τίς ποτε σᾶ σύριγγι μελίξεται ὦ τριπόθητε;
τίς δ' ἐπὶ σοῖς καλάμοις θήσει στόμα; τίς θρασὺς οὕτως;
εἰσέτι γὰρ πνείει τὰ σὰ χείλεα καὶ τὸ σὸν ἆσθμα,
ἀχὰ δ' ἐν δονάκεσσι τεᾶς ἔτι βόσκετ' ἀοιδᾶς.

Who will make music on your pipe, oh thrice
beloved man? Who will put his mouth to your
reeds? Who is so bold? For your lips and
breath live yet, and in these straws the
sound of your song lives on.

Portrait of Henry Parker, Lord Morley, by Albrecht Dürer. Reproduced by kind permission of the Trustees of the British Museum.

CONTENTS

EPILOGUE

APPENDIXES: TEXTS

NOTES ON CONTRIBUTORS

JEREMY MAULE, Fellow of Trinity College and Newton Trust Lecturer in English at the University of Cambridge, was co-editor, with Adrian Poole, of the *Oxford Book of Classical Verse in Translation*. He founded and was general editor of the series Renaissance Texts from Manuscript. His first love was manuscript studies and he shared his many discoveries of works by Ford, Elizabeth Carey, Marvell and Traherne with an enthusiasm and generosity which are remembered by his friends, colleagues and the generation of students he inspired and inspires.

MARIE AXTON, until 1999 Lecturer in English at the University of Cambridge, is a founder and general editor of the Tudor Interlude series and author of *The Queen's Two Bodies*. Her most recent published work is on Shakespeare's *Sonnets* and early French illustrators of Petrarch.

JAMES P. CARLEY, Professor of English, York University, Ontario, is editor of John of Glastonbury's chronicle and has published a number of other documents relating to Glastonbury Abbey. His most recent books, *The Libraries of Henry VIII* and *Glastonbury and the Arthurian Tradition*, will appear in 2000.

DAVID STARKEY is a Fellow of Fitzwilliam College, Cambridge. He has written extensively on political faction in the court of Henry VIII, is general editor of the Post Mortem Inventory of Henry VIII project, and is completing a new biography of Henry VIII.

JULIA BOFFEY is a Reader in Medieval Studies in the School of English and Drama, Queen Mary and Westfield College, University of London. Her research interests include the history of the book in the late medieval and early modern periods, and later Middle English literature, especially lyrics. She is currently working on a collaborative revision of *The Index of Middle English Verse*.

A. S. G. EDWARDS was Helen Cam Fellow at Girton College, Cambridge, in 1998-9. His interests include the history of the book in Britain in the medieval and Renaissance periods, and the history of the study of Middle English. He is general editor of *The Index of Middle English Prose* and currently collaborating on a revision of *The Index of Middle English Verse*.

KENNETH R. BARTLETT, Professor of History and Renaissance Studies, University of Toronto, is author of *The English in Italy, 1525-1558: A Study in Culture and Politics* and *The Civilization of the Italian Renaissance*. He is the founding Director of the University of Toronto Art Centre.

RICHARD REX is a Lecturer in Church History, Cambridge University, and a Fellow of Queens' College. He is the author of *The Theology of John Fisher* and of *Henry VIII and the English Reformation*.

DAVID R. CARLSON, Professor of English, University of Ottawa, has published on Chaucer, the Pearl poet, and John Skelton. His most recent book is *English Humanist Books*.

JAMES SIMPSON is Professor of Medieval and Renaissance Literature, University of Cambridge, and a Fellow of Girton College, Cambridge. He has published widely on late medieval and early modern English literature, including *Piers Plowman* and

Sciences and the Self in Medieval Literature: Allan of Lille's 'Antclaudianus' and John Gower's 'Confessio Amantis'.

SUSANNE WOODS is Provost of Wheaton College and has been Professor of English at Brown University and Franklin & Marshall College. She is author of *Natural Emphasis: English Versification from Chaucer to Dryden* and *Lanyer: A Renaissance Woman Poet*.

RICHARD AXTON is a Lecturer in English, University of Cambridge and a Fellow of Christ's College. He is author of *European Drama of the Early Middle Ages*. With Marie Axton he is founder of the Tudor Interlude series. He has edited the plays of John Rastell and John Heywood.

ABBREVIATIONS

Add.	Additional
BL	London, British Library
BN	Paris, Bibliothèque nationale de France
c.	*circa*
ed.	edited
EETS	Early English Text Society
ES	Extra Series
fol./fols	folio(s)
Forty-six Lives, ed. by Wright	*Forty-six Lives Translated from Boccaccio's 'De Claris Mulieribus' by Henry Parker, Lord Morley*, ed. by H. G. Wright, EETS OS 214 (1943 [for 1940])
Goff	Frederick R. Goff, *Incunabula in American Libraries. A Third Census of Fifteenth-Century Books Recorded in North American Collections* (New York, 1964)
GW	*Gesamtkatalog der Wiegendrucke*, 7 vols (Leipzig, 1925-38); 8- (Stuttgart, 1978-)
Hain	L. Hain, *Repertorium Bibliographicum*, 4 vols (1826-38/repr. Milan, 1948)
Lord Morley's 'Tryumphes', ed. by Carnicelli	*Lord Morley's 'Tryumphes' of Fraunces Petrarcke. The First English Translation of the Trionfi*, ed. by D. D. Carnicelli (Cambridge, Mass., 1971)
LP Henry VIII	*Letters and Papers, Foreign and Domestic, of the Reign of Henry VIII* ..., calendared by J. S. Brewer et al., 21 vols in 33 (London, 1862-1910)
The Exposition and Declaration	*The Exposition and Declaration of the Psalme, 'Deus ultionum Dominus', made by Syr Henry Parker knight, Lord Morey, dedicated to the Kynges Highnes* (London, 1539)
n.d.	no date
NLW	Aberystwyth, National Library of Wales
OS	Original Series
ORL	Old Royal Library
PRO	London, Public Record Office
STC	A. W. Pollard & G. R. Redgrave, *A Short-Title Catalogue of Books Printed in England, Scotland & Ireland and of English Books Printed Abroad, 1475-1640*, 2nd edn rev. by W. A. Jackson, F. S. Ferguson & K. F. Panzer, 3 vols (London, 1976-91)
trans.	translated

AN ATTENDANT LORD? HENRY PARKER, LORD MORLEY

DAVID STARKEY

> No! I am not Prince Hamlet, nor was meant to be;
> Am an attendant lord, one that will do
> To swell a progress, start a scene or two,
> Advise the prince; no doubt an easy tool,
> Deferential, glad to be of use,
> Politic, cautious, and meticulous;
> Full of high sentence, but a bit obtuse;
> At times, indeed, almost ridiculous –
> Almost, at times, the Fool.[1]

At first sight, T. S. Eliot's Shakespearean pastiche applies even better to Henry Parker, Lord Morley than to J. Alfred Prufrock himself. Not that Morley ever got as far as counselling the prince. Instead, his name – otherwise conspicuous by its absence from State Papers – appears as a participant in almost every scene of high court ceremony in the reign of Henry VIII. He attended the coronation in 1509, the Field of Cloth of Gold and the meeting with the Emperor Charles V at Gravelines in 1520, the christening of Prince Edward and the funeral of Queen Jane in 1537, and the receptions of Anne of Cleves in 1540 and the great admiral of France in 1546.[2] His only foreign mission, when he was sent to invest the Archduke Ferdinand with the Order of the Garter in 1523, was purely ceremonial too. Even his writing was ceremonial, since almost all his works were prepared as New Year's Gifts, to be presented to the king, his eldest daughter, or chief minister in the great rituals of gift-exchange which took place each year on 1 January.

And, it is easy to argue, there was precious little substance behind the ceremony. In the obvious sense, this is true: Morley never had independent stature; never took the initiative; never made an impact in the wider world. But politics, especially monarchical politics, needs attendant lords at least as much as Prince Hamlets. And Morley is that greatest rarity: an *articulate* attendant lord. He not only swells a progress or a pageant, but, since he is a writer, he tells us what it felt like to be a participant in the ceremonies – though of the quasi-royal household of Lady Margaret Beaufort rather than the royal court itself. He also gives voice to a whole series of otherwise mute roles: he is an articulate conservative and (what is not quite the same thing) an articulate back-bench peer, even an articulate juryman at state trials. So, listened to carefully, he tells us why conservatives supported Henry VIII's radical policies; why back-bench peers voted for reforming legislation and why nobles found their peers guilty on trumped-up charges. Nor does his self-consciousness desert him as a writer. He tells us why laymen wrote and how their writing (and their reading) helped them to survive the turbulent politics of the reign. No one, least of all Morley, would claim that his pen was mightier than the sword. But it did help to deflect it.

Henry Parker was born in about 1481. His father was Sir William Parker; his mother Alice Lovel, daughter and eventual heiress of William Lovel, in right of his wife Lord Morley. William Parker's origins are unknown. But he was a follower of Richard III and was rewarded for his help in suppressing Buckingham's Rebellion. His service to Richard III led to disfavour under Henry VII: he was never summoned to parliament and, according to later family tradition, 'lived the king's prisoner'. He also twice fell into bouts of insanity. He died in about 1504 and his widow quickly remarried Sir Edward Howard, a younger son of the earl of Surrey.

None of this made for a promising start for Henry, and his position was saved only by the patronage of Lady Margaret Beaufort. Henry had joined her household, probably as a boy. By 1496, when he was fifteen, he was her sewer and, as such, marshalled the service of twenty-five knights at her table on New Year's Day. Shortly after, he married Alice St John, of Lady Margaret's family of the half-blood. For Lady Margaret, even half-blood was thicker than water and his future was assured. Between 1499 and 1503 Lady Margaret received £120 from William Parker's lands for Alice's jointure, and in 1507, after Henry's mother had remarried Sir Edward Howard, Lady Margaret also paid 500 marks to Howard 'to redeem Mr Parker's lands'.[3]

Henry's education continued after his marriage, again supported by Lady Margaret. She paid for his schooling at Oxford and maintained his wife and two children in her household during his absences. When he returned, he resumed an honoured place in her service. At Henry VIII's coronation banquet he acted as her cup-bearer and noted her eager consumption of a cygnet, to which he attributed her death a fortnight later.[4]

It was, or should have been, a flying start. Parker was heir to a considerable fortune and he had a wife who was a member of the extended royal family. No doubt the sudden death of his patroness was a blow, but, according to Lady Margaret's most recent biographers, she had tried to provide for the future by placing him in Henry VIII's household.

I have, however, been unable to find any evidence for this. There is a household list, calendared in *Letters and Papers* under 1516, in which 'Henry Parker' appears as a gentleman usher ordinary of the Chamber and another man of the same name as a page of the chamber ordinary. The evidence of this list has been used, variously, to claim that either Henry himself, or his eldest son, also called Henry, held established positions at court. But the list can be dated, rather precisely, to between 18 March and 1 May 1536. This means that neither of these Henry Parkers can be our man, since by then he had been recognized as Lord Morley for over fifteen years. It is also doubtful whether one of them can even have been his eldest son, since he had been knighted in 1533. And, in any case, the post of gentleman usher was barely suitable for the eldest son of a baron and that of a page of the chamber impossible since it was expressly menial.[5]

Apart from this misdated list, there is nothing to connect Henry Parker senior with any post in the royal household. As we have seen, he attended occasionally at court for special occasions. But that does not make him a courtier. This means that we need to rethink the man and his *milieu*. We also need to explain why, with all his apparent advantages of family and connexion, he should have failed to establish himself at court.

Negatives, of course, are notoriously difficult to prove; but in this case it is relatively straightforward. The young Henry VIII came to the throne with a single mission: war against France. And it would be a good, old-fashioned war, led by the king in person surrounded with his comrades-in-arms – just like the wars of Henry VIII's youthful heroes, Henry V and King Arthur. The two kings, the real Henry and the mythical Arthur, rather tended to merge in his fevered imagination, just as they had in the Malory which he had read as a child. This meant that, for Henry VIII and most of his contemporaries, the pretend war of the jousts ranked almost as highly as the thing itself.[6]

The new tone at court was announced quickly. For six months, according to the chronicler, Edward Hall, the older councillors argued against the king's own participation in the tournament. But by January 1510, Henry VIII could restrain himself no longer. Even so, residual deference to the judgement of his council meant that he rode *incognito*. But a serious injury to his companion, William Compton, the groom of the Stool and his closest friend and body-servant, led to his cover being blown. Thereafter the king was unstoppable and became the star in a brilliant series of jousts and revels that made the Arthurian court live once more.[7]

But jousting is a sociable sport. Arthur had the knights of the Round Table; Henry VIII had a circle of jousting cronies, who supplied his aids and opponents in the lists. And these were the men who won not only the prizes at the end of the tournament; they won also the still more glittering prizes of politics and promotion as well. Most conspicuous was Charles Brandon, who jousted his way from esquire to a dukedom in a mere five years. Brandon's creation as duke of Suffolk also highlights another point. It occurred in 1514, as a reward for Brandon's role in the English victory over the French at the battle of the Spurs.[8]

It had taken Henry VIII almost four years to mount his full-scale invasion of France. But when he finally set sail in 1513, it was at the head of the largest English expeditionary force since the days of Henry V and Edward III. And, as under Edward III, Henry VIII's generals and captains – and the men who performed the deeds of derring-do at sea and on land – were the king's comrades-in-arms in the tournament.

Lady Margaret, with her usual shrewdness, seems to have recognized the way the wind was blowing, and in 1507 paid for Henry Parker to go to London and watch a joust. This, almost certainly, was the tournament organized in celebration of May Day at Kennington, with a sequel in June. A commemorative printed pamphlet was published, which described the two tournaments in verses. Like today's sports-writers, its author lavished extravagant language on the participants. But the poet's real hero was a mere spectator – albeit one who chafed at the role – the future Henry VIII himself. He was then prince of Wales and a youth of sixteen. But, according to the Spanish ambassador, he was 'already taller than his father, and his limbs are of gigantic size'. Size and strength were the two basic physical qualifications for the tournament and Prince Henry was eager to put his natural advantages to the test. The poet-pamphleteer sensed his frustrated enthusiasm:

> Syth our prynce moost comly of stature
> Is desyrous to the moost knyghtly ure
> Of armes to whiche marcyall aventure
> Is his courage.

Meanwhile, he was eager for jousting talk and was willing to bend the rules of etiquette to get it:

And though a prynce / and a kynges sone be he
It pleaseth hym of his benygnyte
To suffre gentylmen of lowe degre
In his presence

To speke of armes and of other defence
Without doynge unto his grace offence.

By the following year, Prince Henry had come off the terraces and on the pitch – or rather the tilt yard. We even have the dates of the fixtures, thanks to Bernard André's Latin *Annals* for 1507/8. These show that from May 1508 the prince threw himself into a constant round of training and display bouts. He did not yet tilt with the lance – that was too dangerous. Instead he rode at the ring. This is defined by one authority as follows: 'the object of this sport was to catch a suspended ring on the point of one's lance. It was far safer than jousting, and hence often preferred. It was also a way of practising for jousting.' Prince Henry would certainly have rather gone the whole hog and tilted for real, but this is as far as he was allowed to go.[9]

It was, however, quite far enough both to signal his intentions and to define his social circle. This included the 'gentylmen of lowe degre', like Brandon himself, who talked the sport with the royal youth, as well as those of higher, even noble rank, like the earl of Essex, who had been chosen to train and initiate the prince into the jouster's art.

On his visit in 1507 Henry Parker must have seen all this. As Lady Margaret's protégé, he was a privileged spectator. He was in a position to witness the prince's enthusiasm at first hand and to overhear his star-struck exchanges with the leading jousters. But neither then nor subsequently did he show any inclination to risk either his neck or his dignity in the lists. And it was the same with the real business of war. Parker took no part in any of the campaigns of the 1510s or 1520s. By the 1540s, his status as peer and landowner meant that he was necessarily involved in the raising of troops. But he never led them himself; instead, for the actual invasion of France in 1544 he delegated this task to his eldest son.

This failure to involve himself in the business of war was wholly exceptional for a member of his caste. The English nobility was, first and last, a warrior élite. It was, and saw itself as being, a true nobility of the sword and lance. Henry VIII's personal enthusiasm for war reinforced this self-image. The result was unusually high levels of noble participation in his wars. In his first French campaign of 1513 only four adult members of the nobility did not serve, either in person or as represented by their heirs. In 1544 the number of non-combatants, including of course Morley himself, was rather greater – but it was still only a handful.[10]

By 1544 Morley, at sixty-three, would have been able to plead the excuse of age – though, as we shall see, he remained exceptionally active in discharging the civilian duties of a nobleman. But that cannot explain his earlier non-involvement. In the dedicatory letter to his *Exposition* of Psalm 93, which was printed in 1539, Morley alludes briefly to the problem. He was, he says, 'unmete to do any bodily service, condigne to so vertuous & excellent a prince'; instead he offers Henry VIII his prayers and his pen.[11] This, probably deliberately, is obscure. Did Morley mean that he was actually disabled? Against this must be set his portrait by Dürer (reproduced above, p. vi). Dürer, notoriously, is an artist who did not flatter his sitters. Yet Morley's portrait, made while he was on embassy in Germany in 1523, shows a face that is exceptionally handsome and youthful for a forty-two-year old. Moreover, the very fact that he was chosen for the embassy suggests that he was a good physical specimen. Was Morley then merely disinclined? Disinclination was not, however, an excuse that usually washed with Henry VIII.

Nor, despite Morley's intellectual interests, is there any trace of the conscientious objections to war felt, for example, by Thomas More at certain stages of his development. Instead, in his 'comparcuyon' of Henry VIII to the Spartan king Agesilaus, Parker singles out the English king's military exploits for especial praise. Agesilaus had succeeded at the age of eighteen and immediately levied just war on the Persians. 'As to there agys', Parker continues, 'it is playne that nyghe unto that same yers oure good kyng Henry toke upon him by just title of right to governe the empyere of Ingland and that schortly after he passid with his puyssaunt army to make war upon the Frenchemen'.[12] And so on.

Finally, then, the reasons for Morley's failure to involve himself in war and the pretend war of the jousts have to remain a mystery. But the consequences are clear. His non-combatant role excluded him from the principal business of the monarchy in the first half of Henry VIII's reign. And, as he could not or would not serve the crown in the only area that mattered, he neither got, nor probably expected, any reward.

The only real exception to this, and it is an important one, is his peerage. His mother, Alice Lovel, died in 1518. She is referred to as Lady Morley. But neither of her two husbands were summoned to parliament in her right; nor was her late brother, Henry, though he too had been acknowledged as Lord Morley. In other words, between Alice's own death and her father's in 1476 almost forty years had elapsed during which the barony lay in abeyance as a parliamentary title. The length of the gap led the editors of *The Complete Peerage* to suggest that in 1518 the barony was formally revived by 'some instrument of creation which has not been discovered'. Helen Miller, however, points out that Morley's was only one of several titles which were restored after a long lapse in the first decade of Henry VIII's reign. And, in each case, the new baron was accorded the precedence of the ancient barony to which he was heir – so that Parker himself was ranked tenth of the barons when he first attended parliament in 1523. This leads Miller to insist that Parker and the rest were peers by inheritance, not new men. Parker's own language, however, tells a rather different story. In the dedication to Henry VIII of his translation of Plutarch's *Lives of Scipio and Haniball*, he refers to himself as 'by your goodnesse Lorde Morlei'.[13] Too much should not be read into this single phrase. But it does seem to suggest that Morley at least thought that he owed his title to the king's favour, rather than to any notion of unimpeachable hereditary right.

Whatever the grounds of Morley's nobility, however, he promptly showed himself conscientious about the discharge of its civil duties. In 1520 he attended the king and queen to the summit meetings with both Francis I and his rival Charles V; in 1521 he was empanelled as a member of the court of the lord high steward to try the duke of Buckingham for treason; and in 1523 he sat in parliament. Parliament was dissolved on 13 August. Four days later Wolsey wrote to Henry VIII enclosing a draft commission for Morley and three others, including Edward Lee, the king's almoner and

Garter king-of-arms, to go to Germany and present the Garter to the Archduke Ferdinand. The offer of the Garter was intended to encourage Ferdinand to be as stout in resisting Luther's heresies on the ground as Henry VIII had been on paper in his *Assertio septem sacramentorum*. The religious element in the embassy meant that the main speaking part was accorded to Lee. But it was Morley who was to deputize for his sovereign and invest the archduke with the accoutrements of the order: the garter, the kirtle, the mantle, and the george.[14]

The leading role in such honorific embassies was, effectively, a perquisite of nobility. Morley seems to have discharged the task with competence and certainly with enthusiasm. His knowledge of French enabled him to communicate with the civic authorities *en route* in the Netherlands. His intellectual interests made him a vivid reporter on the latest words and deeds of Luther, Erasmus, and the papacy in a Germany torn apart by the early Reformation. But the most lasting memorial of the embassy is not Morley's words but the sketch, made by Garter himself or deriving from an original by him, which shows the four ambassadors dining with the archduke on the day of his investiture. Morley, as the senior, sits on Ferdinand's right hand (see frontispiece).[15]

Morley, in his letters home to Henry VIII and Wolsey, had done his best to make an impression. He had flattered the minister assiduously – more fulsomely even than the king.[16] To no avail. It would take a change of circumstances to make more of Morley than a ceremonial tool.

The first step, ironically, was Wolsey's own fall, which opened the way to the Divorce, the Reformation, and the Supremacy. This – in so far as Morley as ever made it – was the making of Morley. The goal of royal policy now shifted, from the enterprise of war to the enterprise of the Reformation. This meant that the chosen instruments of policy changed as well. Instead of soldiers, the king now needed legislators, administrators, judges, and propagandists. It was a world much more suited to Morley's talents and predisposition.

There is also the particular question of the role of the peerage in the changes. This has been overlooked because of Sir Geoffrey Elton's emphasis on the 'parliamentary' solution to the dilemmas of Henry VIII's divorce. According to Elton, the years from 1529 to 1532 were the years without a policy. Then in 1532 Thomas Cromwell joined the king's service and quickly became his leading adviser. He persuaded Henry VIII that the solution to his problems was the royal supremacy and that the best instrument to bring about the supremacy was parliament and, in particular, the house of Commons. We now know that the idea of the supremacy was formulated earlier, by the king himself with the advice and research skills of a handful of clerical councillors. It is also clear that, in this pre-Cromwellian period, coherent practical strategies were employed as well. Circumstances meant that they failed. But that does not mean that they were misconceived. Instead, in the fullness of time, and after the upheavals of Cromwell, Henry VIII was to return to them to produce the more stable and conservative settlement of the 1540s in which Morley, like many others, felt fully at home.[17]

And the lords were central – both to these earlier strategies and to their later, more successful, incarnation. In December 1529, shortly before the prorogation of the first, short session of the Reformation Parliament, a set of 'articles' was drawn up between the king and the nobility 'assembled in this present parliament'. The aim was to settle the vexed question of the extent of the king's feudal rights and the validity of the legal devices, in particular 'uses' or trusts, which were used to defeat them. In the projected settlement, there is no doubt that it was the king who gave most ground: where the land was in trust he limited his claims to a third of the estate. If that benefited the pockets of the nobility, even more was done to flatter their pride in what may have been the associated parliamentary bill drawn up alongside the 'articles'. This would have turned the nobility into an exclusive caste. Their lands would have become inalienable and only they would have been able to entail their lands to their heirs.[18]

In short, in 1529 Henry VIII was engaged in a love-in with his nobility. He had done the same thing before, at the time of his accession in 1509. Then he had reversed the money-grubbing policies of the last years of his father's reign and destroyed the two ministers, Empson and Dudley, most associated with them. Instead, he embraced the aristocratic values of magnificence and magnanimity and surrounded himself with a set of aristocratic favourites as well. The object was to get the nobility on side for his great enterprise of war with France. Now, in 1529, the aim was to line up the nobility in support of the new royal enterprise of the divorce and whatever lay beyond it.

The *quid pro quo* for the agreement over feudal dues was presented in the early summer of 1530. On 12 June a great council – that is, a meeting of the nobility without the house of Commons – was summoned to implement the next step in the king's campaign for a divorce: a letter from the notables of England to the pope. Henry VIII's hope was that the letter would threaten that if Rome refused England would act alone. But substantial opposition forced the king to back down. Instead, the letter as finally agreed conceded that the decision was the pope's but applied heavy pressure on him to find in the king's favour.

Despite the disputes over drafting, the letter was visually impressive, with eighty-odd signatures and seals arranged in eight categories and hanging from the finely written parchment text like bobbins from lace. Eleventh among the barons is Morley's seal and signature 'Harry Morley'. Absenteeism meant that he had a higher place in the 'articles' on feudal rights, where he signs sixth of the barons.[19]

Two years later, at the beginning of the third session of the Reformation Parliament, an attempt was made to get the tandem back on the road. A bill to embody the agreement on feudal dues was read; at the same time, the duke of Norfolk argued once more in a meeting of the great council that the divorce could be decided in England. Neither proposal got anywhere: opposition in the Commons defeated the bill on feudal dues and conservative peers, led by Lord Darcy, blocked Norfolk in the great council.[20]

So the idea of settling the divorce by amicable agreement between the king and his lords proved to be a non-starter. Nevertheless, the role of the Lords in the Reformation Parliament remained important. Cromwell made determined attempts to secure attendance and the Lords' continued to be the setting for the great moments of parliamentary pageantry. The greatest of these took place on 30 March 1534. With the king sitting on his throne and the Commons present, the parliament was prorogued. Then the Lords were sworn to the act of succession, which bastardized the issue of Catherine of Aragon and made Anne Boleyn's daughter Elizabeth heiress of England. On this occasion, Morley sat seventh among the barons.[21]

In this campaign for a legislative reformation Morley was no general. But he was a reliable foot-soldier: always present and (presumably) always voting correctly. And he had his reward. In December 1530 he was appointed to the commission of the peace in Essex, and the following February to the commission in the adjacent country of Hertfordshire as well. As usual, these appointments reflected the location of his lands. Both his seats, Mark Hall and Great Hallingbury, were in Essex, as was the bulk of his estates. But Great Hallingbury was to the extreme west of Essex, lying between Bishop's Stortford to the north and Hatfield Broad Oak (then King's Hatfield) and its forest to the south and east. This carried his influence across the county border into Hertfordshire. Morley remained a leading member of both benches for the rest of Henry VIII's reign. He was also appointed to a host of the other commissions – to oversee drainage, to collect taxes and contributions, to raise troops – on which local government depended. For once, his epitaph gets it right when it emphasizes his local role: 'Essex', it claims, 'was rendered more illustrious by this hero living in it'.[22]

But it is important to read all this correctly. His sudden advancement to the bench in 1530/1, when he was already fifty, was not the belated recognition of a late developer. It was a concrete reward for his attendance in the parliaments and great councils of the Reformation.[23] Circumstances made this attendance newly valuable to the king, so it gained Morley a reward which hitherto had been denied to him. Morley's appointment also suggests that the government was confident he would be enthusiastic in doing their bidding in the locality. The Divorce and Reformation transformed him from a nobody into a (modest) somebody.

With Morley's record of solid service in parliament, the locality and perhaps the study, the king was disposed to scatter other crumbs in his way as well. On 24 March 1534, six days before the taking of the oath of succession, Morley had disputed his precedence in the lords. Garter's draft roll for the parliament gave the order as Rochford, Morley, Dacre and Dacre of Gilsland. But, on the third day of the session, the journal omitted Dacre (who had died earlier in the year, leaving as heir a grandson under age) and transposed Morley and Dacre of Gilsland. The original order was restored on 19 March. Then, five days later on the 24th, Morley sought a formal ruling. It was given in his favour, the lords resolving that 'without prejudice, Lord Morley should hold the higher place, that is, to the left of the illustrious George, Lord Rochford and that the said Lord Dacre shall hold the place to the left of the same Lord Morley'. This issue arose again in June 1536, and once again Morley was vindicated. The question revolved round the date of creation. Precedence within each rank of the peerage depended on the seniority, or original date of creation of the title. The first summons to Morley was 1299 and the first to Dacre comfortably later in 1321. But Dacre of Gilsland was probably arguing that he was also Lord Greystoke by right of his mother; that gave him the upper hand, since the first summons to Greystoke was 1295, four years earlier than Morley. Morley's case was thus by no means straightforward. Both sides clearly cared strongly about the outcome, which is why the issue came up twice. Perhaps Morley owed his double victory to the fact that he was in favour whereas Dacre, who had been put on trial for treason in 1534 but escaped with a verdict of not guilty, remained under a cloud.[24]

Finally, we should not underestimate how, for a man with a temperament like Morley's, sitting in the Lords was its own reward. As indeed it still is. It was like a club, without the drawback of a subscription charge. You were at the centre of affairs – or, at least, it felt as if you were – without the disagreeable necessity of needing to work at it, like a proper councillor. And all these aspects were intensified by the increased length and frequency of the sessions of the Reformation Parliament, which made the Lords (and the Commons too, for that matter) feel more and more like a serious institution of government. So we can guess with what satisfaction Morley dated his letter to Lord Lisle, absent in Calais where he was deputy or governor, 'from London at the parliament'.[25]

But there were other noble duties which were less agreeable. When Dacre of Gilsland was accused of treason by some Scots 'of mean condition' he was informed by the judges that he could not waive his right to trial by his peers in the court of the high steward. Perhaps he was alarmed at the thought of someone like Morley, with whom he was in dispute over precedence, sitting in judgement on him for his life. In the event, Morley was included in the panel which found Dacre not guilty.[26] Morley had earlier sat in judgement on the duke of Buckingham at his trial in 1521. And he was similarly to be empanelled for all the remaining trials for treason of peers in Henry VIII's reign. His record was unique. Eleven peers were in a position to have attended all six trials; but only Morley did so. This record is the more remarkable bearing in mind Morley's relationship to one of the accused. In 1536, he sat in judgement on his son-in-law, George Boleyn, Lord Rochford, and helped to find him guilty. In 1542 he did not flinch from an even more terrible duty. Jane, Morley's daughter and Rochford's widow, was accused of aiding and abetting the treasonable intercourse of Queen Catherine Howard and Thomas Culpepper. The queen and Lady Rochford were not tried by their peers (as Anne Boleyn had been). Instead they were condemned to death by parliamentary act of attainder. Morley duly attended the House for each reading of the bill.[27]

Morley was not, of course, unique in experiencing such dilemmas. The duke of Norfolk was uncle to both of Henry VIII's executed queens and, at the time of the fall of Queen Catherine Howard, strove to distance himself from her by denouncing half his own family. He wrote frantically to the king, declaring that his stepmother was 'ungracious', his brother 'unhappy', and his sister 'lewd'.[28] Morley never engaged, directly at least, in such name-calling. Yet the range of his connexions does present problems. He had close family ties with the Boleyns. As Carley has shown (p. 37 below), we know now that the work he is supposed to have dedicated to Anne Boleyn is a misattribution. Even so, that removes only one of a bundle of apparent contradictions. For Morley was also in the habit of giving the Lady Mary a translation of an improving work each New Year and he and his family were clearly on intimate terms with her. But Mary's mother had been divorced to make way for Anne and Mary herself bastardized in favour of Anne's daughter Elizabeth. What was a Boleyn connexion doing hob-nobbing with Mary? Morley's ties with Thomas Cromwell are even harder to explain. Cromwell, it was commonly supposed, was chief instrument of Anne's advancement; he also boasted of bringing about her fall. And, to even the score, it was Cromwell who forced Mary to acknowledge her bastard status. Despite all this, Morley was on friendly terms with Cromwell as well, presenting him with at least one translation and writing to him with easy familiarity on matters both practical and intellectual. Finally, and above all, there was Morley's over-riding commitment to the king. Henry VIII executed Anne, bastardized Mary, and beheaded Cromwell – as well as decreeing the deaths of Morley's own son-in-law and daughter. Yet Morley served him loyally (which indeed, unless he had wished to tread the steps of the scaffold as well, he could scarcely have avoided doing). But he also went out of his way to dedicate and present the bulk of his literary output to him.

What are we to make of this extraordinary assortment of ill bed-fellows? One reaction would be to deny any sincerity or fundamental seriousness, either to Morley's writings or to his relationships. Another and only slightly less severe verdict would be to see him as a mere turncoat and vicar of Bray, always bending to the prevailing wind. Or he might have been a master of the game of faction politics, with a rat-like intelligence which always knew when to leave the sinking ship.

Actually, my sense is that none of these applies. Not that Morley was rigorously consistent. That would be as anachronistic a verdict as the opposed one of insincerity. But there *is* a sort of coherence in his ideas. As for his relationships, they are muddled because family relationships or the ties of friendship or neighbourliness refuse to fit neat ideological categories – and the more so when, as under Henry VIII, the lines of political and religious division are by no means clear.

There is a final point. We get Morley wrong because we see him in the wrong context. Almost universally he is described as a courtier. But, as we have seen, he was not. He was a backswoodman. In the first half of his life, he was an unimportant backwoodsman; in the second half, a rather important one. And his importance was magnified, for us and probably for his contemporaries as well, by the fact that he was a writer. Writing peers were rather thin on the ground. There was Lord Berners among Morley's elders and the earl of Surrey among his juniors. But Berners was dead by 1533 and Surrey's literary activity was contained in a single decade of astonishing creative activity, between the death of the duke of Richmond in 1537 and his own execution in 1547. Otherwise, Morley was unique. This caused him, in the words of his epitaph, to stand out 'among a throng of nobles like a jewel of great price shining with the splendour of good letters'.[29] But, and this is the issue, a literary backwoodsman is still a backwoodsman. Morley's compositions, although they are addressed to great figures at court, do not make him a courtier. And, although they comment, sometimes directly though more usually obliquely, on the great issues of the day, they do not make him an actor on the political stage. Above all, his writings, although they deal in a broad general culture, do not lift him out of his locality. He might write of England and translate into English, but, again in the words of his epitaph, it was 'Essex that was rendered more illustrious by this hero living in it'. And it is in Essex that we should start to untangle the skein of Morley's relationships and commitments.

For not only was Morley an Essex man, the Boleyns were an Essex family too. Accounts of the Boleyn family suffer from the usual English preference for extremes in social origins. If we are slumming, we emphasize Anne's paternal great-grandfather, Sir Geoffrey Boleyn. This gives us the story of the family's rise from London merchant to queen of England in three generations. If, on the other hand, we are hob-nobbing, we look to Anne's mother, Elizabeth Howard, daughter of the second Howard duke of Norfolk. She connected Anne to some of the bluest blood in England – though, like Henry VIII's own, it was blue only in the female line. But the most important figure in the Boleyn family tree was neither of these. Instead, it was Margaret Butler, Anne Boleyn's paternal grandmother.

Margaret was daughter and co-heiress of Thomas Butler, earl of Ormond. She had married Sir William Boleyn, having, as her eldest son, Sir Thomas, Anne's father. Butler was head of one of the two great Irish families. But he was absentee, preferring to spend his time in England, where he had great estates, centring on his luxurious new house of Beaulieu or New Hall, near Chelmsford in Essex. He was also a great figure at the early Tudor court, as lord chamberlain to Queen Elizabeth of York and mentor to her second son, the future Henry VIII. Ormond was responsible for introducing some of the key figures into the young prince's circle, like his *socius studiorum* or companion in studies, Lord Mountjoy, who was Ormond's step-son, and, through Mountjoy, Thomas More himself. More importantly still, Ormond familiarized Prince Henry with his hero, ancestor, and namesake, Henry V. This he was able to do because of his great age. He had been born in the 1420s, which meant that he had heard memories of the great Henry's exploits during his own boyhood, and was able to pass them on, seven decades and two dynasties later, to Henry VIII in his childhood.[30] Ormond's death without sons in 1515 left Sir Thomas, Anne Boleyn's father, as the principal heir to this vast inheritance.

Beaulieu itself was quickly sold to Henry VIII. He had probably spent happy days there in his youth and it became one of his favourite palaces in the first half of his reign. The other Essex estates, centring on the great lordship of Rochford, became the core of Boleyn's territorial wealth. But Ormond's best bequest was that his influence had given the young Boleyn entrée to the court. He proved himself, for better and for worse, a consummate courtier.

This is the background to the alliances by which Morley linked his family to the Boleyns. By his marriage to Alice St John Morley had several children who lived to adulthood. But only three had much dynastic significance: a son, Henry, and two daughters, Jane and Margery. Henry was probably the eldest. On 18 May 1523 he married Grace, daughter and heiress of John Newport. Newport died eight days after the wedding, and his daughter brought his considerable estates into the Parker family. They centred on Furneux Pelham, which lies to the north-west of Bishop's Stortford, while Morley's house at Great Hallingbury lay to the south-east. So the Newport and Parker lands were adjacent. That explains the marriage in itself.[31]

But both the daughters were to marry into the Boleyn family. Jane was probably the elder and by 1522 she had 'come out' by appearing at court at the entertainments mounted on Shrove Tuesday for the imperial embassy to England. The entertainment consisted of a mock siege of a castle. The besiegers were led by the king; the besieged ladies in the castle were the cream of the beauties of the English court. Each impersonated one of the virtues of the ideal mistress of chivalric tradition. Jane played Constancy. Among her fellow-performers were the two Boleyn sisters: Anne was Perseverance and her sister Mary Kindness.[32] As Eric Ives has nicely observed, the roles have an 'historic appropriateness'. Or, in the case of Jane, irony, as she was to betray her husband and die a traitress to the king.

Within three years of the Shrove Tuesday entertainment, Jane had married George Boleyn, Thomas Boleyn's heir and Anne's brother. In the interim, the Boleyns had taken a major step up in the world. Mary, living out her role of Kindness, had quickly surrendered to the king and become his mistress. Rewards were then showered on her family. The most important was the creation of her father, Thomas, as Viscount Rochford in 1525. The ceremony, on 16 June, was a glittering event. At one and the same time, the king's bastard son, Henry Fitzroy, was made a duke, his cousin, Henry

Courteney, a marquess, and his nephew, Henry Brandon, earl of Lincoln. Two other remoter royal relations were made earls and one a viscount. Boleyn's creation in this exalted company shows that he too had been recognized as a member of the extended royal family.[33] His title was taken from the lordship of Rochford which he had inherited through his mother. Indeed, it was as 'Thomas Ormond de Rochford Chivaler' that Ormond himself had been summoned to sit in the English parliament.[34]

Rochford's promotion turned the marriage of his son and heir and Jane Parker into an affair of some moment. A decade later, Jane herself described some of the circumstances when she recalled in a letter to Cromwell how 'the Kyngys Hyghnes and my Lord my father payed great soms of money for my Joynter ... to the some of too thowsand Marks'. Two thousand marks, or £1333 *6s. 8d.*, was a vast sum of money. That Morley was prepared to pay it showed how much he valued an alliance with the ascendant Boleyns. That he was able to pay it was another matter. For it must have been greatly in excess of his own means. These, according to his assessment for the subsidy, consisted of an income of £233 *6s. 8d.* He was not poor, but he was not rich for a baron either. Hence the king's role in helping to raise the jointure. The king regularly helped with the marriages of his favourites; he also acted as head of the extended royal family to which both parties now belonged.[35]

Some four years later, it was the turn of Margery, Jane's younger sister. In about 1530 she married John Shelton. His father was Sir John, 'a man of great possessions' in Norfolk; while his mother was Anne, sister of Sir Thomas Boleyn and aunt of her namesake, Anne Boleyn.[36]

What are we to make of this double alliance? Jane and George Boleyn had met in the competitive, sexually charged atmosphere of the court. Both were young and attractive. Perhaps indeed they were attracted to each other. But that would have been the least of it. Essentially, as the double match showed, it was a considered alliance between two families, which were already doubly linked, by local connexion and, in the loosest sense, by royal blood. Such intermarriages within the remoter fringes of the royal family were commonplace, as uniting two weak lines made one stronger one. So it was with the Boleyns and the Parkers.

What is much harder to spot, however, is any factional or partisan element in the alliance. A probable portent of things to come occurred in January 1526 when the newly-wedded bliss of Jane and George was interrupted by George's dismissal as the king's page. Pages at court were of two types. Most were low-ranking menials. But a handful were pages in the more modern sense. That is to say, they were boys of good birth and breeding in largely decorative and honorific attendance. George, as Henry VIII's own page, was the most privileged of the lot, with a position in the Privy Chamber, which was the inmost department of the court. But in January 1526, under the cover of the general reform of the royal household known as the Eltham Ordinances, Wolsey succeeded in removing from the Privy Chamber anyone he thought to be hostile or even independent. It is a sort of back-handed tribute to his family's rise that George was one of those dismissed. But he did not fall very far. Jane and he were given an extra £20 a year 'to live on' and he was to be one of the principal attendants on the king's table when he ate in state in public.[37]

With the official installation of Anne as first the king's mistress and then his wife-to-be, the alignment of the Parkers with their Boleyn in-laws became more clear-cut. In

1528 George was restored to the Privy Chamber, but with the adult rank of Gentleman of the Privy Chamber. By 1529/30, with his father's further promotion in the peerage to earldoms of Wiltshire and Ormond, George became a baron as Lord Rochford. He was summoned to parliament and acted as the nobleman at the head of one of the two 'sides' or attendance rotas of the Privy Chamber. Meanwhile, Jane played a similar role as a leading attendant on her sister-in-law, Anne Boleyn. She was especially conspicuous on the visit of Henry VIII and Anne to Boulogne in 1532, when she was one of the select group of English ladies who appeared masked with Anne and danced with the élite of the French court.[38]

Their reception on this visit convinced Henry VIII and Anne that it was safe to proceed. In December, they at last slept together and Anne became pregnant; in January they were married; in March Anne was acknowledged as queen; in May she was crowned and in September Elizabeth was born. Despite disappointment at her sex, the child was proclaimed princess – that is, heir to the throne.

Morley's family played the part in all this that would be expected of family connexions of both the king and, especially, the new queen. Morley's son and heir Henry was one of those dubbed knight of the Bath on the eve of the coronation and, at the subsequent coronation feast, acted as principal servitor from the dresser for his sister-in-law and queen.[39] Rochford himself missed the great day as he was absent on embassy in France, but Jane wrote to tell him of the goings-on, in which the ladies, apparently, took the absence of their husbands and lovers with perhaps excessive equanimity.[40] After the birth of the Princess Elizabeth, it was the turn of the Sheltons to benefit and Sir John and Lady Shelton, senior, were given a leading place in the joint households of the king's daughters: Sir John was made Elizabeth's steward while his wife became Mary's lady mistress or governess.[41]

But of course by this time, if not before, the divisive consequences of the Boleyn marriage were clear to all. And for those at the centre, sides had to be taken, despite many desperate attempts to straddle the fence. At first, the Parkers seem to have followed the logic of their family connexion with the Boleyns by aligning themselves firmly with them. In 1534, for example, Jane played her part in a court coup, by which a royal mistress, who had been set up to rival Anne Boleyn, was removed and replaced by Margaret Shelton. Margaret, usually known as Madge, was both Anne Boleyn's cousin and, through Margaret Parker, her sister-in-law, which made her a safe, unthreatening choice as the temporary receptacle for the king's amorous sighs.[42] More immediately serious were the choices facing the older generation of Sheltons. Their very appointment had been a symbol of the Boleyn triumph and the concomitant humiliation of Mary, the daughter of the disgraced and defeated Catherine of Aragon. Hitherto Mary, as princess, had had her own large separate establishment, most recently based at the old Ormond house of Beaulieu or New Hall. But with Elizabeth's birth all this was forfeit. Her title of princess was transferred to the new royal child; her own household was broken up, and, worst of all, she and the rump of her servants were incorporated into the new, grand establishment set up for Elizabeth, with Sir John Shelton as its chief administrative officer.

Even more controversial was Lady Anne's position. For several years, Mary's principal lady-in-waiting had been Margaret Plantagenet, countess of Salisbury. The countess was of the blood royal, devoted to Catherine of Aragon, and, as the mother of the future cardinal, Reginald Pole, fully sharing in Mary's own devout Catholicism. Now she was dismissed and replaced by Lady Anne. From Mary's point of view it was a horrible reversal. In place of her royal confidant she had a Boleyn gaoler, whose first task was to brow-beat her into submission to her father and – still worse – to her father's new wife and daughter.[43]

But it quickly became apparent that Lady Anne had little appetite for her new role, and both Norfolk and Rochford upbraided her for being insufficiently severe on Mary. Still more striking is the behaviour attributed to Rochford's own wife, Jane Parker. In the autumn of 1535 she is supposed to have been imprisoned in the Tower for leading a demonstration in favour of Mary at Greenwich. The evidence for this is thin and ambiguous.[44] Better vouched for is her part in the fall of the Boleyns the following spring. At least one account identifies her as a 'particular instrument' in the destruction of her husband and sister-in-law; while the imperial ambassador, Chapuys, specifically reports that one of the charges against Rochford was that Anne Boleyn had told his wife that the king was sexually inadequate.

But this last allegation in fact further muddies already murky waters. For Anne Boleyn would hardly have taken Jane into her confidence on such a matter if she had already declared her hostility. If, therefore, we believe this conversation between the sisters-in-law we must surely rule out Jane's earlier involvement in the demonstration in favour of Mary. It is also very unlikely that the Rochfords themselves would have discussed something as sensitive as the king's virility if relations between them had broken down – which would surely have been another consequence of Jane's involvement in the demonstration. Finally Jane, who is supposed to have pursued her husband to the death, is also known to have offered to intercede with Henry VIII for his life.[45]

But if Jane's actions are difficult either to establish or interpret so are her supposed motives. Several have been put forward. One theory has her acting out of outraged jealousy at a homosexual affair between Rochford and the musician Mark Smeaton. This is absurd and is unsupported by a scrap of evidence. Another view also attributes Jane's behaviour to outraged jealousy, but this time at an incestuous affair between Rochford and Anne Boleyn herself. This too is unlikely, unless we accept that the charges of incest against Anne and Rochford were true or even thought to be true. And not even Anne's worst enemies seem to have believed them. Finally, and less dramatically, Jane is supposed to have betrayed Anne because of her family's long-standing loyalty to Mary. This supposed loyalty rather begs the question of why Morley had sought a double marriage alliance with the Boleyns, who were certainly Mary's declared enemies, in 1530 when Margaret Parker had married Anne Boleyn's cousin, if not in 1525, when Jane Parker had married Anne's brother. On the other hand, it is certainly true that by the time of Anne Boleyn's fall Lord and Lady Morley and their daughters were on terms of close acquaintance with Mary, perhaps even of real friendship.[46]

First, then, the facts of the Morley-Mary connexion. In August 1536 Anne, Lady Hussey, was interrogated in the Tower about her recent visit to see Mary at Hunsdon. She replied that she had been there at Whitsuntide, when she had found Lord Morley among the other visitors, perhaps (though the mutilation of the manuscript makes it difficult to be sure) with his wife and daughter as well. Whitsunday in 1536 fell on 4 June. This was just over a fortnight after the execution of Anne Boleyn. It would have been hard to pick a more sensitive time. Under questioning, Lady Hussey claimed that it had been perfectly innocent: she had been accompanying her husband on his way to parliament and had just dropped in to to see Mary.[47] It would be interesting to know what explanation Morley would have offered. At all events, the acquaintance was kept up. In January 1537, Morley made his first recorded New Year's Gift to Mary and the servant presenting it was given a reward of 10*s*. Also giving gifts were both Morley's daughters, Jane, the widowed Lady Rochford, and Margaret, John Shelton's wife. In the following October, Mary acted as godmother to the Shelton's child and gave £1 to the midwife and nurse.[48]

So much for the facts. The crucial questions remain, however. They are: when did the Morleys' connexion with Mary begin and why? The general agreement is that it was long-standing, and went back to the princess's earliest childhood. At first sight, the records of Mary's household seem to bear this out. In 1516 Margaret Parker was one of the new-born Mary's rockers and in 1525 Alice Parker was one of the chamberers assigned to accompany the young princess to Wales when she formally assumed the government of her principality.[49] The coincidence of names is striking. Surely the rocker, who remained in Mary's service for over a decade, was Morley's daughter Margaret, and the chamberer his wife Alice.

In fact, neither identification is tenable. Both cases primarily turn on a point that Morley himself would have relished: that of status. A rocker was a menial servant, who was barely accorded gentry status. The differentiation is clear in a list specifying clothing for Mary's suite in 1525: all her ladies were to be clad in black velvet, except for Mrs Parker and a colleague who were to wear the humbler black damask.[50] Morley's daughter would have been too grand for such a post even in 1516, when her father was only the putative heir to a barony; by 1525, it was unthinkable that she, the daughter of a baron of the blood royal, should have been singled out for inferior dress. There is also the question of age. Margaret Parker would have been about twenty when she married in 1530. That would give her the impossibly young age of five when she joined Mary's service in 1515. The separate identity of the two Margaret Parkers is established by the grant of an annuity of £10 to the rocker, 'for service to the Princess Mary'. Such grants were the normal gesture to a widow or spinster who was leaving the royal service with few or no other means of support. It would have been an absurdity for the nubile daughter of a baron.[51]

Similar points apply to the supposed appearance of Margaret's mother in Mary's household. Once again, the post of chamberer was too humble for a baroness.[52] She is also described incorrectly for her rank. Morley's wife was not Alice Parker but 'Lady Morley'. Finally, it is unthinkable that Lady Morley would have been sent off to Wales alone, leaving her husband languishing in Essex. Instead, in such circumstances, joint appointments were the invariable practice, as with the Sheltons in later, less happy circumstances. And there is no trace of Morley's appointment to Mary's household.

All this means that there is no evidence of Morley's long-standing connexion with Mary either. It is, of course, dangerous to argue from silence. But the records of Mary's various households are pretty complete, and none of Morley's family appears in them until 1533. This suggests a radically different approach. Let us assume instead that the Morley connexion with Mary begins when the evidence suggests it does: in about 1533. This year, as we have seen, was one of great upheaval in Mary's life, with the break-up of her own household; her incorporation into the entourage of her half-sister and the appointment of Sir John and Lady Shelton as her guardians-cum-gaolers. The Shelton's appointment, however disagreeable the circumstances, established one conduit to Morley, since they were the in-laws of his daughter Margaret. But place was to be as important as persons and would suggest a later date still for the commencement of the relationship.

At first, the joint household of the royal half-sisters was peripatetic. It was at Hatfield in February 1534; in October of that year it moved from The More to Richmond, and in October 1535 it was at Eltham.[53] Then, at the end of January 1536, the imperial ambassador Chapuys heard that it was to be moved to Hunsdon. He was distraught at the decision since he had been plotting – with Mary's enthusiastic agreement – to spirit her abroad. Eltham, so near the Thames and the planned embarkation point of Gravesend, had been ideal for the purpose. Hunsdon, deep inland, was much less propitious. Even so, Mary was not to be deterred. She entered into the gung-ho spirit of the thing, and, soon after her arrival at Hunsdon, informed Chapuys that she could easily escape, providing she had drugs to stupefy her women![54]

Henry VIII had acquired Hunsdon House in Hertfordshire from the duke of Norfolk in 1525. Over the next nine years or so he built lavishly, turning the already substantial fifteenth-century manor house into a 'Palayes Royall' at the cost of some £2900. The site, on the watershed between the rivers Lea, Ash and Stort, was high and airy and meet for the 'helthe, conforte & preservacion of [the king's] royal person'. Henry VIII claimed to have 'gret pleasure to resort there',[55] but in practice its healthy situation, modern building and considerable, though not vast, size made it an ideal nursery house for his slowly growing family. It also lay only six miles from Morley's house at Great Hallingbury. This stood on the opposite side of the river Stort, which at this point forms the county boundary between Hertfordshire and Essex. Morley and his messengers were, I suspect, to cross the river several times during the initial eleven months' residence of the king's two daughters at Hunsdon.

To begin with, however, Morley was unable to greet his royal neighbours. This was because he was busy doing the bidding of their father in the last session of the Reformation Parliament. This lasted from 4 February to its dissolution on 14 April. Morley then probably rushed home to present himself at the neighbouring little court. But, only a fortnight later, he was summoned again to London for the trial of Queen Anne Boleyn and Lord Rochford, the mother and uncle of the little princess to whom he had been paying court. Did he remain in London to see the executions and support his daughter Lady Rochford? At all events he was at Hunsdon on Whitsunday, 4 June, when the presence of Morley and his wife among those paying their respects to Mary was noted by Lady Hussey. This too was a fleeting visit as he was back in London from 8 June to 18 July for the emergency parliament which ratified the divorce and execution of Queen Anne, on the one hand, and the marriage and elevation of Queen Jane, on the other.

But, brief though it was, Morley's return home and visit to Mary at Hunsdon on 4 June came, as we have seen, at a momentous time. The destruction of the Boleyns was still hot news. And, even before it got cold, Henry VIII and Cromwell chose a new victim: Mary herself. Huge pressure was brought to bear on her to force her to submit to her father, and acknowledge the validity of her mother's divorce and her own bastardy. Hitherto she had steadfastly refused. Now she was to be broken. We can follow the process in the long series of Mary's letters to Cromwell and Henry VIII, all dated at Hunsdon. They begin on 26 May and they culminate with her unconditional, prostrate submission on or about 14 June.[56] Morley's visit falls almost exactly in the middle. Cromwell's savage personal attack on Mary herself as 'the most ingrate, unnatural and most obstinate person living, both to God and your most dear and benign father' played its part. Still more, probably, did the attack on her friends and supporters. At least two were interrogated and, under questioning, gave lengthy lists of those who had spoken on her behalf.[57] Somewhat later, the extent of Sir Nicholas Carew's communications with Mary, 'about the time the king's council [had] sent her to Hunsdon', was also discovered.[58] Strikingly, Morley's name does not appear in any of these documents. Nor does it in Chapuys' despatches. These were not of course available to the government, which was just as well as they document not only those who were lobbying for Mary but those actively plotting for her as well – like Lord Darcy, who was executed after the Pilgrimage of Grace, and Lord Montague, the countess of Salisbury, the marquess of Exeter, and Sir Nicholas Carew, all of whom went to the block in their turn. The inference is clear: Morley had become (rather recently, I would guess) a personal friend of Mary's. But he was not a political ally.

This inference is confirmed by Morley's own account of one of his conversations with Mary at Hunsdon. It comes in the preface to his translation of the Exposition of Psalm 36 (or 37 in the Authorized Version) by Johannes de Turrecremata, which he had presented to Mary, most likely, on New Year's Day 1538.[59] The preface begins with Morley's recollection of the visit: 'I apon a certeyn tyme waytynge on your Grace at Honesdon.' As usual, he recalled, they had talked 'of thynges touchynge to vertue' and Mary had 'greately commend[ed]' the Psalm that was the subject of Turrecremata's work. The Psalm, as Morley goes on to explain, deals with the worldly fortune of the ungodly, and its instability in the face of God's invincible justice. 'I myself', the psalmist sings, 'have seen the ungodly in great power: and flourishing like a green bay-tree'. So had Anne Boleyn flourished in the days of her power. But then, the Psalm continues, 'I went by, and lo, he was gone; I sought him, but his place could no where be found'.[60] For 'he' read 'she'. For Anne Boleyn had forfeited the throne of England for a coffin made out of a bow chest in the Chapel of St Peter *ad Vincula* in the Tower. It takes little to imagine Mary murmuring the words in bitter satisfaction. But now she too was facing a crisis. Its outcome was to give her worldly felicity – but at what price? Morley's preface continues with a quotation from Seneca on the meaninglessness of the outward trappings of power – the 'purple robes and golden garmentes'. These were soon on Mary's mind as well. Faced with her father's offers to reconstitute her household and refresh her wardrobe, she found herself protesting to Cromwell that 'the king's favour is so good clothing to her, she desires no more'.[61]

Morley's preface thus takes us very close to his real conversations with Mary and to Mary's real concerns in that summer of 1536. It also shows why nobody in power cared two hoots about the fact that Morley and Mary had met or about what they had said when they met. Morley had waited on Mary as a neighbour, not as a partisan. They had discussed virtue, not politics. And virtue, especially otherworldly virtue, was a safe topic of conversation even under Henry VIII.

Mary left Hunsdon in December 1536, when, as a mark of her restoration to favour, she travelled *via* Richmond to spend Christmas at her father's court at Greenwich. But she seems to have been back at Hunsdon in March 1537 and again in September. Both these occasions, revealingly, show her contacts with local people. In 1538 there was another long stay, which included Christmas.[62] On 8 December Mary wrote to Cromwell from Hunsdon about the arrangements for the forthcoming festivities. She took for granted that she would be remaining at Hunsdon and asked for an increase in her quarterly allowance of £40 from the king: 'as this quarter of Christmas must be more chargeable than the rest, especially considering the house that I am in'. Cromwell obliged by arranging for an augmented payment of £100. We can imagine that 5*s.* of this went to Morley's servant when, on New Year's Day, he presented his master's now-usual gift of a book. Unfortunately, imagine is all that we can do, as Mary's accounts for 1539, with their list of rewards given for bringing New Year's Gifts, are missing.[63]

It seems certain that the gift was made, for my chronology of Morley's friendship with Mary fits well with Carley's revisionist dating of the books Morley gave her as New Year Gifts. I date their acquaintance-ripening-into-friendship to Mary's lengthy and frequent visits to Hunsdon in 1536-8 *and not before*. Similarly, Carley has shown that none of Morley's surviving gifts to Mary can be dated before 1537. But no fewer than six survive for the period 1537-47. It is, of course, conceivable that earlier presentations were made. But it does seem very strange that there should be a survival rate of zero for the pre-1537 gifts as against one of over half for the post-1537 volumes. Much safer, I think, is to assume that the sequence starts with Morley's ripening acquaintance with Mary in 1536-7. Inspired by his recent conversations with Mary, Morley may well have begun work on his first translation for her in the autumn of 1536 and had it presented the following New Year. The only problem is that on 1 January 1537 his servant was given a reward of 10*s.* However, on the two known occasions when Morley presented books, in 1543 and 1544, the reward was limited to half that amount (books, after all, were not all that valuable, especially little, do-it-yourself ones!).[64] The first time that Morley's servant is given 5*s.* is January 1538 and I would be inclined to place the *terminus a quo* then.[65]

So far, I have being trying to present Morley's relationships – personal and literary alike – in terms of 'natural' categories, like locality, rather than voluntaristic ones, like political affiliation. Another sort of 'natural' relationship in Tudor terms was service. This explains the otherwise strange fact – strange, that is, in terms of both religious commitment and social status – that Morley wrote as a familiar friend to Ralph Morice, archbishop Cranmer's rather radical secretary and eventual biographer. 'Fellow Raf', the usually punctilious nobleman began, before going on to ask Morice to secure Cranmer's discreet intervention in a local religious dispute in Harlow.[66] The term 'fellow' normally denotes fellow-servant. And this indeed Morice was by hereditary descent, as it were. His father, James, was clerk of the works to Morley's old patroness and mistress, Lady Margaret Beaufort. Morley thus addressed the son as 'fellow', as he would once have called his father, when they were both servants in Lady Margaret's household. James Morice had shared Lady Margaret's piety, and this piety, as was not uncommon, transmuted into his and his family's early interest in evangelical religion. His three sons also followed their father into successful careers of service: William, first with Richard Pace, the king's secretary and later with the king himself;

Ralph with Cranmer, to whom he was recommended by Lord Rochford; and Philip with Cromwell.[67] Much about Morley that is now lost is probably to be explained by his 'fellowship' with this band of brothers and his consequent hot-line to their diverse employers.

But finally, of course, it is Morley's attitude to his 'natural' lord, Henry VIII, that most matters. This underpins, or perhaps undermines, almost everything that he wrote or did, and it forms the substance of the rest of this book. I shall therefore try to be brief and sketch out no more than a few general principles. Henry VIII's great achievement was the break with Rome. Here there is an obvious inconsistency in Morley's attitude, between the vigour of his denunciation of 'the Babylonicall seate of the Romyshe byshop' in his *Exposition and Declaration of the Psalme, Deus ultionum Dominus* of 1539, and his equally passionate embrace in 1555 of 'the golden worlde [which] shall in processe come again' following Mary's restoration of the papal obedience.[68] But this inconsistency was, after all, no more than the inconsistency of his country and his class and arguably, if we take her submission to Henry VIII seriously, of Mary herself. Much more interesting and revealing are the continuities.

The first is a more-or-less vigorous anticlericalism. This is clear from his early despatches from Germany, where he comments complacently on the rude caricatures ('abominable pictures') of the pope and clergy that were in circulation. It also clear, as he sent a copy home to the king, 'which I think your highness will laugh at', that he expected that Henry VIII would enjoy them too.[69] For a pervasive anticlericalism was part of the *zeitgeist*. It was shared, not only by the king and his noble companions like the duke of Suffolk, but also by such important intellectual influences on Henry VIII as More and Erasmus, when they were in certain moods and on certain subjects.

The second continuity is Morley's conservative approach to doctrine and ritual. At first sight, this seems to sit uneasily with his anticlericalism. But, like most of the great names of his time, he found it easy to combine the two. And the traditionalism, like the anticlericalism, appears (often in the same sentence!) in those early letters from Germany. These are filled with disapproval of the lewd doctrines of Luther and his followers and their intention to 'subvert all aunsient faith'. Morley also knows exactly who is to blame for letting things get out of hand. It is the German princes who have failed in their duty to suppress errant doctrine: 'forasmuch as by the long sufferance of the princes that heresy is so rooted, that without peril to themself it is not to be commoned of'. Henry VIII, on the contrary, has been exemplary, and the only hope of orthodoxy lay in 'God's help and the assistance of your grace and other like princes'.[70]

Morley's view of the secular power as the bulwark of orthodoxy forms the third continuity in his thought. It survived all the vicissitudes of Henry VIII's reign and even lingered into Morley's sunset years under Mary. It is also wholly consistent with his English patriotism.

This English patriotism is the fourth continuity in Morley's life and work. His principal intellectual activity of translation from Latin and the romance languages into English is his life-long tribute to the English language.[71] But in his *Exposition and Declaration of the Psalme, Deus ultionum Dominus*, he goes much further and comes near to a modern doctrine of nationalism – English nationalism. Hitherto England had been in subjection to Rome. But Henry VIII, divinely inspired and determined 'to rule and nat to be ruled', had severed the bonds and 'set the Englysshe nation at fredoome and lybertie'. These are revolutionary thoughts which inspired Morley to revolutionary language – so revolutionary, indeed, that it anticipates later struggles and regimes. It was a Year One ('England is newe born'); it was a war of liberation to the death ('for where as there is nothing more swete than libertie, nothynge more bytter than bondage, in so moche that death hath ofte ben chosen to advoyde servitude'); Henry VIII was the great leader ('*Pater patriae*, that is, the father of our countrey'); Hail to Henry! ('you are our beautie, you are oure honour, you are our glorie'). Henry the Great, the English Augustus, Scipio, Cyrus, Saladin.[72]

And all this, it must be remembered, from a deeply conservative backwoods peer, the Essex man of his age. Some have speculated that Morley uttered these thoughts only under pressure, to protect himself from the charges of treason which his conservative leanings and contacts might otherwise have inspired. As we have seen, Morley's contacts hardly bear this construction. And, in any case, his prose seems to tell a different story. For in the *Exposition* Morley rises to heights of eloquence, originality, and ease of expression which he never attains elsewhere and which few other contemporary writers begin even to match.

Once again, therefore, we need to throw overboard our politico-religious prejudices about the period. Take, for example, Morley's sustained commitment to expanding both the English language and the body of thought available in English by his sequence of translations. The manifesto for this new confidence in the capacity of English was the preface, written by Sir Brian Tuke, to William Thynne's printed edition of Chaucer. In the preface, Tuke presents an elegant brief history of language, from the classical tongues through to the vernaculars of his own Europe. For him, there are two measures of the maturity of a language. The first is a regular grammar and an abundant vocabulary; the second is a notable literature. English, he proclaims, in his own times has acquired both. On the one hand, many have busied themselves in 'the beautifyeng and bettryng of thenglysh tonge', and, on the other, the present edition of Chaucer (complete, he claims, and prepared from the best texts), makes available the flower of English literature, which, like Homer to the Greeks or Cicero to the Romans, serves as a touchstone of excellence.

Now there is no doubt that this was in some measure an officially inspired edition: Thynne was clerk of the king's kitchen; Tuke was treasurer of the king's chamber; and the printer was the king's printer. It also appeared in 1532, the same year that the act of Annates fired the opening salvo against Rome. And the preface ends by lauding Henry VIII, in whom 'is renewed the glorious tytell of Defensor of the christen faithe, whiche by your noble progenytour, the great Constantyne, sometyme kyng of this realme & emperour of Rome, was nexte god and his apostels chefely maynteyned'.[73] This is the appeal to history, indeed to some of the same history, by which the royal supremacy itself was shortly to be justified.

But, and this is the important thing, Tuke, the author of this precocious radicalism, was himself impeccably religiously conservative. There is abundant visual testimony to this in his portrait by Holbein. It is inscribed with verses from the Book of Job; and pendant round his neck, hanging from his heavy golden chain of knighthood, is a crucifix. It is unusually large; it also bears the badge of the Five Wounds of Christ. Veneration of the Five Wounds was a sign of a 'high-temperature' religiosity. The Five Wounds were also the banner of the Pilgrims of Grace in their socially and religiously conservative revolt of 1536.[74] But, as Tuke's career and writings show, rebels had no monopoly of religious conservatism. Morley's life and writings are testimony to the same fact.

The *Exposition*, with its vehement nationalism and anti-papalism is, at first sight, a little harder to fit into this kind of pattern. The work nearest to it in tone and content is, as has long been realized, Richard Morison's *An Invective Ayenste the Great and Detestable Vice, Treason*. This was published in the same year, 1539, and also denounces, though frontally rather than indirectly, the king's former intimates who were executed in 1538-9 after the so-called Exeter conspiracy. Perhaps significantly, indeed, one of the three surviving copies of the *Exposition* is bound up with the *Invective* (London, British Library, 292. a. 3).[75] Now Morison, of course, was as far as could be from a conservative. True, his career had begun in Reginald Pole's household in Padua. But he had quit it promptly and returned to England to put his new-fangled Aristotelian scholarship at the service of the government. Once in England, his ability to write to order, his gift for the killer-phrase, and his willingness to kick men when they were down had quickly made him the chief royal propagandist. The covers of the British Library volume thus put the fastidious Morley in strange and rather vulgar company. But not so strange. For the work which defines the militantly nationalistic propaganda of these years was not by Morison, but by that very different figure, Cuthbert Tunstall, bishop of Durham.

It took the form of a court sermon, preached before the king on Palm Sunday, 1539. Palm Sunday was one of the days of estate. These were the principal feast days of the Church which were also the main occasions of court ceremony. In front of an unusually well-attended court, the king wore his robes and participated in heightened ceremony, both in the chapel and the chamber. This combination became particularly potent after the Reformation, when the Royal Supremacy combined the headship of Church and state in the king's person. Tunstall's sermon lived up to the occasion. It was a call to resist the ungodly mission which Cardinal Pole had launched against Henry VIII. 'Be nothing afraid', he exhorted his listeners, 'thou hast God on thy side. ... Only take an English heart unto thee and mistrust not God'. The sermon was immediately put into print by the king's printer so that it could reach an even wider audience.[76]

What gave the language of the sermon an added piquancy, however, was Tunstall's own position. He was a gentleman born and a prince by virtue of the palatine status of his bishopric. He was a scholar of European repute, who had dealt on equal terms with More and Erasmus. And he was a known theological conservative. Elton, taking the partisan view of support for the Reformation, remarks with surprise on this testimonial from one of his 'political opponents' for Cromwell's policies. This rather gets the order of priorities wrong. Tunstall was supporting not the minister but the king. And he was doing so freely because he was riding high in the king's favour at this point – higher indeed than Cromwell.

The previous summer Tunstall had been summoned to court to act as the king's theological councillor in devising a reply to an important initiative from the German Lutherans. The letter setting out the initiative had arrived in August, when the king was on progress. Tunstall accompanied the king, and, for several weeks, was virtually alone with him. Together they worked through the proposals, and the result was a comprehensive rejection of Lutheranism. This rejection led directly to the act of Six Articles, which, in turn, heralded the fall of Cromwell and the 'conservative reaction' of 1539/40.[77]

The reaction was comprehensive, in both religion and politics. The English church was committed to doctrinal orthodoxy; there was also a new political settlement which highlighted the role of the nobility. In particular, a new noble-dominated council, the privy council, became, in the aftermath of the fall of the low-born minister, the governing body of England.[78] Under, of course, the king. And under a king who remained, if anything more emphatically than before, Supreme Head of the Church. For the Supremacy was all the stronger, since, with Cromwell dead and Cranmer gagged, it could be fully supported by the broad body of sensible, conservative opinion – like Tunstall and Morley. It was, in short, a return to the settlement which had been envisaged in 1529. Even the issue of Uses, which had been the carrot for noble support in 1529, was reopened, and a new act enshrined the royal concessions which had been offered but rejected a decade earlier.

So Morley was not being as wilfully selective as it might appear when, in the account of eucharistic miracles he presented to Mary, now Queen, he included 'your worthy fathers dayes' in the times of 'plentye'. These were the ages when orthodox religion had given England treasure in heaven and earthly prosperity as well. Both had been destroyed by the disastrous changes under Edward VI, which had debauched religion and debased the coinage. But now, under Mary, he trusted, the 'golden worlde' would return, with the host on the altar and the pound in your pocket. But it would also return *because of* Mary.[79]

Here there is an interesting doubleness in Morley's thought. The catastrophes of Edward VI's reign had convinced Morley, along with many others, that the papal obedience was not something that could be dispensed with. Instead (as More had seen from the first) it was the only rock on which orthodoxy could stand. That was the logic of Morley's position. But his language tells a different story. England could trust in better times, he tells Mary, because of 'the hope that we have in God and you, swete, delycate, red rose, the very maynteyner off faythe'. In other words, Morley, even at his most orthodox, and even after the experiences of Edward VI's reign, remained at heart a believer in the Supremacy. He could not of course call it that. Instead, he gave the 'strong' interpretation to the queen's title of 'Defender of the Faith'. Though Philip and Mary had 'the greatest parte of Christendome under your subjectyon', Morley wrote, 'this one tytle ... of the Defendoresse off the Faithe ... [surpass]yth all the rest of your tytles and croun[es and i]s the very precyous gemme'. In other words, under Mary, as under Henry, the crown remained the only effective bulwark against heresy. Fortunately, perhaps, death spared Morley from having to confront the implications of the Elizabethan Supremacy. But I have the inkling that he – like most of his class – would have conformed.

NOTES

1 T. S. Eliot, *Collected Poems, 1909-1962* (London, 1963), p. 17.

2 *Rutland Papers*, ed. by W. Jerdan, Camden Society 21 (London, 1842), 35 and *LP Henry VIII* III.i.906/1; XII.ii.911, 1060; XIV.ii.572/3 (vi); XV.14; XXI.i.1384/ii.

3 G. E. Cokayne, *The Complete Peerage of England, Scotland, Ireland, Great Britain and the*

United Kingdom, ed. by V. Gibbs *et al.*, 13 vols in 14 (London 1910-59) [hereafter GEC] ix, 220-3; M. K. Jones & M. G. Underwood, *The King's Mother* (Cambridge, 1992), p. 114.

4 Jones & Underwood, *King's Mother*, pp. 165, 236-7.

5 *LP Henry VIII* II.i.2735, re-dated by D. Starkey, 'The King's Privy Chamber, 1485-1547' (unpublished Ph.D. dissertation, Cambridge, 1973), p. 426 n. f. A possible identification for one of these other Henry Parkers is suggested by S. T. Bindoff in *The History of Parliament: The House of Commons, 1509-1558*, 3 vols (London, 1982) III, 57-8.

6 D. Starkey, 'King Henry and King Arthur', *Arthurian Literature*, 16 (1998), 171-96.

7 D. Starkey, *The Reign of Henry VIII: Personalities and Politics* (London, 1985), pp. 47-8.

8 S. J. Gunn, *Charles Brandon, Duke of Suffolk, 1484-1545* (Oxford, 1988).

9 For all this, see Starkey, 'King Henry and King Arthur', pp. 185-6.

10 H. Miller, *Henry VIII and the English Nobility* (Oxford, 1986), pp. 137, 157.

11 *Forty-six Lives Translated from Boccaccio's* De Claris Mulieribus *by Henry Parker, Lord Morley*, ed. by H. G. Wright, EETS OS 214 (1943 [for 1940]), 168 and see below, pp. 232-3.

12 Below, p. 227.

13 GEC IX, 221 n. k; Miller, *Henry VIII and the English Nobility*, p. 12; *Forty-six Lives*, ed. by Wright, p. 162. See also Marie Axton, 'Lord Morley's "*Tryumphes of Fraunces Petrarcke*": Reading Spectacles', below, pp. 174-5.

14 *State Papers, Published under the Authority of His Majesty's Commission, King Henry VIII* 11 vols (London, 1830-52) I, 120-1; J. Strype, *Ecclesiastical Memorials*, 7 vols (London, 1816) I, 65-71.

15 Miller, *Henry VIII and the English Nobility*, p. 87; College of Arms, Vincent MS 152, p. 178, reproduced as the frontispiece to this volume.

16 *Forty-six Lives*, ed. by Wright, p. xvi.

17 For some of this, see D. Starkey, 'Court, Council and Nobility in Tudor England', in *Princes, Patronage and the Nobility*, ed. by R. G. Asch & A. M. Birke (Oxford, 1991), pp. 175-203.

18 S. E. Lehmberg, *The Reformation Parliament, 1529-1536* (Cambridge, 1970), pp. 94-7.

19 J. J. Scarisbick, *Henry VIII* (London, 1968), p. 259; Edward, Lord Herbert of Cherbury, *The Life and Raigne of King Henry the Eighth* (London, 1649), p. 306; *LP Henry VIII* IV.iii.6044.

20 Lehmberg, *Reformation Parliament*, pp. 134-5.

21 Miller, *Henry VIII and the English Nobility*, pp. 120-8; *LP Henry VIII* VII.391.

22 *LP Henry VIII* IV.iii, 6803/12; V.119/11; *Forty-six Lives*, ed. by Wright, pp. xxii-iii, xlvi n. 2. The paraphrase in GEC IX, 224 n. c gives the right nuance of the original Latin of the epitaph.

23 Some care is also needed here as there is no evidence that Morley was ever summoned to a council meeting as such. Instead, the lists of noblemen, including Morley, calendared in *LP Henry VIII* as summonses to (great) councils, are more likely to be draft lists of those to be impanelled for the court of the high steward for the trial of peers (compare *LP Henry VIII* X.834 with the actual panel for the trial of Rochford and Anne Boleyn, *LP Henry VIII* X.876/6, and *LP Henry VIII* XI.5 with the panel for the trials of Darcy and Hussey in 1537, *LP Henry VIII* XII.i.1207/20).

24 J. E. Powell & K. Wallis, *The House of Lords in the Middle Ages* (London, 1968), pp. 572-3; Miller, *Henry VIII and the English Nobility*, pp. 51-7.

25 *The Lisle Letters*, ed. by M. St Clare Byrne, 6 vols (Chicago & London, 1981) I, 5c.

26 GEC IX, 21-2 and see n. 24 above.

27 Miller, *Henry VIII and the English Nobility*, pp. 44-5, 157. See also James Simpson, 'The Sacrifice of Lord Rochford. Henry Parker, Lord Morley's Translation of *De Claris Mulieribus*', below, pp. 153-69.

28 *State Papers* I, 721 (*LP Henry VIII* XVI.1454).
29 Perhaps his known expertise as a bookman, as well as his conservative religious views, explain why his fellow peers put Morley on the committee to consider the abortive censorship bill for 'books containing false opinions' in 1545 (S. E. Lehmberg, *The Later Parliaments of Henry VIII, 1536-1547* (Cambridge, 1977), pp. 222-3).
30 GEC X, 131-3; Starkey, 'King Henry and King Arthur', pp. 191-3.
31 GEC IX, 224-5.
32 *LP Henry VIII* III.ii p. 1559 and see E. W. Ives, *Anne Boleyn* (Oxford, 1986), pp. 47-8.
33 Powell & Wallis, *The House of Lords*, pp. 560-2. Of the new earls, Rutland's mother was descended from Edward IV's sister, while Cumberland's father had (like Morley himself) married into the St Johns. The viscount was Robert Ratcliffe, Lord Fitzwalter, whose wife descended from the Staffords on one side and the Woodvilles on the other.
34 GEC X, 132 n. d.
35 *Original Letters Illustrative of English History*, 1st series, ed. by H. Ellis, 3 vols (London, 1824) II, 67-8; *LP Henry VIII* IV.ii p. 1331.
36 *House of Commons, 1509-1558*, ed. by Bindoff, III, 312.
37 *LP Henry VIII* IV.i.1939/14 and see Starkey, 'King's Privy Chamber', pp. 149-64.
38 *LP Henry VIII* IV.ii.4403; V p. 305; GEC X, 140-1; BL, Add. MS 9835, fols. 24-6 (*LP Henry VIII* V.927), discussed in Starkey, 'King's Privy Chamber', pp. 185-201; Ives, *Anne Boleyn*, p. 200.
39 *LP Henry VIII* VI.562 i & ii.
40 *LP Henry VIII* VI.613.
41 *LP Henry VIII* VII.372.
42 Ives, *Anne Boleyn*, pp. 242-3.
43 P. Freidman, *Anne Boleyn*, 2 vols (London, 1884) I, 266-8, 272.
44 *LP Henry VIII* IX.566 and cf. Ives, *Anne Boleyn*, p. 339.
45 Ives, *Anne Boleyn*, pp. 376-7.
46 The ground is gone over by G. W. Bernard, 'The Fall of Anne Boleyn', *English Historical Review*, 106 (1991), 584-610 and E. W. Ives, 'The Fall of Anne Boleyn Reconsidered', *English Historical Review*, 107 (1992), 651-64.
47 *LP Henry VIII* VII.1036; XI.222.
48 F. Madden, ed., *Privy Purse Expenses of the Princess Mary* (London, 1831), pp. 7, 42.
49 *LP Henry VIII* II.ii p. 1473; D. M. Loades, *Mary Tudor* (Oxford, 1991), pp. 346, 348.
50 *LP Henry VIII* IV.i.1577/13.
51 *LP Henry VIII* IV.iii.5406/5.
52 Rather nicely, Mary's own correspondence in 1536, the year when her acquaintance with Morley was most intense, contains a revealing remark about the status of chamberer. She would, she wrote to her father on 21 July, 'rather be a chamberer, having the fruition of the King's presence, than an Empress away from him' (*LP Henry VIII* XI.132).
53 Freidman, *Anne Boleyn* I, 266-8; II, 36, 122.
54 *LP Henry VIII* X.99, 307.
55 *History of the King's Works*, ed. by H. M. Colvin *et al.*, 6 vols (1963-82), IV, 154-5.
56 *LP Henry VIII* X.968, 991, 1022, 1083, 1108, 1109, 1129, 1133, 1136.
57 Ibid., 1134/1, 4.
58 *LP Henry VIII* XIV.i.190.
59 *Forty-six Lives*, ed. by Wright, pp. 170-1.
60 Psalm 37. 36-7.
61 *LP Henry VIII* XI.6.
62 Madden, *Privy Purse Expenses of Mary*, pp. lxxvii-viii, lxxxii-iii.
63 *LP Henry VIII* XI.1269 misdates Mary's letter to 1536. Madden, *Privy Purse Expenses of*

Mary, p. lxxxiii establishes the correct year by reference to her accounts. The missing accounts for 1539 are noted by Madden on p. 82.

64 Madden, *Privy Purse Expenses of Mary*, pp. 7, 97, 143.

65 Ibid., p. 51.

66 *LP Henry VIII* VI.1600-1.

67 D. MacCulloch, *Thomas Cranmer* (New Haven & London, 1996), p. 18; Jones & Underwood, *King's Mother*, p. 279.

68 See below, pp. 232, 258.

69 *LP Henry VIII* III.ii.3390.

70 *LP Henry VIII* III.ii.3390, 3546.

71 In his earlier translation of Petrarch's *Trionfi*, Morley was inspired by emulation of the French translator Simon Bourgouyn and by his conviction that what a Frenchman had done an Englishman could do at least as well. This attitude looks back to the fierce, but punctilious, competitions between the French and English Courts which Glenn Richardson has identified as characterizing the periods of Anglo-French peace in the first half of Henry VIII's reign. (See G. J. Richardson, 'Anglo-French Political and Cultural Relations during the Reign of Henry VIII' (unpublished Ph.D. dissertation, London, 1996), especially chapter 3.) It also looks forward to the strident English nationalism of the Reformation, of which the *Exposition* is one of the most hectic flowers.

72 See below, p. 232.

73 W. Thynne, ed., '*The Works of Geoffrey Chaucer*, introduced by W. W. Skeat, fac. edn (London, n.d.), pp. xxii-iv.

74 J. Rowlands, *Holbein: The Paintings of Hans Holbein the Younger* (Oxford, 1985), pp. 144-5; the Pilgrims' banner is reproduced on the cover of A. Fletcher, *Tudor Rebellions* (London, 1968).

75 *Forty-six Lives,* ed. by Wright, pp. li n. 7; lxxxi n. 4.

76 Cited in G. R. Elton, *Policy and Police* (Cambridge, 1972), p. 190.

77 R. McEntegart, 'England and the League of Schmalkalden' (unpublished Ph.D. dissertation, London, 1992), pp. 256-85.

78 See n. 17 above.

79 See below, p. 258.

THE WRITINGS OF HENRY PARKER, LORD MORLEY

A Bibliographical Survey[1]

JAMES P. CARLEY

ON 3 JANUARY 1538 John Husee wrote to his master Arthur Plantagenet, Viscount Lisle, describing the annual presentation of New Year's gifts at Court:

> The King stood leaning against the cupboard, receiving all things; and Mr. Tuke at the end of the same cupboard, penning all things that were presented; and behind his Grace stood Mr. Kingston and Sir John Russell, and besides his Grace stood the Earl of Hertford and my Lord Privy Seal. There was but a small Court.[2]

He also observed that Cromwell singled him out to the king who, in turn, made gracious comments to him: 'It was gently done of my Lord Privy Seal to have your lordship in remembrance, setting the matter so well forward.' The scene recreates vividly both the ritual of the New Year's Day gift-giving ceremony and the potential for favour which lay behind it. The nobility and clergy were all expected to exchange gifts with the monarch and there was a strict hierarchy; the ultimate aim was to have one's contribution singled out, in order that one's interests ('the matter') might be forwarded in the following months. The 1538 scenario shows Cromwell as quite literally the power behind, or rather beside, the throne.[3]

A similar ceremony took place in the households of Henry's children and the same protocol determined the value of gifts given and received.[4] As a rule the nobility presented jewels, clothing, plate or money.[5] Henry Parker, Lord Morley, thus stands out as anomaly among this group: clearly, he took himself seriously as a writer and translator and considered his own efforts worthy of presentation to patrons or potential patrons. Over approximately twenty-five years he presented books as New Year's gifts to Henry (six survive and several are lost), to Mary (eight survive and there may have been more), and Thomas Cromwell (one survives and there are references to others). In some cases, there was a close link between the book and desires for patronage: for example, when he gave Cromwell a copy of Niccolò Machiavelli's *Istorie Fiorentine* and *Il Principe*, he ended his letter with a request: 'I pray youe ... to tender me in suche things as Maister Rycharde Croumwell schall sew to youre Lordschip for me.'[6] His inspiration for translating Petrarch's *Trionfi* into English for Henry VIII came from an example at the French court, where – as he pointed out – the translator of this text into French was well rewarded for his efforts.[7] His presentations to Mary, to whom he appears to have been genuinely devoted,[8] seem more disinterested and on one occasion he assured her that in spite of his gift and its flattering introduction he did not 'loke to have favour of youe'.[9] At the end of his life, too, one daughter long since executed, his son and wife more recently deceased but his beloved Mary safely enthroned, Morley bade his adieux to the life of the court, observing:

Manuscript copies of the Writings of Henry Parker, Lord Morley

Work	Date	Hand	Decoration
Petrarch, 'Tryumphes'	before 1547		
'Plutarch', 'Lives of Scipio & Haniball'	1522-35	later court hand	strapwork initials
'Plutarch', 'Lyff of Kyng Agesylayus'	*c.* 1538	later court hand	strapwork initials
Plutarch, 'Life of Thesius'	1542-46/7	calligraphic later court hand	strapwork initials with scrollwork and decoration
Plutarch, 'Lyfe of Paulus Emilius'	1542-46/7	calligraphic later court hand (as 'Lyfe of Thesius')	strapwork initials with scrollwork and decoration
'Exposition and Declaration'	*c.* 1539		
Paolo Giovio, 'Commentarys of the Turke'	1536-41	Hand C	strapwork initials
Boccaccio, 'Of the ryghte renoumyde ladyes'	1542-46/7	Hand C	strapwork initials with scrollwork and decoration
Masuccio Salernitano, 'Tale'	1544-46/7	Hand C	strapwork initials with scrollwork and decoration
'Thomas Aquinas', 'Angelical Salutacion' &c.	1537-47	Italic hand	decorated initials with scrollwork and other decorations
Johannes de Turrecremata, 'Exposition of Psalm xxxvi'	1538-40 or 1543	Hand C	strapwork initials with scrollwork
Erasmus, 'Laude unto the Virgyn Mary'	1537-47	Hand C	strapwork initials with scrollwork
Preface to Rolle's Latin Psalter	1538-40 or 1543	Hand C	strapwork initials with scrollwork
'Tytylles of the Salmes' &c.	1541 or 1544-46/7	calligraphic later court hand	strapwork initials with scrollwork and grotesques
Seneca, 'Epistles'	1537-47	calligraphic later court hand	strapwork initials with decoration
Cicero, 'Dreme of Sypyon'	1548-53	Hand C	strapwork initials
Miracles of the Sacrament	1555-6	later court hand	

Printed	Recipient	Provenance
c. 1553/4-56 J[ohn C[awood]	1. Henry VIII 2. Henry Fitzalan, Lord Maltravers	1. MS Lost 2. Lost presentation copy in Arundel/ Lumley Library
	Henry VIII	O.R.L. 1199. Now BL, Royal MS 17 D.xi
	Thomas Cromwell	Cromwell → NLW Now Aberystwyth, NLW 17038C
	Henry VIII	O.R.L. 1189. Now BL, Royal MS 17 D.ii
	Henry VIII	O.R.L. → Oxford. Now Bodleian Library, Laud MS misc. 684
1539. Thomas Berthelet	1. Henry VIII	1. MS Lost
	Henry VIII	O.R.L. 997 → Earl of Arundel. Now BL, Arundel MS 8
	Henry VIII	O.R.L. → Duke of Devonshire. Now Chatsworth, Devonshire Collection MS
	Henry VIII	O.R.L. Now BL, Royal MS 18 A.lxii
	Mary Tudor	O.R.L. Now BL, Royal MS 17 C.xvi
	Mary Tudor	O.R.L. Now BL, Royal MS 18 A.xv
	Mary Tudor	O.R.L. Now BL, Royal MS 17 A.xlvi
	Mary Tudor	O.R.L. Now BL, Royal MS 2 D.xxviii
	Mary Tudor	O.R.L. Now BL, Royal MS 17 C.xii
	Mary Tudor	O.R.L. Now BL, Royal MS 17 A.xxx
	Mary Tudor	O.R.L. Now BL, Royal MS 18 A.lx
	Mary Tudor	O.R.L. → BL. Now Add. MS 12060

And I humbly praye your gracyous magestie not to thinke that I do tell this as S. Jerome writeth to that noble lady Salvina after that sorte, that the Grekes do, to have the more grace of you, in telling an untrue tale. God be my judge such kinde of speche I never used to that vertuous person of yours. The love and the truth that I have borne to your highnes from your childhod is a wytnes for me afore God, and your magestie, for the which I have receyvyd of you, my most gracious Lady and Maistres, a rewarde more precyous then golde or stone, that is libertye to end myne olde dayes in quyet.[10]

Reginald Pole's Legatine Register contains an absolution for schism for Morley, dated 23 March 1555, in which Morley is described as having resisted schism.[11] Scholars have assumed that when Morley died a year later in November 1556 he was 80 years old and that he was thus born in 1476. The evidence is taken from an epitaph composed by his grandson now kept in the tower of the church at Great Hallingbury ('Vixit annos 80, obiit anno domini 1556, mense Novembris').[12] This is one of a group of six brasses to Morley, his wife and grandparents (five written by Morley himself), all engraved at the same time, and meant to be affixed to a marble tomb in the church. Nevertheless, as the entry in *The Complete Peerage* notes without specifying: 'the dates are mostly erronious'.[13] For example, the brass to his paternal grandmother states that she died in 1440 at age 70, whereas the brass to his father does not have him born until 1464 (i.e. dying 1520 at age 56). In fact, Morley's father seems to have died before 1506 rather than 1520 as is stated on the brass and his mother's will is dated 9 April 1518, although her brass has her dying in 1528. Doubtless, the calculations on Morley's brass are also inaccurate, as indeed *The Complete Peerage* implies when it notes that he was 'aged 33 and more in 1519' (p. 221). In BL Add. MS 12060, fol. 21^v, Morley describes New Year's festivities which occurred in Lady Margaret's household when he was 'of the age of fyftene yeares'. The year must have been 1496, since the occasion was to celebrate William Smith's elevation to the see of Lincoln (and Smith was translated in January 1496).[14] In this case Morley would have been born in 1481. His description of his age might possibly have been rounded off by a year or so, but it is highly unlikely that he would say he was fifteen when he was in fact twenty, especially since part of the point of the story was to emphasize his youth. This redating, taking approximately five years off his age, makes more sense of the other events of his life and in particular renders the Dürer portrait, drawn in 1523, somewhat more credible; as Carnicelli has observed: 'Dürer was not given to idealized portraiture. ... The face is lean and handsome, *extremely youthful in appearance* considering Morley's forty-seven years' (my emphasis).[15]

Morley's career may have been a relatively undistinguished one, as Stephen Gunn has observed,[16] but it is in another sense remarkable that he managed to survive the various potential crises in his life: close association with Mary at a particularly dangerous time, intermarriage with the Boleyns, possible links with the Pilgrimage of Grace,[17] cultivation of Cromwell as a patron, disgrace of his daughter. His New Year's gifts, moreover, mirror the complex negotiations between individuals, patrons, and factions which constituted the web of his life and the Tudor world in general.[18]

The Writings of Henry Parker, Lord Morley

NEW YEAR'S GIFTS TO HENRY VIII

A. Manuscripts

1. **London, British Library, Royal MS 17 D.xi.** 'Lives of Scipio and Haniball.' Translation of the *vitae* – written by Donato Acciaiuoli in spite of the attribution to Plutarch,[19] – in Plutarch, *Vitae illustrium virorum*: pr. Venice, 1491 (Goff P-833), fols lxviii^{r}-lxxix^{v}.[20]

40 + iii leaves.[21] 275 × 190 (190 × 120) mm. Front and back flyleaves taken from a 14th-cent. copy of Peter Comester's *Historia scholastica*. 34-46 lines per page. Paper. 1522-35.[22] Old Royal Inventory Number 1199.

Written in a somewhat cursive later court hand, possibly by a professional scribe. Fols 1, and i-iii at end blank, although borders are marked for written text. Strapwork W, infilled with leaf, on fol. 3^{r} and three other elaborate capitals. Text ends fol. 40^{r}26.

On fol. 2^{r} there is a scribble in lead-point: 'Worke wysely quod Wyngffeld'.[23]

Preface printed in *Forty-six Lives*, ed. by Wright, pp. 161-2. Fols 38^{v}-40^{r} contain 'The comparing together of thes twaine noble emperours Haniball and Scipio'.[24]

2. **London, British Library, Arundel MS 8.** 'The Commentarys of the Turke.' Translation of Paolo Giovio, *Commentario de le cose de' Turchi*: pr. Rome, 1535 (H. M. Adams, *Catalogue of Books Printed on the Continent of Europe, 1501-1600, in Cambridge Libraries*, 2 vols [Cambridge, 1967], G-680) &c.[25]

ii + 35 + iii leaves. 280 × 195 (195 × 125) mm. Catchwords on fols 12^{v}, 26^{v}. Ruled for 27-28 ll. per page. Paper. 1536-41.[26] Old Royal Inventory Number 997.

Written in anglicana formata by C.[27] Strapwork T with decorative motif on fols 1^{r} and 3^{r}. Text ends fol. 35^{v}21.

Preface printed in *Forty-six Lives*, ed. by Wright, pp. 160-1.

3. **Chatsworth, Devonshire Collection MS.** 'Of the ryghte renoumyde ladyes.' Translation from Boccaccio, *De claris mulieribus*: pr. Ulm 1473 (*GW* 4483) &c.[28]

i + 47 + i leaves. 245 × 195 (185 × 138) mm. Ruled for 31 ll. per page. Vellum. 1542-46/7 (Henry is 'of ... Irelonde Kynge'). Heavily cropped. Leaf missing between fols 3 + 4.

Written in anglicana formata by C. Strapwork initials with scrollwork and grotesques, animals or flowers on almost every folio.[29] The royal monogram HR VIII is found in the scrollwork of the capital T on fol. 1^{r}; the scrollwork of the capital M on fol. 12^{v} contains the first words of the Angelical Salutation: aue maria gra*tia*.[30] Text ends fol. 47^{r}10.

Complete text printed in *Forty-six Lives*, ed. by Wright, pp. 1-159.[31]

4. **London, British Library, Royal MS 17 D.ii.** 'Lyfe of Thesius.' Translation of the Plutarch *vita* in the Latin version of Lapo da Castiglionchio (Lapus Florentinus Minor): pr. *Vitae illustrium virorum* (1491), fols 1^{r}-5^{r}.

38 + i leaves. 255 × 190 (180 × 115) mm. Some remnants of old foliation in bottom right margins. Ruled for 22 ll. per page. Vellum. 1542-46/7 (Henry is 'of ... Irelonde Kynge'). Old Royal Inventory Number 1189.

Written in a self-consciously calligraphic later court hand by the same scribe as Laud misc. 684, described below. Strapwork A, with scrollwork and animal or grotesque

Fig. 1. London, British Library, Royal MS 17 D.II, fol. 1^{r}. The scribe of 17 D.II was also responsible for Laud misc. 684. This decorative motif turns up in other manuscripts. Reproduced by kind permission of the British Library Board.

heads on fol. 1^{r}; strapwork L with scrollwork and rose on fol. 3^{r}. Text ends on fol. $38^{r}2$.
Preface printed in *Forty-six Lives*, ed. by Wright, pp. 162-3.

5. Oxford, Bodleian Library, Laud MS misc. 684 (S.C. 1280). 'Lyfe of Paulus Emilius.' Translation of the Plutarch *vita* in the version of Leonardo Bruni Aretino: pr. *Vitae illustrium virorum* (1491), fols ci^{r}-cv^{r}.
i + 39 leaves. 190 × 148 (140 × 93) mm. Ruled for 23 ll. per page. Vellum. 1542-46/7 (Henry is 'of Irelond Kynge').

Written in a self-consciously calligraphic later court hand. Strapwork T with marigold on fol. 1^{r}; strapwork A, with scrollwork and animal and grotesque heads on fol. 1^{v}; decorated T with Tudor rose on fol. 3^{r}. Text ends fol. $38^{r}13$. Although ruled, the front and back pastedowns, as well as fols i, 39, are blank apart from later additions. Original green velvet binding.[32]

Preface printed in *Forty-six Lives*, ed. by Wright, pp. 164-5.

6. London, British Library, Royal MS 18 A.LXII. 'Tale from Massuccyo Salernytano.' Translation of the 49th tale from Masuccio Salernitano, *Il Novellino*: pr. Naples 1476 (Hain 10884) &c.; ed. by A. Mauro (Bari, 1940).
14 + i leaves. 255 × 190 (155 × 120) mm. Foliation beginning B1 on fol. 9 visible in bottom right margins (the first gathering is of 8). Ruled throughout for 19 ll. per page. Vellum. 1544-46/7.[33]

Written in anglicana formata by C. Strapwork S with scrollwork on fol. 2^{r}; strapwork F with profile male and grotesque head on fol. 4^{r}; strapwork F with

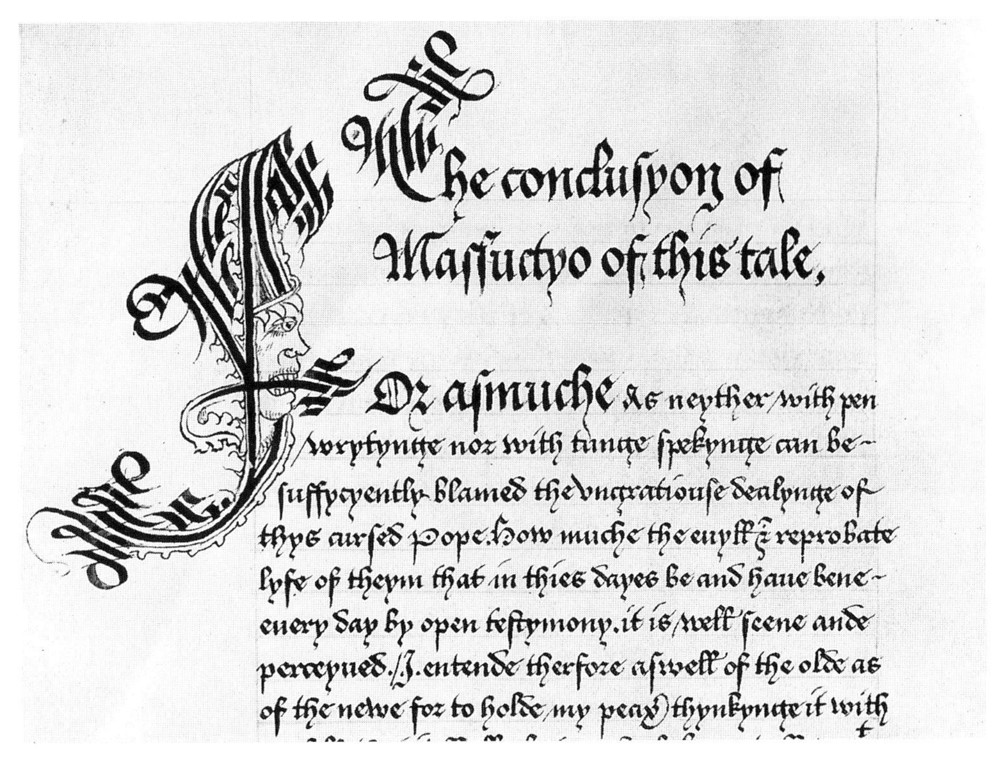
The conclusyon of
Massuctyo of this tale,
Forasmuche as neyther with pen
wrytynge nor with tunge spekynge can be-
suffycyently blamed the ungratiouse dealynge of
thys cursed pope. How muche the euyll & reprobate
lyfe of theym that in thies dayes be and haue bene-
euery day by open testymony. it is well seene and
perceyued. I entende therfore aswell of the olde as
of the newe for to holde my peax thynkynge it with

Fig. 2. London, British Library, Royal MS 18 A.LXII, fol. 12^{v}. This illustrates the hand of the scribe (C) responsible for seven of Morley's presentation manuscripts. Reproduced by kind permission of the British Library Board.

scrollwork on fol. 5^{r}; strapwork F with profile male head on fol. 12^{v}. Folio 1^{r} blank. Text ends fol. 13^{r}18. On fol. 14^{r} the following note occurs in a contemporary hand: 'The sven [deleted] seven gyftes of the holy ghoste are compared unto seven operations effectes of a fyer.'

Ed. by F. Brie, 'Die erste Übersetzung einer italienischen Novelle ins Englishe durch Henry Parker, Lord Morley (ca. A.D. 1545),' *Archiv für das Studium der neveren Sprachen und Literaturen* 124 (1910), 46-57 (pp. 49-57); preface printed in *Forty-six Lives*, ed. by Wright, pp. 165-6.

Lost

7. 'Tryumphes of Fraunces Petrarcke.' Translation of Francesco Petrarca, *Trionfi*: first pr. Venice 1470 (Goff P-371).[34]

In the dedicatory epistle to Lord Maltravers accompanying the printed edition of his *Tryumphes of Fraunces Petrarcke* (1553-6) Morley stated that he did 'translate the sayde booke to that moost worthy kynge our late soveraygne Lorde of perpetuall memorye kynge Henrye theyghte [...] what his highnes dyd with it, is to me unknowen ... '.[35]

8. 'The Exposition and Declaration of the Psalme, *Deus ultionum Dominus*.'
Thomas Berthelet's printed edition of 1539 reproduces what must have been the dedicatory epistle to the manuscript earlier presented to Henry VIII: 'I than offer unto your hyghnesse this newe yere, dere and dred soveraygne lorde, this psalme of king Dauid, *Deus ultionum dominus*, with a briefe declaration of the same, moste humbly praienge your high accustomed goodnes to accepte it in gree, & not to regarde the rudenes, but rather the faithfulnes of me your subject, that wylleth with the very harte, as he writeth, goodnes, and all goodnesse to you.'[36]

B. Printed Work

The Exposition and Declaration of the Psalme, 'Deus ultionum Dominus', made by Syr Henry Parker knight, Lord Morley, dedicated to the Kynges Highnes. London: Thomas Berthelet, 1539. (*STC* 19211).

Survives in 3 copies on paper: London, Lambeth Palace 1553.07(3); British Library, 292.a.33(2); Oxford, Bodleian Library, Mason CC.37. The Berthelet border ('A compartment with cherubic head above and 1534 in the sill') was used in a number of books published from 1534 up to 1569.[37]

NEW YEAR'S GIFTS TO MARY TUDOR

1. **London, British Library, Royal MS 17 C.XVI.** 'The Angelical Salutacion set forthe by Thomas Alquine.' Adaptation and translation from various authors including Aquinas. 'The Stature and Forme and lyfe of ouer blessed Lady and of ouer Savior Criste Jesu brevely discryved by Sayncte Anselme.' Translation of portions of a version of the *Epistola Lentuli*, pr. among the works of Anselm: see T. A. & J. P. Gabler, *Kleinere theologische Schriften*, 2 vols (Ulm, 1831), II, 662.

i + 12 leaves + i + paper flyleaf. 206 × 140 (136 × 99) mm. Ruled for 22 ll. per page. Vellum. 1537-47.[38]

Written in a English italic hand. Decorated S with scrollwork and animal or grotesque heads and marigolds on fol. 2^{r}; decorated B with animal or grotesque heads and flowers on fol. 4^{r}; decorated M with marigolds on fol. 10^{v}. Folio 1^{r} contains a full-page drawing of the Virgin with crown and sceptre holding the Child.[39] Text ends on fol.12^{r}7.

Preface printed in *Forty-six Lives*, ed. by Wright, pp. 172-3.

2. **London, British Library, Royal MS 18 A.XV.** Translation of the Exposition of Psalm xxxvi from Johannes de Turrecremata, *Expositio super toto Psalterio*: pr. Rome 1470 (Goff T-517) &c. Translation 'in an Italion Ryme called Soneto' of a *Carmina de utilitate psalmorum* attributed to Maffeo Vegio da Lodi: ed. by E. Flügel, 'Verschollene Sonette', *Anglia* 13 (1891), 72-6 (pp. 74-5); E. P. Hammond, *English Verse between Chaucer and Surrey* (Durham, N. C., 1927), p. 391.[40]

i + 9 + v leaves. 250 × 200 (175 ×105/124) mm. Written leaves ruled for 29 ll. per page. Paper. 1538-40 or 1543 (Edward is commended, but no queen mentioned: 'accepte my good wyll that I do beare unto youe, next youre victoriouse father ... your swete and noble, towarde brother Prynce Edward').

Written in anglicana formata by C. Strapwork T on fol. 1^{r}; strapwork I with scrollwork on fol. 2^{r}; strapwork T on fol. 3^{r}. Text ends on fol. 9^{r}.25.

Preface printed in *Forty-six Lives*, ed. by Wright, pp. 170-1.

3. **London, British Library, Royal MS 17 A.XLVI.** 'Laude or prayse to be saide unto the Virgyn Mary mother of Chryste Jesu'. Translation of Erasmus, *Paean Virgini matri dicendus*: first published in *Lucubratiunculae* (Antwerp, 1503) and subsequently printed with other works.

ii + 22 + ii leaves. 188 × 138 (123 × 88) mm. Gatherings of 8; quire signatures. Ruled for 19 ll. per page. Vellum. 1537-47.

Written in anglicana formata by C. Strapwork T, strapwork S with scrollwork containing the initials MA on fol. 1^{r}; strapwork T, strapwork M containing the phrase 'aue ma' on fol. 4^{r}. Text ends on fol. 22^{r}.16.

Preface printed in *Forty-six Lives*, ed. by Wright, pp. 171-2.

4. **London, British Library, Royal MS 2 D.XXVIII.** Prefatory letter by Morley to Richard Rolle of Hampole's Latin Psalter.[41]

4 leaves. 220 × 145 (155 × 110) mm. Vellum. 1538-40, or 1543 ('to pray, fyrst for your moste royall father ... next for your moste exellent and towarde brother, the Prynce, and thyrde, for youe').

Written in anglicana formata by C. Strapwork T with scrollwork containing the initials MA on fol. 3^{v}. Text begins fol. 3^{v}, ends fol. 4^{r}.15.

Erased inscription on fol. 85^{r}: To Sir Jh – – – this booke be delveryed.

Preface printed in *Forty-six Lives*, ed. by Wright, pp. 168-9.

5. **London, British Library, Royal MS 17 C.XII.** 'Tytylles of the Salmes of David.' Athanasius, Preface to exposition of the Psalms, Latin tr. by Angelo Poliziano: pr. Paris, 1507 &c.

23 + i leaves. 206 × 153 (140 × 100) mm. Gatherings of 4; quire signatures. Ruled for 19 ll. per page. Paper. 1541 or 1544-46/7 (Morley salutes 'ouer nobyll Quene and your swete brother').

Written in a self-conscious calligraphic later court hand. Fols 1^{r}, 3^{r}+^{v} blank. Strapwork initials with scrollwork and grotesques on fols 2^{r} &c. Text ends on fol. 23^{r}.15.

Preface printed in *Forty-six Lives*, ed. by Wright, pp. 169-70.

6. **London, British Library, Royal MS 17 A.XXX.** 'The foure-score twelfth Epistle of Senecke, joyned to the same parte of the eighteenth Epistle of the said auctour.' Translation from Seneca *Epistulae morales*, letter 91, linked to a passage from letter 120.[42]

19 + iii leaves. 166 × 121 (95 × 69) mm. Ruled for 12 ll. per page. Paper. 1537-47.

Written in a self-conscious calligraphic later court hand. Strapwork I on fol. 1^{r}; strapwork T with profile male head on fol. 4^{r}. Text ends fol. 19^{r}.4.

Ed. by Carlson, below, pp. 247-50; preface printed in *Forty-six Lives*, ed. by Wright, pp. 173-4

Jayne makes a tentative but almost certainly mistaken identification with no. 2197 in the Lumley catalogue ('Senecaes epistles, some of them translated into English. manuscript').[43]

7. **London, British Library, Royal MS 18 A.lx.** 'The dreme of Sypyon, taken owt of the syxte boke of Cicero, intytlyd *De republyca.*' Translation of the *Somnium Scipionis* section of Cicero's *De re publica*: ed. by K. Ziegler, rev. edn (Leipzig, 1969), pp. 126-36.

i + 7 + vi leaves. 250 × 175 (190 × 125) mm. Ruled for 34-5 ll. per page. Vellum. 1548-53 (Mary is addressed as 'Prynces' and Edward as 'Kyng').

Written in anglicana formata by C. Ruled throughout except for first and last leaf. Strapwork T, M on fol. 1^r; strapwork T, W on fol. 2^r. Text ends on fol. 7^v.22.

Ed. by Carlson, pp. 241-6 below; preface printed in *Forty-six Lives*, ed. by Wright, pp. 174-5.

8. **London, British Library, Add. MS 12060.** Account of the Miracles of the Sacrament.

i + 23 leaves. 234 × 155 (165 × 105) mm. 1^4, 2^4, 3^4, 4^4, 5^4, 6^4 (lacks 1; stub showing). Ruled for 25 ll. per page. Vellum. 1555-6.[44]

Written in a professional later court hand. No decorated initials. Leaf missing at end. Ed. by Carley & Rex, below, pp. 253-69; preface and prologue printed in *Forty-six Lives*, ed. by Wright, pp. 175-84.[45]

NEW YEAR'S GIFT TO THOMAS CROMWELL

Aberystwyth, NLW MS 17038C. 'The Lyff of the Good Kyng Agesylayus.' Translation of Xenophon's *vita* in the Latin version by Battista, son of Guarino Veronese, rather than that of Antonio Pacini da Todi (Morley calls him Anthony Tudartyn) as early printers thought.[46]

1 + 35 leaves. 262 × 185 (135 × 91) mm. Ruled for 22 ll. per page, except for the last ruled for 23 lines. Paper. *c.* 1538.[47]

Written in a somewhat cursive later court hand. Strapwork initials on fols 1^v, 2^r, and 5^v. Text ends fol. 35^r10, followed by a larger 'Amen'. Rebound in full morocco with gilt tooling in the nineteenth century.

Fol. i is an addition, containing a letter of presentation dated at Ludlow, 20 Nov. 1602, to Edward La Zouche from William Kenrick. On fol. 1^r there are pen trials reproducing 'Gramatice partes quot sunt octo' in different forms, and the phrase 'monye makethe my ...'. This phrase also occurs erased in the upper margin of fol. 11^r.

Dedicatory letter and 'The comparcuyon of oure most dere and gratyous soverayne lord kyng Henry to this Agesylayus kyng of the Lacydymones', ed. by Carley, below, pp. 226-9.

PRINTED BOOK PRESENTED TO HENRY FITZALAN, LORD MALTRAVERS

The tryumphes of Fraunces Petrarcke, translated out of Italian into English by Henrye Parker knight, Lord Morley. London: John Cawood, 1553/4-56 (*STC* 19,811).[48]

Survives in 5 copies on paper: London, BL, C.13.a.7(2) (formerly 232.f.29, George III's copy); BL, G.10713; private collection, olim London, Sion College K.12.5/P.44 E;[49]

Oxford, Bodleian Library, 40 P.57.Jur; San Marino, Calif, The Huntington Library, RB 47870.[50]
Ed. by D. D. Carnicelli, *Lord Morley's 'Tryumphes'*.[51]

TEXTS MISATTRIBUTED TO MORLEY

1. **London, British Library, Harley MS 6561.** 'The Pistellis and Gospelles for the LII Sondayes in the Yere.' Translation by George Boleyn of Jacques Lefèvre d'Etaples, *Epistres et Evangiles des cinquante et deux sepmaines de l'an*, in the printed edition of Simon Du Bois (Alençon, 1530-2).[52]

i + 202 fols; back flyleaf taken from a medieval service book. 185 × 125 (145 × 90) mm. Ruled throughout for 30 ll. per page. Vellum. 1532-3.[53]

Written in high-grade bastard secretary with elements of italic. Marking the beginning of the preface on fol. 2ʳ is a coroneted lozenge with Anne's arms situated in a square frame. In the lower corners of the frame and left and right under the coronet a cipher (made up of the letters HENREXSL) occurs. Fol. 2ᵛ has 14 ll. of text. A title-page occurs on fol. 3ʳ, contained in an architectural border of gold, with Anne's arms in a roundel at the top. On fol. 3ᵛ there is another architectural border with corner medallions representing the four evangelists; St Peter and St Paul form part of the design of the side pillars. Within the border is a miniature of the Crucifixion with the Virgin Mary, St John and Mary Magdalen at the foot of the cross. Fol. 4ʳ has another architectural border: Anne's arms form the decoration of the opening initial of text. Throughout the text there are initials of three related designs. Text ends near bottom of damaged fol. 202ᵛ.

Preface printed in *Forty-six Lives*, ed. by Wright, pp. 187-8.

In spite of the fact that the dedication page has suffered considerable damage, the nineteenth-century antiquary John Holmes was able to decipher a reference to 'the perpetuall bond of blood' which united the translator/donor and his patron.[54] Examining the possibilities he concluded that the author must have been Morley – Morley was George Boleyn's father-in-law – and this attribution has been generally accepted. Later, using ultraviolet light Wright was able to read the whole preface, in the first sentence of which the author declared himself Anne's 'moost lovyng and fryndely brother'; Wright concluded that brother was being used metaphorically and upheld Holmes's attribution. In fact, there is no indication that the term is being used in any but the literal sense and the fit is perfect. Anne's brother George was fluent in French and served in France on several diplomatic missions. Like Anne he was sympathetic with the strain of French evangelical thought exemplified by this work and, of course, he formed part of Anne's intimate coterie. Harley represents the level of manuscript suitable for him to have commissioned and there is a cipher on fol. 1ᵛ which almost certainly contains the letters of his name.

2. **London, British Library, Royal MS 17 D.XIII.** Henry Parker, Knight. Commentary on Ecclesiastes. Presented to Edward Seymour, Duke of Somerset.

103 leaves + modern flyleaves at front and back. 280 × 190 (175 × 140) mm. Apart from preface, ruled for 23 ll. per page; gatherings of 8 (except for m (10) and n (3) with quire signatures in lower middle margin. Paper. 1548-9.[55]

Written in a idiosyncratic calligraphic later court hand by a non-professional scribe. Strapwork F on fol. 3^{r}; strapwork H on fol. 7^{r}. Text corrected by scribe. Text ends fol. 103^{v}17.

Preface printed in *Forty-six Lives*, ed. by Wright, pp. 184-7.

The Commentary on Ecclesiastes is the only manuscript attributed to Morley not to have been prepared as a New Year's gift. Noting that the style is almost 'Johnsonian' in its cadences Wright described it as 'the most comprehensive exposition of Morley's views on life'.[56] Similarly Carnicelli concluded that 'By his insistence that man must resign himself to fate, that he is an insignificant creature who must learn that true happiness lies in learning to control his wishes, and by his firm belief that man should make the best of a highly imperfect world, Morley reveals himself as an experienced and stoical courtier who had achieved much wisdom.'[57] Although Wright may well have been correct when he maintained that the Commentary is more moderate in *tone* than the earlier *Exposition and Declaration*, it is nevertheless considerably more radical theologically. Like the *Epistle of Godly Consolacion* (*STC* 4407 [London, 1550]), the Commentary lauds 'true preachers' and the fact that the 'furderaunce of the Gospell' will lead to the obedience of the nation to the king as spiritual head. Dismissing the monastic life – 'Salomon callith the austerite of lyffe vanyte, condempninge therby the observacions of the monkes of the charterhowse' (fol. 17^{v}) – it also condemns the invocation of saints and the 'feynynge' of purgatory (fol. 80^{r-v}). As theology the Commentary thus contradicts some of Morley's fundamental beliefs,[58] and unlike the *Exposition and Declaration* cannot be excused as the work of a Nicodemist.[59] It is difficult, then, to reconcile this text with Morley's other writings,[60] and the very identification of the author as 'Henry Parker, Knight', may provide evidence that he was not the author. In all his other presentation texts Morley gave his name as Henry Parker, Knight, Lord Morley, although elsewhere his signature appears as 'Henry, Lord Morley'; or 'Harry Morley'. Indeed, it would have been inaccurate for him not to include Morley in any formal document and Henry Parker, Knight cannot be an abbreviated form of Henry Parker, Knight, Lord Morley. Nor does it seem possible to assume that this was a scribal error, since this omission would immediately have stood out to Morley if he had seen the manuscript and it is hard to imagine that he would not have examined the preface before he presented the book. It is likely therefore that this text was written by somebody else. The most obvious possibility is Morley's son Henry (d. 1553), made a Knight of the Bath at the time of Anne Boleyn's coronation in 1533.[61] If Morley's son were author, moreover, it would explain some of the similarities with Morley's own work, both in phrasing and in the very gesture of making this sort of presentation. The son, in other words, could well be imitating the father. There are, however, no indications that Morley's son held more advanced views than his father, and both Parker's own sons fled to the Continent in Elizabeth's reign. The question of authorship thus must remain problematic, although it does seem unlikely that Morley himself was the author.[62]

If these two texts are removed the Morley canon holds together much more coherently. 'The Pistellis and Gospelles' cannot be reconciled with his conservative religious stance: nothing about this Lefèvre text would have appealed to Morley. In the case of the Commentary on Ecclesiastes the advanced evangelical stance goes against everything we know about Morley's religious position. The doctrinal oddity is compounded by the fact that it would have made nonsense for him to have made a bid for Somerset's patronage only to oppose the bill for clerical marriage almost immediately afterwards.[63]

REFERENCES TO LOST WORKS

In the preface to his translation of Seneca's epistles Morley stated that he was 'wont yerely' to present Mary a 'poore translacion'. Likewise, in the preface to the translation of the *Somnium Scipionis* Morley described his earlier offerings, suggesting this to be an annual occurrence and affirming himself 'accustomed allways afore this present tyme, either to send youe sum notable worke concernynge sum Christen doctours wrytynge in the Laten tonge, or ells sum of their workes by me translated into our tounge'.[64] Assuming that he began this practice around 1537 and continued it into Edward's reign, there would have been approximately a dozen New Year's gifts to Mary in the years before her coronation rather than the seven which survive.[65]

When he was compiling his *Index of British Writers* John Bale had access to the royal collection at Westminster and in his entry for Morley he gave two titles: 'Henricus de Morle, eques auratus ac regulus, scripsit comedias ac tragedias plures. *Ex bibliotheca regis.* / Vitas sectarum. *Ex relatione quorundam.*' In his list of books *Ex bibliotheca Anglorum regis*, moreover, he listed 'Liber vite sectarum domini de Morley'.[66] Presumably one can identify 'Liber vite sectarum' as an omnibus title for the Plutarch Lives, with 'secta' being used in the sense of set. The entry under Morley's name is somewhat more problematic, but most modern scholars have assumed that this provides evidence for lost plays written by Morley. If these were in the royal library, of course, they must have been presented by Morley to Henry, and this would indeed have been an odd sort of gift. It is much more likely, however, that there is a mistake here and that the reference *Ex bibliotheca Anglorum regis* pertains to the 'Vitas sectarum' as the later entry in the *Index* suggests; the authority for the 'comedias ac tragedias plures' thus being the far less reliable *Ex relatione quorundam.*[67]

MANUSCRIPTS OWNED BY MORLEY OR POSSIBLY ASSOCIATED WITH HIM

1. **London, British Library, Harley MS 4775.** s.xv^{2}. *The Gilte Legende*: excerpts ed. by Richard Hamer in *Three Lives from the Gilte Legende* (Heidelberg, 1978); manuscript described on pp. 31-2.

Morley's signature – 'Harry Morley' is found on fol. 263^{r} along with the motto 'Quis prohibeat sperare meliora' below his name.[68] His wife has signed both as 'Alys Seynt Jhon' and 'Alys Morley'.[69] The names of Harry St John (fol. 5^{r}); John St John (fol. 109^{v}, 263^{v}); Margaret St John (fol. 263^{r}); Oliver St John (fol. 263^{r}); William St John (fol. 263^{v}); Kathryn Parker (fol. 263^{r}) Francis Parker (fol. 263^{r}); Elizabeth Parker (fol. 263^{r}) also appear. Presumably this manuscript came to Morley through the St John connection.

2. **London, British Library, Royal MS 15 A.XIII.** Justinus, Epitome of Pompeius Trogus's lost *Historiae Philippicae*: ed. by O. Seel, Teubner (1972). s.xiv.

Given by Morley to Henry FitzAlan, twelfth Earl of Arundel (d. 1580): the inscription on front flyleaf (fol. 1^{r}) reads: 'ex dono Henrici Domini Morley'. On fol. 105^{r} there is an inscription in a fifteenth-century hand: 'S[a]maule Wode Clarke'. No. 1394 in the Lumley catalogue.[70]

3. **Durham, University Library, Cosin MS V.II.15.** Boethius. *De consolatione philosophiae*, trans. by John Walton: ed. by M. Science, EETS OS, 170 (London, 1927). s. xv^{2}.

On fol. 112^{v} Morley has written '[...] secundum Harry Morley'. Other later names which occur are Edmund Mariet; R. Rychardson; Rychard Buckley; T. Perkyns; J. Thornehull; 'Willelmus Browne 1612';[71] 'Geo: Davenport 1664'.

4. **Leiden, University Library, Vossius MS Q. 9.** John Lydgate et al. Anthology of Middle English Verse.[72] s.xv^{2}.

'D. Morley' occurs on fol. 1^{r} in a sixteenth-century hand. On fol. 116^{r} there is an inscription in a slightly earlier hand: 'lowe good and drede schame / drserr[sic] lowe and kepe the (?) name / quod John Kyng of Dommowe / for thysse boke ysse hysse.'[73] Since Dunmow, Essex is located within a very few miles of Morley's principal estate at Great Hallingbury, it is likely that there was a link with Morley.[74]

DATING

When did Morley's habit of giving books begin and how did it originate? According to his own testimony he was inspired by a French example:

> one of late dayes that was grome of the chaumber with that renowmed and valyaunte Prynce of hyghe memorye, Fraunces the Frenche kynge, whose name I have forgotten, that dydde translate these tryumphes [of Petrarch] to that sayde kynge, whyche he toke so thankefully, that he gave to hym for his paynes an hundred crounes, to hym and to his heyres of inheritaunce to enjoye to that value in lande for ever, and toke suche pleasure in it, that wheresoever he wente amonge hys precyous jewelles, that booke was alwayes caryed with hym for his pastyme to loke upon, and as muche estemed by hym, as the rychest diamonde he hadde: whiche sayde booke, when I sawe the coppye of it, I thoughte in my mynde, howe I beynge an Englyshe man, myght do as well as the Frenche man, dyd translate this sayde worke into our maternall tounge, and after much debatyng with my selfe, dyd as your Lordshyppe doth se, translate the sayde booke to that moost worthy kynge our late soveraygne Lorde of perpetuall memory kynge Henry theyghte, who as he was a Prynce above all other mooste excellente, so toke he the worke verye thankefullye, merveylynge muche howe I coulde do it, and thynkynge verelye I hadde not doone it, wythoute helpe of some other, better knowynge the Italyan tounge then I: but when he knewe the verye treweth, that I hadde traunslated the worke my selfe, he was more pleased therewith then he was before ...[75]

It is, in fact, possible to determine the identity of the Frenchman whose name Morley had forgotten by the time of Mary's reign. The first French prose translation of Petrarch's *Trionfi* – rather than the commentary by Bernardo Illicino – was undertaken at the end of the fifteenth century and published by Barthélemy Vérard in 1514.[76] Slightly later Simon Bourgouyn made a translation into verse which circulated only in manuscript and in 1538 Jean de Meynier, baron d'Oppède's verse translation was published.[77] Of these translators only Simon Bourgouyn occupied a position which could be described as a 'grome of the chaumber': in his translations from Lucian, published in 1529, he is identified as 'escrivain et varlet de chambre du roi'.[78] It must be he therefore to whom Morley was referring.

Four copies of Bourgouyn's translation survive – Paris, Bibliothèque nationale de France, fonds français 2500 + 2501 (hereafter F1), fonds français 12423 (hereafter F2); Paris, Bibliothèque de l'Arsenal, 6480 (hereafter A); private collection (hereafter P)[79] – but there is considerable dispute about dating of the translation: at one extreme, Eberhard König dates it to *c.* 1500, at the other Franco Simone would place it at around 1530.[80] P is a large book, measuring 308 × 222 mm, and, as König shows, was almost certainly owned by Anne de Polignac. F1, now bound as two volumes, is lacking the Triumph of Love and begins (fr. 2501) with the second Triumph. It is a small book, measuring 158-60 × 102-105 mm, its miniatures extracted.[81] If there had been an indication of early ownership, this was lost when the preliminary material was removed. Like P, F2 is a large book, measuring 315 × 220 mm, and contains six full-page miniatures. As in the case of F1 the original ownership is uncertain.[82] Based on the miniatures by Godefroy le Batave, Myra Orth has concluded that A cannot have been completed until 1522 or later: Dürer is the inspiration for several of the miniatures and in particular his Triumphal Cart of Maximilian, not published until 1522, 'is the direct source for the figure of Cleopatra (Dürer's "Gravitas") and the inspiration for several others.'[83] She has also pointed out that there are hints of royal ownership since there are added verses addressed to 'an unnamed prince'.[83] Although she stops short of identifying this prince as Francis I she does observe that one of the miniatures contains lizards, which it is 'tempting' to identify with Francis's salamander.[85] In other words, it is likely that this book was prepared for Francis.[86]

Bourgouyn's name is not found in the household accounts until 1523, where he appears as a valet de garderobe, paid 120 livres tournois.[87] In 1524 and 1525 he appears in the accounts among the 'gens de metier' and then he disappears from the household records.[88] In the second half of the 1520s, however, Francis created a new position of 'autres valets de chambre' to accommodate various of his writers and artists and, as noted above, Bourgouyn described himself as such in 1529.[89] 'Valet de chambre' translates into English as 'grome of the chaumber' and Morley presumably saw Francis's copy of Bourgouyn's translation after *c.* 1526 when Bourgouyn received this title.[90]

According to Morley's description the book he saw was not part of the travelling library as such but was rather kept among the jewels and other treasures.[91] Unique in its diminutive size (122 × 85 mm) and 'restrainedly luxurious', A fits this description precisely – i.e. a larger book like the others would probably not have been found among the jewels. The most likely occasion for Morley to have seen the book would have been during Wolsey's mission to Amiens in 1527, when Morley's son formed part of the entourage.[92]

Morley indicated that he thought long and hard about his translation of the *Trionfi* for Henry and much debated with himself before undertaking it. Nevertheless it must have been a product of the late 1520s or very early 1530s, since it would seem to predate his other translations for Henry.[93] Although the king reacted in surprise that Morley could undertake such a chore, and with pleasure that he had done so,[94] Henry did not provide rewards equivalent to those received by Bourgouyn. Nevertheless, Morley decided to keep on with his translating activities and he next produced his version of the 'Lives of Scipio and Haniball'.[95] Once again his model may have been Bourgouyn, who had earlier translated this and other Plutarchian works for several well-placed patrons.[96]

As the various prefaces indicate, all Morley's surviving presentation manuscripts were New Year's gifts. Relatively little concrete information concerning the New Year's gifts obtained from and presented to Henry VIII survives and there are specific records from only nine New Year's Days out of a total of thirty-eight in Henry's reign. Materials relating to gifts presented or received on six different New Year's Days are calendared in *LP Henry VIII* and one other uncalendared example survives in the Treasurer of the Chamber's Accounts for 1543/4 (BL, Add. MS 59900). At New Year 1529 Morley's servant received 20*s*. for bringing a gift to Greenwich;[97] in 1532 the Lords, including Morley, received a selection from gilt cups, cruses, and goblets, and one salt;[98] for 1533 there is an account of plate received from goldsmiths for New Year's gifts in which Morley figures;[99] at New Year 1539 Morley's servant received 20*s*. for bringing a gift to Greenwich;[100] again at New Year 1540 his servant received 20*s*. for a gift brought to Greenwich;[101] at New Year 1541 his servant was given 13*s*. 4*d*. for bringing a gift to Hampton Court;[102] and at New Year 1544 his servant was given 20*s*. for bringing a gift to Hampton Court.[103]

A. Jefferies Collins has listed the four known surviving New Year's Gift Rolls in Henry's reign.[104] According to the 1532 Roll (PRO, E.101/420/15) Morley received a gilt cup with a cover and presented 'a boke covered with purple saten'. The 1534 Roll (PRO, E.101/421/13) records that Morley received a gilt cup with a cover and gave 'a boke covered with crimsin velvet'. The 1539 Roll (Washington, Folger Shakespeare Library, Z.d.11) shows Morley receiving a gilt cruse and giving 'a boke covered withe grene velvet'.

Only the now lost *Tryumphes* (presuming my dating to be accurate) and the surviving BL, Royal MS 17 D.XI ('Lives of Scipio and Hannibal') were presented to Henry before Henry's assumption of the title of Supreme Head in mid-January 1535. If we assume that Morley presented no other books to Henry before January 1536 then it is possible that the *Tryumphes* is the book covered with purple satin from 1532 and the 'Lives of Scipio and Hannibal' the book covered with crimson velvet from January 1534, but it is more likely that at least one of these 'bokes' corresponds to a lost book. Two other works (BL, Arundel MS 8, the 'Commentarys of the Turke', and the *Exposition and Declaration of the Psalme*, '*Deus ultionum Dominus*') can be shown to have predated Henry's assumption of the kingship of Ireland. The latter, stridently antipapal in tone, would seem to stand in response to Paul III's excommunication of Henry late in 1538 and may well be the book in green velvet to which reference is made in 1539 gift roll. Printed later in the same year, it would almost appear to be a 'commissioned' work and it is not impossible that Cromwell suggested the project.[105]

For the period after 1541 four books survive. In this group Chatsworth ('Of the ryghte renoumyde ladyes') stands categorically apart: it is by far the most elaborate and lavishly produced, with particularly delicate decorated capital letters on almost every folio. In the preface Morley observed that if by chaunce it [this manuscript] shulde cum to the handes of the ryght renomyde and moste honorable ladyes of your Highnes moste tryhumphaunte courte, that it shulde be well acceptyde to theym to se and reede the mervelouse vertue of theyr oune sexe, to the laude perpetuall of theym. And albeit, as Bocas wrytethe in hys proheme, he menglyssheth sum not verey chaste emongste the goode, yet hys honeste excuse declarethe that he dyd it to a goode entent, that all ladyes and gentlewomen, seynge the glorye of the goode, may be steryde to folowe theym, and seynge the vyce of sum, to flee theym.[106]

When and what circumstances would Morley decide that the ladies of Henry's court needed to contemplate the chastity and eschew the 'vice' of their antique sisters?

Morley's daughter, Jane, was a principal witness against her husband George Boleyn, Lord Rochford, at the time of his trial in 1536. After his execution, she regained royal favour and was a member of the household of Henry's next three queens. As matron of the queen's suite to Catherine Howard she was deeply implicated in the Thomas Culpeper affair, for which treachery she was condemned to death, her father being present in the lords at the time of her attainder.[107] With Catherine herself she was executed on Tower Green on 13 February 1542.[108]

The great superiority of Chatsworth to all the other presentation manuscripts establishes that it must have been prepared for a very special occasion and the form of address indicates that it was presented after June 1541. Given the situation over the Christmas season 1541/42 – Henry had been informed of his wife's adultery on All Souls' Day and things went from bad to worse for the rest of the winter – the presentation of a book on female virtue and vice at this time is inconceivable.[109] His daughter's actions would, moreover, have rendered Morley himself especially vulnerable to royal displeasure and disgrace. Politically, a much more astute time to placate in this manner and at such expense would have been shortly after the crisis had passed but before Catherine had been forgotten in the joys of a new marriage, that is New Year's Day 1543.[110] What the translation of *De claris mulieribus* in its luxurious format may well represent is a 'public' repudiation by Morley of his daughter's actions and an act of submission to Henry. Without mentioning Lady Rochford, in this case, Morley tacitly condoned the punishment of female promiscuity and espoused the need to control the behaviour of the ladies at court. Chatsworth would seem, then, to be a witness to the absolute power of politics in Tudor court life: like Thomas Boleyn, Morley had not only to submerge private grief but also to dissociate himself from his own flesh and blood in order to salvage his position and maintain his alliances.[111]

There are very few clues concerning the order of presentation to Henry of the other three post-1541 books. In the preface to the Life of Theseus (BL, Royal MS 17 D.II) Henry is addressed in a slightly unusual way. Elsewhere he is called 'moste myghty and moste Christen Kynge' or 'most mighty and most pusant prince', but here Morley refers to him as 'moste victoryus'; this epithet might seem particularly appropriate to the period after the capture of Boulogne in 1544, i.e January 1545.[112] The 'Tale from Massuccyo Salernytano' (BL, Royal MS 18 A.LXII) cannot have been presented until after Henry's marriage to Catherine Parr in July 1543, since she is greeted, and must therefore date to January 1544, 1545, or 1546.[113]

Morley dedicated 'The Lyff of the Good Kyng Agesylayus' to Thomas Cromwell as the 'right honorable Baron ... Lord Pryvy Seall', which means that it must have been presented after July 1536 but before Cromwell's execution in 1540. In 1537 Morley was involved in a particularly vitriolic dispute with the Prior and Chapter of Norwich concerning the priory of Aldeby.[114] Although a letter dated 25 March makes clear that Cromwell had assisted Morley in the matter, the monks continued to offer resistance and the Chapter wrote a letter of protest on 15 April. On 21 April Morley wrote again to Cromwell 'praying your Lordshipp further to goo thorowe with me and not to forsake me in this my sute'. Morley triumphed in the long run, since the manor was his by 1547, but the precise details of what occurred after the letter of 21 April are unknown. Nevertheless, Morley would have felt a strong indebtedness to Cromwell during 1537, and New Year's Day 1538 may well have been the occasion when he presented the Life of Agesilaus to him, especially since in 'The comparcuyon of oure most dere and gratyous souerayne lord kyng Henry to this Agesylayus kyng of the Lacydymones' Morley stated that Henry has ruled '*wellnere*' thirty years and the thirtieth year of Henry's reign began on 22 April 1538.[115]

There is not a great deal of evidence concerning books owned by Mary Tudor and the eight manuscripts presented to her by Morley represent the single largest group of her books.[116] It has generally been assumed that Morley's friendship with Mary dated back to her childhood; that his daughter Margery was one of her rockers and that by 1525 his wife Alice was a chamberer in her household.[117] Starkey, however, has shown that this was not the case and that Morley's intimacy with Mary did not begin until 1536 when she was moved to Hunsdon, only six miles from Great Hallingbury. With his wife and one of his daughters Morley was at Hunsdon on Whit Sunday in 1536 and presumably ran the risk of arrest.[118] In Mary's Privy Purse Expenses there are records of gifts to his servant in January 1537 (10*s*.); 1538, 1540, 1543, and 1544 (5*s*.).[119] In 1543 and 1544 it is stated specifically that the servant brought a book and no doubt the same is true on the other occasions. BL, Royal MS 18 A.LX ('The dreme of Sypyon') was presented during Edward's reign, and Add. MS 12060 (Account of the Miracles of the Sacrament) after Mary acceded to the throne. In three prefaces – those found in Royal MS 2 D.XXVIII (Rolle's Psalter), Royal MS 17 C.XII ('Tytylles of the Salmes of David'), and Royal MS 18 A.XV (Johannes de Turrecremata) – Morley includes the rest of the royal family in his salutation. There was a strict and formal hierarchy of greeting in these cases which could not be violated (or individuals omitted): first came king, then queen, then prince, and finally Mary. Only one of these three manuscripts, Royal MS 17 C.XII, was written when Henry was married: 'next God and your moste Christen father and ouer nobyll Quene and your swete brother I most honor, moste love, and praye for'. If the reference is to Catherine Howard then this manuscript would have been presented in January 1541. However, the studied insistence on Mary's relationship to Henry, her 'heyghe, excellent bloude' and the fact that she is a 'myghty kynges douter' perhaps fits in better with her restoration to second place in the succession in 1543. In this case the gift would fall into the period 1544-6. Royal MS 18 A.XV must have been presented between wives (i.e. in 1538, 1539, 1540, or 1543) since the greetng reads 'my goode wyll that I do beare unto youe, next youre victoriouse father, oure naturall and leage Lorde, and your swete and noble, towarde brother Prynce Edward, afore all creatures alyve'. The preface, which opens with an evocation of Morley's previous stay at Hunsdon, emphasizes the risks of false felicity, and this might possibly indicate the period when the Court was in mourning for Jane Seymour.[120] In the preface to Royal MS 2 D.XXVIII Morley undertakes 'allways to pray, fyrst for your moste royall

Father, oure sovereygne Lorde and Kynge, next for your moste exellent and towarde brother, the Prynce, and thyrde, for youe'. Immediately afterwards, however, he adds 'the children of hys Grace to cum'. The mention of future children indicates that there was a wife in the offing. On 6 October 1539 a marriage treaty between Henry and Anne of Cleves was concluded and there were elaborate preparations for her arrival in England, which took place on New Year's Day 1540. As is well known, Henry was deeply disappointed in what he saw. Late in 1539, however, would be just the period that future progeny would be in the public mind and would fit very well with the writing of this preface for presentation on New Year's Day 1540.[121] There are two indications that the Seneca translation came late: first Morley observed that he was 'wont yerely' to give books; secondly he pointed out that Mary stood 'by his [Henry's] favour and love in most high felicitye'. This text was almost certainly produced, then, after Mary's 1543 re-instatement. Forms of address establish that the Account of the Miracles of the Sacrament must have been presented in 1555 or 1556. Loades has observed that:

> As long as Philip remained in England, [Cardinal] Pole confined himself mainly to his ecclesiastical and diplomatic duties, but after the king's departure in August 1555, his role quickly and dramatically increased. He was given discretionary membership of the 'Select Council', which was to keep Philip in touch with English affairs, and was regularly accommodated at court in order to console Mary with his presence and advice. He was never sworn as a privy councillor, but was regularly consulted about a wide range of business. Michieli believed that he had been specifically briefed by the king to protect Mary from the quarrels and deviousness of her normal council ...[122]

This corresponds precisely to the situation Morley describes on fol. 10[r-v] of the Account of the Miracles: 'your highnes ... folowyng the wise counsell of the unculpable vertuous cardinall your cosyn, whose conversatyon and life is knowen to be through Cristendome without spotte, I say that your highnes in folowing his counsell, and with your godly wyt together, the golden worlde shall in processe come againe'. In other words, it is likely that this treatise was presented to the queen in January 1556.

HANDS AND DECORATION

Although all the surviving manuscripts were prepared for presentation they vary considerably in professionalism of script and ornateness – as well as quantity – of decorated intials. Morley made use of several scribes. C, whose most lavish product was Chatsworth ('Of the ryghte renoumyde ladyes'), wrote two other texts destined for Henry (Royal MS 18 A.LXII ['Tale from Massuccyo'], Arundel 8 ['Commentarys of the Tuke']) and four for Mary (Royal MS 2 D.XXVIII, fols i, 1-3 [preface to Rolle], (Royal MS 18 A.XV [translation and exposition of Psalm xxxvi], Royal MS 17 A.XLVI ['Laude or prayse unto the Virgyn'], Royal MS 18 A.LX ['The dreme of Sypyon']). One of these, Royal MS 18 A.LX, can be dated to a period after Henry's death in 1547. Royal MS 17 D.II and Oxford, Bodleian Library, MS Laud misc. 684 were both written by a single individual in a rather amateurish hand.

In terms of decoration there seem to be a number of standard motifs which link the whole series: rose, pomegranate, marigold, a characteristic profile male head, animal and grotesque heads, all drawn freehand.[123] The appearance of the rose is self-

Fig. 3 & 4. London, British Library, Royal MS 17 C.xi, fol. 2^{r} and Chatsworth, Devonshire Collection MS, fol. 35^{r}. This illustrates the recurring grotesque head, pomegranate and rose motifs. Reproduced by kind permission of the British Library Board and the Duke of Devonshire and the Chatsworth Settlement Trustees.

explanatory and the use of the marigold probably stood as a tribute to Mary, whose badge was the marigold. Morley himself was portrayed holding a pomegranate in the drawing by Dürer of 1523: Carnicelli describes this as a 'symbol of the unity of the church and of resurrection and hope in immortality'.[124] It was also Catherine of Aragon's badge and it is somewhat surprising that the pomegranate featured so prominently in the design of Chatsworth, presented *c.* 1543 and in difficult circumstances. In particular the crowned M on fol. 11^{v} reads almost like a tribute to Mary: out of the crown are a pair of stems with a rose on the left and a pomegranate on the right; below, between the shafts of the M are found a pair of marigolds. Chatsworth also contains the royal monogram HR VIII and the opening words of the Angelical Salutation in the scrollwork of decorated initals (as does Royal MS 17 A.xlvi), and two of the books presented to Mary (Royal MS 2.D.xxviii and Royal MS 17 A.xlvi) have the initials 'ma' in the scrollwork.

LATER PROVENANCE

For the most part, the manuscripts presented to Henry VIII are in an excellent state of repair and there are very few marginal notes or other signs of readership. On fol. 2^{r} of Royal MS 17 D.xi there is the inscription 'Worke wysely quod Wyngffeld'. Royal MS 18 A.lxii contains on fol. 14^{r} the note that 'The seven gyftes of the holy ghoste are compared unto seven operations effectes of a fyer' in a contemporary hand which

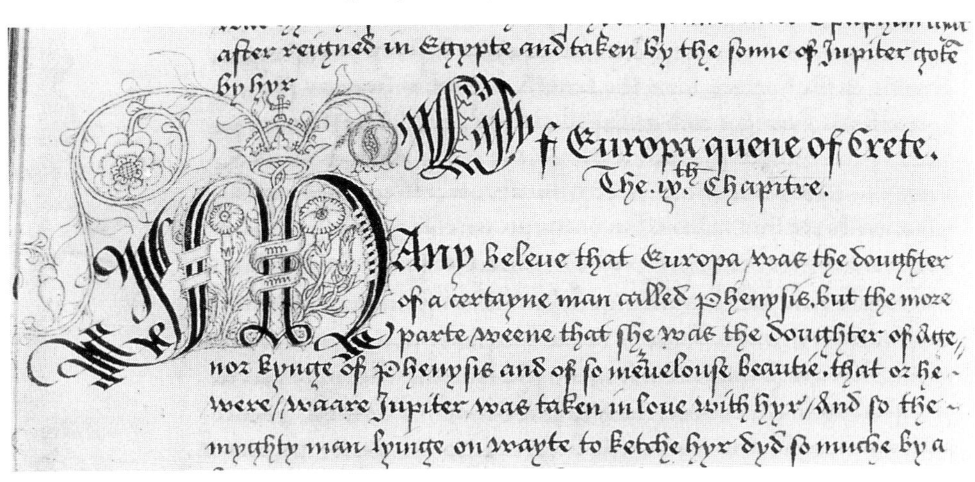
after reigned in Egypte and taken by the sonne of Jupiter gote
by hyr

Of Europa quene of Crete.
The .iiij.th Chapitre.

Many beleue that Europa was the doughter
of a certayne man called Phenysis, but the more
parte weene that she was the doughter of Age-
nor kynge of Phenysis and of so mervelouse beautie that or he
were// waare Jupiter was taken in loue with hyr/ And so the
myghty man lyinge on wayte to fetche hyr dyd so muche by a

Fig. 5. Chatsworth, Devonshire Collection MS, fol. 11ᵛ. Crowned M with rose and pomegranate, marigolds between the shafts. Reproduced by kind permission of the Duke of Devonshire and the Chatsworth Settlement Trustees.

closely resembles but is not identical to that of Henry himself. The statement does not pertain, as far as I can tell, to anything in the text and, as in the case of the inscription in Royal MS 17 D.XI, there is no way to ascertain how or why it was inserted. More enlightening, perhaps, is Morley's own description of Henry's response to one book. According to his account Henry received his translation of the *Tryumphes* 'verye thankefullye, merveylynge muche howe I coulde do it, and thynkynge verelye I hadde not doone it, wythoute helpe of some other, better knowynge the Italyan tounge then I: but when he knewe the verye treweth, that I hadde traunslated the worke my selfe, he was more pleased therewith then he was before'.[125] If this doesn't exactly establish Henry as a careful reader, it does at least seem to show that he took a polite interest in what was in the book.

Three of the manuscripts presented to Henry have royal inventory numbers: Royal MS 17 D.XI ('Lives of Scipio and Haniball') = 1199; Arundel MS 8 ('The Commentarys of the Turke') = 997; Royal MS 17 D.II ('Lyfe of Thesius') = 1189.[126] Books which were in the Upper Library at Westminster Palace in 1542 carry numbers from 1 to 910 and those arriving soon after Henry's death were numbered 911-1450. Therefore, the three Morley manuscripts must have come to Westminster when books from other libraries, primarily Hampton Court and Greenwich, were being integrated into the main Westminster collection. The number in Arundel 8 indicates that it fell into the 'c' range – for *Commentarys* – and the other two appear under 'l' for *Lyfe*. Unlike the others Arundel 8 was subsequently abstracted from Westminster: presumably it was acquired directly by Thomas Howard, 2nd Earl of Arundel (1585-1646), since there is no sign of another earlier, non-royal, owner.

In the case of Chatsworth substantial trimming has taken place and if there had been an inventory number it would have been removed at the time of the cropping. Although Narcissus Luttrell's name has been associated with the manuscript, the first authenticated post-Henrician owner is Edward Wynne of Chelsea, in the catalogue of whose library it appears in 1786. Later owned by James Bindley, Sir Peter Thompson, Richard Heber, and Thomas Thorpe, it was then acquired by Sir Thomas Phillipps, in whose collection it was numbered MS 10416.[127] It was bought for the 9th Duke of Devonshire in 1898 for £98.[128] Like Chatsworth, Royal MS 18 A.LXII ('Tale from Massuccyo') has been trimmed, but this was not extensive enough to have eliminated any putative inventory number. My suspicion, therefore, is that the manuscript remained at Hampton Court or Greenwich during the years shortly after Henry's death and that it was not amalgamated into the main royal collection until considerably later.[129]

Bodleian, Laud misc. 684, which remains in its original covers, shows no signs of an inventory number and presumably therefore never got to Westminster. On the front pastedown there is an inscription 'Liber Roberti Hare 1559'. At the bottom of the page Hare has written 'Gutta cavat lapidem non vi sed sepe cadendo';[130] on the back pastedown 'Ipse deus simul atque volam me servat opinor, / Hoc sentit, moriar, mors ultima linea rerum'.[131] In the lower margin of fol. 1^r is found 'Liber Guilielmi Laud Archiepiscopi Cantuariensis et Cancellarii Universitatis Oxon. 1633'.[132] Hare (d. 1611), who amassed a considerable collection of manuscripts, may have obtained this manuscript directly from the royal library through his connection with William Paulet, marquis of Winchester, Lord High Treasurer to Mary and Elizabeth, into whose service he had entered by 1556.[133]

All but one of the books Morley gave Mary have remained in the royal collection. London, BL Add. MS 12060, the one that escaped, has the signature of Richard Rushbrooke (Resbrooke) on fols 1^r and 8^v in a late-sixteenth/early-seventeenth-century hand.[134] On a front flyleaf there is an inscription: 'Ex dono Elisaei Ashpoole Rectoris de Bardfield magna Comitatu Essexiae Anno Domini 1694'; also 'A.C to Margaretta Phillippina [V]ale 1773'. Later it was owned by Samuel Butler, Bishop of Lichfield, and was bought by the British Museum from Thomas Butler in 1841. On fol. 23^v occurs the following Latin tag and translation, probably in the hand of Ashpoole:

> Tantum Religio potuit suadere nugarum
> Whatt can't religion doe. Men fools are made,
> When knaves are priests, and they the fools perswade.

On fol. 1^r of the Xenophon presented to Cromwell (Aberystwyth, NLW MS 17038C) – which consists almost entirely of pen trials reproducing 'Gramatice partes quot sunt octo' in different forms – and erased in the upper margin of fol. 11^r the phrase 'monye makethe my ...' is found in a contemporary script. This same phrase, rendered as 'mony makithe myrthe / quod Pears', appears (perhaps in the same hand) on fol. 263^r of London, BL, Harley 4775 which, as has been described above, was associated with Morley and his family. Slightly lower on fol. 263^r the same individual has written 'Remember the ende of thy faythfull frynde quod R. Pears'. That the same, elsewhere unattested, adage – 'mony makithe myrthe' – is found in both manuscripts indicates that they are likely to have been together at some point and that the phrase was presumably added in NLW 17038C before the manuscript was presented to Cromwell rather than afterwards.

After Cromwell's fall his books were sequestered along with his other goods, but the chronology of their absorption into the royal collection is not clear. Although Cromwell's house at the Austin Friars was seized on 10 June 1540 there were still books in the library as late as 11 April 1545, when Ralph Sadler wrote to the Council concerning books belonging to the Office of Arms which had been held by Cromwell:

> Neither Duresme [Cuthbert Tunstall] or he remember finding any such books; but of all such books, records, letters and writings as they found they delivered a calendar to the King. Except certain treaties delivered into the treasury of the Exchequer and a few books had into the King's library, all remain in the late lord Crumwell's library in the Augustynes.[135]

There is evidence that NLW 17038C was one of the books which got into the royal library. On fol. i^{r} there are a number of pen trials and the draft of a letter dated 20 November 1602 from Ludlow and addressed to Edward La Zouche, 11th Baron Zouche of Harringworth, president of Wales (appt. June 1602). The author of this letter was one William Kenrick, clerk of the Court of the Council, who 'happeninge upon this smale boke', which he took 'to be the verey same booke that was first dedicated and presented', determined that he would offer it 'instead of other presents' to La Zouche. In the letter Kenrick does not explain where he 'happened' upon the book and there is no indication of how it got to Ludlow. The name Kenrick does, however, come up in connection with another book, one which had been in the royal library before Henry's death. The presentation copy to Henry of John Leland's *Genethliacon Illustrissimi Eädverdi principis Cambriae*, printed by Reyner Wolfe in 1543, now survives as Clare College, Cambridge, O 6 26. Printed on vellum, it is still in the original binding: dark green morocco and on both front and back a Tudor rose surmounted by the royal crown within a frame stamped in gold and HR at the margins.[136] How the book got to Clare is unknown, but on the back flyleaf the name Roland Kenrick occurs twice, the second time in the version 'Rolandi Kenrik et amicorum 1568'.

Although nothing is known about Roland Kenrick's origins, apart from the fact that he was probably an Anglesey man, it can be established that he entered the service of Thomas Moyle, surveyor general of the Court of Augmentations, by 1550.[137] After Moyle's death in 1560 he was active in civic life in Beaumaris, Anglesey, and was returned as an MP for Anglesey in 1572. In the same year the second wife of Sir Richard Bulkeley was accused of adultery and of attempting to poison her husband. The first of her alleged lovers was 'one William Kendricke a young gallant'; apparently she 'declared to Rowland Kenericke, the father of the sayd William that shee would marrie his sonne William when her husband Sir Richard should die'.[138] William Kenrick, then, was the son of Roland, who in turn can be shown to have possessed the presentation copy of Leland's *Genethliacon*. Roland must have acquired at least one other book from the royal collection (i.e. the Life of Agesilaus, absorbed into the collection at some point after Cromwell's fall) which subsequently passed to his son William, who later decided to present it to La Zouche.

COMMENTARY

Unlike the somewhat impersonal prefaces to Henry, couched in respectful generalities, Morley addressed Mary in direct and specific terms. On more than one occasion he referred to her proficiency in Latin.[139] In his translation of Angelo Poliziano, for example, he noted that he had 'not moche alteryd from the sence', as Mary could confirm by consulting the Latin. Concerning his translation of Cicero's *Somnium Scipionis*, he pointed out that Mary would have already seen the Latin version. When he gave her Rolle's Latin commentary on the Psalms he assumed that she would read it. In the preface to 'The Angelical Salutacion' he observed that:

skante ye were cum to xij yeres of age, but that ye were so rype in the Laten tonge, that rathe dothe happen to the women sex, that youer Grace not only coulde perfectly rede, wright and constrewe Laten, but farthermore translate eny harde thinge of the Latin in to ouer Inglysshe tonge. And amonge all other youer most vertuus ocupacions I have sene one prayer translatyd of youer doynge of Sayncte Thomas Alquyne that, I do ensuer youer Grace, is so well done, so neare to the Laten that when I loke uppon yt, as I have one of the exemplar of yt, I have not only mervell at the doinge of yt, but farther, for the well doynge, set yt as well in my boke or bokes as also in my pore wyfes, youer humble beadwoman, and my chyldern. ...

Morley's copy of this text, which was obviously made in multiple 'exemplars' for wider distribution, is not known to survive, but another one does. London, BL Add. MS 17012 is a lavishly produced Book of Hours which belonged to a lady of the court of Henry VII and Henry VIII. Functioning as a kind of *album amicorum*, it contains the signatures of various individuals, including Henry VII and Queen Elizabeth, Henry VIII and Catherine of Aragon. On fols 192^{v}-194^{r} has been added (rubrication lacking; text but not title in same hand as what went before) 'The prayor of Saynt Thomas of Aquune translatyd oute of Latyn ynto Englyshe by þe most excelent *Prynses* [deleted] Mary, doughter to the moste hygh and myghty Prynce and Prynces Kyng Henry the viii and *Quene Kateryne hys wyfe* [deleted][140] in the yere of oure Lorde God ml ccccc xxvii: and the xi yere of here age'.[141] The following note has been added in the bottom margin of fol. 192^{v}: 'I have red that no body lyvethe as he shulde doo but he that foloueth vertu and I rekenyng you to be on of them I pray you to remembre me yn your devocyons / Marye [word illegible]'.

Mary's personal devotion was intense and the Morley presentations fit neatly into this context.[142] Like her father Mary was deeply attached to the Psalms – Morley observing 'that yt is manefestly knowen to all those that knowe your vertuous lyfe that daly ye exarcyse your selfe in the Salmes, in saynge with your chaplen the service of the daye'[143] – and three of Morley gifts pertain to the Psalter. According to Morley, Mary especially commended Psalm 36 to him, which led him to translate the Turrecremata commentary (Royal MS 18 A.xv). Particularly interesting is the presentation of a medieval manuscript of Rolle's Latin Psalter. Morley claimed to be rather diffident about giving her 'suche an olde boke', and the manuscript has no illuminations or other elegant features, but he himself had read the text – observing that the author did not name himself in it – and he assumed she would too: 'thoughe percase sum that knowythe not what a preciouse thyng ys hyde in thys so rude a letter ... yet that hyghe and exellent wytt of yours wyll in the redynge of this exposition of thys Psalter deme all other wyse'. The value of the book, quite clearly, was devotional rather than antiquarian and this gift foreshadows the manner in which a variety of monastic manuscripts would be rescued (and sometimes hidden) by recusant collectors in the second half of the sixteenth century.[144] Nor was this the only medieval manuscript given to Mary. Cambridge, Queens' College, MS 13 is an early-fifteenth-century copy of Augustine's *Soliloquia*, which was presented to Mary by her chamberlain Lord John Hussey.[145] BL, Royal MS 2 B.III, a late-thirteenth century illuminated Psalter, was given to her by Ralph Pryne, grocer of London. Most famous is Royal MS 2 B.VII, Queen Mary's Psalter (s. xiv in), which was rescued from export by the London customs-officer, Baldwin Smith, and given to the Queen, who had it elegantly rebound. These gifts of old manuscripts suggest that Mary was a collector of this sort of material by choice rather than happenstance.

Two of the texts presented to Mary concern the Virgin, Morley specifically addressing Mary herself as 'the secunde Mary of this wourlde in vertue, grace and goodenes'. The description of her namesake's intellectual and physical characteristics may well stand as a comparison and tribute to Mary: 'she was not only apte to learne but thereunto she lovid learnynge and specyally she gave all her mynd to study holy scripture ... she had browne fayer eyes, a right aspecte, blake browis, a meane nose, her face long, her fayre handis and fingers longe. She was of a meane stature ...'[146] Mary was personally devoted to the Eucharist,[147] and it is significant that Morley's last and most personally revealing work was his Account of the Miracles of the Sacrament.[148] Including personal reminiscences of his boyhood in the household of Lady Margaret Beaufort, his travels, and his opinions about Richard III, it also represents an attempt to understand the sweep of English history in light of the revolution which had just passed – the period when 'this your realme was brought to that sedytion, that first they denyed the head of the Church, the Pope's Holynes, next wolde have no saintes honored but threwe vile matter at the Crucifyx, and, adding mischeife to myscheife, denyed the sevyn sacramentes of the Church'.[149] This kind of behaviour caused Morley to observe that 'I can thynke noone other but that the ende of the worlde hastythe apasse accordynge as Christe saide, that ther shulde cum fals prophettes in the ende of the wourlde that with their false techynges shulde seduce many.'[150] This position is similar to that of protestant apocalyptic thinkers such as John Bale, but comes from the other end of the religious spectrum.

At first glance the Account of the Miracles of the Sacrament looks like an original composition but for the most part it is, as Morley himself states, a set of translations. The originality, such as it is, comes from the choice and arrangement of materials. Altogether Morley gives fifteen exemplary tales concerning the miraculous nature of the Eucharist. The general model for the design of the work is doubtless the *De veritate corporis et sanguinis Christi in eucharistia* (Cologne, 1527) of John Fisher, to whom Morley refers in the text as 'so good a man, and so devine a clerk'. In six cases Morley uses the same exempla as did Fisher, who discussed miracles in the preface to book III of *De veritate*. Although he could possibly be translating *De veritate* in his two accounts from Cyprian (nos 1 + 2), and the one from Augustine (no. 4), in the others (the story from John Chrysostom (no. 3), from Bede (no. 10), Edward the Confessor (no. 11)) he must have gone back to Fisher's source texts since he includes details not present in *De veritate*.[151] Morley's other main model was Hartmann Schedel's highly popular world chronicle, *Liber cronicarum* (Nuremberg, 1493), from which he took four tales (nos 7, 8, 9, 12). The *Liber cronicarum* was well known in England and would have been a natural source for him,[152] but Morley had a particular reason for including these stories, since he had, as he observes, seen the very bridge at Maastricht where the first of the two miracles described by Schedel occurred.

For two accounts, which form a kind of matching pair (nos 13 + 14), Morley's source appears to have been his own experiences in the household of Lady Margaret.

One of his most treasured memories was the New Year's Day when he, as Lady Margaret's sewer, had twenty-five knights in his train and he provides a unique insight into the 'magnificence' of her domestic arrangements. It would seem likely, however, that Morley also consulted Fisher's *A mornynge remembraunce had at the moneth mynde of the noble prynces Margarete countesse of Rychemonde & Darbye* (London, 1509) when writing his descriptions and there are parallels in general structure and in specific details. Even if there are some differences between the two versions, then Morley presumably used Fisher's printed account to remind himself of his youthful experiences and to provide a *point de départ*.[153]

Although he himself had been in a vulnerable position in his youth, his own father having been standard bearer to Richard III at Bosworth Field, Morley was fortunate to find a place in Lady Margaret's household and prospered under her. Lady Margaret approved of loyalty, moreover, and encouraged another member of her household, Sir Ralph Bigod, in his support of Richard III, his former master. From Bigod, so Morley maintained, he heard that Mass had not been celebrated in Richard's camp on the morning of Bosworth Field. This, by Morley's reckoning, was a direct result of the murder of the Princes in the Tower. In only one other 'contemporary' source, that of the Continuator to the *Crowland Chronicle*, is there a reference to the episode of the postponed Mass: 'Mane die Lunae illucescente aurora – cum non essent capellani de parte regis Ricardi parati ad celebrandum.'[154] Morley thus appears to be an independent source for details about Richard III as well as Tudor reaction to him.[155]

In his discussion of Lady Margaret's virtues Morley quotes from an epitaph in honour of Matilda (Edith), wife of Henry I. The monks of Crowland considered Matilda to be a special patron and these verses are incorporated into the *ps*. Peter of Blois section of the Crowland chronicle.[156] The chronicler found his material on Matilda, who was buried at Westminster, in the monastic records and did not himself compose the epitaph.[157] Nevertheless, it would seem likely that Morley's source was the Crowland chronicle which must therefore have been available for his inspection. This is signficant for two reasons. First, if he examined the Crowland chronicle and quoted verses from it it might also be the source for his information on Richard's failure to celebrate Mass, or at least it might have refreshed his memory about Bigod's statements in his childhood. Secondly, the question of the composition and survival of the Crowland chronicle is an extremely complex one and any new evidence concerning readership/ownership has the potential of signficantly changing our understanding of the history of the text. In particular, it does not seem to have circulated widely in the early Tudor period.[158] It is not known how many copies of the chronicle were prepared, but by 1506 the monastery itself no longer possessed one.[159] In modern times only one medieval copy, British Library, Cotton MSS, Otho B.XIII, badly damaged in the fire of 1731, survives.[160] When William Fulman prepared his edition (published 1684), however, there was a second, more ornate, manuscript in the possession of Sir John Marsham, which probably did not contain the later continuations.[161] Nothing is known of the earlier history of the Marsham copy but Otho B.XIII was owned in Elizabeth's reign by William Cecil, Lord Burghley (1520-98).[162] Morley might therefore have seen or owned either of these manuscripts. Since it is known that they had left the monastery well before the dissolution, moreover, it is possible that Lady Margaret provides a link. She had strong connections with Crowland, being a member of the confraternity, and in his chronicle commissioned by the monastery in 1506 Sir John Harrington concludes with a eulogy to her.[163] It could well be that she had been given a copy of the chronicle and that Morley got access to it through this channel.[164] It is otherwise hard to imagine how he hit upon such an obscure source so many years later.

Athough consistently loyal to Mary and a follower of her cause Morley had a long history of ingratiating himself with others in positions of power. Soon after Mary came to the throne Henry Fitzalan, twelfth earl of Arundel (1511?-1580), became great master and lord steward to Mary. It is perhaps at approximately this time that Morley decided to rededicate his translation of Petrarch's *Trionfi* – originally presented to Henry VIII – to Arundel's son Henry Fitzalan, Lord Maltravers (1538-1556), whom he called in his dedicatory epistle 'the mooste towarde younge gentle Lorde Matravers'. In Cawood's printed edition two other short texts follow, one seemingly directed to Arundel and one to Maltravers. Unlike the *Tryumphes*, which was not a new piece of work, these two appear to have been written for the occasion. The second, addressed to Arundel, is Morley's epitaph to himself.[165] In this he extolled his friendship with Arundel and bequeathed his heart to him:

Epitaphium Henrici Parkeri Equitis Domini Morley, quod ipse adhuc vivens composuit & suo sepulchro inscribi viscit.

Ciste parum quaeso viator & pauca hee verba lege, cum inter mortales dalcius nihil est quam amicitia vera teste invoco Jesum Christum eternum judicem me inclitum Henricum Comite Arundel, tam ardenter dum vita comes fuit amasse. Ut moriens hoc cor meum sibi familieque sue commendabam felicem me rudicans quod nec ipsa mors qui cuncta consumit rapit calcat suppeditat non potuit qui pars mei corporis divinissima ut puta sedes animi immortales in loco ubi tam fidelis et carus amicus quiesset ibi, & cor meum quiesseret. Divi deipari virgine Mariae praecare quietem. Vive & vale.[166]

The epitaph makes perfectly good sense in the context of Arundel's elevation and it is not, moreover, the only example of Morley's wooing of Arundel: he gave at least one medieval manuscript to him.[167]

The first and longer added text – 'Vyrgyll in his Epigrames of Cupide and Dronkenesse' – appears to be intended for the young heir rather than the father, but it is slightly difficult to understand why Morley chose this particular poem.[168] Warning against excess in love and wine, Morley's amplified version of the Latin text recommends 'measure' and concludes: 'So use both wyne and wemen that ye be not to nyse. / If that ye note this doctryne, doubtles ye shall do well.' Certainly if, as K. R. Bartlett argues, this volume was published as a statement of support for a marriage between Maltravers and Princess Elizabeth, a 'plot' hatched in 1554, this is an odd tribute to the allurements of the Queen's younger half- sister.[169]

Generally speaking Morley eschewed print[170] and he is not known elsewhere to have recycled old material. The *Tryumphes* is, therefore, an anomaly. In the epistle to Maltravers he condemns the 'common reader' who prefers 'dunghill' matter and would rather have 'a tale prynted of Robyn Hoode' than the edification offered by Petrarch's writing. (The reference to Robin Hood is a commonplace one and was used, for example, by Richard Taverner in his condemnation of secular reading.) Morley also censures the printers who cater to the debased taste of the general public: 'what prynter wyll not saye, that he may winne more gayne in pryntynge of a merye jeste, then suche lyke excellente workes, suerlye (my good Lorde) very fewe or none, whyche I do lamente at my harte'. This may suggest that he did not prepare the *Tryumphes* for publication as such but that he gave a manuscript to Maltravers.[171] The reason for the presentation is impossible to determine, but the 'Vrygyll in his Epigrames of Cupide and Dronkenesse' does seem particularly well suited to a young man about to embark on matrimony (albeit not with a royal princess): 'Let Venus serve to multiply our nature that doth excel.' Maltravers married Anne Wentworth in April 1555; the previous New Year's Day might provide the appropriate occasion.

If Morley presented a manuscript the impetus for publication must have derived from the Arundel household rather than Morley. Four of the five surviving copies of the *Tryumphes* have been bound up with Twynne's *Physicke Against Fortune*, printed by Richard Watkyns in 1579.[172] Since so many sheets remain unbound and unsold it would seem that after printing the text, Cawood did not distribute it widely, perhaps as a result of Maltravers' death on 30 June 1556.[173]

CONCLUSION

As Morley states himself, the original inspiration for his Petrarch translation came from a French example, an individual who can be identified as Simon Bourgouyn, valet de chambre to Francis I. By my dating the resulting translation of the *Tryumphes* presented to Henry VIII is the first translation of this text into English and is a significant landmark in the introduction of Petrarchism into Tudor England. At some point soon afterwards Morley decided to translate selected Plutarch Lives in emulation of Bourgouyn's earlier work. Once again he was one of the pioneers on the English scene.[174] The first of these, his Life of Scipio and Hannibal, must have met with a positive reception since Morley continued sporatically to translate Plutarch, and also to use his translations tailored to the tastes of different individuals as a means of soliciting patronage, for the rest of his life.[175]

By nature, the presentation of a manuscript as a New Year's gift indicates a restricted audience and Warren V. Boutcher has observed 'Morley is in fact disdainful of the medium of print, and very clearly distinguished the world of printers, profit and popular taste from the closed aristocratic circles of Erasmian readers'.[176] Without doubt, Morley's target audience was a tightly-knit court circle, beginning with the recipient him/herself. In the preface to Royal MS 17 C.XII he constructed an imaginary dialogue with Mary envisaged as principal, perhaps even sole reader. In Royal MS 2 D.XXVIII, he was equally intimate, exhorting Mary 'in Goddes name sumtyme to loke upon thys when your Grace hathe leysure'. Elsewhere, he imagined a wider readership. The translation of Boccaccio, although presented to Henry, was directed in part to the ladies of the court. In the preface to the translation of Seneca's Epistles he observed that he was not necessarily writing for Mary herself, who sits in 'highe felicitye, but for other, whiche harde fortune bloweth here and there'. Not only was his intended audience those less fortunate than Mary, it was those less educated: 'let them loke that can knowe the Latyne tong, of this golden epistle of this vertuous Senecke; those that can but rede the mother tong, to loke on this my poore translacion'.[177] In his penultimate surviving work, the translation of *Somnium Scipionis* section of Cicero's *De re publica*, presented to Mary during Edward's reign, he envisaged an even wider audience: 'as muche as I have doone in the translatynge the best I can, and woll gladly have don it better, to that extent that all those that be the Kynges your brother subjectes myght not onely heere it, but also folowe and understand it as well as the noble Romayne Macrobius that dyd expounde it'.[178] Does this suggest by this stage in his career he was contemplating the publication of his works,[179] or was he simply imitating prefaces he would have seen in printed books?[180] Do we see in Morley a reflection of the movement from manuscript culture to the printed book or simply the mouthing of a new rhetorical strategy reflecting the ubiquitousness of a developing technological process?

NOTES

The research on Morley's French counterpart, Simon Bourgouyn, was funded by a grant from the N. R. Ker Memorial Fund and I am very grateful to the Committee for the award. A full study of Bourgouyn will appear elsewhere. I should like to thank Marie Axton, Rolf Bremmer, Jon Hunt, Lisa Jefferson, Jennifer Loach, Myra Orth, Richard Rex, Glenn Richardson, and J. B. Trapp for their assistance with specific points.

1 The section on New Year's gifts to Henry VIII is a revised version of Ch. X in *Order and Connexion: Studies in Bibliography and Book History*, ed. by R. C. Alston (Cambridge, 1997), pp. 159-76. Some of the material on the New Year's gift to Cromwell will appear in '"Plutarch's" Life of Agesilaus: a Recently Located New Year Gift to Thomas Cromwell by Henry Parker, Lord Morley', in *Prestige, Authority and Power in Late Medieval Manuscripts and Texts*, ed. by F. Riddy (York, 2000), pp. 159-69.

2 *The Lisle Letters*, ed. by M. St Clare Byrne, 6 vols (Chicago & London, 1981), no. 1086 (V, 10).

3 R. McEntegart, 'England and the League of Schmalkalden 1531-1547' (unpublished Ph.D. dissertation, University of London, 1992), p. 208, n. 43, has pointed out that at New Year 1538 Cromwell was in an even more dominant position than usual.

4 Mary's New Year's Gift List of 1557 has been printed in D. Loades, *Mary Tudor: a Life* (Oxford, 1989), pp. 358-69.

5 See P. Glanville, 'Plate and Gift-Giving at Court', in *Henry VIII: a European Court in England*, ed. by D. Starkey (London, 1991), pp. 131-5 (pp. 132-3): 'The King's gifts were stereotyped, and their preparation was entrusted to a small group of London goldsmiths working to regular annual contracts at fixed rates. The King's greater subjects, however, were expected to be more lavish and more imaginative. ... The 1532 New Year Gift Roll records a characteristic mixture of practicality and luxury. Most of the bishops gave money; while the earls gave principally goldsmiths' work, including a gold trencher plate and rosewater flagon, a gold dog-choke and a pair of gilt collars for greyhounds.'

6 See K. R. Bartlett, 'Letter of Henry Parker, Lord Morley, to Thomas Cromwell', p. 231 below. [*LP Henry VIII* XIV.1.285.] Richard Cromwell (alias Williams) was Thomas Cromwell's nephew, the son of his sister Catherine.

7 *Lord Morley's 'Tryumphes'*, ed. by Carnicelli, p. 78.

8 See J. K. McConica, *English Humanists and Reformation Politics Under Henry VIII and Edward VI* (Oxford, 1965), p. 157: 'His unwavering devotion to the Princess Mary, even at times when such loyalty must have risked disfavour, silences the accusation of mere trimming which his persistent compliments to those in power might otherwise imply.'

9 See *Forty-six Lives*, ed. by Wright, p. 168.

10 Account of the Miracles of the Sacrament, below, p. 263.

11 Douai, Bibliothèque municipale, MS 922.II, fols 51^v-52^r. I thank Thomas F. Mayer for this reference.

12 See *Forty-six Lives*, ed. by Wright, pp. xlvi-vii, n.3.

13 G. E. Cokayne, *The Complete Peerage of England, Scotland, Ireland, Great Britain and the United Kingdom*, ed. by V. Gibbs et al., 13 vols in 14 (London 1910-59), 9, 224, n. c.

14 See M. K. Jones & M. G. Underwood, *The King's Mother: Lady Margaret Beaufort, Countess of Richmond and Derby* (Cambridge, 1992), p. 158.

15 *Lord Morley's 'Tryumphes'*, ed. by Carnicelli, p. 5.

16 See S. J. Gunn, 'Henry Bourchier, earl of Essex (1472-1540)', in *The Tudor Nobility*, ed. by G. W. Bernard (Manchester & New York, 1992), pp. 134-79 (p. 154): 'he was not even appointed to the commission of the peace until 1530, when he was well into middle age, and all his obvious loyalty brought him only one stewardship of crown lands, tentative royal assistance in a dispute with the canons of Norwich, and the chance to purchase at the normal price some monastic estates in 1540'. For a modification of Gunn's assessment, see now Starkey, 'An Attendant Lord? Henry Parker, Lord Morley', above, pp. 7-8.

17 In 1537, for example, he complained to Cromwell that the canons of Norwich 'demaunde, yf I were attaynted of treason, what my bondes shoulde availe them for the payment of their rent'. Quoted in *Forty-six Lives*, ed. by Wright, p. xxviii.

18 In the following discussion I do not deal with Morley's own shorter poems, on which see Carlson, 'Morley's Translations from Roman Philosophers', below, pp. 139-40, and Woods, 'Ryding Ryme', below, pp. 201-11. As Carnicelli observes (*Lord Morley's 'Tryumphes'*, p. 174, n. 9), these poems are not without merit; his '"Never was I lesse alone," has become something of an anthology piece, an example of the work of the "courtly makers" in the court of Henry VIII'.

19 On the attribution to Plutarch, found in the early printed editions and accepted by Morley, see V. R. Giustiniani, 'Sulle traduzioni latine delle "Vite" di Plutarco nel quattrocento', *Rinascimento*, N.S. 1 (1961), 3-62 (p. 25); D. A. Russell, *Plutarch* (London, 1973), p. 148; and J. Maule, 'Plutarch', below, pp. 107-11.

20 Wright argued that Morley made use of this edition in his translations from Plutarch: see *Forty-six Lives*, ed. by Wright, p. lxi. It is, in fact, a reprint of the Venice 1478 edition (Goff P-832). For other early editions see Giustiniani, 'Sulle traduzioni latine', pp. 44-5.

21 Until very recently it was not normal British Library practice to number blank leaves and I have used lower-case roman numerals to indicate unnumbered leaves. The distinction between roman and arabic numbers, however, has no bearing on the actual structure of the codex.

22 Henry is addressed as 'King Henry, of that name th'Eight, King off Englonde and of Fraunce, Defendour of the faith, Lorde of Yrlonde etc.', but not Supreme Head of the Church of England, which title was added to his style on 15 January 1535. He was awarded the title of Defender of the Faith in October 1521.

23 It is not clear to which of the twelve Wingfield brothers this refers. On the various members of this family see J. M. Wingfield, *Some Records of the Wingfield Family*, London, 1925); J. Blatchly, 'The Lost and Mutilated Memorials of the Bovile and Wingfield Families at Letheringham', *Proceedings of the Suffolk Institute of Archaeology*, 33 (1973-6), 168-94; H. M. Nixon, 'French Bookbindings for Sir Richard Wingfield and Jean Grolier', in *Gatherings in Honor of Dorothy E. Miner*, ed. by U. E. McCracken & L. M. C. Randall (Baltimore, 1974), pp. 302, 305; G. J. Undreiner, *Robert Wingfield: Erster staendiger englischer Gesandter am deutschen Hof (1464?-1539)* (Freiburg, 1932).

24 According to Morley, Henry VIII could be compared to Scipio primarily in terms of the virtue of meekness. In 1544 Anthony Cope dedicated *The historie of two the moste noble capitaines of the worlde, Anniball and Scipio* to Henry and Edward (*STC* 5718). In Elizabeth's reign Gabriel Harvey observed that Cope's history 'gives a notable light to Livie; & was worthie to be dedicated to King Henrie the VIII': see L. Jardine & A. Grafton,

'"Studied for Action": How Gabriel Harvey Read His Livy', *Past and Present*, 129 (1990), 30-78 (p. 57).

25 Paulo Giovio (1483-1552) was the bishop of Nocera. The dedicatory epistle to the Italian version of the *Commentario*, from which Morley translated, is dated to 22 Jan. 1531. A Latin translation was pubished in Paris in 1538. Paul Ashton published an English translation in 1546.

26 Henry is 'suppreme heede' but only 'Lorde of Irelonde'. By 'The Act for the Kingly Title' of 18 June 1541 he assumed the title of King of Ireland: see S. G. Ellis, *Tudor Ireland* (London & New York, 1985), p. 139; also *Handbook of British Chronology*, 3rd edn, ed. by E. B. Fryde, D. E. Greenway, S. Porter, & I. Roy, rpt with corrections (Cambridge, 1996), p. 43.

27 C designates the single scribe responsible for seven of Morley's manuscripts, the most elaborate of which is the Chatsworth manuscript, on which see below.

28 Morley used the Louvain edition of 1487 (*GW* 4485): see *Forty-six Lives*, ed. by Wright, pp. lxix-lxxi.

29 Strapwork initials occur on fols 1^{r}, 3^{r}, 4^{r}, 4^{v}, 6^{v}, 7^{r}, 7^{v}, 8^{v}, 9^{v}, 10^{v}, 11^{v}, 12^{r}, 12^{v}, 13^{v}, 14^{v}, 15^{r}, 16^{r}, 17^{r}, 18r^{r}, 19^{r}, 20^{r}, 20^{v}, 21r^{r}, 22^{r}, 23^{v}, 24^{r}, 24^{v}, 25^{v}, 26^{v}, 27^{r}, 27^{v}, 28^{v}, 29^{r}, 30^{v}, 31^{r}, 31^{v}, 32^{r}, 32^{v}, 33^{v}, 35^{r}, 36^{r}, 37^{r}, 38^{v}, 39^{r}, 42^{r}, 43^{v}, 44^{r}, 45^{r}, 45^{v} and 46^{r}. Human or grotesque heads (alone or in other combinations) are found on fols 4^{r}, 4^{v}, 9^{v}, 12^{r}, 12^{v}, 17^{r}, 19^{r}, 20^{v}, 22^{r}, 23^{v}, 24^{v}, 27^{v}, 29^{r}, 30^{v}, 31r^{r} 32^{r}, 33^{v}, 36^{r}, 37^{r}, 38^{v}, 39^{r}, 42r^{r}, 43^{v}, 45^{r}, 45^{v} and 46^{r}. There are birds (alone or as part of a scene) on fols 8^{v}, 16r^{r}, 20^{r}, 20^{v} (pecking fruit), 21^{r}, 22^{r} (examining a pear), 28^{v}, and 33^{v}. Flower and fruit motifs include the rose, pomegranate and marigold and occur (alone or as part of a design) on fols 1^{r}, 4^{r}, 6^{v}, 8^{v}, 9^{v} (marigold in the mouth of a human figure), 10^{v}, 11^{v} (where a rose and pomegranate grow out of a crown with orb; below nestling between the shafts of the M are a pair of marigolds), 12^{v}, 13^{v}, 16^{r}, 17^{r}, 20^{v}, 21^{r} 22r^{r}, 24^{r}, 24^{v}, 25^{v}, 27r^{r}, 27^{v}, 28^{v}, 30^{v}, 31^{r}, 31^{v}, 32^{v}, 33^{v}, 35^{r}, 38^{v} (marigolds in the mouth of a grotesque), 44^{r}, and 46^{r}. Animal or snakes are found (alone or as part of the design) on fols 3r^{r} (monkey), 4^{r}, 7^{v} (dragon), 20^{r}, 24^{v}, 27^{v}, 31^{r}, 32^{v}, and 33^{v} (lion).

30 Wright misreads 'gra*tia*' as 'pro'. None of the other examples of scrollwork contain initials, but the H on fol. 4^{r} and the M on fol. 11^{v} contain two sets of five minims in the scrollwork.

31 On the confusion of this version with a Middle English verse translation see J. M. Cowen, 'The Translation of Boccaccio's *De Mulieribus Claris* in British Library MS Additional 10304 and *The Forty-Six Lives Translated from Boccaccio* by Henry Parker, Lord Morley', *Notes and Queries*, 243 (1998), 28-9.

32 All the other surviving manuscripts presented by Morley have been rebound.

33 It must have been written after 1541 (Henry is adddressed as 'King of Englond, Fraunce and Irelande'). Morley, moreover, sends greetings both to 'Quene Katheryn' and to Prince Edward: it is unlikely that he would have alluded to Catherine Howard during the period of her disgrace in January 1542 and so the reference must be to Catherine Parr whom Henry married in July 1543. This work was chosen presumably because it shows the betrayal by Pope Alexander III of the emperor Frederick Barbarossa. See John N. King, *Tudor Royal Iconography: Literature and Art in an Age of Religious Crisis* (Princeton, 1989), p. 130, who has observed that Frederick Barbarossa 'possessed special appeal at the Tudor court during the Reformation, because his excommunication and alleged betrayal by the pope could be interpreted as precursors to Henry VIII's conflicts with Clement VII and Paul III'.

34 On early Italian editions and late French versions possibly known to Morley see *Lord Morley's 'Tryumphes'*, ed. by Carnicelli, pp. 28-37; also Marie Axton's corrections to Carnicelli in 'Lord Morley's *Tryumphes of Petrarcke*'.

35 See *Lord Morley's 'Tryumphes'*, ed. by Carnicelli, p. 78.

36 Reprinted from the 1539 edition in *Forty-six Lives*, ed. by Wright, pp. 167-8; also *The Exposition and Declaration*, ed. by Rex, below, pp. 232-3.

37 See R. B. McKerrow & F. S. Ferguson, *Title-page Borders used in England & Scotland 1485-1640* (London, 1933), no. 30. The same border was used even later with the date deleted. In *Tudor Royal Iconography*, pp. 80, 145, n. 35 and in 'Henry VIII as David: the King's Image and Reformation Politics' (*Rethinking the Henrician Era*, ed. by P. C. Herman (Urbana & Chicago), 1994, pp. 78-92), pp. 86-7, J. N. King has argued mistakenly that the date on the border proved that Morley had originally written the text in 1534.

38 Presented to Lady Mary. Mary was insistent that she be styled princess even after her demotion in 1533 (she had been given the title Princess of Wales when she was nine) and in 1534, for example, she had instructed a gentleman of her household not to receive any writing from the court in which she was not so named. Later in the same year she formally objected to the withdrawal of her title as princess: see Loades, *Mary Tudor*, pp. 82-3. During the crisis over her submission in 1536 Lady Hussey was arrested for addressing her as princess. It is virtually impossible therefore that Morley would address her as the 'Lady Mary' rather than princess until after 1536, when she had submitted to her father. Henry, rather than Edward, is named as king, which gives a terminus ad quem of 1547.

39 On this drawing see King, *Tudor Royal Iconography*, p. 198: 'A pen-and-ink drawing of the Madonna and Child conflates the figure of Mary as Queen of Heaven, wearing a crown and holding a scepter, with the Woman Clothed with the Sun ...'.

40 Hammond observes that this poem is not found in early printed editions of Maffeo Vegio's works. She also discusses Morley's use of the term 'soneto'.

41 My description is of the added Morley preface, not of the Psalter itself – on which see Hope Emily Allen, *Writings Ascribed to Richard Rolle Hermit of Hampole and Materials for his Biography* (New York, 1927), p. 166. On confusion of the manuscript with BL, Royal MS 18 B.XXI see *Forty-six Lives*, ed. by Wright, p. lvii.

42 On Morley's numbering of the letters and its relationship to Erasmus's edition see Carlson, 'Morley's Translations', below, n. 40, 43.

43 *The Lumley Library: the Catalogue of 1609*, ed. by Sears Jayne & F. R. Johnson (London, 1956), p. 248.

44 Although described as queen of England, France, Naples, Jerusalem, and Ireland, Mary is called princess of Spain. It must therefore have been completed after she married Philip in 1554, but before he acceded to the Spanish throne as Philip II in January 1556.

45 For a description and discussion see R. M. Warnicke,'The Lady Margaret, Countess of Richmond (d. 1509), as Seen by Bishop Fisher and by Lord Morley', *Moreana*, 19, no. 74 (1982), 47-55; also Warnicke, 'Lord Morley's Statements about Richard III', *Albion*, 15 (1983), 173-8.

46 See Giustiniani, 'Sulle traduzioni latine', pp. 33-4.

47 For a detailed discussion of the dating and subsequent history of the manuscript see my '"Plutarch's" Life of Agesilaus' (n. 1, above). Owned by Halliwell-Phillips, it was subsequently lost from view and modern descriptions have been based on Horace Walpole's observations in the *Catalogue of the Royal and Noble Authors of England*.

48 Cawood is described in the colophon as 'Prynter to the Quenes hyghnes', to which office he received the grant on 29 December 1553: see *Calendar of Patent Rolls*, Philip & Mary, i. 53. Maltravers died in August 1556.

49 Sold at Sothebys as Lot 50 on 13 June 1977: see Axton, 'Lord Morley's *Tryumphes of Petrarcke*', below, p. 199, n. 65.

50 For the history of the various copies see *Forty-six Lives,* ed. by Wright, pp. l-li. For a 'Bibliographical History of Morley's *Tryumphes*' see *Lord Morley's 'Tryumphes'*, ed. by

Carnicelli, pp. 163-4. Carnicelli points out that in three copies (BL C. 13.a.7, the Bodleian copy, and the former Sion College copy) the *Tryumphes* is bound with Thomas Twyne's *Physike Against Fortune* (1579), which is a loose translation of Petrarch's *De remediis utriusque fortune*. Although the Huntington copy is now free-standing, it too was bound with Twyne's *Physike* when Richard Heber acquired it from Saunders in 1832. Heber had the two works separated and individually bound; he then sold the Twyne. (I thank Thomas V. Lange, Curator of Early Printed Books and Bindings, The Huntington Library, for this information.) The Grenville copy was sold at the British Museum Duplicate Sale of 1832: it is listed as no. 558 in the sale catalogue. For the title-page compartiment see McKerrow & Ferguson, no. 83: the first use in a dated book is 18 December 1554.

51 Carnicelli states that all five existing copies are identical and he prints 'arbitrarily' from the Huntington Library copy. For a discussion of the Roxburghe Club edition of 1887 (ed. by Stafford Henry, Earl of Iddesleigh and J. E. T. Loveday, based on a transcript by J. Payne Collier), see *Lord Morley's 'Tryumphes'*, ed. by Carnicelli, p. 164.

52 For reasons why it must derive from this edition see my '"Her moost lovyng and fryndely brother sendeth gretyng": Anne Boleyn's Manuscripts and their Sources', in *Illuminating the Book: Makers and Interpreters*, ed. by M. P. Brown & S. McKendrick (London, 1998), pp. 261-80 (p. 263). The same article provides a detailed description of the manuscript.

53 The form of address and the heraldic devices indicate that it was presented to Anne Boleyn during the brief period after she was created marquess of Pembroke on 1 September 1532 but before March 1533 when she was recognized as queen. It is almost certainly a New Year's gift.

54 For a more detailed analysis of the authorship question see '"Her moost lovyng and fryndely brother sendeth gretyng"', pp. 267-8.

55 Seymour is described as 'Protectour'.

56 *Forty-six Lives*, ed. by Wright, pp. xciv-vi (p. xcvi).

57 *Lord Morley's 'Tryumphes'*, ed. by Carnicelli, p. 16.

58 See, for example, the position articulated in the preface to Erasmus's *Paean* where St Gregory is cited to 'confute and blame theym that do not honour to the holy saynctes in heven' (*Forty-six Lives*, ed. by Wright, p. 171).

59 On this term see Perez Zagorin, *Ways of Lying: Dissimulation, Persecution, and Conformity in Early Modern Europe* (Cambridge, Mass., 1990).

60 See Rex, 'Morley and the Papacy', below, p. 96: 'If this work indeed proceeds from the pen of Henry Parker, Lord Morley, then his religious utterances must be seen as determined entirely by the prevailing wind.'

61 In their *Catalogue of Western Manuscripts in the Old Royal and King's Collections*, 4 vols (London, 1921), II, 253, G. F. Warner & J. P. Gilson note that '[T]he present work is distinctly Protestant in tone, both preface and commentary, and is perhaps by his son.'

62 There were other well placed Henry Parkers in the period but there is no indication that any of them had a literary bent. One Roger Parker, who was the son of Henry Parker of Frith Hall, Essex, was a Marian exile and patron of Bartholomew Traheron.

63 In a private communication Jennifer Loach suggested that if Morley were the author then it would support the theory that the coup of 1549 was initially thought to be a catholic one.

64 See Carlson, 'Roman Philosophers', below, p. 131; also Starkey, 'An Attendant Lord?', pp. 14-16, on when he first became intimately acquainted with Mary.

65 One of the manuscripts presented to Mary (London, BL, Add. MS 12060) is known to have left the royal library after her death and others may also have done so.

66 See *Index Britanniae Scriptorum: John Bale's Index of British and Other Writers*, ed. by R. L. Poole & Mary Bateson; rpt with an intro. by C. Brett & J. P. Carley (Cambridge, 1990), pp. 166, 515.

67 On the putative plays see *Lord Morley's 'Tryumphes'*, ed. by Carnicelli, pp. 16-17: 'Bale's similar description of Sir Thomas More as a writer of comedies in his youth suggests that both More and Morley dabbled to some extent in drama and are perhaps to be linked with the group of playwrights who flourished in the early Tudor court. ... We can only conjecture about Morley's lost comedies and tragedies and about his connection with this "school" of early Tudor writers of interludes. ... If Morley was in fact the author of comedies and tragedies, the probability is strong that his tragedies resembled the medieval moralities and that his comedies had all the earmarks of the New Learning.'

68 For a partial list of signatures in Harley 4775 see C. E. Wright, *Fontes Harleiani: a Study of the Sources of the Harleian Collection of Manuscripts Preserved in the Department of Manuscripts in the British Museum* (London, 1972), p. 245, and the references cited. For other examples of Morley's signature see *inter alia* London, British Library, Cotton Vitellius B.XX, fols 285v, 286v. On the use of this motto by the Parker family see *Elvin's Handbook of Mottoes*, rev. R. Pinches (London, 1971), p. 168. For a more detailed study of this manuscript see my '"Plutarch's" Life of Agesilaus' (n. 1, above).

69 Morley was married to Alice St John, daughter of John St John of Bletsoe. She inherited a copy of Gower from Lady Margaret Beaufort: see Jones & Underwood, *The King's Mother*, p. 241. John St John received a copy of *The Canterbury Tales*: see Boffey & Edwards, 'Books Connected with Henry Parker, Lord Morley and his Family', below, p. 70.

70 London, British Library, Royal MS 20 C.VIII (Honoré Bouvet, *Larbre des batailles* (s.xv in); executed for Jean, duc de Berry) owned by Humphrey Lloyd and then Lumley (no. 1179 in the Lumley catalogue), contains an 'Epitaphium Henrici Parkeri equitis domini Morlei' – on which see below, n. 166. It is possible that Morley owned the manuscript, but it is more likely that he added the epitaph to a manuscript already owned by somebody else associated with the Arundel circle.

71 On William Browne and his collection of medieval manuscripts see A. S. G. Edwards, 'Medieval Manuscripts Owned by William Browne of Tavistock (1590/1?-1643/5?)', in *Books and Collectors 1200-1700*, ed. by J. P. Carley & C. G. C. Tite (London, 1997), pp. 441-9.

72 For a description of the contents see J. A. van Dorsten, 'The Leyden "Lydgate Manucript"', *Scriptorium*, 14 (1960), 315-25 (pp. 322-3).

73 Van Dorsten names John Kyng as an owner previous to Morley and Thomas Andrew as a later owner (*c.* 1600?). He gives Antony Kynwellmarshe (s.xv/xvi), Pyatt, Recherd Pryntys (s.xv/xvi), John Thomas Wyf (?), Humfrydus Bertun (?) as users. Dr A. I. Doyle has kindly provided me with a more complete reading and better dating in some cases than that provided by van Dorsten and would date Thomas Andrew's signature to s.xv/xvi. See also Boffey & Edwards, 'Books Connected with Henry Parker, Lord Morley', below, p. 72. Rolf Bremmer, who has examined the signature under ultra-violet light, reads as 'D. Morley' or just possibly 'D. Marley'. He informs me that there are extensive marginal annotations by Franciscus Junius the Younger.

74 London, British Library, Royal MS 19 B.x (Aldobrandinus, *Le Régime de santé*) has 'the Lorde Morley's armys' drawn on a front flyleaf and on fol. 157v is found 'the Lorde Morley's best'. Janet Backhouse ('Sir John Donne's Flemish Manuscripts', in *Medieval Codicology, Iconography, Literature, and Translation: Studies for Keith Val Sinclair*, ed. by P. R. Monks & D. D. R. Owen (Leiden, 1994), pp. 48-53 (p. 52, n. 26)) has suggested that the connection is with Henry Lovel (d. 1489), who succeeded to the title in 1476. Lovel was the brother of Morley's mother. The manuscript was in the royal library before 1550 and contains the royal inventory number 'No. 1299'.

75 *Lord Morley's 'Tryumphes'*, ed. by Carnicelli, p. 78.

76 See P. Chavy, *Traducteurs d'autrefois, Moyen Age et Renaissance: dictionnaire des*

traducteurs et de la littérature traduite en ancien et moyen français (842-1600) (Paris, 1988), p. 1089; also F. Simone, *The French Renaissance*, trans by H. Gaston Hall (London, 1969), pp. 235-43. On the attribution to Georges de la Forge see Simone, pp. 231, 315, n. 53.

77 *Lord Morley's 'Tryumphes'*, ed. by Carnicelli, p. 33, cites de la Forge and Meynier d'Oppède as possible inspirations for Morley, but is unaware that the former translation appeared before 1536. He does not mention Bourgouyn. Wright, *Forty-six Lives*, p. ci, n. 1, states categorically that '[t]he work in question must have been *Les Triu[m]phes Petrarque traduictes de la[n]gue Tuscane en Rhime francoyse par le Baron D'opede*, Paris, 1538'. Both Wright and Carnicelli therefore assume that Morley's translation dated from the late 1530s or after and Carnicelli states (p. 11), that '[i]t seems likely that Morley made it some time after his retirement to Essex in 1536 or 1537, during the years when his interest in Italian literature prompted him to read and annotate Machiavelli's *Istorie Fiorentine* and *Il Principe* and send them to Cromwell as gifts'.

78 On this edition see B. Moreau et al., *Inventaire chronologique des éditions parisiennes du xvie siècle*, 4 vols (Paris/Abbeville, 1972-92), III, 1833.

79 For descriptions of F1, F2, and A see E. Pellegrin, *Manuscrits de Pétrarque dans les bibliothèques de France* (Padua, 1966), pp. 453-6, 458-61, 424-8. On A see also M. D. Orth, 'The Triumphs of Petrarch Illuminated by Godefroy le Batave (Arsenal, Ms. 6480)', *Gazette des Beaux Arts* (Dec. 1984), 197-206; on P see E. König & G. Bartz, *Boccaccio und Petrarch in Paris* (Munich 1997), pp. 279-309. Much more work needs to be done on the dating of Bourgouyn's translation and the following discussion is a preliminary one. In 'Lord Morley's "Tryumphes of Fraunces Petrarcke"', below, pp. 176-7, M. Axton argues that Morley saw Bourgouyn's work at the time of the Field of the Cloth of Gold in 1520.

80 König & Bartz, *Boccaccio und Petrarch in Paris*, pp. 285, 304-9; Simone, *The French Renaissance*, pp. 218-19.

81 I owe the information on the removed miniatures to Myra Orth.

82 In 'Illustrations of Petrarch's *Trionfi* from Manuscript to Print and Print to Manuscript' (*Studies in Fifteenth-Century Printed Books Presented to Lotte Hellinga*, ed. by Martin Davies [London, 1999], pp. 507-47 [p. 545]), J. B. Trapp has observed: 'Among the French manuscripts of Simon Bourgouyn's verse translation of the *Trionfi* one, made for an unknown patron, possibly in the early 1510s, has six full-page miniatures. Some are based on the woodcuts first published by Capcasa in 1493, and re-used in Venice in 1497, 1500, 1503, 1508 and 1515.

83 Orth, 'The Triumphs of Petrarch', p. 201. As she also observes (private communication), it cannot have been produced much later, since Godefroy le Batave does not seem to have been working later than 1526.

84 Orth, 'The Triumphs of Petrarch', pp. 199-200.

85 Orth, 'The Triumphs of Petrarch', p. 202. In a private communication Orth has noted that (i) Godefroy had worked exclusively for the king and his mother up to that point; (ii) there are several missing folios which could include an owner's bifolium at the beginning.

86 This does not imply, of course, that Bourgouyn undertook the translation for Francis: he may have first written it more than a decade earlier.

87 Paris, Archives nationales KK 98, fol. 10^{r}.

88 Paris, BN, fonds français 21,499, fol. 108^{v}; Paris, Archives nationales J964, fol. 7^{v}.

89 Although he was appointed a valet de chambre in 1526, Clément Marot had to petition the king in verse to receive his salary. Obviously the situation was similar for Bourgouyn, since he does not appear in the household after 1525, although he does turn up in other records. See Glenn Richardson, 'The Privy Chamber of Henry VIII and Anglo-French Relations, 1515-1520', in *The Court Historian* 4.2 (August 1999), pp. 119-40.

90 It is possible that Morley would also translate 'valet de garderobe' as 'groom of the chamber'. However, Francis was engaged in war during the winter of 1524-5. He was captured at the battle of Pavia (24 February 1525) and did not return to France until 17 March 1526. (See R. J. Knecht, *Francis I* (Cambridge, 1982), pp. 176-91.) It is highly unlikely that Morley would have seen the book during this period: although some visitors did see the Blois library they did not get access to the private holdings as such.

91 An inventory of Francis's books at Blois taken in1518 still survives and this includes an alphabetical list of eighteen books which Francis carried with him when he travelled, the last one of which is 'Triumphes de Pétrarque. Escript à la main. Couvert de veloux biguarré et ferré partout'. See H. Omont, *Anciens inventaires et catalogues de la bibliothèque nationale*, 1 (Paris 1908), pp. 56-7. This manuscript was not described as 'historié' (a category normally noted) and so it seems unlikely that it describes one of the surviving copies of Bourgouyn's translation. (I thank Dr Orth for this observation.) On Francis's travelling library in general see T. Kimball Brooker, 'Bindings commissioned for Francis I's "Italian library" with horizontal spine titles dating from the late 1530s to 1540', *Bulletin du bibliophile*, 1997, no. 1, 33-91 (pp. 43-5).

92 Morley's name does not appear among the name of the lords officially taking part in the delegation (see *The Chronicle of Calais*, ed J. G. Nichols, Camden Soc. 35 (London, 1846), p. 38) but this does not rule out the possibility of his presence. He was present at the Field of the Cloth of Gold (see J. G. Russell, *The Field of the Cloth of Gold* (London, 1969), p. 201) but this was before A was illustrated and more importantly before Bourgouyn was described as a 'grome of the chaumber'. (If Morley were referring to 1520 in his description of seeing the French translation, then he must have got further news of Bourgouyn's career later in the decade, and added 'groom of the chamber' to his subsequent description of the unnamed Frenchman.) Alternatively, even though Morley does not appear in any other recorded diplomatic missions (see Gary M. Bell, *A Handlist of British Diplomatic Representatives 1509-1688* (London, 1990)), he may have gone to France on unofficial business and Francis was known to have shown his books to interested visitors. Morley's son-in-law, George Boleyn, was a member of several missions to France and both his son and daughter were present when Henry met with Francis at Calais in October 1532: for a list of lords present, which does not include Morley, see P. A. Hamy, *Entrevue de François premier avec Henry VIII, à Boulogne-sur-Mer, en 1532* (Paris, 1898), pp. L-LIX.

93 Perhaps the most likely date for the presentation would be just after Wolsey's fall, when Morley would have been looking for a new patron and when there were many perquisites available. See also Starkey, 'An Attendant Lord?', on the importance of the Divorce and Reformation in the process: as he observes (p. 6), 'the King now needed legislators, administrators, judges and propagandists'.

94 Of course, Morley's prefaces contain a certain amount of flattering self-dramatization and it would be foolhardy to take every detail as literally accurate.

95 Axton, 'Lord Morley's "Tryumphes"', below, pp. 174-5, suggests that the 'Lives of Scipio and Hannibal' comes before the translation of the *Trionfi*.

96 See the forthcoming study by Myra Orth and myself. Morley does not state that he got the idea for the Plutarch translations from Bourgouyn but, given that Bourgouyn was a pioneer in the translation of Plutarch's Lives into French and the first to translate the *Trionfi* into French verse and that Morley occupies the equivalent position in English, it is unlikely that Morley chose to translate Plutarch independently.

97 *LP Henry VIII* v p. 307 (Treasurer of the Chamber's Accounts). As Muriel St Clare Byrne, *The Lisle Letters*, II, 22, has observed: 'There was a graduated scale of tips, the amount received being determined by the master's rank. Ordinary knights' servants, as for example Russell's, Kingston's, Palmer's, Thomas More's, received only 13*s*. 4*d*. [in 1534].'

98 *LP Henry VIII* v.686 (p. 327): see below for further detail.
99 *LP Henry VIII* VI.32 (p. 14): he was amongst those who received gilt cups and so forth purchased from John Freman.
100 *LP Henry VIII* XIII.2.1280 (p. 538) (Treasurer of the Chamber's Accounts: BL, MS Arundel 97, fol. 54^v^).
101 *LP Henry VIII* XVI.1280 (p. 179) (Arundel 97, fol. 109^v^).
102 *LP Henry VIII* XVI.1489 (p. 699) (Arundel 97, fol. 166^r^).
103 Add 59900, fol. 69^v^.
104 See his *Jewels and Plate of Queen Elizabeth I: the Inventory of 1574* (London, 1955), p. 248. The only roll in which Morley's name does not appear is that for 1528 (PRO, E.101/420/4) which is incomplete and lists only gifts from Henry. The form of layout of the rolls seems to have been standardized under Thomas Cromwell. Up to around 1649 when they were dispersed, the rolls were preserved in the Jewel House (p. 247).
105 Neville Williams (*The Cardinal & The Secretary* (London, 1975), p. 203) has argued that this tract was one of the most interesting 'elaborations' to Cromwell's preamble to the Act in Restraint of Appeals: 'since he [Morley] emphasized the novelty of Henry's kingship. He praised him as "an ark of all princely goodness and honour" who was not only "the noblest King that ever reigned over the English nation" – a phrase that speaks volumes – but was also "*pater patriae*, that is the father of our country; one by whose virtue, learning and noble courage, England is newborn, newly brought from thraldom to freedom". This paternalism lay at the heart of much of Cromwell's social and economic legislation ...'
106 See *Forty-six Lives*, ed. by Wright, p. 3.
107 See H. Miller, *Henry VIII and the English Nobility*, Oxford, 1986, p. 157: 'Morley, it is true, was still exceptionally active in civilian life, following up his attendance at every trial by peers with an outstanding record of regular attendance in parliament; he was even present in the house of lords for each reading of the bill passed in 1542 to attaint his daughter, lady Rochford, and Katherine Howard.'
108 See J. J. Scarisbrick, *Henry VIII* (London, 1968), pp. 431-3; also L. B. Smith, *A Tudor Tragedy: the Life and Times of Catherine Howard* (London, 1961), pp. 167-70, 177, 178, 189, 190, 200, 202, 204-5. Smith refers to Lady Rochford as 'a pathological meddler, with most of the instincts of a procuress who achieves a vicarious pleasure from arranging assignations' (p. 167). A detailed (and perhaps less polemical) study of Lady Rochford would yield interesting information about the workings of court factions during Henry's reign.
109 In any case, Morley would not have had time to undertake the translation and have Chatsworth produced between the eruption of the crisis in November 1541 and New Year's Day 1542: the topic would not have presented itself to his mind until Henry was willing to entertain the charges against his wife very late in 1541.
110 Nor is there any reference to the queen in his salutation, which might have been expected if it were presented after Henry's marriage to Catherine Parr.
111 On this topic see James Simpson, 'The Sacrifice of Lady Rochford', below, pp. 154-5.
112 At the close of the preface Morley also prays 'your most victorius parson well to accept yt'. It should be noted, however, that Morley calls Henry victorious on more than one occasion in his dedicatory epistles to Mary.
113 Given the state of Henry's health, this does not seem a likely gift for January 1547.
114 On the dispute see *Forty-six Lives*, ed. by Wright, pp. xxvi-viii. (After her husband's execution in 1536 Morley's daughter pleaded with Cromwell to act as an interecessor for her: see *LP Henry VIII* x.1010, 1251.)
115 In the dedicatory letter to the Life Morley observed that Cromwell had been 'in other urgent causys of myne a schyld inexpungnable'. There are no surviving records of Cromwell's

patronage of Morley later in 1538. Independently, Sir Geoffrey Elton suggested to me that New Year 1538 would be the most likely time for the gift. Jennifer Loach (private communication) raised the possibility that the extended discussion of councillors in the Life should be seen in the context of the discussion of 'counsel' of the later 1530s. In particular it could well be a reaction to the claim of the Pilgrims in 1536 that the council was being packed by men of low birth and the replies to this claim by Sir Richard Morison and others. See also K. R. Bartlett, 'Morley, Machiavelli and the Pilgrimage of Grace', below, pp. 77-85.

116 On her printed books see T. A. Birrell, *English Monarchs and Their Books: from Henry VII to Charles II* (London, 1987), pp. 21-3.

117 See Loades, *Mary Tudor*, pp. 346, 348.

118 In June 1536 Anne Grey, Lady Hussey, wife of the former chamberlain of Mary's household, was sent to the Tower for conspiring to secure Mary's recognition as heir apparent; at Hunsdon she had referred to Mary as Princess rather than the Lady Mary. During the course of her interrogation Lady Hussey indicated that Lord and Lady Morley and their daughter had been as Hunsdon at the same time. In January 1537 Mary stood as godmother to Morley's grandchild. The second wife of Morley's son Henry was the daughter of Sir Philip and Lady Jane Calthorpe, both of whom had served in Mary's household.

119 See *Privy Purse Expenses of the Princess Mary 1536-1544*, ed. by F. Madden (London, 1831), pp. 7, 51, 82, 97, 143. (The January accounts for 1539, 1541 and 1542 are missing.) In December 1537 there was a gift of 3*s.* 4*d.*, which Wright, *Forty-six Lives*, p. liii, n. 1, speculates was connected with Mary's role as godmother.

120 See Loades, *Mary Tudor*, pp. 114-15, on Mary's reaction to Jane Seymour's death: 'Thus Mary lost a good friend, and was too "accrased" to attend the first stage of the obsequies. ... The court passed Christmas 1537 in mourning, and the usual festivities were much curtailed, so although Mary seems to have been present at Greenwich, there was little opportunity for her to preside at her father's side, even if he had been disposed to allow her to do so.'

121 Henry married Catherine Howard on 28 July 1540, a matter of weeks after the annulment of his marriage to Anne of Cleves. Catherine Parr's husband, Lord Latimer, was still alive on New Year's Day 1543; after he died Henry married her, 12 July 1543. Morley's greeting (to a king wifeless but about to embark) cannot therefore refer to either of these cases.

122 *Mary Tudor*, p. 319.

123 On the use of pattern book alphabets in this period see J. J. G. Alexander, *The Decorated Letter* (New York, 1978), pp. 25-7. See also Erna Auerbach, *Tudor Artists* (London, 1954) and C. P. Christianson, *Memorials of the Book Trade in Medieval London: the Archives of Old London Bridge* (Cambridge, 1987). Although in many cases artists appear to have employed stencils or templates this does not appear to be the case in the Morley series of books. Paul Christianson has observed (private communication): 'Freehand decoration was a professional skill for some scribes and may have been a speciality for some scribal artists who did decorative work exclusively on jobs where textwriters were providing the text (but not the decoration of initials).'

124 *Lord Morley's 'Tryumphes'*, ed. by Carnicelli, p. 5.

125 *Lord Morley's 'Tryumphes'*, ed. by Carnicelli, p. 78.

126 On the libraries of Henry VIII and a detailed account of the significance of the numbering system see my 'Marks in Books and the Libraries of Henry VIII', *PBSA*, 91 (1997), 583-606.

127 The Life of Agesilaus was also owned by Phillipps, catalogued as MS 9375.

128 For details concerning the owners of the manuscript see *Forty-six Lives*, ed. by Wright, pp. lxiii-lxiv.

129 There are a number of Henrician books which share this fate and it would be interesting to determine the sequence by which books were brought to Whitehall.
130 See H. Walther, *Proverbia Sententiaeque Latinitatis Medii Aevi*, 6 pts. (Göttingen, 1963-9), no. 10508.
131 Horace, *Epistulae*, 1, 16, 78. For 'servat' the correct reading should be 'solvet'.
132 The original Laud classification was H 17 and this is marked in the upper margin of fol. 1ʳ.
133 See *The History of Parliament: the House of Commons 1558-1603*, ed. by P. W. Hasler, 3 vols (London, 1981), II, 254-5. Hare also owned one of Wolsey's books, British Library, Harley MS 1197, fols 402-13, which probably entered the royal library at the time of Wolsey's fall.
134 Possibly R. Rushbrooke, BA, Cant 1576-7, who was rector of Hepworth, Suffolk, 1578-9.
135 See *LP Henry VIII* xx. 1.506. The presentation copy to Cromwell of Elyot's *Dictionary* (BL C.28.m.2) was at Westminster by *c.* 1550 and carries the inventory no. 1064.
136 Dr Robert Costomiris first drew my attention to this book.
137 On Kenrick see *The History of Parliament: the House of Commons*, II, 393.
138 See 'History of the Bulkeley Family (NLW MS 9080E)', ed. by E. Gwynne Jones, with an introduction by B. Dew Roberts, *Transactions of the Anglesey Antiquarian Society and Field Club* (1948), 1-99 (pp. 17-18). I thank Dr Ceridwen Lloyd-Morgan, National Library of Wales, for this reference.
139 On the Venetian ambassador, Giovanni Michieli's, commendation of her skill in Latin see Loades, *Mary Tudor*, p. 331. Juan-Luis Vives recommended Latin in his *De institutione Fominae Christianae*, commissioned by Catherine of Aragon for Mary: see Loades, *Mary Tudor*, pp. 32-3. The presentation copy to Catherine of this work survives as Oxford, Bodleian Arch B.e.30. Much later, Mary was part of the team assembled under Nicholas Udall to translate Erasmus's *Paraphrases*.
140 References to the pope have also been deleted throughout the text.
141 Two years earlier when Mary was despatched to Ludlow Catherine expressed herself pleased that Richard Fetherston would replace her as Mary's Latin tutor: 'As for your writing in Latin, I am glad that ye shall change from me to Master Federston, for that shall do you much good to learn by him to write aright.' Quoted in Garrett Mattingly, *Catherine of Aragon* (New York, 1941), p. 220.
142 Thomas Paynell also appealed to 'Lady' Mary's piety when he presented a translation from St Bernard for her as a New Year's gift: *A compendious & a moche frutyfull treatyse of well livyng, contaynyng the hole summe and effect of al vertue* (London: Thomas Petyt, n.d.) (*STC* 1908). Paynell claimed that he decided to present this work to Mary because of her learning and her inclination 'to the observacion of Chrystes lawes'. (I thank Dr Rex for this reference.)
143 Royal MS 17 C.xii, fol. 1ᵛ: printed in *Forty-six Lives*, ed. by Wright, p. 169.
144 On this topic see my 'Monastic Collections and their Dispersal', in *The Cambridge History of the Book in Britain*, volume 4 (1557-1695), ed. by John Barnard & D. F. McKenzie, forthcoming.
145 See M. R. James, *A Descriptive Catalogue of the Western Manuscripts in the Library of Queen's College Cambridge* (Cambridge, 1905), pp. 14-16; also G. D. Hobson, *Bindings in Cambridge Libraries* (Cambridge, 1929), p. 14.
146 Royal MS 17 C.xvi, fols 10ᵛ, 11ʳ.
147 See Loades, *Mary Tudor*, p. 245. Her father, and her great-grandmother Lady Margaret Beaufort as well, shared this devotion and it is worth noting that in the conclusion to his translation of a 'Tale from Massuccyo Salernytano', dedicated to Henry, Morley observed: 'take example of theyr juste and feythfull workes. whereby we worthely may communycate

the holy and moste blessyde sacrament of the aulter to our salvation' (Royal MS 18 A.LXII, fol. 13r).

148 In this work he repudiated the heretics in Henry's reign who 'wolde not the Ave Maria to be sayde'; it is a nice touch that he encoded a reference to the Angelical Salutation in one of the initials of Chatsworth, a manuscript presented during a time of great personal stress.

149 See below, p. 254.

150 From the preface to his translation of Erasmus *Paean*; printed in *Forty-six Lives*, ed. by Wright, p. 172.

151 For his use of examples from the *Golden Legend* and Gregory the Great, both probably suggested by his reading of *De veritate*, see Rex, 'Morley's Religion', p. 100. Morley owned a manuscript of the English translation of the Golden Legend: see above, p. 39.

152 For example, Richard Rex has discovered in the Cambridge University Library a copy of Fisher's *De veritate*, on a back flyleaf of which there are notes in a late-sixteenth-century hand. These concern 'Miracula circa Euch. ex Chronicis Nurenbergae' and refer to some of the same examples as used by Morley.

153 On the disparities between the two accounts, primarily in tone rather than fact, see Warnicke, 'The Lady Margaret, Countess of Richmond' (n. 45 above), pp. 53-4.

154 *The Crowland Chronicle Continuations: 1459-1486*, ed. by N. Pronay & J. Cox (London, 1986), p. 180.

155 See Warnicke, 'Lord Morley's Statements' (n. 45 above), p. 178: 'Given the context of Morley's remarks, the "Account" must surely be also accepted as evidence that even those contemporaries who had daily contact with and remained friendly to the loyal servants of Richard III genuinely believed him guilty of a "horrible offence" againsts his nephews.'

156 Morley does not include two earlier lines on Matilda: 'O regina potens Anglorum linea regum / Scotos nobilitans nobilitate tua.' He also omits the two succeeding lines: see below, pp. 264, 268-9, n. 56. The chronicle is a mid-fifteenth-century forgery. The continuations were written slightly later in the century: see Antonia Gransden, *Historical Writing in England ii. c. 1307 to the Early Sixteenth Century* (London, 1982), pp. 490-2.

157 It also survives independently the final section of an earlier manuscript of unknown provenance (s.xi-xiii) containing a wide range of disparate materials (now Oxford, Bodleian Library, MS Laud lat. 86, fol. 133r). William Camden almost certainly saw Laud lat. 86 and quoted three historical poems, including this one, on fol. 133r+v of his *Remains*: see William Camden, *Remains Concerning Britain*, ed. by R. D. Dunn (Toronto, 1984), pp. 296-7.

158 See *The Crowland Chronicle Continuations*, ed. by Pronay & Cox, pp. 1-105. They observe (p. 99): 'The work is also important because it is wholly independent. All the other chronicles and "histories" of the Tudor period are inter-related from More and Vergil all the way to Shakespeare. ... The Crowland Continuator, however, remained unknown until the very end of the Tudor period. ... It thus has a double importance. First, that it gives us an independent witness to the mood of the times which was to be exploited so skilfully and effectively by the device of the "official history" which the Tudor regime adopted from continental humanism, as one of the means for political indoctrination and legitimation. Second, that because Tudor historical writers remained unaware of it and therefore made no effort to counter or explain away what the Continuator had recorded, its emergence in the seventeenth century gave people an impetus to re-examine Tudor history, and to wrestle with the issues which it raised.'

159 *The Crowland Chronicle Continuations*, ed. by Pronay & Cox, p. 102.

160 Only eight folios of Otho B.XIII survived the fire: *The Crowland Chronicle Continuations*, ed. by Pronay & Cox, p. 103. BL, Arundel MS 178 contains a partial copy of the early section (not including the verses on Matilda) made in the sixteenth century.

161 *The Crowland Chronicle Continuations*, ed. by Pronay & Cox, p. 40. This copy was supposedly stolen by Obadiah Walker, Master of University College, Oxford: see *Ingulph's Chronicle of the Abbey of Croyland*, tr. Henry T. Riley (London, 1854), p. ix.

162 I thank Dr C. G. C. Tite for this information.

163 *The Crowland Chronicle Continuations*, ed. by Pronay & Cox, p. 102; see also Jones & Underwood, *The King's Mother*, p. 136.

164 On manuscripts owned by members of Morley's extended family see Boffey & Edwards, 'Books Connected with Henry Parker, Lord Morley', below, pp. 69-75.

165 Morley also wrote an epitaph for Sir Thomas West, Lord La Warre (d. 1544), known as a devout Catholic: see *Forty-six Lives*, ed. by Wright, p. xlviii. He was responsible for the epitaphs to his grandmothers, his father and mother, and his wife, which survive in the parish church at Great Hallingbury: see above, p. 30.

166 This is followed by eight further lines on the mutability of the world, translated from 'Auctores incerte' [sic]. The typesetter clearly had trouble with the Latin. In fact, this is a rewrite of a much more conventional earlier epitaph which survives on fol. 1[r] of Royal MS 20 C.VIII:

Epitaphium Henrici Parkeri equitis Domini Morlei, quod ipse adhuc vivens composuit et suo sepulchro inscribi jussit.

Ciste parum quaeso viator et pauca haec verba lege, lectaque pectore repone tuo. Fui, ut tu, homo mortalis infinitis obnoxius incommodis, morbis scilicet et malis. Nec dubium, quin ut sum et tu aliquando futurus sis, cibus vermibus, pulvis et cinis. Cur igitur per fas et nefas cura tibi paras, cum in tam exiguo tumulo, corpus tuum quiescet, sicut et ego hic quiesco? Cur tirio et astro te adornas, in puncto temporis ad nihilum venturum, quemadmodum vento veniente minaci et flores decidunt, et omnis decor eorum evanescit, et non potius animam immortalem virtutibus ac bonis operibus studes Deo commendare? O immemor tuae salutis, utinam saperes, et intelligeres, atque novissima tandem pervideres sed nil amplius moror, quin obsecrem, ut nulla manus sepulchrum hoc violet, donec a summo coelo, personet angelica tuba. Chare viator precare quietem. Vive et vale.

167 See above, p. 40.

168 Pr. *Lord Morley's 'Tryumphes'*, ed. by Carnicelli, pp. 159-60. As Carnicelli has observed (p. 11), the *ps.*-Virgilian *De venere*, to which Morley provides an *amplificatio* in eight eight-line stanzas, can be found in the Lyon edition of 1529.

169 See 'The Occasion of Lord Morley's Translation of the *Trionfi*: the Triumph of Chastity over Politics', in *Petrarch's Triumphs: Allegory and Spectacle*, ed. by K. Eisenbichler & A. A. Iannucci (Ottawa, 1990), pp. 325-34.

170 Although *The Exposition and Declaration of the Psalme, Deus ultionum Dominus* was printed, Morley himself gave Henry a manuscript copy and there is no indication that he was responsible for the printed version.

171 As with his other manuscript presentations, however, he anticipates more than one reader, requesting Maltravers 'to defende it [his translation] agaynst those that will more by envy then by knowledge deprave it, and then I do not feare but those that knowe and can speake the Italian, will beare with the simple translation, and commende the worke, as it is so muche commendable ...' (*Lord Morley's 'Tryumphes'*, ed. by Carnicelli, pp. 78-9).

172 See above, n. 50. For a discussion of how Watkyns acquired the sheets see Axton, 'Lord Morley's "Tryumphes of Fraunces Petrarcke"', below, p. 192.

173 The reference in the Lumley catalogue, no. 1778 – 'Francis Petrarkes triumphes englished by Henrie Parker lorde Morley, anglice' – must describe a printed text since manuscripts are signalled as such in the catalogue. I thank Marie Axton for this reference.

174 Thomas Wyatt completed his translation of Plutarch's *Quyete of Mynde* late in 1527; his dedicatory letter to Catherine of Aragon is dated 31 December 1527. Concerning

this work, Patricia Thomson ('Sir Thomas Wyatt: Classical Philosophy and English Humanism', *The Huntington Library Quarterly*, 25 (1961/2), 79-96 (pp. 79-80)), has observed: 'As the first rendering of Plutarch in English ... *Quyete of Mynde* is as much a pioneer work as Wyatt's Italian sonnets, octaves, and tercets. It is an early example of the prose essay in English. It gives Wyatt a place, albeit a humble one, in the humanist movement of Henry VIII's England.'

175 According to P. Neville Sington, translations of classical texts were one of the easiest, and safest, ways to court royal favour in the 1540s: see her 'Press, Politics and Religion', in *The Cambridge History of the Book in Britain*, volume 3 (1400-1557), ed. by L. Hellinga & J. B. Trapp, forthcoming.

176 'Florio's Montaigne: Translation and Pragmatic Humanism in the Sixteenth Century' (unpublished Ph.D. dissertation, University of Cambridge, 1991), p. 47. See also J. W. Saunders, 'The Stigma of Print: a Note on the Social Bases of Tudor Poetry', *Essays in Criticism*, 1 (1951), 139-64 (p. 154): 'And when Henry Parker, Lord Morley, wrote lines to "hys Posteritye" ... or Robert Smith, the martyr, wrote an *Exhortation to his children*, it was the succeeding generation, and communication by manuscript, that they had in mind.'

177 On the topic of bilingual translations in the period, see D. Carlson, 'Alexander Barclay and Richard Pynson: a Tudor Printer and his Writer', *Anglia*, 113 (1995), 283-302 (p. 297, n. 28)

178 The Henry Parker who wrote the Commentary on Ecclesiastes makes the same point: 'I have permitted ... thes my annotacions to comme into other mens handes, which, although they be simple and breff, yet unto thoose that have no better, or that have ben deluded affore tyme wyth false gloses and exposicions they maye be occasion of better knowlege'.

179 And, if it were he who initiated the publication of the *Tryumphes*, then this would represent the culmination of the process. Note, however, that he uses the term 'heere' rather than 'read'.

180 Almost fifty years ago Saunders argued ('The Stigma of Print', p. 164) that 'In the past the answers [about the evolution of English poetry in the sixteenth century] have perhaps been wrong because the right questions have not been asked. One question which it is suggested must in future be asked in any discussion of a particular Tudor poet is "Did he write for a manuscript audience or for a printed-book audience?"'

BOOKS CONNECTED WITH HENRY PARKER, LORD MORLEY, AND HIS FAMILY

JULIA BOFFEY & A. S. G. EDWARDS

THE WRITINGS of Henry Parker, Lord Morley reveal the range of his reading, whether in the form of explicit references or citations from identifiable sources.[1] We are concerned here, however, less with his use of that reading than with some reconstruction of the materials that may have been more generally available to him, and with the range of books that can be circumstantially linked with his name or otherwise shown to have been circulating within his circles of family relationship.

The starting point for such enquiry must be Morley's marriage to Alice St John. This marriage brought him into a family of keen book collectors who can be linked in their turn, as we will see, to another notable book collector, Margaret Beaufort. Morley's wife Alice was the daughter of John St John of Bletsoe, grandson of Margaret Beauchamp of Bletsoe. After the death of her first husband Sir Oliver St John in 1437, Margaret Beauchamp married John Beaufort, 2nd Duke of Somerset. The daughter of this marriage was, of course, Margaret Beaufort, mother of the future Henry VII, whose patronage was of some significance to the St John family. These relationships by marriage lead to much of the information we can recover about books possibly available to Morley.

One main documentary source of information about manuscripts and/or printed books owned by the St John family survives. In Balliol College, Oxford, MS 329, on fol. 172, is an unheaded list of books and texts in what has been described as 'a contemporary hand'. It occurs in a manuscript evidently owned by the St John family: the names 'John Seynt John' and 'Olever St. John' occur on fols 20^{r} and 166^{v} respectively. That the manuscript, as noted on fol. 66^{v}, appears to have been preserved within or in proximity to 'the sead manour of Astwicke in the countie of Bedfordshire' suggests a connection with Bletsoe (also in Bedfordshire) and hence with one of the Oliver St Johns who were respectively Margaret Beauchamp's husband and younger son (the former died in 1437; the latter in 1497). This younger son inherited the family property of Lydiard Tregoze in Wiltshire, and may have had less connection with Bedfordshire than the elder son, John St John of Bletsoe, who was to be Alice St John's grandfather. But whatever the nature of the connection, there are plausible grounds for linking the list with the St John family and so with books to which Alice St John and Henry Morley may have had access. We have transcribed the list below with attempts to identify the works there noted:[2]

[1] 'Bochacius de casu virorum illustrium': either Boccaccio's Latin original or John Lydgate's *Fall of Princes* (IMEV 1168; STC 3175)

[2] 'The Sege of Troy': possibly Lydgate's *Troy Book* (IMEV 2516; STC 5579)

[3] 'Sanke Royall': presumably the *Queste del Saint Graal* or the *Estoire dou Graal*
[4] 'Boicius de Consolacione': possibly Chaucer's prose (IPMEP 43) or John Walton's verse translation of Boethius (IMEV 1597; STC 3200)
[5] 'de Regimine principum / Secreta Secretorum': possibly John Lydgate and Benedict Burgh's translation (IMEV 935)
[6] 'The Romaunce of Partenope': (IMEV 4081, 4132)
[7] 'Rommant de la Ros': presumably a manuscript version of *Le Roman de la Rose.*
[8] 'Brut þe croniculis': the *Brut* (IPMEP 374)
[9] 'Seynt Kateryne of Seene': possibly *The Orchard of Sion* (IPMEP 561; STC 4815)
[10] 'The pylgrymage o þe sowle' (STC 6473; IPMEP 75)
[11] 'The tales of Caunterburye': (IMEV 4019; STC 5082 etc.)
[12] 'The booke of chevallerie': possibly Vegetius, *De Re Militari*
[13] 'The booke of þe salutacioun of owre lady'
[14] 'Egidiris de Regimine principum': i.e. Aegidius Romanus' work of this title, surviving uniquely in Middle English prose in John Trevisa's translation in Bodleian Library MS Digby 233
[15] 'Legenda Aurea': (STC 14508, 24873, 24880; IPMEP 567, 682)
[16] 'Maister of þe Game': (IPMEP 775)
[17] 'Pontus': presumably one of the various prose versions of the romance *King Ponthus* (STC 20107 etc; IPMEP 476)
[18] 'Maundeville': i.e. *Mandeville's Travels* (STC 17246-17254; IPMEP 232, 233, 239, 599)
[19] 'The booke of þe .iij. kynges of Coleyne', surviving in English in both verse and prose (STC 5572-75; IPMEP 290, SIMEV *854.3)
[20] 'The Revelicioun of Seynt Brigiede' (IPMEP 312)
[21] 'Sydrake': presumably *Sydrak and Boccus* surviving in both verse and prose (IMEV 772, 2147; STC 3186-88a; IPMEP 684)
[22] 'Bartholomew in twey bokis of ij volemys': presumably John Trevisa's translation of Bartholomaeus Anglicus, *De proprietatibus rerum* (STC 1536-7; IPMEP 785)

The grounds for connecting this list with books in the St John family's possession are circumstantial, but of some weight. There are a number of correspondences between the titles in this list and other manuscripts containing names of St John family members. Balliol MS 329 itself could correspond to [5] 'de Regimine principum Secreta Secretorum' since it includes Lydgate and Burgh's translation of the *Secreta Secretorum*, on fols 80-126, which seem to have circulated as a separate booklet. Elsewhere, '[1] Bochacius de casu virorum illustrium' reflects a form of the title often given to John Lydgate's *Fall of Princes*; Bodley MS e Musaeo 1 of this work has the name 'Elysabethe Seynt John' on fol. 1.[3] [11] 'The tales of Caunterburye' can be presumably connected with the 'booke of velom of Canterbury Tales in English' which Margaret Beaufort (d. 1509) bequeathed to John St John, sometimes conjecturally identified with the Devonshire manuscript of Chaucer's poem (on which see below).[4] [12] 'The booke of chevallerie' may be identifiable with a copy of Vegetius, *De Re Militari*, a manuscript of which, CUL Add. 8706, has the name 'J. Saint John' on fol. 1^r.[5] Such correspondences suggest that this list seems to provide a proper basis for drawing conclusions about the family's book-collecting activities.

One obvious problem in assessing this list is determining whether it records manuscript and/or printed books. At least three of the books – [12] 'The booke of chevallerie' , [14] 'Egidiris de Regimine principum' and [16] 'Maister of þe Game' – are not recorded in any early printed English edition. A third, [20] 'The Revelicioun of Seynt Brigiede' survives in this title only in manuscript, although there are various early printed texts associated with St Bridget. Most of the others that can be identified were printed in the fifteenth century ([1], [8]-[11], [15], [18]-[19], [22]), one of these ([10]) only in such an edition. Two survive only in relatively late printed editions, one ([21]), if it is verse from [1537?], if prose from an edition of [1535?];[6] the other [4] (if this could refer to Walton's translation) from 1525.[7] Such editions seem likely to postdate this list. These points, together with the fact that a St John name has been found in only one early printed book (see below), suggest the likelihood that at least the majority of these books are manuscripts.[8]

Nearly all the books seem to be in English. Several are certainly ([1], [2], [6], [11]) or probably ([4], [5]) or possibly ([21]) in verse. Only [3] 'Sanke Royall' and [7] 'Rommat de la Ros' seem likely to have been in French.[9] The lack of any works certainly in Latin offers some insight into the cultural sensibilities of a late medieval noble family.[10]

The nature of the works represented in this list , which may well reflect the accumulated taste of more than one generation, illuminates certain cultural continuities. A number of popular literary works appear, by Chaucer (*The Canterbury Tales* ([11]), Lydgate (probably) (his *Fall of Princes* ([1]), and his *Troy Book* ([2]), and various romances: *Parthenope* [6], *Ponthus* [17], and *The Romance of the Rose* [7]. Others are theological or devotional works of various kinds: Boethius ([4]), the translation of Deguileville, *The Pilgrimage of the Soul* ([10]), the saint's life of Katherine of Siena ([9]), the *Legenda Aurea* ([15]), *The Three Kings of Cologne* ([19]), *The Revelation of St Bridget* ([20]), and the unidentified 'booke of þe salutacioun of owre lady' ([13]). Several works are concerned with kingship and governance: Lydgate's translation of the *Secreta Secretorum* ([5]), the item which is probably a translation of Vegetius, 'The booke of chevallerie' ([12]), and 'Egidiris de Regimine principum' ([14]). Different kinds of instructional works are represented by the encyclopedia of Bartholomaeus Anglicus [22], the hunting treatise, *The Master of Game* [16], the *Brut* chronicle [8], *Mandeville's Travels* [18], and the quasi-encyclopedic *Sydrak and Boccus* [21]. Most of these works are in Middle English and offer testimony to the growing prominence of the vernacular even within elevated circles.

The manuscripts and early printed books discussed here seem very likely to have been available to Morley through the connections of his wife's extended family (this is by no means to rule out the possibility that his own family possessed copies of a similar range of works, of course).[11] Tracing such family connections leads to further manuscripts which confirm the clear predilection for English books, particularly of a literary or a pious cast, some of which are associated with Lady Margaret Beaufort. Alice St John's father, Sir John St John of Bletsoe, became Lady Margaret's chamberlain in 1504 and was one of the executors of her will; Alice, like Morley himself, served in Lady Margaret's household, and Sir John St John of Lydiard Tregoze, the grandson of another of the children of Margaret Beauchamp, was another household servant.[12] Her will includes a bequest to Sir John St John of Lydiard Tregoze 'a booke of velom of

Canterbury Tales in Englische', and to 'Maistres Parker', presumably Alice herself, 'a booke of velom of Gower in Englisshe'.[13] *The Canterbury Tales* may be linked to [11] on the Balliol list, and 'Gower in Englisshe' is possibly Bodley MS 902, a manuscript of Gower's *Confessio Amantis* which has the names of 'Katherin Sent Jhon' (fol. 9^{r}) and 'Jane Sent John' (fol. 80^{v}).[14] Another literary manuscript possibly owned by Morley himself is Leyden, Vossius UL 9, a collection mainly of Lydgate's works and associated Chauceriana, which has the name 'H. Morley' (fol. 1^{r}).[15]

The interrelationship of the various families, and their desire to preserve the visibility of this, is marked by the additions made in a book of hours which Margaret Beauchamp had commisioned around part of a dismembered manuscript originally made for John Beaufort Earl of Somerset, Margaret Beaufort's grandfather. Now BL, Royal MS 2. A.xviii, these include family obits and notes such as one in the calendar for April relating to Alice St John's aunt, Margaret: 'hac die margareta Seint John Abatissa de Shaftesbury fuit consecrata [1460]'.[16]

A similar instance of this desire to register family relationships seems to be constituted by the notes made by a variety of hands in BL, Harley MS 4775, a finely-produced copy of the English prose *Gilte Legende*, which includes on the end flyleaf (fol. 263^{r}) the names of 'harry morley', 'alys morley', and 'alys sent john' (both names presumably referring to Henry Parker's wife); 'marget saynt John', 'oluyer saynt [John]', 'wyllaym seynt John', 'John Seynt John' (various of her St John relatives); and, possibly from the next generation, 'Elyzabeth parker', 'frauncis parker', and 'katheryn parker'.[17]

Other hitherto unnoted connections may be made between surviving books and Morley's St John relatives by marriage. The name 'Oliver Sent ihon' appears in Sion College, Arc. L. 40. 2 /E. 1, which is a Wycliffite Old Testament (fol. 124^{r}).[18] A copy of Anthony Woodville's translation of Guillaume de Tignonville's *Dits des philosophes*, printed by Caxton as *The dictes or sayengis of the philosophres*, contains the inscription 'Olyver Seynt', to which has been added 'Joh[?n]', in two sixteenth-century hands.[19] A manuscript of *The Master of Game*, BL, Harley MS 5086, in which it is collocated with such texts as *The Book of Marshalsy* and *The Babees Boke*, contains the names of 'henricus parker' and 'Margera. parker', in what appear to be sixteenth-century hands.[20]

More remotely, it is possible to relate the St Johns to other families whose ownership of manuscripts (some of which duplicate those in the Balliol MS 329 list) can be documented. Elizabeth St John, one of the daughters of Oliver St John and Margaret Beauchamp, married as her first husband William Lord Zouche, whose grandson John married Margaret Willoughby. The copy of the *Brut* which is now Glasgow, Hunterian Library, MS 230 includes some rhyming proverbs ascribed to one or more Willoughbys, and on fols 245^{v} and 246^{r} a number of inscriptions which conclude 'quod Zowche'.[21] Sir Henry Willoughby owned a manuscript of Lydgate's *Fall of Princes* in the sixteenth century[22] as well as a copy of Trevisa's translation of Bartholomaeus Anglicus's *De proprietatibus rerum*.[23] In addition he can be linked to copies of Gower *Confessio amantis* and of Trevisa's translation of the *Polychronicon*.[24] Successive generations of St Johns married earls of Kildare,[25] whose library, when recorded in 1518 and again in 1525-6, included with its many Latin and French books a number of English ones: the *Polychronicon*; 'Bocas the Fall of Princes'; 'Arthur'; 'The Siege of Thebes'; 'The

Chronicles of England'; 'The feetis of armes of chyvalry made by Christyn de Pyce'.[26] The connections in the marriages made by Henry and Alice Morley's children confirmed further extensive networks of shared literary or bibliographical interest: their daughter Jane, for example, was married to George, viscount Rochford, brother to Anne Boleyn and translator and commissioner of de luxe manuscripts.[27]

It is instructive to contrast what can be gleaned about book ownership in the Morley circle with the activities of other contemporary or near contemporary collectors. Gerald Fitzgerald is one, of course, with an extensive library suggesting wide interest in books in Latin and several vernaculars. At the other extreme is the more dedicated, specialist library of Roger Townsend, a lawyer whose books largely reflect his professional interests (although even here there are echoes of the interests of the Morley circle in the form of a copy of some version of the *De regimine principum*).[28] James Morice, Clerk of Works to Margaret Beaufort, left a record of some twenty-three books, in sixteen volumes, in his possession. All of them appear to have been printed books, many by Caxton and the majority in English, including copies of Gower's *Confessio amantis* and the *Canterbury Tales* as well as Lydgate's *Temple of Glass* and the *Royal Book* and a version of Aesop. Clearly Morice was a collector in a new style, unable to draw on the resources of established noble manuscript libraries of the kind in existence in Morley's circles.[29]

Closer in style to the range of books we have suggested as available to Morley through his family connections is the 'library' noted in Bodleian, Fairfax MS 10, fol. 1^{v}, a manuscript of Nicholas Trivet's chronicle which was seemingly owned in the later fifteenth century by a Bedfordshire family, the Broughtons.[30] A number of the titles here replicate those in the St John list of Balliol MS 328: 'The pylgrymage of the soule', 'Boicius de consolacione philosophie', 'The talys of Caunterbury', 'Egidius de regiminis principis et al.'. There seem as well to be a number of works which Caxton printed: 'Legenda sanctorum', 'Ryal', 'Speculum vite Christi', 'The Fablys of Isope', 'The Chesse'. Some of the other works survive only in manuscript, however: 'Hocklyf de Regimine' (Hoccleve's *Regiment of Princes*), 'Incendium amoris' (Rolle's work of this title), 'The sege of Jherusalem a part' (a romance surviving in several versions in verse and prose); and it may be that the collection recorded here represents a library the manuscript core of which was subsequently enlarged by members of later generations after the invention of printing.

Such evidence of manuscripts and books that can be related in various ways to Morley does suggest some discernible trends. Chief of these is the way in which books available to Morley through family connections seem to represent an interest in works in the English vernacular. Also noteworthy seems the continuity of this interest in works in both manuscript and printed forms. Such trends serve, in their turn, to remind us of the extent to which Morley's own writing draws on earlier English literary traditions.

NOTES

1 For some account of his reading see *Forty-six Lives*, ed. by Wright, pp. lxxi-lxxix.

2 For an earlier printing of this list and description of the manuscript in which it occurs see R. A. B. Mynors, *Catalogue of the Manuscripts of Balliol College, Oxford* (Oxford, 1963), pp. 339-40.

The following abbreviations are used in square brackets to identify the texts: IMEV: *The Index of Middle English Verse*, Carleton Brown and Rossell Hope Robbins (New York, 1943); SIMEV: *A Supplement to the Index of Middle English Verse*, Rossell Hope Robbins & John L. Cutler (Lexington, Ky., 1965); IPMEP: *Index of Printed Middle English Prose*, R. E. Lewis, N. F. Blake, A. S. G. Edwards (New York, 1985).

3 For a description of this manuscript see *Lydgate's Fall of Princes*, ed. H. Bergen, EETS ES 124 (1927), pp. 77-9. Morley himself refers to 'The Fall of Prynces' in his enumeration of Boccaccio's works at the beginning of his translation of the *De claris mulieribus* (*Forty-six Lives*, ed. by H. G. Wright, 3/1).

4 See J. Manly & E. Rickert, *The Text of the Canterbury Tales*, 8 vols (Chicago, 1940), I, 621-2.

5 For description see G. Lester, ed., *The Earliest English Translation of Vegetius' De Re Militari*, Middle English Texts 21 (Heidelberg, 1988), pp. 19-20. We assume that this is the work referred to, rather than the printed edition by Caxton of the *Book of Fayttes of Armes and of Chyvalrye* (1489; STC 7269).

6 See IPMEP 684.

7 Durham, University Library, Cosin MS V. II. 15, a copy of Walton's verse translation of Boethius, contains on fol. 112^{v} the note '[...] secundum Harry Morley'. We are grateful to Professor Carley for this information.

8 It is possible that some of the entries in the list refer to French printed editions.

9 On the different versions of the Grail story, see Jill Mann, 'Malory and the Grail legend', in *A Companion to Malory*, ed. Elizabeth Archibald & A. S. G. Edwards (Cambridge, 1996), pp. 203-20, and on later English circulation of the *Roman*, Julia Boffey, 'English Dream Poems of the Fifteenth Century and their French Connections,' in *Literary Aspects of Courtly Culture*, ed. D. Madox & S. Sturm-Madox (Cambridge, 1994), pp. 113-21.

10 The entries indicating Boethius and *The Three Kings of Cologne* could possibly refer to Latin versions of the *De consolacione philosophiae* and John of Hildesheim's *Historia trium regum*, but this seems on balance unlikely.

11 Surviving books with evidence connecting them to members the Morley and Lovel families include BL, Royal MS 19. B.x, a French *Regime de Santé* (see G. F. Warner & J. P. Gilson, *Catalogue of Western Manuscripts in the Old Royal and King's Collections*, London, 1921, II, 327), and BL, Harley MS 6324, a fragmentary copy of *The Master of Game*, with the name of 'henry lovell' (recoverable under ultra-violet light) on fol. 78^{r}. We are grateful to Dr Carol Meale for this information. See also Carley, 'The Writings of Henry Parker, Lord Morley', above, p. 60 n. 74.

12 For most of the above, see Michael Jones & Malcolm Underwood, *The King's Mother: Lady Margaret Beaufort, Countess of Richmond and Derby* (Cambridge, 1992).

13 C. H. Cooper, *The Lady Margaret: a Memoir of Margaret, Countess of Richmond and Derby*, ed. J. E. B. Mayor (Cambridge, 1874), pp. 129-35.

14 For description see G. G. Macaulay, ed., *The Complete Works of John Gower*, 2 vols (Oxford, 1899-1902), I, cxxxviii-cxl.

15 We are indebted to Dr A. I. Doyle for knowledge of this inscription. It is read as 'D. Morley' by J. A. van Dorsten, 'The Leyden "Lydgate Manuscript"', *Scriptorium*, 14 (1960), 315-25 (p. 310), where the manuscript is described.

16 Some entries are transcribed in F. Madden,'Genealogical and Historical Notes from Ancient Calendars, &c,' *Collectanea Topographica et Genealogica*, 1 (1834), 277-80. For a full description and bibliography see Kathleen L. Scott, *Later Gothic Manuscripts, 1390-1490*, 2 vols (London, 1997), II, 127-32.

17 See James Carley, 'Plutarch's Life of Agesilaus: A Recently Located New Year Gift for Thomas Cromwell by Henry Parker, Lord Morley', in *Prestige, Authority and Power: Proceedings of*

the Seventh York Manuscripts Conference, ed. Felicity Riddy, forthcoming.

18 For description see N. R. Ker, *Medieval Manuscripts in British Libraries: I, London* (Oxford, 1969), pp. 287-8.

19 Information from Dr Meg Ford: the volume is BL, C. 10. b. 2 (STC 6828).

20 It also contains inscriptions which relate it at what would seem to be the same period to 'Rawfe parker de fullham gent. & Etheldred vxor eius' (verso of second flyleaf).

21 SIMEV 106.5 and 1628.8.

22 See H. Bergen, ed., *Lydgate's Fall of Princes*, EETS ES 124 (1927), 81-4; this manuscript is now in the Taylor Collection in Princeton University Library.

23 On this manuscript see R. W. Mitchner, 'Wynkyn de Worde's Use of the Plimpton Manuscript of De Proprietatibus Rerum', *The Library*, 5th ser. 6 (1951), 7-18.

24 The former is Nottingham, University Library, MS Mi LM 8, the latter is in the Martin Schøyen collection. For discussion see Kate Harris, 'Ownership and Readership: Studies in the Provenance of the Manuscripts of Gower's Confessio Amantis', D. Phil. thesis, University of York, 1993, pp. 186-8, 195-6.

25 Elizabeth, daughter of Oliver of Lydiard Tregoze married Gerald Fitzgerald, 8th earl, and Elizabeth, sister of John Zouche, married Gerald Fitzgerald 9th earl (d. 1534). See further Donough Bryan, *Gerald Fitzgerald, the Great Earl of Kildare (1456-1513)* (Dublin, 1933).

26 See *Historical Manuscripts Commission, 9th Report;* appendix, pp. 288-9, and for some discussion, Julia Boffey, *Manuscripts of English Courtly Lyrics in the Later Middle Ages* (Cambridge, 1985), pp. 140-1.

27 See James P. Carley, '"Her moost lovyng and fryndely brother sendeth gretyng": Anne Boleyn's Manuscripts and their Sources', in *Illuminating the Book: Makers and Interpreters: Essays in Honour of Janet Backhouse*, ed. by M. Brown & Scott McKendrick (London, 1998), pp. 261-80.

28 C. E. Moreton, 'The "Library" of a Late Fifteenth-Century Lawyer', *The Library*, 6th series, 13 (1991), 338-46.

29 See J. C. T. Oates, 'English Bokes Concernyng to James Morice', *Transactions of the Cambridge Bibliographical Society*, 3 (1959-63), 124-32.

30 The list is printed by Ruth Dean, 'An Essay in Anglo-Norman Paleography', *Studies Presented to M. K. Pope* (Manchester, 1930), pp. 79-87.

MORLEY, MACHIAVELLI, AND THE PILGRIMAGE OF GRACE

K. R. Bartlett

To intellectual historians, Henry Parker, Lord Morley, usually appears either as an insignificant translator of limited gifts[1] or as the instrument through which Thomas Cromwell discovered Machiavelli, a reputation evidenced by a letter of 13 February 1537 to the then Lord Privy Seal in which the *History of Florence* and *The Prince* are recommended for study, and copies of them included in the package, together with Morley's own marginal notations.[2]

Much has been made of this moment, although its importance has been reduced, despite Cardinal Pole's placing Machiavelli and Cromwell together among the damned.[3] It is now known that Machiavelli's texts were read in England and used by others before that letter of recommendation from Morley to Cromwell was sent. Also, Cromwell's own time in Italy has been much better documented[4] and with it the probability that his familiarity with the works of the ill-fated Florentine second chancellor antedated Morley's gift of early 1537.[5]

However, the question of the context of Morley's exhortation to Cromwell to study and use Machiavelli has not been addressed. I have argued elsewhere that Morley had his translation of Petrarch's *Trionfi* printed to influence a political conspiracy centred on a plot to marry the princess Elizabeth to Lord Maltravers to secure a purely English royal alternative to Philip and Mary after the Spanish marriage threatened the integrity of the English crown.[6] What I now propose is that Morley's recommendation of Machiavelli to Cromwell was a consequence of the Pilgrimage of Grace and offered, in an oblique way, a confirmation of the need for princes occasionally to break their words, as Henry had done with the rebels, and a pledge of loyalty to Cromwell's policies and the Henrician reform, despite Morley's own conservative position in matters of religion. It is an explanation of how an elderly aristocrat, described as 'a member of the conservative Erasmian group, and a man eminently sympathetic to [Sir Thomas] More's own position'[7] could also be a profiteer in monastic property, a close adherent of the Boleyns[8] before their declared Protestantism and a supporter of Thomas Cromwell and the succession of Elizabeth, despite his friendship with and sympathy for Mary Tudor and the old faith.

The Pilgrimage of Grace was one of the most dangerous insurrections against the Tudors. It arose from social and economic as well as from religious disaffection, largely sparked by the dissolution of the monasteries. The threat to Henry VIII was particularly great because it represented a widespread revolt in the North, and included the nobility, gentry, and priests as well as common men. It was galvanized by religion; indeed, the symbol of the revolt was the five wounds of Christ, and the rebels' oath specifically rejected the Crown's own oath of supremacy.[9]

The rising began in Lincolnshire on 1 October 1536 but soon spread all across the North as far as the Scots border. It was in reality three separate insurrections: the Lincolnshire Rising, which had ended by 18 October; the Pilgrimage of Grace, which was to last until the end of that year; and later revolts in the North-West and the East Riding of Yorkshire, which began with the new year, 1537. The rebels' oath required them to protect the Roman Church and to demand that the King drive the heretics from his council, naming Thomas Cromwell and Archbishop Cranmer, among others. It was, then, a traditional medieval 'restorative' revolt, attempting to save the kingdom by rescuing the king from the control of evil counsellors, and sworn to stop the social, economic, and religious change occasioned by the Henrician Reformation, with its attendant destruction of monastic life and alienation of church property.

The size of the Pilgrimage of Grace and the defection of several leading northern magnates made the situation extremely perilous. About thirty thousand rebels were in arms; York and Hull were taken; Lord Darcy handed Pontefract Castle to the rebels, and his fellow northern peer, Lord Hussey, joined the revolt, as did Sir Thomas Percy and the abbots of Jervaux and Bridlington. It required the loyal nobility – the Dukes of Norfolk and Suffolk, the Marquis of Exeter, and the Earls of Shrewsbury, Arundel, Derby, and Huntington – to suppress the Pilgrims, and then only after a negotiated settlement with them had been abrogated by Henry to purchase more time.[10]

Had the revolt been simply another rising for religion and against low-born, wicked counsellors, it might not have been the threat it was. However, in addition to its size and the involvement of all social groups including the nobility, there was a greater danger, connecting the rebels to elements of the Catholic faction at court and leading magnates who retained sympathy not only for the old religion but also for the memory of Queen Catherine of Aragon and for her daughter, Mary Tudor. It was with this group that Morley might have been reasonably seen to sympathize, and it was to signal his loyalty and commitment to the King's cause that he sent Cromwell his books by Niccolò Machiavelli, requesting, 'I most hartely pray youe to schew the very wordes unto the Kynge'.[11]

The religious and social conservatives who sympathized with the revolt spread beyond the fastness of the north of England into court faction and learned opposition. It has been suggested that 'compelling signs exist that the noble and gentry supporters of Mary Tudor joined forces with Catholic lawyers from the inns of court in revolt against Cromwell's administration'.[12] The rebel lords Darcy and Hussey promised Eustace Chapuys, the ambassador of Charles V, that if the Emperor should invade England the nobility, the clergy and the still Catholic people would rally to the Emperor out of respect for religion, Queen Catherine, Mary Tudor, and the old ways and out of hatred for the King's present counsellors and the alterations in the Church.[13]

The strength of the conservative nobility, both in the country and at court, should not be discounted. Northern lords such as Darcy and Hussey were supported by Lords Neville, Latimer, and Lumley, as well as by the brothers of Northumberland, although the Earl himself remained aloof. Even among those magnates who remained outside the revolt, there were doubts as to the depth of their loyalty and real fear concerning their ultimate position. Great peers, such as the Duke of Norfolk, the Marquis of Exeter, and the Earl of Derby, did waver, especially Exeter, whose royal blood was such a threat that he and others with Yorkist connections were eventually brought down and executed, once the danger of the Pilgrimage had passed.

Many of those who felt some sympathy with the cause of the Pilgrimage of Grace had been associated with the Catholic court party and had been close to Queen Catherine and Mary Tudor, a party with which Lord Morley was also associated. He kept his close attachment to Mary Tudor and to a conservative Catholicism, despite his willingness to dispossess the Pope in England and trade in monastic property. It was this continued association with the Catholic faction which occasioned his letter to Cromwell and his gift of his own annotated copy of *The History of Florence* and *The Prince*.

There can be no doubt about Morley's affection for and attachment to Mary Tudor. His many translations dedicated and offered as gifts to her reflect a constant service, even at a time when it was dangerous to his career, if not his life, to put such loyalty in writing.[14] In his eight manuscripts dedicated to Mary Tudor, he reflects his own religious conservatism and his discomfort at her circumstances after the divorce. The translation of Erasmus's *Paean Virgini matri dicendus* contains a passage reflecting his sorrow at the decline in the worship of the Virgin and refers to Catherine's daughter as a second Mary of this world in virtue, grace, and goodness.[15] He makes complimentary remarks about Bishop Fisher in his life of the Lady Margaret, in whose household Morley had served.[16] And, of course, in the 1570s his grandson was to become a notorious recusant and exile for the old religion as a pensioner of Philip of Spain.[17]

Given his known religious beliefs and his conservative social views, it would have been reasonable to suspect Morley of harbouring sympathy with the Pilgrims. Morley himself appears to have had no difficulty in dispossessing either the Pope or the monasteries. In fact, he was one of the signatories of a letter from the English nobility to Clement VII expressing their adherence to Henry's position in his great matter and requiring the Pope to grant the King's divorce, despite his own earlier adherence to Queen Catherine's cause and his continued sympathy with her daughter.[18] He wrote eloquently against the primacy of the Bishop of Rome and in favour of universal access to scripture by all Christians. In this, he was not deviating from the conservative position of faith that Erasmus and even Thomas More would have accepted, although the issue of the royal supremacy would have divided them.

Furthermore, Morley appears not to have mourned the passing of the monasteries. He actively worked to acquire former ecclesiastical property and recovered some which he himself had given to a priory of his own foundation at Beeston. The oath of the Pilgrims, then, would not have held any emotional or even religious attraction to him.

In political matters Morley was also committed to the Crown and its position. He was an unquestioning servant of Henry VIII and he appears to have had the most cordial relations with Thomas Cromwell; hence the letter and the books of Machiavelli with their reference to services in the past and deference due. Never is there the slightest indication that he shared the opinion of the Pilgrims regarding Cromwell, Archbishop Cranmer, and others; and, despite his own ancient title, he equally seems not to have held Cromwell in contempt because of his low birth. Moreover, although he had been close to Queen Catherine, he was joined to the Boleyns by the marriage of his daughter, Jane, who married the brother of Anne Boleyn, George, Viscount Rochford.[19] This union brought Morley even closer to the Tudors through marriage. He himself had married Alice St John, a kinswoman of Lady Margaret.[20]

This devotion to the Crown and to the Tudors, the express hostility to the papacy and support of the dissolution of the monasteries, the connection with the Boleyns and the cultivation of Thomas Cromwell's favour should have put Morley outside suspicion during the dangerous months of the Pilgrimage of Grace. However, it appears not to have done so altogether. Any possibility of another ancient, conservative, Catholic family wavering at a moment when other great lords were made uncomfortable by a series of events which seemed to challenge the foundations of their mental universe had to be addressed. Whether Cromwell implied to Morley that he wanted assurance of absolute loyalty is unknown; but Morley obviously felt compelled by the events of late 1536 and early 1537 to make such a declaration, and the use of Machiavelli as a vehicle for subtle counsel was a brilliant choice.

It must first be stated that Morley and Cromwell both exhibited some of the symptoms of italophilia. Cromwell had spent much time in Italy in his youth and knew the language and culture and probably even the texts that Morley forwarded with his advice. Equally, Morley knew Italian well enough to make important translations of rather difficult texts, such as Petrarch's *Trionfi*, although there is no evidence whatsoever that he travelled to the peninsula or had any formal tuition in the language. He himself states that in contrast to Cromwell's personal experience of Italy he has none: 'Youre lordschip, I have oftentymes harde you say, hath bene conversant among them. Sene theyere factyons and maners. And so was I never.'[21] Possibly Morley's residence at the imperial court or even his participation in the Field of the Cloth of Gold brought him into contact with Italian nobles and scholars surrounding the Emperor or Francis I, or with some of the French nobles who had travelled through Italy during the campaigns of Charles VIII, Louis XII, and Francis himself. Regardless of the genesis of their knowledge, Morley and Cromwell would have shared a common bond in their Italian interests. Morley, then, chose well in his offering of the texts by Machiavelli.

Sir Henry Ellis is certainly correct in identifying the 1532 printing of the *History of Florence* and *The Prince* as the one sent by Morley to Cromwell.[22] Both were printed by Giunta in the same type and same format in that year and were often bound together, as they were, presumably, in the Morley book. Also, it was not inappropriate to send both texts, since the lessons of the former could be extended by those of the latter.

The letter opens with Morley's observation that Machiavelli had revealed the pretensions of the papacy, despite the History's commission by Clement VII. The Florentine's anticlericalism and anti-papal perspective obviously delighted Morley, and he recommended these to Cromwell. He remarked that the war between Florence and the papacy at the time of the Pazzi Conspiracy illustrated how the Holy See meddled with sovereign powers and how effectively the Florentines under the leadership of Lorenzo de'Medici dealt with Pope Sixtus IV in his attempts to impose his family's hegemony over parts of central Italy.[23] If the unanointed Lorenzo de'Medici ruling a city state like Florence could have accomplished this, think how a great King, like Henry VIII, might succeed in the face of papal arrogance and pretension.[24]

The sending of Machiavelli by Morley to Cromwell might have been dismissed as a minor literary anecdote or as a reference to the condemnation of the Florentine by Cardinal Pole, who put Cromwell and Machiavelli in the same pit of hell, associating the two of them in a way not intended by Morley. However, this letter is more significant. What is seldom noted is Morley's guidance of Cromwell to the eighth book of *The History of Florence*. It is the book in which the author discusses the greatest threat to the rule of Lorenzo de'Medici, the Magnificent, at the time of the Pazzi Conspiracy and the cause of that threat as factional division and internal conflict which brought about the intervention of foreign powers, including both the papacy and the kingdom of Naples. There is a specific lesson here which Morley wanted Cromwell to consider.[25]

The parallels to the events of the Pilgrimage of Grace and northern rebellions are obvious, if superficial. Civil discord brought about grave consequences from which Florence just managed to survive, largely through the brilliance and courage of its chief citizen, Lorenzo de'Medici. The loyalty of most of the people of the republic and the criminal behaviour of the Pazzi conspirators resulted in the commons rallying to their uncrowned prince and mercilessly destroying the rebels and their supporters. Henry VIII as an anointed king and as a figure every bit as heroic as Lorenzo will also prevail but he, too, must stand firm against the treachery of great families and the conspiracy of priests more loyal to the Pope than to their religious vows and their native city.

Even the inclusion of *The Prince* in this double volume of Machiavelli adds a lesson. The Duke of Norfolk was forced by the strength of the Pilgrims to negotiate a truce which was proclaimed by a herald and promised a redress of many of the Pilgrims' demands, including the restoration of the monasteries and a general pardon of all those who had risen against the Crown, and the summoning of a Parliament to hear complaints. Clearly, Norfolk and Henry could not ever have entertained adhering to this humiliation brought about by insurrection.[26] The King broke his word and moved against the rebels, bringing down the insurgent lords and the other leaders of the revolt. Punishment was swift and certain, justified by a quite separate incident in the East Riding. Regardless of their promises, then, Henry and Norfolk never planned to permit the revolt to have succeeded in any way and only waited for the merest pretext to exact vengeance, once the loyal forces were sufficiently strong to suppress the revolt, impose order, and execute the leaders. Machiavelli's advice in *The Prince* is, of course, to do exactly that. How a prince should keep his word was a lesson not lost on Morley, Cromwell, or Henry.

This very act of ruthlessness, though, must have made Morley nervous, given the ambiguity of his own connections with certain of the rebels and with the focus of their cause, Mary Tudor. Completely loyal though he was, Morley felt the need to witness for his allegiance not just to the King but to the very minister whom the Pilgrims wanted to see destroyed and whose policies had resulted in the suppression of the monasteries and the social changes attendant upon that royal revolution. Machiavelli's texts were evidence that Morley knew the dangers of rebellion, conspiracy, and disloyalty while recognizing the rewards and virtues of adherence to King and minister. As with his use of his translation of Petrarch's *Trionfi*, Morley was letting Italian literature serve as the oblique instrument of his counsel, the admission of his complete allegiance to the King's policy as executed by Thomas Cromwell.

If Morley had been the only writer of the period of the rebellions of 1536-7 who relied on the exemplum, advice, and effect of Machiavelli, this letter to Cromwell might be seen to have been overvalued in its subtlety. Reference to the Pazzi Conspiracy and the apposite advice of the Florentine second chancellor regarding relations with the Holy See could be dismissed as eccentric comments from a nervous peer wishing merely to curry favour rather than offer good counsel. However, at exactly the same time as Morley was composing his letter covering his gift of Machiavelli's works to Cromwell, another prominent Tudor writer, the Protestant apologist and Cromwell familiar, Richard Morison, was applying the lessons of the same two books in his own advice to Cromwell.

Morison, like Cromwell, had spent a part of his youth in Italy, as a student at Padua where he studied law and where he was a resident in Reginald Pole's household. [27] He used very much the same terminology in his *Apomaxis calumnarium convitiorumque* (1537),[28] his reply to Cochlaeus on the matter of the royal divorce, as Morley had used in his letter to Cromwell, appealing to the Florentine as a prefiguration of his own counsel: 'Niccolò Machiavelli, who most diligently in his writing in Italian discussed events in Italy.'[29] Machiavelli is useful and appropriate, and the example of the Florentines can be applied to the condition of England. The year before the *Apomaxis* was printed, Morison had written a polemic against the rebellions, *A Lamentation in which is showed what Ruin and Destruction cometh of Seditious Rebellion* (London, 1536). This text is a classic work of propaganda directed against the rebels of the Pilgrimage of Grace and full of zeal for the necessary and exemplary restoration of order which will certainly follow.

But again in that critical year of 1536 Morison had produced *A Remedy for Sedition* (London, 1536) in which he refers to Machiavelli by name and cites him with approbation, especially the passages in the *Discourses* referring to the loss of reverence and obedience among the people. This has been identified[30] as an important Machiavellian moment in English political thought, one in which the experiences and method of the Florentine were applied to the English crisis of 1536. Similarly, the Italian experience recorded in Machiavelli applied to a parallel situation in England is a model which Morley himself employed in his letter to Cromwell.

The matter of the Florentine's *History* was also an example of the consequences of conspiracy and rebellion, a lesson that Morley in his letter and gift is swearing he has learned. He will not rebel or offer sympathy to the insurgents. His loyalty remains firm and he is witnessing for it through the distant experience of the Florentines. The exempla of the Greeks and Romans were useful, as Machiavelli himself attests; but, as his friend and fellow Florentine, Francesco Guicciardini, notes in his *Ricordi*, the ancients should not be quoted at every instance, since contemporary politics offer a more useful guide in many instances.[31]

The effect on Cromwell of Morley's letter and gift can be judged from Morley's role after the suppression of the rebellion. He was appointed to the panel sitting in judgement on the noblemen who took up arms against the Crown. The condemnation of Lords Hussey and Darcy was in part the judgement of Morley, who was offered by Cromwell an opportunity not just to swear his allegiance and his hatred of rebellion but to help to preclude it by punishing his fellow peers in an exemplary manner. The execution of those nobles stood as witness to the error and pointlessness of rebellion, and their deaths should not be mourned any more than the terrible fates of the Pazzi conspirators in Florence over half a century earlier should have been the cause of any distress.

This appointment of Morley to the bench of nobles examining and condemning the rebel peers was certainly a test of his true commitment to the King's and Cromwell's cause. His connections with these conservative Catholic lords were well known, especially with Hussey, with whose wife he had earlier been briefly arrested. It was also a test that had been administered before, when, in what must be seen as a act of personal cruelty as well as a test of loyalty, Morley had been named by Henry to sit on the panel to judge his own son-in-law, George Boleyn, Lord Rochford, and his former friend, Queen Anne. The decision of that court was, of course, to find them guilty of incest and treason and require their execution. As in his subsequent condemnation of Hussey and Darcy, Morley had to prove his loyalty through the blood of others. Machiavelli might have inspired Cromwell to effect this cruel trial of Morley's allegiance: he writes in chapter seventeen of *The Prince* that 'a prince should not worry if he incurs reproach for his cruelty so long as he keeps his subjects united and loyal'.[32]

NOTES

1 J. K. McConica, *English Humanists and Reformation Politics Under Henry VIII and Edward VI* (Oxford, 1965), p. 157.

2 Public Record Office. SP1/143. fol. 74[r-v]. Printed in Sir Henry Ellis, *Original Letters Illustrative of English History* (London, 1846), III, 63-7. H.G. Wright, in his edition of *Forty-six Lives*, redates this letter to 1539, and is followed in this by Sir Geoffrey Elton. However, A. G. Dickens accepts Ellis's dating (February 1537), as does James Carley, noting that Morley requested assistance from Cromwell in a dispute concerning the prior and chapter of Norwich in January 1537 and acknowledges that help in March 1537. There is no evidence of any similar connection in 1539. Also, the circumstances of the letter relate much more reasonably to the earlier date. See Carley, '"Plutarch's" Life of Aqesilaus: A Recently Located New Year's Gift to Thomas Cromwell by Henry Parker, Lord Morley', in *Prestige, Authority and Power in Late Medieval Manuscripts and Texts*, ed. by Felicity Tiddy (York, 2000), p. 84 n. 21.

3 'Est autem ... liber inscriptus nomine Machiavelli, ciusidam Florentini, indigni prorsus, qui tam nobiliem civitatem patriam habeat. Sed ut ubique Satanas suam prolem habet, suos filios, qui se miscent inter filios dei, quod tandiu erit. ...' Also R. Pole, 'Apologia ad Carolum Quintum', in *Epistolarum Reginaldi Poli ... collectio* (Brescia, 1744), I, 137-52.

4 See A. J. Slavin, 'The Gutenberg Galaxy and the Tudor Revolution', in *Print and Culture in the Renaissance*, ed. by G. Tyson & S. Wagonheim (Newark, 1986), pp. 90-109; and the same author's 'The Tudor Revolution and the Devil's Art: Bishop Bonner's Printed Forms', in *Tudor Rule and Revolution*, ed. by D. J. Guth & J. W. McKenna (Cambridge, 1982), pp. 11-12 and 12n.

5 Bishop Bonner as early as 1530 asked to borrow from Cromwell some Italian books, writing 'wher ye willing to make me a good Ytalion promised unto me, longe agon, the Triumphes of Petrarche in the Ytalion tonge. I hartely pray you at this tyme by this beyrer, Mr Augustine his servant, to sende me the said Boke with some other at your devotion; and especially, if it please you, the boke called Cortigiano in Ytalion'. Ellis, *Original Letters*, II, p. 178. It is interesting and significant that Cromwell owned in England a copy of Castiglione's *Courtier*, a book which appeared in print only in Venice in 1528.

6 K. R. Bartlett, 'The Triumph of Chastity Over Politics: the Occasion of Lord Morley's Translation of Petrarch's *Trionfi*', in *Petrarch's Triumphs: Spectacle and Allegory*, ed. by A. A. Iannucci (Ottawa, 1990), pp. 335-53.

7 McConica, p. 152.

8 Morley's daughter, Jane, married George Boleyn, Lord Rochford, Queen Anne's brother as early as 1526.

9 John Guy, *Tudor England* (Oxford, 1990), p. 149.
10 Ibid., pp. 149-51.
11 See transcription of the complete letter below, pp. 230-1.
12 Guy, p. 151.
13 *LP Henry VIII* VII. 1206. See also Guy, p. 151.
14 McConica, p. 157.
15 BL, Royal MS 17 A.XLVI.
16 McConica, p. 155.
17 See A. Loomie, *The Spanish Elizabethans: the English Exiles at the Court of Philip II* (New York, 1963), p. 95 and p. 95n.; also see K. R. Bartlett, *The English in Italy, 1525-1558: a Study in Culture and Politics* (Geneva, 1991), pp. 62-3 and p. 63n.
18 *Lord Morley's 'Tryumphes'*, ed. by Carnicelli, p. 6.
19 The common belief, however, that Morley's earliest translation was dedicated to Queen Anne has recently been corrected. James Carley has reattributed *The Pistellis and Gospels for the 52 Sondays in the Yeare* to Anne's brother, George, Lord Rochford, Morley's son-in-law. See J. Carley, '"Her moost lovyng and fryndely brother sendeth gretyng": Anne Boleyn's Manuscripts and their Sources', in *Illuminating the Book: Makers and Interpreters*, ed. by Michelle P. Brown & Scot McKendrick (London, 1998) p. 263.
20 See M. K. Jones & M. G. Underwood, *The King's Mother: Lady Margaret Beaufort, Countess of Richmond and Derby* (Cambridge, 1992), pp. 114, 241, 280.
21 Ellis (n. 2 above), p. 64. (See appendix 2 below, pp. 230-1, for complete text of Morley's letter.)
22 Ibid., pp. 63-4.
23 Ibid., pp. 65-6.
24 The events of the Pazzi Conspiracy against Lorenzo de' Medici are complicated but significant as a parallel to be drawn with England. Enmity had arisen between Pope Sixtus IV and Florence over a number of issues, particularly the rule of the city of Imola in the Romagna, a territory subject to the Church. The Florentines wished to see the Romagna remain weak and divided rather than united under the authority of the Pope's family, one of whom he wished to transfer to Imola. Lorenzo de'Medici thwarted papal policy and refused a necessary loan to acquire the city.

Simultaneously, within Florence the Pazzi, a family of great wealth and ancient nobility, believed themselves dishonoured by the rule of the Medici and their use of lesser families as agents for their policy. To gain favour with the Pope and work against the Medici hegemony the Pazzi lent the required money to Sixtus and became involved with the papal nephew to whom Imola had been promised. This group became increasingly anti-Medicean to the point that a conspiracy was hatched in 1478 to murder Lorenzo and his brother Giuliano, a plot which included several members of the Pazzi family as well as the archbishop of Pisa.

Paid assassins struck in the cathedral at mass, killing Giuliano but only wounding Lorenzo. The response from the people of the city was equally violent, killing many of the chief conspirators, including the archbishop of Pisa, and suspending their bodies from the windows of the Palazzo della Signoria. Other conspirators were hunted down and caught by Lorenzo's agents.

Furious, Pope Sixtus declared war not on Florence but on Lorenzo and used the armies of his ally the King of Naples to attack Florentine territory. In great danger, Lorenzo went alone in 1479 to Naples, the capital of his enemy, and convinced King Ferrante to abandon the Pope. By 1480 Lorenzo had achieved a separate peace with Naples, leaving Sixtus without the means to wage war against Florence. See N. Machiavelli, *The History of Florence and the Affairs of Italy*, ed. by F. Gilbert (New York, 1960), Book VIII, chapters 1-4.
25 M. Dowling states that there is no parallel between the Pazzi Conspiracy and the propaganda

needs of Cromwell. However, she fails to look at the passage recommended by Morley in the context of the Pilgrimage of Grace. See M. Dowling, *Humanism in the Reign of Henry VIII* (London, 1986), p. 200.

26 Cf. J. A. Williamson, *The Tudor Age* (London, 1975), pp. 146-8.

27 For Morison, see W. G. Zeeveld, *The Foundations of Tudor Policy* (Cambridge, Mass., 1948); K. R. Bartlett, *The English in Italy: a Study in Culture and Politics* (Geneva, 1991); D. S. Berkowitz, *Humanist Scholarship and Public order: Two Tracts Against the Pilgrimage of Grace by Sir Richard Morison* (Washington, 1984); C. R. Bonini, 'Richard Morison: Humanist and Reformer Under Henry VIII', unpublished Ph.D. thesis, Stanford University, 1974.

28 The *Apomaxis* was printed in 1537 but actually composed earlier, perhaps in 1535; see Zeeveld, p. 158.

29 '... Nicholao Macchavello, qui diligentissime res gestas in Italia, Italorum sermone perscripsit.' *Apomaxis*. sig. X2^{v}. Quoted in F. Raab, *The English Face of Machiavelli* (London, 1964), p. 34.

30 Raab, pp. 38-9.

31 Francesco Guicciardini, *Maxims and Reflections of a Renaissance Statesman*, trans. by M. Domandi (New York, 1965), *ricordo* 110, series C, p. 68.

32 N. Machiavelli, *The Prince*, trans. by G. Bull (Harmondsworth, 1961), p. 95.

MORLEY AND THE PAPACY
Rome, Regime, and Religion

RICHARD REX

IT IS PERHAPS merely a curious coincidence that the two most extensive pieces of original composition which survive from the hand of Henry Parker, knight, Lord Morley, both concern the papacy. Coincidence though it is, it is nonetheless remarkable that one of these writings is a vitriolic polemic against the Bishop of Rome, while the other is an equally strongly argued polemic in his favour. This stark contrast is at one level easily explained: the former work was written in the wake of Henry VIII's Break with Rome, while the latter was written after Mary Tudor's reconciliation with Rome. But the fact that Morley wrote on both sides of one of the sixteenth century's most divisive controversies raises unavoidable questions about his own religious views and commitments. Was he a Protestant who conformed under Mary only to save his skin? Was he a Catholic who conformed under Henry only to save his skin? Or was he a neutral, cynically writing to please whatever regime held the reins of patronage? Or was he simply an obedient subject, dutifully informing his conscience according to that of his sovereign? This paper will endeavour to answer these questions and provide a credible account of Morley's religious views by examining his writings for and against the papacy and by looking more broadly at what can be ascertained from his other translations and prefaces.

Morley's antipapal invective, *The Exposition and Declaration of the Psalme, Deus Ultionum Dominus* (STC 19211), dedicated to Henry VIII, was one of only two of his works to be printed in his lifetime. The original manuscript does not survive. It is, moreover, the only product of Morley's pen which (as far as we can tell) was entirely his own effort. The colophon informs us that it was printed at London by Thomas Berthelet in 1539. This was a year which saw a renewed burst of antipapal propaganda in England even as Henry VIII sought to establish the general catholicity of his religious position in the eyes of the international community. This curiously double-edged propaganda offensive was in fact devised to counter one and the same diplomatic threat: the danger that Francis I and Charles V, now reconciled through papal meditation in a ten-year truce of June 1538 after decades of intermittent but bitter conflict, might demonstrate their new-found accord in an attempt to execute the bull of excommunication which Pope Paul III had promulgated against Henry VIII late in 1538. The English regime's response was thorough and wide-ranging. The relatives of Cardinal Reginald Pole, who had found that his obedience to the universal church outweighed his loyalty to his cousin the king, were swept up in the court purge of suspect nobles which is known to historians as the 'Exeter conspiracy'. How real a likelihood there was of the Marquis of Exeter and his connections leading a Yorkist coup against the king under a papal banner is open to question, but truth was not always paramount in Tudor treason trials, and the messy and slightly panicky series of arrests and executions conducted in late 1538 and early 1539 was given retrospective legitimacy and final summation in the most extensive Act of Attainder in English Parliamentary history, a private statute (31 Henry VIII, c. 15) rushed through in the Parliament of May 1539.[1] Taxes were raised to meet the perceived threat of invasion, and Henry VIII began the construction of the massive series of coastal forts whose remains can be seen to this day at various sites along the south coast.

It was in this highly charged atmosphere that the regime launched a propaganda offensive on two fronts: a renewed series of attacks on the moral authority of the papacy, combined with a clamp-down on doctrinal and liturgical deviation. Until the summer of 1538, the evangelical faction had been making the running in religious policy, under the firm and committed leadership of Thomas Cromwell and Thomas Cranmer. Not only had the authority of the pope been cast aside, but indulgences had been abolished, the doctrine of purgatory had been watered down, doubt had been cast on relics and miracles, pilgrimage had been effectively prohibited, the Bible had been published in English, and monastic life was well on the way to disappearance.[2] The culmination of this reforming programme was a series of well-publicized acts of official iconoclasm in 1538, as England's leading shrines were systematically dismantled, with the proceeds carted off to the royal coffers.[3] It was the destruction of the shrine of Thomas Becket at Canterbury, an episode which 'shocked the conscience of Christian Europe' (to borrow the immortal words of F.E. Smith), that provided the motive or at least the occasion for the papal excommunication of Henry, which passed through the Roman Consistory on 17 December 1538, but had been under discussion since Paul III set up a committee to consider sanctions against Henry on 25 October 1538.[4]

The worsening international situation, combined with shifts in the balance of power at court, led Henry to take measures aimed simultaneously at stemming the advance of evangelical ideas at home and restoring his damaged credibility abroad. John Lambert was very publicly tried and burned for his denial of the real presence in the eucharist.[5] On 1 October 1538 a commission was established to investigate Anabaptist heresy.[6] Proclamations enjoined all clergy and laity to observe traditional liturgical ceremonies. In Lent, the French ambassador, returning to his home country, was said to have described Henry as 'Catholic in all that does not bring him profit or hurt the Holy See'.[7] Henry himself ostentatiously crept to the cross on Good Friday 1539.[8] The culmination of this programme was the passage of the Act of Six Articles in May 1539, reiterating traditional doctrines of eucharistic presence and sacrifice, as well as traditional practices like auricular confession and clerical celibacy.[9] Henry and Cromwell clearly hoped that this programme would avert the risk of concerted action against England from France, Spain, and the Empire.

At the same time, however, Henry made it clear both at home and abroad that this demonstration of liturgical and doctrinal conservatism was not to herald any rapprochement with Rome. Cuthbert Tunstall (Bishop of Durham) and John Stokesley (Bishop of London), two of the episcopal bench's leading scholars (both of them known internationally for their learning thanks to puffs in Erasmus's much-published correspondence[10]), set their names to an open letter to Reginald Pole which laid out the familiar political, theological, legal, and historical grounds for the Break with Rome.[11] Much of this material also found its way into a Palm Sunday sermon Tunstall published in 1539 which simultaneously attacked the papacy and defended traditional ceremonies.[12] Antipapal pageants were held on the Thames, and the executions of men like Sir Adrian Fortescue sent out a clear message about the risks of a shrewdly undefined treason.[13] Cromwell's favourite author, Richard Morison, drafted an upbeat opening address for the 1539 Parliament which emphasized the king's role in overthrowing papal tyranny.[14] In addition to this, Morison produced another vernacular pamphlet in support of the king, *An Invective ayenste the Great and Detestable Vice, Treason* (STC 18111-3), which set out to justify the executions of those implicated in the Exeter conspiracy. As H.G. Wright pointed out in his study of Morley, it is significant that one of only three surviving copies of the *Exposition and Declaration* is bound together with a copy of Morison's *Invective*.[15] Both were of course printed by the king's printer, Thomas Berthelet, who published a great deal of what was obviously official propaganda in the 1530s.[16] The *Invective* appeared very early in 1539. Zeeveld reckons that Morison's pamphlet was what Henry VIII enclosed with a letter to his representative at the Imperial Court, Thomas Wyatt, on 13 February 1539.[17] Later that year Morison produced yet another timely propaganda piece, *An Exhortation to Styrre all Englyshemen to the Defence of theyr Countreye*.[18]

This is the context in which Morley's *Exposition and Declaration* appeared. That the work was printed can be confidently ascribed to a decision by Henry VIII or Cromwell rather than to Morley himself, who otherwise showed no desire whatsoever to immortalize himself in print. At the very least, the government reckoned his exegetical effort useful. But it is worth asking why Morley made this highly, indeed doubly, uncharacteristic foray into biblical exegesis. Not only was it unusual for Morley to write something entirely from his own imagination, it was also unusual for a layman to venture into the realm of theology. Thomas More and Henry VIII were obvious exceptions to this rule in the English context, yet even they had stopped short of scriptural commentary. Finally, this was the only strictly religious work among the seven surviving writings which Morley presented to Henry VIII. His other offerings were predominantly heroic or moralistic in character. It is tempting to suppose that the *Exposition and Declaration* was more in the nature of a commission than of a voluntary offering.

There are several reasons why Morley might, towards the end of 1538, have been anxious to establish his credentials as a faithful subject. The most obvious was a patriotic desire to do his bit for king and country in a crisis. Yet he might also have felt a little exposed in the aftermath of the Exeter conspiracy. Among the many common threads which link the unfortunate victims of this episode (for the men and women involved seem to have been more conspired against than conspiring), one was connection with Catherine of Aragon and her daughter, Mary Tudor. Although it has now been shown that Morley was not, as was once thought, connected with Catherine of Aragon, he had recently become acquainted with her daughter, Mary Tudor.[19] Moreover, his own daughter was the widow of George Boleyn, Viscount Rochford, who had been executed for treasonable relations with his sister Queen Anne in 1536. Morley was in fact just the sort of man likely to be swept up in the purge of 1538-9: an aristocrat of the old school with potentially suspect family and personal ties. The *Exposition and Declaration* looks like an effort to establish or defend his position as a loyal subject in the fevered context of late 1538. Its references to unspecified 'jeoperdies' which 'the kinges highnes hath escaped only by the helpe of God', to betrayal by friends and subjects whom the king had 'entierly trusted & loved', to the

Bishop of Rome's machinations against the king, and to the papacy's role in setting princes at each other's throats look distinctly like allusions to the 'Exeter conspiracy' and to the papally brokered Franco-Imperial peace which was seen as a potential prelude to a crusade against England.[20] Whether Morley thought of it himself, or whether (more probably) it was suggested to him by Thomas Cromwell, New Year 1539 was a particularly timely moment to clarify his adherence to the king's religious policy.[21] As for the means he chose to achieve this, Henry VIII's piety was characterized by an abiding concern for the book of Psalms,[22] and a commentary on a psalm – especially a short commentary – must have seemed a sure way to attract his notoriously finite capacity for attention.

Psalm 93 (Vulgate numbering, which still prevailed in Henry VIII's Church of England) is a psalm of the vengeance of the Lord against the oppressors of his people. By Jews it was interpreted as a prayer for vengeance against Christians, and by Christians as a prayer for vengeance against their own persecutors.[23] Morley's unprecedented and (as far as I know) unparalleled variation on this theme is to read the psalm as a vindication of Henry VIII against the now overturned oppression of the papacy.[24] In a manner obviously calculated to appeal to the king's self-image, Henry VIII is presented in the *Exposition and Declaration* as a biblical deliverer who had 'set the englysshe nation at fredoome and lybertie', releasing her 'from the captivite Babylonical'.[25] The identification of Henry VIII with David which Morley makes at several points was becoming a commonplace. Henry's Davidic self-image has been expounded recently by both Tudor-Craig and John King.[26] More striking still is the Messianic picture of Henry VIII as Christ himself. Morley goes out of his way to expound 'Christ' as 'annoynted kyng', and applies to Henry VIII personally the concluding section of the psalm (*Beatus homo ...*), which was traditionally interpreted generally of all Christians and specifically of Jesus Christ. In what amounts to a hymn of praise for Henry, the king is credited with priestly and prophetic as well as royal qualities, for revealing the word of God to his people and leading them out of darkness and blindness into light.[27] Morley, like evangelical advocates of Henry's regime, casts his hero in the mould of the Old Testament judges and kings. Richard Morison, for example, likened Henry to David, Jehosophat, Amazias, Josias, and Ezechias.[28] But where the evangelical writers list kings noted for the suppression of idolatry and the promulgation of God's word, Morley lists leaders victorious in battle over their enemies, along with the enemies over whom they triumphed: Moses, Joshua, Gideon, Sampson, David, Hezekiah, Asa, and Judas Maccabees (this last, of course, drawn from a book which most Reformers demoted to the level of apocrypha). As if to emphasize his point, Morley adds four later Christian rulers: Constantine, Theodosius, Henry V, and Henry VII. These four were, from the point of view of traditional religious values, not only good Christians but good Catholics, whose personal fidelity to Christ earned them the favour and protection of providence, above all in battle.

The Messianic encomium of the king is matched by the apocalyptic denunciation of the pope. Morley runs the gamut of antipapal invective, and the ferocity of his rhetoric is still striking, especially for a man of such conservative and temperate habits and beliefs. The papacy is the 'seate of Sathan', the 'sect of Sathan', 'the monstruous hydra', a 'tyraunte', a 'bloud sucker', a 'deceyvour', 'this dronken strompette, soused in the bloudde of sayntes and martyrs'. It seeks 'to bryng in his subjection, all the pryncis of the worlde', sets princes together by the ears, fleeces Christians of their wealth, and sets 'princis subiectes ayenst their soveraines'. Rome itself is identified with 'the poluted citie of Babylon', following the Apocalypse, which is cited on this very point. The pope himself is 'the Babylonicall byshoppe', the 'adversarie' and 'ennemye' of God; Morley hints that the papacy is the abomination of desolation, talking of the popes' 'triumphant thrones, wherin they syt as gods'. He sits not in the see of Peter, but in 'this chaire of pestilence'. Morley excoriates 'the false doctrine, the wylye wayes, the abhomynable hypocrysye, the detestable ydolatrye of this wycked monster of Rome'.[29] His polemic is a glossary of evangelical buzzwords and catchphrases.

Strong stuff, and it is not hard to guess where it all came from. The Break with Rome had been followed by one of the heaviest preaching offensives in English history, perhaps the first time the pulpit had been used so extensively, so continuously, and so systematically to support a controversial royal policy. The initial series of high-profile sermons from the kingdom's premier pulpit, Pauls' Cross, had been followed up with royal letters commanding the preaching up of the king, and the denigration of the pope, in every parish. After the final abolition of every vestige of papal authority in 1536, Cromwell's vicegerential injunctions of that year formalized the requirement for anti-papal preaching every Sunday and feast day for three months, and once a quarter thereafter.[30] A gentleman like Morley would have had a regular diet of antipapal vitriol from the likes of Cranmer, Latimer, and Shaxton on his visits to the Chapel Royal. Such evangelical preachers made the intellectual running in this field, following the Continental Reformers in their unhesitating identification of the papacy with Antichrist.

As early as 1534 this identification had surfaced in the semi-official propaganda tract *A Mustre of Scismatyke Bysshopes of Rome* (STC 23552), the work of Thomas Swynnerton (pubished under the pseudonym of John Roberts). As Swynnerton was one of Cromwell's evangelical protégés, we can take it that this doctrine was already far from unwelcome in official circles.[31] But it was Thomas Cranmer who first publicly aligned Henry's regime behind this consensus doctrine of sixteenth-century Protestantism. He was reported by the imperial ambassador, Eustace Chapuys, as having identified the pope as Antichrist in a public sermon on Sunday 6 February 1536.[32] In a letter of the same date to Charles V himself, Chapuys reported that the sermon had lasted 2 hours, with three-quarters of it devoted to antipapal invective.[33] His report is confirmed by information which had reached Reginald Pole at Venice by 24 March 1536, when he wrote to Aloysius Priolus to say that he had learned from a letter from England of 25 February that three bishops had preached against the authority of the pope, led by Cranmer, who had stated 'The Bishop of Rome is the Antichrist, he who will precede the Day of Judgement and the end of the world'.[34] The doyen of Henrician propagandists, Richard Morison, stated that 'the kyngdome of Antichriste' was 'the reigne undoubtedly of the byshope of Rome' and that the papacy was 'that abhominable hore, which hitherto these many yeres, hath soused al kyngedomes in the dragges of Idolatrye, of Hypocrisie, of al errours'.[35] In his unpublished address to the 1539 Parliament, he further had described the papacy as 'that stronge strompet of babylon'.[36] Nor was this too strong for Henry's own ears. The king himself, in a conversation reported by the French ambassador referred to the pope as an 'abomination', the 'son of perdition', and the Antichrist.[37] Perhaps caution kept this fundamental

Protestant teaching out of the official formulations of the faith of Henry's Church. It was only under Edward VI and again under Elizabeth that the doctrine was in effect to attain the status of dogma in the Church of England.[38]

Yet the wealth of the vocabulary stands in marked contrast to the poverty of the substantial critique. The thrust of Morley's attack is political rather than doctrinal. Morley writes of the 'word of God' (with the clear implication that he intends to understand the Bible by this term), yet the papacy's offence against the word of God, the idolatry and heresy of which it stands accused, consists in nothing more than exalting its own political claims in opposition to those of anointed kings. In making the essence of his critique of the papacy political rather than doctrinal, Morley is able to cut off the antipapal invective from its potentially destabilizing implications for traditional religion. We can see similar tactics in the use of the Antichrist doctrine in Richard Sampson's commentary on the Psalms. Like Morley, Sampson based the identification on the pope's political usurpations rather than on theological deviations.[39] And, like Morley, he was anxious to safeguard traditional doctrines and practices as far as possible. To an extent even more marked than that of another conservative's justification of Henry VIII (namely Stephen Gardiner's *De vera obedientia*), Morley's work steers discussion away from the Petrine claims and the Petrine texts. Gardiner brushes aside the suggestion that Peter might be the rock upon which Christ builds his church: Morley does not so much as mention this embarrassing interpretative tradition.[40] On one level the *Exposition and Declaration* is unquestionably a fierce antipapal polemic; on another, it is a damage-limitation exercise. By restricting antipapal polemic to the realm of politics, Morley sought to preserve traditional religion in the Church of England from the corrosive effects of evangelical theology. What is remarkable about the nature of Morley's attack on the papacy, then, is its predominantly political character. The besetting sin of the papacy is worldly ambition, the usurpation of the rights of princes. Even when the sensitive Morley nods towards the Reformation by employing the buzzwords of contemporary evangelical theology, he does so in a political context. If the Bishop of Rome is a 'serpent' prepared to devour God's 'holy worde', his motive in so doing is 'to maynteyne his power'.[41] Nevertheless, in a work which was probably designed to convince the king of its author's unflagging loyalty, the wholehearted antipapal vitriol cannot have done Morley any political harm.

The exclusively political scope of Morley's critique of the papacy is evident not only in the *Exposition and Declaration*, but in his other allusions to the subject in Henry's latter years. When he forwarded a copy of Machiavelli's *Istorie Fiorentine* and *Il Principe* to Thomas Cromwell in February 1537, he pointed out in his covering letter that he had annotated the margins at those places where the author 'touches any thing consernyng the Bysschop of Rome'. Morley adduces the *Istorie Fiorentine* as evidence for the papacy's history of endemic and malevolent interference in the affairs of princes, culminating in the war between the papacy and King Ferdinand of Naples in the later fifteenth century. Morley urges Cromwell 'to note well what the Florantyns dyd agaynst the Romysche Bysschop and how lyttle they reputyd his cursynges', and observes that their example constitutes a valuable justification for Henry's break with Rome.[42] But while this information was doubtless music to the ears of Cromwell and Henry (if Cromwell brought it to the king's attention, as Morley hoped), it also shows us the way in which Morley understood the Break with Rome, seeing it not as we tend to do in the context of the European Protestant Reformation, but in the context of recurrent medieval quarrels between Church and State. While those two stories can be tied and told together in certain views of history, for Morley they are clearly separate stories. By setting Henry's Break with Rome in the context of medieval diplomatic history, its radicalism can be obscured or disguised, leaving the possibility of the sort of reconciliation which had always resolved such confrontations in the past.

Much the same tendency to restrict the quarrel between Henry and Rome to the political domain can be seen in the comparison of Henry with Agesilaus with which Morley closed his dedication to Cromwell of Plutarch's life of Agesilaus: 'Now last of all, where Plutarke breffly praysys Agesylayus for obsserving religyon, what laude schall and may all Chrystendome geve unto kyng Henry that, where treuth was taken away and error bare rule by usurping of the spyrytuall bysschop of Rome, hathe and dothe dayly by devyne wysdome as a most chrysten relygyus prynce reforme the same by worde whiche is groundyd by the word of God, by dede in schewing hymsellf the very trew mynster of god to se the worde of god mayntaynyd?'[43] Although this dutifully deploys the catchphrases of official propaganda, it still manages to refrain from any specific charge against the papacy other than that of usurpation. A similar theme is sounded in the dedication to Henry VIII of Masuccio's tale of Alexander IV and Frederick Barbarossa. Although here Morley even goes so far as to describe the pope as 'that false Antecriste', the only specific charge against him is breach of faith with the Emperor in betraying him to the Turks.[44]

Morley's second extensive discussion of the papacy was composed in an entirely different context. Presupposing that his account of the *Miracles of the Sacrament* was, like his other writings, a New Year's gift, we can show quite convincingly that it was written in time for New Year 1556. The address to the manuscript is made to Queen Mary as married to Philip of Spain, and the precise royal style employed enables us to date it more precisely still. Shortly before the marriage, Philip was made King of Naples by his father, Charles V, in order to equate his rank with that of his new wife, and in Morley's address Mary is called Queen of Naples. This gives us a *terminus a quo* of 25 July 1554.[45] As she is styled 'Pryncesse off Spayne', we can be sure that the manuscript was presented before that time, shortly after New Year 1556, when Charles V formally abdicated in favour of his son, who thereupon became Philip II of Spain.[46] While this leaves both 1555 and 1556 as possible dates for the presentation, the prologue's allusion to Mary as 'folowyng the wise counsell of the unculpable vertuous cardinall your cosyn' points towards the later date.[47] For it was thought that, when Philip himself left England in August 1555, he commended Cardinal Pole to the queen as an impartial councillor in his absence.[48] Morley's praise of Pole's 'wise counsell' suggests that he may have been aware of the king's recommendation, and his failure to mention Philip himself, the queen's husband, as a source of advice, which would have been inexplicably tactless at New Year 1555, when Philip was at court, makes perfect sense for New Year 1556, when he had left the country.

Unlike Morley's *Exposition and Declaration* for Henry VIII, the *Miracles of the Sacrament* was not a wholly uncharacteristic production. Although it was unusual in being so largely his own work, it stood in the line of almost exclusively religious works which he offered to Mary Tudor. Indeed, on one occasion on which Morley offered her a secular work (a translation of Cicero's *Somnium Scipionis*), he felt it necessary to justify his departure from custom in a prologue, which emphasized the moral worthiness of the work.[49] There is no hint that Morley's relations with Mary were ever anything but cordial, so there is no need to conclude that his decision to compose an original work on this occasion reflected anything other than his own free choice. Whereas the *Exposition and Declaration* was written at one of the tensest conjunctures in the history of Henry VIII's reign, and its fevered tone reflects this, the *Miracles of the Sacrament* reads more calmly. Although it is still a polemical work, it lacks the bitterness of the *Exposition and Declaration*. Its tone is that of something written after the end of a story rather than in the midst of one. The claims advanced here, that the *Miracles of the Sacrament* expresses the 'real' Morley, and that the *Exposition and Declaration* is a piece of temporizing, are inevitably vulnerable to the charge of simplification and special pleading. Yet the fact that Morley was clearly in a very hazardous position under Henry, whereas he was in no way threatened under Mary, makes it plausible to conclude that the *Miracles of the Sacrament*, rather than the *Exposition and Declaration*, reflects his true convictions about the papacy. This can be seen in details as minute as his brief but warm reference to John Fisher in the later work: 'I do ensure your highnes that doctour fysher then bishopp of rochester being her [i.e. Lady Margaret Beaufort's] ghostly father, shewyd me not long before his death, that he had writen her liffe, which I suppose is in your graces hande; then if yt so be, oh, good Jhesu how joyous wolde yt make me to se and to reade it, writen by so good a man, and so devine a clerk as that bishop was.'[50] The final comment might be mere pious convention, but the entirely offhand revelation that Morley had spoken with Fisher – martyred for his refusal to accept the royal supremacy – 'not long before his death' rings true, and speaks volumes for his continuing loyalty to a friend whom he would have known since his boyhood in Lady Margaret's household.

That said, it is nonetheless remarkable that Morley's *Miracles of the Sacrament* lays just as much emphasis as the *Exposition and Declaration* on the political rather than the doctrinal aspects of communion with Rome. The argument from providence as revealed in history is simply reversed. In the *Exposition and Declaration*, Morley had exclaimed: 'Let England I say, put other nations in memorie, of the great falle, that the estate of Chrstendome toke, whan kynges began to obey the lewde doctrine of priestis, whan pristes presumptuously toke upon theym, to rule goddis worde after theyr fantasyes, and not theyr lustes, accordyng to his lawes.'[51] The argument of the prologue to the *Miracles of the Sacrament* is the exact opposite. Now it is disobedience to the see of Rome that has brought providential chastisement and vengeance upon the kingdoms of this world, from the Byzantine Empire to the Kingdom of Bohemia. The only structural difference between the arguments is that the providential case of 1539 is merely asserted, whereas its converse of 1555 is amply substantiated. In 1555, as in 1539, heresy is seen as essentially political. The first heresy, separation from Rome, is a strictly political act. Further strictly doctrinal heresies, among the Greeks as among the Bohemians and the Tudor English, stem from this root of rebellion.

Nobody can read the prologue to the *Miracles of the Sacrament* without being struck by Morley's decisive allegiance to a figure who is once more 'the Popes Holynes' (as he had been in 1523[52]) rather than 'the Romysshe bysshop'.[53] His Romanism is, indeed, disturbingly unscrupulous. In his account of the mythic King Lucius, he makes, apparently from his own imagination, the claim that this first of Britain's Christian monarchs was actually baptized at Rome. And in equal but opposite fashion, his account of the heretic Pelagius suppresses his source's inconvenient statement that Pelagius had come to Britain from Rome![54] Yet for all this papal triumphalism, the Petrine claims and the Petrine texts are as conspicuous by their absence from the *Miracles of the Sacrament* as they are from the *Exposition and Declaration*. The politics of providence underpin Morley's call to unity with Rome just as they had underpinned his call to autonomy under Henry. The reversal in his appraisal of the *Donation of Constantine* illustrates this fundamentally political approach to the question. In the *Exposition and Declaration* he refers dismissively to 'the tyme that Sylvester chalenged by gyfte, that that Constantyne never gave hym' as the beginning of the papacy's fall through the pollution of temporal possessions.[55] Yet by 1555 he has recovered what was presumably his original conviction that Constantine 'commaundyd ... S. Sylvester the Pope to be the head of all the bishoppes in the worlde'.[56] In each case, Morley traces papal primacy to the *Donation of Constantine* rather than to the New Testament or even to the primitive church. Although I have argued elsewhere for the view that the papacy was not a spiritual irrelevance for the people of early Tudor England,[57] Morley's religious writings offer no support for this view. He is clearly happy in communion with Rome, and I shall be arguing that he is not really happy out of communion with Rome. But from the point of view of the Roman curia, his understanding of the spiritual role of the papacy would have seemed sadly defective. His attachment to the papacy seems to have been based on history and human law rather than theology and divine law. And if Morley was representative of opinion at large, even simply of educated lay opinion, then this makes it easier to understand how the Break with Rome was possible even if it was not greatly welcome. Stephen Gardiner evinced a similar theological shallowness in his reaction to the reconciliation with Rome in late 1554. As Jean-Pierre Moreau notes in his study of English reactions to the 'schism', Gardiner's sermon in Parliament on the reconciliation dwells exclusively on the worldly historical and political dimensions of the Roman obedience, paying no more attention to the Petrine texts in 1554 than he had done in 1535.[58]

For all his renewed loyalty to the papacy, Morley never lost his respect and admiration for Henry VIII. Even as he addresses Mary, his recollections of the old king are favourable. Henry is 'your most victorious father' and 'your worthy father', and his days are included in a nostalgic invocation of a merry England which existed before the Reformation brought down the chastisement of divine providence.[59] The only point at which even a hint of criticism is voiced is in his curious tale of a Gothic king of Spain, Theodoricus, whose crimes are distinctly reminiscent of Henry's: 'he utterly despised the sea of Rome and sayd that to hym appertayned only to make all the ecclesiastycall lawes, and usyd his lyffe so dissolutely that by the permissyon of God the Sarasyns ... entryed Spain'. Yet this figure, who seems to be a conflation of Theodoric II with Rodrigo, last King of the Goths, was nevertheless – again like Henry – 'a very valiaunt prynce of his person and dyd many notable actes with his owne hande'.[60] Morley was content to forgive his former master – and thus by extension himself – a great deal. In a pointed fashion, Morley included in his *Miracles of the Sacrament* a story of Richard III's last day on earth, which he had derived from Sir Ralph Bigod, who had passed from Richard's service to that of Lady Margaret Beaufort. Morley drew particular attention to the fact that even after his move into the Tudor entourage, Bigod could never bear to hear ill spoken of his former sovereign lord, and that Lady Margaret herself had used to praise Bigod's sterling loyalty to Richard's memory.[61]

Moving beyond the question of Morley's attitude to the papacy, there can be little serious doubt as to the essential conservatism of his religious views. H. G. Wright's account of them, however, was confused, partly as a result of the curious arrangement of his material in his introduction to Morley's translation of Boccaccio's *De claris mulieribus*. When discussing Morley's dedications to Mary, Wright notes his devotion to Mary and the Blessed Sacrament, but makes no effort to reconcile this with the very different picture of a definitely Protestant, if socially conservative, evangelism which emerges in his discussion of the commentary on Ecclesiastes dedicated to the Duke of Somerset in the early years of Edward VI. This work attacks monastic vows and free will, dismisses the pope as a heretic, appeals to 'the aucthorite of Godes worde', and gives a strongly Lutheran account of the life of man amid the vicissitudes of the world. Indeed, the preface subtly but distinctly affirms the central evangelical doctrine of certainty of grace, by rejecting the scholastic interpretation of Ecclesiastes 9:1: 'But there were none that more abused the said boke then the scoles of our divines, which made a mater of conscience agaynst God of this place: "Man knowyth not whether he be worthy of love or hatered", greatlye disquietyng with the wresting of the said texte the consciences of all men, extinguishinge the most assurid faythe in Christ with all other godlye knowlege, and teaching nothing elles but that we owght to doubt of the grace and love of God towardes us.'[62] This context helps us to understand the comment that follows soon after, namely that Christ is 'our onlye mediator and salvacion, frelye yeven us of God'. For although that remark is quite compatible with Catholic theology, coming after such a distinctively evangelical piece of exegesis it must be read as an affirmation of justification by faith alone and a denial of the cult and intercession of the saints. If this work indeed proceeds from the pen of Henry Parker, Lord Morley, then his religious utterances must be seen as determined entirely by the prevailing wind. However, it has been pointed out by James Carley that the preface to this work is signed simply 'Henrye Parker, knight', whereas every other work is signed 'Henry Parker, knight, Lord Morley'.[63] While this is but a slight discrepancy, it is remarkable in one clearly so punctilious as our author in matters of title and style. As the doctrinal position of this work is so diametrically opposed to that of Morley's writings, the onus of proof must therefore be judged to lie with those who might wish to argue that Morley was indeed its author.

Nor is there much to support the contention that Morley would have had any particular desire to ingratiate himself with the Protector. Somerset's reforming religious policy was made obvious even in 1547, and all the signs are that Morley did not endorse it. The absolution which Morley secured from Cardinal Pole in 1555 described him as having resisted schism.[64] This claim can hardly have referred to his record under Henry VIII, but it could be justified by his record under Edward VI. While only three secular peers (the Earl of Derby with Lords Dacre and Windsor) accompanied eight conservative bishops (led by Tunstall) in opposing the Book of Common Prayer and the Act of Uniformity (which received its third reading on Tuesday 15 January 1549), Morley was to vote with that group against the bill for clerical marriage (third reading on Tuesday 19 February 1549) and against the bill for abolishing sundry books and images (third reading Saturday 25 January 1550).[65] It is unlikely that a man opposed to clerical marriage would have been supporting the Book of Common Prayer, and it may be that Morley abstained from the votes on the latter. In any case, divisions were still relatively rare occurrences in Parliament, and voting against government bills of any kind is not the sort of activity we associate with a man angling for favour and patronage. Morley's record of assiduous attendance at the House of Lords tails off towards the end of Edward VI's reign, perhaps because of age and infirmity. However, it is interesting to note that both he and Lord Wharton made over proxies to the Duke of Northumberland early in March 1552, a few weeks before the Second Uniformity Bill and the bill to deprive Cuthbert Tunstall of the bishopric of Durham.[66] It is quite possible that Northumberland was encouraging these two peers to absent themselves because they had already given earnest of their conservative sympathies. However, as Morley appeared in Parliament only a few times thereafter, it would be risky to over-interpret what might have been a perfectly innocent administrative arrangement.[67]

Consideration of Morley's other manuscripts reveals two predominant religious concerns: an interest in the Psalms, and devotion to the Virgin Mary. Besides the *Exposition and Declaration*, three of Morley's offerings were related to the Psalter, all of them dedicated to Mary Tudor between 1537 and 1544. Although offerings of this kind must always mediate to some degree between the interests of the donor and those of the recipient, the fact that Morley should be sufficiently familiar with a variety of commentaries on the Psalms suggests that he was himself attached to the Psalter as a medium of prayer and devotion. This was by no means uncommon. Morley clearly knew that Mary too employed the Psalter in her devotions, as his offerings are explicitly designed to her assist her therein. In his prologue to a translation of Athanasius on the scope of the Psalms, he remarks to Mary 'that daly ye exarcyse your selfe in the Salmes, in saynge with your chaplen the service of the daye'.[68] And Mary's father, Henry, was well known for his devotion to the Psalter. His personal Psalter, highly ornate, still survives,[69] and he commissioned (directly or indirectly) commentaries on some or all of the Psalms from such varied authors as Erasmus, John Fisher, John Longland, and Richard Sampson (all of them personally acquainted with him, and the last three particularly close to him at various stages of his religious life[70]). Although, as we can see, Morley's religious beliefs and practices were profoundly traditional in nature, this clearly did not exclude a serious concern with scripture, which helps to explain why, despite his essential conservatism, he seems to have assimilated the evangelical habit of referring to the Bible as 'the word of God'.

Morley's devotion to the Virgin Mary is apparent in two of his other offerings to Mary Tudor. One is a translation of Erasmus's *Paean in Praise of the Virgin*. The other included both a commentary on the Ave Maria by Thomas Aquinas and an account of the life of the Virgin ascribed to Anselm. Marian devotion was of course one of the most widespread aspects of traditional Catholicism, so there is no surprise in Lord Morley's and Lady Mary's shared attachment to her patron saint. And Morley inevitably makes the most of the potential for flattery in presenting his earthly patroness as 'the secunde Mary of this wourlde'.[71] Nevertheless, Morley's devotion should not be characterized as merely conventional piety. The Anselmian text seems to have been particularly important to him, as in both prologues he cites with obvious feeling Anselm's remark that 'only to thynke that Mary is mother unto God passith all altitude that either may be thought or spoken'.[72] The prologue to the Erasmian text is notable for its slight polemical edge. Morley takes the trouble to censure those who 'do not honour to the holy saynctes in heven', taking the traditional side in a debate which troubled the Church of England in the later 1530s and 1540s. In order to discredit the opponents of the cult of the saints, Morley maintains that their position is at the top of a slippery slope which declines into repudiation of the veneration of the consecrated host (which implicitly undermines the real presence in the eucharist, a doctrine to which Henry VIII was unshakeably attached): 'we have clerkes in our tyme that dar affyrme that to honour hyr is a dymynysshynge of the honour of Godd, and so, fallynge frome one hereticall opynyone to another, at last deny the honoure due to God hymsellf in the moste holy and dyvyne sacrament of the aulter'.[73]

This slide down the slippery slope was described in slightly more detail some years later in the prologue to the *Miracles of the Sacrament*:

> first they denyed the head of the Church, the popes holynes, next wolde have no saintes honored but threwe vile matter at the crucifyx, and adding mischeife to myscheife, denyed the sevyn sacramentes of the Church, some of them willing to have but thre, some none at all. And by ther desertes fyll into so reprobable a will, that they not only expulsed the name of the precyous Mary, mother to Christ, out of ther common prayers but therunto wolde not let the Ave maria to be sayde.
>
> This was greatly to be lamentyd but this that folowith moche more, for the most devine holy sacrament of the aulter, the very sancta sanctorum which all Cristen realmes hath belevyd to be really the very body of Christ, these heretyckes without sence or wytt, more abhomynable then Machomet the false prophete, hath so despised yt and handlyd yt, and in such an herytycall sorte, that as the excellent Maro sayeth to tell yt
>
> Animus meminisse orret: luctuque refugit
>
> and by ther false doctryne as moche as in them was, hath condemnyd all the kinges in Cristendome and ther progenitours with ther subjectes to be no better then idolaters. ...

This comprehensive indictment of the Reformation attack on traditional religion is noteworthy for two reasons. First that it now identifies the top of the slippery slope as the Break with Rome. Second that, notwithstanding this, no blame is attached to Mary's father, but rather to 'these heretyckes', and that all the other heretical measures listed were measures implemented by Edward VI's regime rather than Henry's. Henry VIII's offence was, as it were, political rather than doctrinal, and England's subsequent lapse into heresy was the providential punishment for that political offence. Morley is plainly anxious to minimize Henry VIII's personal responsibility for what ensued, and thus by extension to minimize any personal responsibility of his own for following his late master so loyally. The advantage of this strategy is that it avoided the embarrassment of condemning the Queen's father for heresy.

The remaining major element in Morley's religious world, as far as it can be reconstituted from his surviving writings, is his devotion to the sacrament of the altar, which is attested by his last work, the *Miracles of the Sacrament*. There is no reason to suppose that Morley had ever, even in what were presumably for him the dark days of Edward VI, faltered in his belief in that Catholic doctrine according to which the 'spyrytuall man ... by faithe and by hys worde dothe consecrate in fourme of breade the moste blessyd body of God'.[74] We have already noted his concern that attacks on the cult of the saints would undermine respect for and thus belief in the real presence.

The *Miracles of the Sacrament* is expressly intended to refute those who 'hath taken opinion against the devine and holy sacrament of the aulter, that it shuld not be really the precious body of God that was borne of the blissyd virgin Mary and also have despised the holy masse'.[75] It sets out to demonstrate the truth of Catholic eucharistic doctrine on the grounds of the powerful miracles which have been worked through or in the presence of the consecrated eucharistic host. Morley relates twelve miracles drawn from a range of authorities from Cyprian to his own memory.

The appeal to miracles in defence of the real presence was by no means irrational nor even unusual. In the context of a doctrine which was itself admittedly contrary to the ordinary canons of natural science, there is nothing surprising in the attempt to substantiate it with phenomena which themselves transgress the boundary of the natural. To put it another way, the doctrine of transubstantiation relied for its credibility not on its rationality but on divine power, and miracles were at once the expression and the confirmation of that power. Transubstantiation itself was explicitly presented in oxymoronic terms as an ordinary, predictable miracle. As a focus of sacred power, the consecrated host must be expected to produce miraculous effects in its environment, acting in this regard much in the same way as a relic, only more efficaciously in that it was at once more certain than ordinary relics and more powerful as it was a relic of Christ himself.[76] Thus the appeal to miracles had been made by Catholic polemicists against Wyclif and the Lollards. At the time of the 'Earthquake Council' which condemned Wyclif's doctrines in 1382, a knight named Sir Cornelius Cloune claimed to have been converted from his former Wycliffite views on the eucharist by seeing a consecrated host bleed.[77] And Thomas Netter's monumental refutation of Wyclif related a prodigy he had witnessed at the trial of the Lollard John Badby in 1410. Just as Badby had averred that he would rather venerate a spider than the consecrated host, 'a huge and horrible spider lowered itself from the ceiling and landed directly on the blasphemer's lips, and, as he spoke, managed to find its way into his polluted mouth'.[78]

In popular Catholic culture on the continent eucharistic miracles were traditionally associated with the conviction of Jews of heresy, blasphemy, and sacrilege. In the sixteenth century the traditional miracles associated with Lollards and Jews were experienced by anxious and troubled Catholic communities amid heretical denials of their doctrine, or, worse, sacrilegious assaults on their rites. Catholic historiography records these miracles, and Catholic polemic regularly compiled lists of eucharistic miracles such as that here presented by Morley in order to establish the truth, antiquity, and divine sanction of perhaps their most distinctive doctrine.[79] While discussions of literal and figurative speech might preoccupy the theologians, popular devotion or scepticism was aroused and sustained by practical manifestations of sacred power, whether for Catholics in the self-defence or tragic self-vindication of the assaulted host, or for Protestants in the successful challenging of its sacred power through desecration with impunity.[80] As so often, Morley's aristocratic simplicity is a better testimony to what really mattered in religion than the more considered and reflective writings of professional theologians like John Fisher and Richard Smyth.

Having said that, even professional theologians regarded the argument from miracles as a respectable one, and Morley almost certainly took his immediate departure from none other than John Fisher's handling of the matter in his lengthy refutation of the

Swiss Protestant Johannes Oecolampadius, a work devoted entirely to the defence of the real presence in the eucharist. Fisher included the argument from miracles as the 'sixth corroboration' of Catholic doctrine in the preface to book III of his *De veritate corporis et sanguinis Christi in Eucharistia.*[81] Although Fisher's account is much briefer than Morley's, it is remarkable that of the eleven miracles Morley derives from literary sources, five are among those referred to in Fisher's text: both of the miracles taken from Cyprian and that from Augustine, and references to the texts Morley gives from Bede and Chrysostom. The two miracles from Cyprian are given by Fisher in full, and Morley's versions are reasonably close renderings of exactly the texts which Fisher cites. That is, Morley had no need to look at an edition of Cyprian for the stories he gives.[82] The same is true of the story of the tribune Hesperius drawn from Augustine's *City of God*, for Fisher gives all of the story that Morley gives. Morley's citation from Chrysostom is the same text cited by Fisher about a priest who was granted a vision of angels while he celebrated Mass. Besides these, Fisher gives one eucharistic miracle from Gregory the Great's *Dialogues*. Morley uses the same source, but gives two other miracles instead. In addition, Fisher also points his readers to the *Golden Legend* for a range of further miracles in the lives of the saints, referring among others to Edward the Confessor's life. The *Golden Legend* gives the story of the eucharistic vision shared by King Edward and Earl Leofric in much the same terms as Morley, and is probably his immediate source. Thus we can probably credit Fisher not only with inspiring Morley's compilation, but also with providing, directly or indirectly, half of its raw materials.

Those examples that were drawn from original sources came from texts that were well enough known. The Bede miracle comes from his *Ecclesiastical History*. For the story of how St Clare's prayer before the reserved host saved her convent from the depredations of marauding Saracens, Morley refers us to a text he calls the *Cronaca Cronicarum*. This turns out to be Heinrich Schedel's *Liber Cronicarum*, a popular fifteenth-century world history. It transpires that this source also contains Morley's other three miracles, the dancers of Magdeburg, the broken bridge at Utrecht (or Maastricht as Morley has it), and the deathbed of Hugh of St Victor. Given Morley's admiration for Fisher, and the derivative character of his scholarship, it is most likely that his *Miracles of the Sacrament* was inspired by Fisher's *De veritate*, which was widely owned and read in Tudor England. Thus Morley's sources for his miracles are not obscure, and do not compel us to overpraise his scholarship. He is, incidentally, apparently unaware of the native English tradition of anti-Lollard miracles in this vein, some of which were associated with the cult of the Holy Blood of Hailes.[83]

Morley's religious position is close to that of popular religion. He is not a theologian. Although he is a pious and literate layman from the highest level of society, his religion is that of the people, a religion of miracles and worship, of practice rather than theory, of ritual rather than doctrine. All this is in keeping with Eamon Duffy's picture of traditional religion.[84] When Morley takes issue with the Reformation, it is the saints and the sacraments that concern him, not justification and authority. His is a functioning and functional religion. The crude providentialism of his attack on and defence of the papacy, and his trust in clear and simple miracles, both testify to this. Morley is, in short, a traditional and typically unheroic religious figure. His career offers an interesting parallel to that of the clergyman Stephen Gardiner. Neither of them had any time for the Protestant Reformation. Both of them were unwaveringly loyal to Henry VIII. Despite their disquiet at religious change following the break with Rome, they made the best of it. Each was obliged to give earnest of his loyalty by penning a vigorous defence of Henry's proceedings. In this adjustment they were certainly assisted by their fundamentally political view of the role of the papacy. However, they shared a firm attachment to the real presence, and thus at bottom to the traditional symbol structure of medieval Catholicism, at whose heart that doctrine lay. Therefore, under Edward VI, they made their dissent from the religious policy of the regime ever more clear. With the restoration of Mary, they found themselves vindicated. The restoration of the Mass was the issue of paramount importance to them, but they were comfortable too with the reconciliation with Rome, even if they still took a fundamentally political view of the papacy's role. Had Morley lived to a prodigious old age, he might have discovered the inner resources to stand with Viscount Montague and the bishops in opposition to Elizabeth's restoration of a Protestant settlement. But given his record of temporizing and compromise, he was probably fortunate that his conscience was not put to the test yet again. Like Stephen Gardiner, he would have accounted himself doubly lucky to be able to die a loyal son of both his Mother Church and his mother country.

NOTES

1 For the so-called conspiracy, see M. H. & R. Dodds, *The Pilgrimage of Grace 1536-1537 and the Exeter Conspiracy 1538*, 2 vols (Cambridge, 1915), II, 296-328, esp. p. 311.
2 The latest survey of the Henrician Reformation is to be found in Diarmaid MacCulloch, 'Henry VIII and the reform of the church', in *The reign of Henry VIII: Politics, Policy and Piety*, ed. by MacCulloch (London, 1995), pp. 159-80. For a fuller account, with some slight differences of interpretation, see Richard Rex, in *Henry VIII and the English Reformation* (London, 1993). George Bernard offers a very different vision of the 1530s in forthcoming papers on Thomas Cromwell and on the religion of Henry VIII.
3 For Henrician iconoclasm see R. Whiting, 'Abominable idols: Images and image-breaking under Henry VIII', *Journal of Ecclesiastical History* 33 (1982), 30-47. For the events of 1538 see Eamon Duffy, *The Stripping of the Altars: Traditional Religion in England, c. 1400-c. 1580* (New Haven & London, 1992), pp. 407-10; Rex, *Henry VIII and the English Reformation*, pp. 97-8; and Peter Marshall, 'The Rood of Boxley, the Blood of Hailes and the Defence of the Henrician Church', *Journal of Ecclesiastical History* 46 (1995), 689-96.
4 See *LP Henry VIII* XIII.ii.684 for notice of the papal consistory of 25 October to consider reaction to the desecration of Becket's shrine; and *LP Henry VIII* 13.ii.1087 for a note of the bull of excommunication. The text of the bull is in D. Wilkins, *Concilia Magnae Britanniae et Hiberniae*, 4 vols (London, 1737), III, 840-1.
5 See Foxe, *Acts and Monuments*, ed. by G. Townsend, 8 vols (London, 1843-9), V, 229-34 for an account of Lambert's trial.
6 *LP Henry VIII* XIII.ii.498. The commissioners were Cranmer, Gardiner, Robert Barnes, Edward Crome, John Stokesley, Richard Sampson, Richard Gwent, Nicholas Heath, John Skip, and Thomas Thirlby.
7 *LP Henry VIII* XIV.i.585, Cardinal Farnese to Cardinal Brindisi, 22 March 1539.
8 According to John Worth, who reported this to Lord Lisle on 15 May 1539. See *The Lisle Letters*, ed. by M.St C. Byrne, 6 vols (Chicago & London, 1981), V, no. 1415, p. 478.

9 See G. Redworth, 'A Study in the Formulation of Policy: the Genesis and Evolution of the Act of Six Articles', *Journal of Ecclesiastical History* 37 (1986), 42-67.

10 For Erasmus's opinions of these two men see *Contemporaries of Erasmus*, ed. by P. G. Bietenholz with T. B. Deutscher, 3 vols (Toronto, 1985-7), III, 289-90 and 349-54.

11 *A Letter written by Cutbert Tunstall and J. Stokesley somtyme Byshop of London, sente vnto R. Pole, Cardinall* (London: R. Woulfe, 1560. STC 24321). Although the letter survives only in this edition of 1560, the nature of the text suggests that it was probably printed in 1539 for propaganda purposes. Simply to have sent Pole a private letter of this length and to this effect would have been too obviously wasted effort by this stage.

12 *A Sermon of Cuthbert Bysshop of Duresme, made upon Palme Sondaye laste past* (London, 1539), sig. A.viii.[r-v].

13 See Richard Rex, 'Blessed Adrian Fortescue: a martyr without a cause?', *Analecta Bollandiana* 115 (1997), 307-53, esp. 332-41.

14 London, BL, Cotton MS Titus B i, fols 109-114.

15 *Forty-six Lives*, ed. by Wright, p. lxxxi, note 4. BL, 292.a.33 binds together the Morison followed by the Morley.

16 John Guy, *Christopher Saint German on chancery and statute*, Selden Society supplementary series, 6 (London, 1985), pp. 22-3.

17 W. Gordon Zeeveld, *Foundations of Tudor Policy* (Cambridge, Mass., 1948), p. 229, referring to *LP Henry VIII* XIV.i.280, with a supporting reference to *LP Henry VIII* XIV.i.233. As the *Invective* was presumably produced at the earliest very late in 1538, Berthelet must have turned it around in very short order. Morley's effort must also have been turned around quickly.

18 Zeeveld, *Foundations of Tudor Policy*, p. 231.

19 See David Starkey, above, pp. 14-15, revising the views advanced in J. K. McConica, *English Humanists and Reformation Politics under Henry VIII and Edward VI* (Oxford, 1965), pp. 154-7.

20 *Exposition and Declaration*, sig. A6[v].

21 While it is not possible to be absolutely certain that the *Exposition and Declaration* was presented to the king at New Year 1539, this year seems far more probable than the other two possibilities, 1538 and 1537. There is simply no obvious reason why Morley should have written such a piece for New Year 1538. New Year 1537 might have been plausible, as Morley's known conservative sympathies could have made it worth his while emphasizing his loyalty in the wake of the Pilgrimage of Grace (and the *Exposition and Declaration* goes out of its way to uphold the king's right to choose what councillors and ministers he pleased, arguably a response to the Pilgrims' grievance over Henry's low-born councillors). However, if it had been produced then, it would probably have been printed among the responses to the Pilgrimage in early 1537, rather than being inexplicably delayed for two years.

22 See for example P. Tudor-Craig, 'Henry VIII and King David', in *Early Tudor England: Proceedings of the 1987 Harlaxton Symposium*, ed. by D. Williams (Woodbridge, 1989), pp. 183-205, esp. pp. 195-6. See also Richard Rex, *The Theology of John Fisher* (Cambridge, 1991), pp. 81-2, for Henry VIII's requests to Erasmus and John Fisher for a commentary on the psalms.

23 The classic late medieval psalm commentary was Iacobus Perez de Valencia, *In Psalmos Dauidicos lucubratissima expositio* (Paris: Regnault, 1533), fol. CLXXVII[v]. Perez refers to Rabbi Kimhi's interpretation of the psalm as a prediction regarding Christian persecutions of Jews. A commentary with which Morley was almost certainly acquainted was that of Juan de Torquemada (Iohannes Turrecremata), Psalm 36 of which he translated and dedicated to Mary Tudor. Torquemada, apparently following Perez, also applied Psalm 93 to persecutors.

See his *Expositio in Psalterium* (Paris, 1513), fols cxiii^{r}-cxiiii^{v}. The theme of the Lord's vengeance is also central to the commentaries on Psalm 93 by Ludolph of Saxony and Franciscus Titelmannus. See Ludolph of Saxony, *In Psalterium expositio* (Venice: O. Scotus, 1521), fols 89^{r}-90^{r}; and F. Titelmannus, *Elucidatio in omnes Psalmos* (Antwerp: M. de Keyser, 1531), fols 247^{v}-251^{r}. I have been unable to find any echo in Morley's exposition of evangelical or Protestant commentaries, such as those of Bugenhagen or Bucer.

24 Richard Sampson's interpretation of Psalm 93, found in the second part of his psalm commentary, applies the psalm traditionally enough to divine vengeance against tyrants. See Richard Sampson, *Explanationis Psalmorum secunda pars* (London, 1548), fols cxxxvii^{r}-cxxxviii^{v}.

25 *Exposition and Declaration*, sig. A2^{v} (see below, p. 232).

26 Besides Tudor-Craig, 'Henry VIII and King David', see also John N. King, *Tudor Royal Iconography: Literature and Art in an Age of Religious Crisis* (Princeton, 1989), pp. 70-89. King discusses Morley's *Exposition and Declaration* in this context (p. 80), and elsewhere points out that Morley even likens Henry to Judith (p. 219).

27 *Exposition and Declaration*, sig. B5^{r-v} (see below, p. 236).

28 Richard Morison, *An Exhortation to Styre all Englyshe Men to the Defence of theyr Countrye* (London, 1539), sigs. B6^{r}-B8^{r}.

29 *Exposition and Declaration*, sig. B3^{v} (see below, p. 235).

30 For the preaching campaign of 1535 see Susan Wabuda, 'Bishop John Longland's mandate to his clergy, 1535', *The Library*, 6th series, 13 (1991), 255-60; and also Rex, *Henry VIII and the English Reformation* (above, n. 2), pp. 29-31 . For the 1536 Injunctions, see *Documents Illustrative of English Church History*, ed. by H. Gee & W. J. Hardy (London, 1896), pp. 269-74, esp. p. 270.

31 For the career of this minor reformer, see *A Reformation Rhetoric: Thomas Swynnerton's Tropes and Figures of Scripture*, ed. by Richard Rex (Cambridge, 1999), pp. 6-22.

32 Chapuys to Cardinal Granvelle, 10 Feb. 1536, *LP Henry VIII* x.283.

33 *LP Henry VIII* x.282.

34 See R. Pole, *Epistolarum Collectio* (Brixiae, 1744), I, no. 27, 440-9, at p. 444.

35 *Exhortation*, sigs. D5^{r} and D3^{r}.

36 London, BL, Cotton MS Titus B I, fol. 111^{r}.

37 Marillac to Montmorency, 6 July 1540, *LP Henry VIII* xv.848.

38 See Christopher Hill, *Antichrist in Seventeenth-Century England* (Oxford, 1971), pp. 1-40.

39 Richard Sampson, *In Priores Quinquaginta Psalmos Daviticos, familiaris explanatio* (London, 1539. STC 21679), sig. A2^{v}-A3^{r}.

40 *Obedience in Church and State*, ed. by Pierre Janelle (Cambridge, 1930), p. 157. I owe this insight into Gardiner's strategy to Mr C. D. C. Armstrong.

41 *Exposition and Declaration*, sig. A5^{r} (see below, p. 233).

42 *Forty-six Lives*, ed. by Wright, p. xxxi. The Machiavelli might alternatively have been sent in February 1539. The date is immaterial for the argument developed here, but I accept James Carley's argument for the earlier date, advanced in the article cited in the next note.

43 James P. Carley, '"Plutarch's" Life of Agesilaus: a Recently Located New Year's gift to Thomas Cromwell by Henry Parker, Lord Morley', in *Prestige, Authority and Power in Late Medieval Manuscripts and Texts*, ed. by F. Riddy (York, 2000).

44 *Forty-six Lives*, ed. by Wright, p. 166. This gift was probably presented to Henry VIII in his last years, some time between New Year 1544 and New Year 1546.

45 For Philip's royal title and his marriage to Mary on 25 July 1554, see David Loades, *Mary Tudor: a life* (Oxford, 1989), pp. 223-6.

46 Loades, *Mary Tudor*, p. 260.

47 *Miracles of the Sacrament*, fol. 10^{r-v} (see below, p. 258).

48 See Carley, 'The Writings of Henry Parker, Lord Morley', above, p. 45.

49 *Forty-six Lives*, ed. by Wright, pp. 174-5. Morley gave a similar excuse for the translation of a couple of Seneca's epistles which he dedicated to her (see below, p. 247).

50 *Miracles of the Sacrament*, fol. 20^{v} (see below, p. 263).

51 *Exposition and Declaration*, sig. $B6^{r}$ (see below, p. 236).

52 See the excerpt from Morley's letter to Wolsey printed in *Forty-six Lives*, ed. by Wright, p. xvii.

53 See Rex, 'The crisis of obedience: God's Word and Henry's Reformation', *Historical Journal* 39 (1996), 863-94, at p. 880, on the decision by Henry VIII's council to change the official appellation of the pope to 'Bishop of Rome' in December 1533.

54 *Miracles of the Sacrament*, fol. 8^{r} (see below, p. 257).

55 *Exposition and Declaration*, sig. $A7^{v}$ (see below, p. 234).

56 *Forty-six Lives*, ed. by Wright, p. 178.

57 Rex, *Henry VIII and the English Reformation* (above, n. 2), pp. 31-6.

58 J.-P. Moreau, *Rome ou l'Angleterre? Les réactions politiques des catholiques au moment du schisme, 1529-1553*, Publications de l'Université de Poitiers, Lettres et sciences humaines, 22 (Paris, 1984), p. 144. The 'pragmatic' nature of Gardiner's attachment to Rome (nonetheless genuine for all its pragmatism) is also noted by Glyn Redworth, *In Defence of the Church Catholic: the Life of Stephen Gardiner* (Oxford, 1990), p. 321, who there refers in his turn to the similar views of J. A. Muller, *Stephen Gardiner and the Tudor Reaction* (London, 1926), pp. 234-5 and 300 and R. H. Pogson, 'The legacy of schism: confusion, continuity, and change in the Marian clergy', in *The Mid-Tudor Polity, c. 1540-1560*, ed. by J. Loach & R. Tittler (London, 1980), pp. 116-36, at p. 119.

59 *Miracles of the Sacrament*, fols 9^{r}-10^{r} (see below, pp. 257-8). See also fol. 23^{r} for a reference to Henry as 'the worthy prynce your father'.

60 *Miracles of the Sacrament*, fol. 7^{r-v} (see below, p. 257).

61 *Miracles of the Sacrament*, fols 19^{v}-20^{r} (see below, pp. 262-3).

62 *Forty-six Lives*, ed. by Wright, p. 186. This text is unquestionably Protestant. It is almost inconceivable that it could have been written by anybody who did not personally adhere to the doctrine of justification by faith alone and to its theological corollary, certainty of being in a state of grace.

63 Carley, 'The Writings of Henry Parker, Lord Morley', above, p. 38.

64 See Carley, 'The Writings of Henry Parker, Lord Morley', above, p. 30 n. 11.

65 *Journals of the House of Lords* (n.p, n.d.), I, 331, 343, and 384. Morley was extremely assiduous in his attendance at the House of Lords. The journals of this period record dissent from bills, but neither the number of votes in favour nor the number of abstentions.

66 *Journals of the House of Lords*, I, 409, 416-18, and 421.

67 *Journals of the House of Lords*, I, 432-8 for his few appearances in the last Parliament of Edward VI, and p. 456 for a token appearance under Mary.

68 *Forty-six Lives*, ed. by Wright, p. 169.

69 For Henry's Psalter see Tudor-Craig, 'Henry VIII and King David' (above, n. 22), pp. 193-6.

70 For Fisher and Erasmus, see above, n. 21. Fisher was virtually Henry's chief theological adviser until the divorce controversy ruined their relationship. Longland was Henry's confessor from around 1520. And Sampson was Dean of the Chapel Royal from 1522 until 1540 (*ex inf.* Fiona Kisby: see her dissertation on 'The Royal Household Chapel in Early Tudor London', London Ph.D. 1996, Appendix 1). Sampson's commentary (see above, n. 38) is dedicated to Henry. In addition, Richard Taverner dedicated to Henry his translation of Wolfgang Capito's *Epitome of the Psalmes or Briefe Meditations* (London, 1539; STC 23709). As Taverner was in the king's personal service (see McConica, *English Humanists* (above, n. 19), p. 183), this effort may also have been at royal command. Alexander Alesius

had dedicated a new Latin translation and exposition of the first 25 Psalms to Henry VIII in 1536, but it is unclear whether the gift ever reached its intended recipient. For an edition of this text see Gotthelf Wiedermann, *Der Reformator Alexander Alesius als Ausleger der Psalmen. Dissertation* (Erlangen, 1988), at pp. 141-246.

71 *Forty-six Lives*, ed. by Wright, p. 172.

72 Prologue to the translation of Erasmus (*Forty-six Lives*, ed. by Wright, p. 171). Compare the prologue to the translation of Aquinas and Anselm (*Forty-six Lives*, ed. by Wright, p. 173): 'only to thinke of the Virgin that she ys the mother of God excedis all height that, nexte God, maye be thought or spoken'.

73 *Forty-six Lives*, ed. by Wright, p. 171.

74 From the preface to Masuccio (*Forty-six Lives*, ed. by Wright, p. 166).

75 *Miracles of the Sacrament*, fol. 11^{r} (see below, p. 258).

76 See Duffy, *Stripping of the Altars* (above, n. 3), pp. 95-100, for popular beliefs and practices regarding the elevation of the consecrated host; and pp. 101-7 for eucharistic miracles. Miri Rubin, *Corpus Christi: the Eucharist in Late Medieval Culture* (Cambridge, 1991) is the authoritative account of eucharistic piety as a whole. G. J. C. Snoek, *Medieval Piety from Relics to the Eucharist: a Process of Mutual Interaction*, Studies in the History of Christian Thought, 63 (Leiden, 1995), presents a full and fascinating account of the consecrated host as apotropaic and thaumaturgic relic. The wide appeal of such stories (and the relative poverty of Morley's collection) can be seen from, for example, Raymond of Capua's *The Life of St Catherine of Siena*, trans. by G. Lamb (London, 1960), which records two eucharistic miracles in the life of that saint (pp. 284-91).

77 See *Knighton's Chronicle*, ed. & trans. by G. N. Martin (Oxford, 1995), pp. 260-3.

78 Thomas Netter of Walden, *Doctrinale Fidei Catholicae*, 3 vols (Venice, 1757-9; facsim. Farnborough, 1967), II, 386-7. Roger Dymmok also invokes the testimony of eucharistic miracles against the Lollards. See *Rogeri Dymmok Liber contra XII errores et hereses Lollardorum*, ed. by H. S. Cronin (Oxford, 1922), pp. 99 and 110.

79 Rubin, *Corpus Christi*, pp. 108-29, discusses the medieval use of host miracles to teach eucharistic doctrine, tracing this as far back as Paschasius Radbert. Rubin also presents a fascinating sample of such miracle stories, which again shows up the paucity of Morley's collection. See K. P. Luria, *Territories of Grace: Cultural Change in the Seventeenth-Century Diocese of Grenoble*, Studies on the History of Society and Culture, 11 (Berkeley & Oxford, 1991), p. 134, for the abiding significance of eucharistic miracles in Counter-Reformation doctrine and devotion.

80 For examples and discussion of ritual desecration of the host, see R. W. Scribner, 'Ritual and Reformation', in his *Popular Culture and Popular Movements in Reformation Germany* (London, 1987), pp. 103-22, at pp. 110-14; see also his comment in 'Reformation, carnival and the world turned upside-down' (ibid., pp. 71-101) that profanation of the host represents the converse of host miracles (p. 96); and see also N. Z. Davis, 'The rites of violence', in her *Society and Culture in Early Modern France* (London, 1975), pp. 152-87, at pp. 156-8, 171, and 179-81.

81 Morley, if I am correct, would have been using one of the 1527 editions of the *De Veritate*, but for modern readers it is more convenient to consult John Fisher, *Opera Omnia* (Würzburg, 1597; facsim. ed. by Gregg Press, 1967), pp. 921-3.

82 For the details of the sources discussed in this paragraph, see the edition (below, Appendix 7) of the *Miracles of the Sacrament*, fols 11^{v}-19^{r} (pp. 259-62), and the relevant notes.

83 For which see Duffy, *Stripping of the Altars*, pp. 102-5.

84 Duffy, *Stripping of the Altars*, pp. 278-98.

WHAT DID MORLEY GIVE WHEN HE GAVE A 'PLUTARCH' *LIFE*?

JEREMY MAULE

If in Arthur of Britain, Huon of Bordeaux, and such supposed chivalry, a man may better himself, shall he not become excellent with conversing with Tacitus, Plutarch, Sallust and fellows of that rank?

William Cornwallis, *Essayes*, 'Of the Observation of Things'

WHAT I TELL YOU THREE TIMES IS TRUE: Morley's gifts of 'Plutarch' lives in translation amount to a practice sufficiently repetitive to be interesting. Three such donatives survive among his gifts to King Henry VIII, and one to his chief minister, with unremittingly upward glances at Henry still. In this quality his Plutarch *Lives* resemble Morley's more theologically directed gifts to Henry's daughter, Mary, which he specifically recognized as having sufficiently common features to make the odd exception worth remarking upon.[1] To King Henry, Morley dedicated *Lives* of Scipio and Hannibal (before 1535), of Paulus Aemilius, and of Theseus (both the latter after 1541); and (at one remove, to his chief minister Cromwell) a *Life* of Agesilaus that invoked quite specifically 'comparcuyon of oure most dere and gratyous soverayne lord kyng' with the Spartan king whose biography it presented. The purpose of this paper is to explore the nature of the truths that such an 'excellente clerke' as Plutarch could be seen to offer, as the work was selected for treatment and passed from the hand of its noble translator to or towards his monarch.

These lives take their place, of course, in a wider spectrum of Morley's gift-giving and of his advices. Like much in that range of writing they are seen through the veil of translation, and their explicitudes, when they come, shelter behind the walls of commentary or of commendation. But it seems clear that all the doctrine thus obliquely directed was chosen by Morley for a sense of its 'excellent' qualities – he is fond of the word, and repeats it often – and that this excellence was one that his own taste (more restrained than Lord Berners's, perhaps,[2] though rangy enough) took to exclude the 'mery jeste', or the 'tale prynted of Robyn Hoode, or some other dongehyll matter'.[3] It was a taste in which the noble and the 'renomyde' found space to negotiate with the 'morall', the 'storyall' and the 'clerckely', and it found a way of facing rulers by asking them to face up to others of their kind.

Yet in the literature which enabled him to do so, Morley had other writer-ruler relationships in front of his eyes, relationships that threatened to bring the mind 'out of quyate'. He knew what Seneca said – and he knew what happened to Seneca. The examples of other vicious emperors – Commodus, Heliogabalus – stood over against the simpler panegyrical mode that he might seek to co-opt from Claudian, when addressing Queen Mary. There is a danger to the modern critic reviewing Morley's *Lives* (in reviewing *any* life-writing presented to Henry VIII) in reaching too quickly for applications too easily allegorical of Henry's reign and its turbulent politics. McConica's verdict, for example, that Morley's body of translation 'forms a running commentary on the momentous events of the day' looks too uncautious, because too easily *current*.[4] The graver policy of Morley's life-writing tends rather, as in his 'Prolog' to the Life of Paulus Aemilius, to offer an Aristotelean 'meane' as 'the best part'.[5] Henrician narratives that enjoy hindsight, as Steven Gunn has recently cautioned, 'often tend to the factional explanation',[6] and the same is as true of later Tudor historiography, which often capitulates too easily to an urge to discover historical allegory, quickly reaching for applications and interpretations predominantly hindward in cast. Sometimes, it is true, such allegories seem unavoidable, as with the bitter force of Surrey's great anti-Henrician sonnet on the luxury and cowardice of Sardanapalus, 'Th'Assyryan kinge'. But to read Morley's *Lives* demands a more cautious hermeneutic. Their application, if one were wished, lay safely in the future, in the moulding and improving prolepsis of *example*. The moralism of humanist pedagogy – even at its most panegyrical – is often guarded. That is not to say that Morley did not imagine his *Lives* might have their use: it is rather to insist, with him, that such use was still to come.

Yet for all these difficulties, there are perspectives and considerations that do seem to shed light on Morley's giving of a 'Plutarch' life. The initial choice of subject; the rhetoric of exemplarity and of explicit comparison; the occasional sense of difficulties in reading ancient histories; the tendency to extrapolate from the various incidents of lives not always self-consistent a dominant or even a single virtue: all these are manoeuvres that appear more than once in Morley's *Lives*. I shall try in this essay by a number of routes to recover the nature, the weight of Morley's presented biographies. The main example considered is the pair of lives twinned and compared in London, British Library, Royal MS 17 D.XI, *The Lives of Scipio and Haniball* (hereafter R), which seems to have been one of the first of such gift-biography-translations. What forms of living do these *Lives* inculcate? And what type of giving do they represent? I review in turn some of the ways in which these lives of Scipio and Hannibal were received in the century or so from their first appearance in humanist print; something of the particular appeal of the two great generals to the Renaissance reader and artist; and (more speculatively) some of the contexts to which Morley's own choice of the *Lives* may have spoken, and the morals that he points in the practices of his own translation. But first I consider what weight the name of 'Plutarch' brought to Morley's choice of source-text and what extra textual freight it carried in the sixteenth century.

CAPACIOUS PLUTARCH

All the model lives that Morley chose to point at Henry as 'lawdabyll', as 'none in my simple opinion that more owght to be noted' and the like, come on as the work of Plutarch; though as it happens, two of his four choices were the work of other authors. All came through the relatively new medium of print, and, as Morley is careful to explain in his prefaces, through the filter of Latin: Plutarch (and Xenophon, the real author of the Agesilaus) had written in Greek (he is 'the great clerke and Grecian', 'the excellent Grecian'), but '*Plutarchi vitae*' is the book from which Morley works. That work was at its *largest* in the century after 1470, and also at its most eclectic. The story behind Morley's 'all the lyves of the nobyll Romayns and Gresyans' is complicated, but is worth recovering before we consider his use of them.

Plutarch's works had been lost to the medieval world. His *Lives* were recuperated into epitome in the fourteenth century, and a series of spirited attempts to recover and expand the Greek manuscript tradition followed in the 1390s (Salutati's correspondence with Chrysoloras gives the passionate flavour of this interest). Finally, in the humanist circles around Leonardo Bruni before 1444 and Guarino thereafter, the collaborative work of rendering the strong exemplary and moral appeal, the experiential wisdom, of the *Lives* began its large task.[7] There were 50 lives in the Greek manuscripts: 22 pairs (one a double, where two Spartan kings match the two Gracchi), and four singles. The contents of the Strassburg edition (*c.* 1473-5) give a good idea of the collaborative flavour: at least thirty-six years' work goes into the collection. The unity of the enterprise should not be exaggerated, however. Textual access to crucial manuscripts remained haphazard, and other Latin translations ran alongside the ones finally printed.[8]

In addition to those lives now gradually gathered and rendered, Plutarch was known from ancient authors to have written at least twelve others. Of these, the most disastrous loss from antiquity was that of Scipio: Scipio Africanus, esteemed by Plutarch the greatest man Rome had produced, was to have been matched with Epaminondas, the greatest man of Greece. No trace of either Life survived, however, and to supply this loss the man who had already translated into Italian Bruni's Latin narrative of the Florentine people from the beginnings down to 1404 on the instruction of the *Signoria* set to work. His name was Donato Acciaiuoli, and the flavour of his civic humanism has become known through the masterful account of Eugenio Garin.[9]

How Acciaiuoli's supplement ever came actually to be mistaken for Plutarch is at first sight hard to conceive. The text itself makes no such pretensions. For one thing, Hannibal was Simply Not Greek – and hence no proper topic for a parallel in the famous series of Greeks and Romans. However, the order of that pairing had turned tail in the fifteenth century, and the switch of emphasis from Plutarch's determined fronting of Greeks to the Italian humanists's reordering of the manuscripts in order to privilege the Latin (hence Morley's 'Romayns and Gresyans') perhaps goes some way to explain it. If Scipio leads, rather than Epaminondas, it's easier to see why one might reach for Hannibal.

Acciaiuoli's working practice as an historian is also visibly different from Plutarch's own, particularly with respect to his source-texts. Some the Florentine silently assimilates, until whole clauses of Livy cut and pasted start to show. Yet at the same time he is a much more anxious citer, parading *auctores* with at least intermittent care, and offering the occasional dab at discrimination between them: as Morley translates (R, fol. 22^{r}),

> This acte I finde not among the Auncyent writers but in Trogus / which remembrith it | Lett the reader give credence therto as it lyketh him.

Several of these citations contain explicit references to sources dating well after Plutarch's own time of writing (as here to Justin's compilation of Trogus) as well as one to Plutarch's own life of one of the Gracchi. Plutarch's methods (even if reliance on the unmanageable scroll tended to lead him to base most of a section on a single source) show a much sharper sense of the range of evidence and a subtler set of criteria for discrimination between conflicting reports.[10] Acciaiuoli, by contrast, cites sources rather doggedly (Livy, Polybius, and 'Emilius' the author of the Augustan *De viris illustribus* usually attributed to Nepos, for example), though he can be a careful reporter of different traditions (as of the circumstances of Scipio's exile). The nearest Acciaiuoli comes to Plutarch, perhaps, is to the simpler manner of his moralism, in the closing 'Comparisons' between paired *Lives*.[11] But neither Acciaiuoli's style (already reported by the time of Erasmus' *Anti-Ciceronianus* as the subject of rather picky philological comment) nor the relative crudity of his moralized politics could long have deceived a careful reader of Plutarch.

Nor is there any evidence that Acciaiuoli wished to do so. He himself knew the real Lives of Plutarch well enough: by May 1465 he had already translated the lives of Alcibiades and Demetrius, and completed a Life of Charlemagne.[12] He was certainly not faking Plutarch: he was simply undertaking his own life-writing by way of plugging a known gap, and an important one. If the result is, at some level, disappointing, it is because other humanist biographies written in response to Plutarch's lives had already, earlier in the fifteenth century, attempted a more emulous and engaged imitation of their original. Bruni, for example, had welded a Plutarchan sharpness of anecdote to the nuanced, characterizing power of Sallust to produce a memorable life of Cicero.[13] Acciaiuoli's Life of Scipio, though not without an ability for learned dilation (on the foundation of Capua, for example) and some challenging signs of original research,[14] nevertheless betrayed some errors of haste, in the copy overlooked by Ammannati in 1467. The first draft was finished by 26 February 1467, and a revised version by 5 November 1468.[15]

By now, print was to hand: the great project of bringing Plutarch home into Latin and rounding it out was ready for it. The *editio princeps*, prepared by Giannantonio Campano and printed by Ulrich Han (Rome ?1470-1, Goff P-830) has no titles. But Acciaiuoli's dedication of the Scipio-Hannibal to Piero de Medici includes the following explicit – one might have thought unmistakable – words: 'constitui animo duorum prestantissmorum ducum Scipionis et Anibalis gesta, quae ex uariis auctoribus tum Graecis tum Latinis collegeram, presenti uolumine complecti'. After that, however, the carelessness of print and perhaps the slow development of titles and apparatus in the incunable as a whole are really the explanation of a mounting confusion and vagueness as to the work's real authorship. The next edition was printed at Strassburg (*c.* 1473-5, Goff P-831). It still retained the preface, something the 1478 and 1491 Venetian editions (Goff P-832, P-833) were to abandon; but confusingly added a misleading incipit to the life of Scipio for the first time – an incipit which is also an explicit attribution of the work to Plutarch himself: 'Plutarci historiographici greci de vita atque gestis Scipionis Africani traducti in Latinum linguagium per Donatum Accaiuolum Incipit feliciter.' And this transpired while Acciaiuoli was still alive!

From there the course was set fair for a century's worth of the pleasant acceptance of 'Plutarch's' Scipio and Hannibal. This success can be read in a number of ways. Most simply, perhaps, it is a testimony to the slow development of certain features of print para-text, above all to the minimal presence of titularity. There is a way, too, in which the worthiness of the subjects themselves (it is one of the topics in both dialectical and rhetorical treatments of proof) may have effectively offered confirmation of authorship, *ex auctoritate ad auctorem*, so to speak. In a circular reinforcement, the simple greatness of the two opponents worked to 'confirm' Plutarchan authorship and

Plutarchan authority worked to confirm the way in which the 'twain noble captaines' (R, fol. 38^{v}), 'Thies two dukes' (R, fol. 40^{r}), were to be fitly lessoned.

COUNSELLING PLUTARCH

We have seen, then, how the humanist labour of gathering the Plutarch *vitae*, which often came to light in smaller manuscript groups, of translating them from Greek to Latin, and of rounding out their number by filling in the known gaps and adding other great figures (from Homer to Charlemagne) was completed virtually at the same moment that printing began in the West. As a result of this coincidence, Plutarch's *fortuna* was ready for a spectacular new phase. But it should not be assumed that the phase would necessarily be a further episode in a triumphantly progressive history of humanist scholarship. More than the culture-gap of England and Italy measures the distance between the learned diligence of the republican Acciaiuoli and the prince-pleasing efforts of the English baron: the story of the texts that they share is on almost any view incapable of being presented as a narrative of cultural progression. The hard work of humanist philology may have brought Plutarch's biographies back into attention and freshly into Latin; but it was incapable of policing the canonicities of its own enthusiasm. The efforts involved in gathering Plutarch, in completing him (in filling the missing comparisons, supplying the Scipio he was known to have written) inevitably led on to an effort at supplement. In such generous aggregations, quickly multiplied by print, and further diffused into the various vernaculars, the stricter scholarly notion of an 'authentic Plutarch' was bound, for a while at least, to be submerged.

The role of print, then, is here best understood as a step-change in the speed at which errors could be propagated. It provides the defining moment for that small invention of tradition which gave a hundred years of textual life to 'Plutarch's' *Lives* of Scipio and Hannibal. One does not suppose that the serious scholars were ever much deceived as to the authorship of the work. The book in which they appeared might include other lives than Plutarch's, other lives even than those Plutarch was known (as in the case of Scipio Africanus, though not of Hannibal) at least to have written once, even if they were lost: but did anyone ever suppose they were reading Plutarch's *Life* of Homer or Virgil – or Charlemagne? Though the first two of these examples might still be read as offering the possibility of a Plutarchan parallel in the literary sphere, all these last three lives are part of a group firmly blocked off by white space at the end of the long list of contents in the early print folios of the *Lives*. But Scipio and Hannibal, more confusingly, sit in the middle of the main run of authentic *Lives*, sandwiched between the pairs of Pelopidas/Marcellus and Philopoemen/Quintus Flaminius; and, as we have seen, their own *incipits* unblushingly assign their authorship to Plutarch. So for a century or so after 1478, the lives of these two great generals travelled in Latin – and thence into Spanish, French, and English vernaculars – as Plutarch's work. The best of commanders by the best of biographers is a pleasing recipe in any market; and for Acciaiuoli, at least, Scipio stood not only for military success, but as a supreme example of a ruler's care for the state: 'nihil ... in hac vita preclarius, nihil excellentius, nihil sanctius quam in administranda republica patrie sue pietatem officiumque prestare'.

Not all readers of these new Lives, however, were ready to travel so optimistically, or so anachronistically, in the slipstream of such exemplary greatness. If Morley were really the 'eminently Erasmian personality' of McConica's portrait,[16] the uncomplicated willingness to urge the example of a Scipio or (more cautiously) of a Hannibal on his 'most Crysten kynge' might look like a sad dereliction from Erasmian duty. 'Hic quem legis', Erasmus had warned the Christian prince at whom his own *Institutio* was directed in 1516, 'ethnicus est; tu qui legis Christianus'.[17] But this careful Christian discrimination is likely to have detained neither Morley nor his monarch. As Robert Aulotte, the great scholar of the *Moralia*'s after-life in Renaissance France, has remarked, in this 'exceptionelle et quasi universelle floraison' of Plutarch it was exactly the timelessness that appealed, the claim to offer an 'identité fondamentale de la nature humaine', to discover 'l'homme rattaché à l'homme dans l'infini du temps et la diversité des époques'.[18] This enlarged encyclopaedia of human greatness and human error, then, is the work from which Morley draws out his smaller draughts of 'princes and conquerours', of rulers and generals in action and policy, and draws them 'in to ouer maternall tongue'. It will not have worried him that the 'boke intytelyd *Plutarchi vitae*', as he calls it in the Paulus Aemilius preface, carried more in it than was strictly Plutarch's, any more than 'Cicero's *ad Herennium*' or 'Seneca's *Octavia*' or epistles to St Paul might have worried him. Such big names then simply carried more baggage than is now allowed them: Plutarch was more largely, but not differently, imagined as a result. As far as Morley was concerned, each of his four New Year's gifts might fairly claim to be 'wretten', as his Cromwell dedication puts it, 'by the Famus clerke Plutarke in the greke tounge and traunslatyd out of Greke into Latyn and drawen out off Latyn into Englysche by me'.[19]

How humanist, in any case, should we want Morley to be? If we decline to press home the errors of Morley's 'Plutarch' ascription, and look instead at what is more typical of his *Lives* as a small gift manuscript of Plutarch, and particularly of 'counselling' Plutarch as an appropriate text for a ruler, the picture is both less barbarous and more continuous. For while the confusions of paratext and the cursory informations of the early printed editions of the Latin translations of the *Lives* were probably to blame for Morley's errors of ascription,[20] it is also worth stressing how much in keeping Morley's manuscript gift Plutarchs lay with the typical 'Plutarch' manuscript of the century or so before his own. As Pfeiffer's lists make clear, few of the Greek manuscripts of *Lives* circulating in the humanist period agreed in their contents, and an editorial grasp of the divergent recensions of the three 'books' in which the *Lives* travelled was to emerge only gradually. Moreover, few contained the majority of Plutarch's parallels: 10, 13, 15, 8, 6, or even 2 were the more typical contents of a Plutarch *Lives* manuscript.[21] In this respect, Morley's pairs and singles resemble more closely the manuscripts in which their source-texts travelled than they do the compendious editions so laboriously put together across three generations of Greek-teaching in fifteenth century Venice and Florence, or the early printings at Venice and Frankfurt. These early printed 'complete' *Vitae* gave that slow assembly by the humanists (almost half a century in the making) immediately wider transmission, virtually at the moment of its completion. Yet it is in similar selections from those lives for the smaller scale of dedicatory gift-work (so similar, in Bourgouyn's case, as to invite further enquiry) that Plutarchan biography typically continues to show at

French, Hapsburg and Hungarian courts throughout the fifteenth and sixteenth centuries.

Both the size and shape, then, of Morley's little *Lives* bespeak a continuity of practice hardly interrupted, even though textually funded, by the invention of printing. What is also striking is their relative plainness, unillustrated by any of the attractive and luxurious illuminations that can be found in the Milanese Plutarch manuscript described by Charles Mitchell, for example, where SPQR swirling on a pennant is the only Roman touch in a fine field of Late International Gothic plate-armour.[22] The Morley manuscripts are neat but drab; only an infrequent penwork initial offers an attempt at decoration, and even the scribe's competence as a copyist is moderate at best.[23]

Nevertheless, Morley's 'Plutarchs' offer a small witness to the larger phenomenon of vernacular humanism – that is, 'the translation and adaptation of classical works for the entertainment and instruction of noble and unprofessional readers'.[24] In this company, their classicism, such as it is, is an unexclusive affair, and the measure of this accommodation is embedded from the start in vocabulary-choices. One of its opening decisions, to translate *miles* as 'knight', sits comfortably (and probably unconsciously, though the point had been debated as early as the 1440s, between Leonardo Bruni and Alfonso de Cartagena)[25] with other more traditional narratives of the chivalric virtues. Thus the young Hannibal (R, fol. 4^r) sets to to learn 'the feates of warr' and accustom himself to 'knightly pointes', as does the young Scipio 'in all other knightly paines taking' (R, fol. 24^r) before an opportunity arises to exhibit his 'great minde to prove the Fortune of the bataile' (R, fol. 19^v). And Scipio's father and uncle, as they 'lefte greate ensample of Faith and temperaunce to their knightes that lyved' (R, fol. 24^r), move similarly away from Acciaiuoli's own republican register.

Considered technically, Morley's translation is less fluent at finding the English in which to meet and match Latin syntax than it is in working its lexical cross-overs towards a more chivalric idiom. At a number of points, Morley's gift-translation looks syntactically challenged: one spots the shifts of gear, for example, as the requirements of an ablative absolute strike him just too late in the sentence. One misconstrual just gives up the unequal struggle and rests in the following garble:

> But Scipio well amendid as of the untrue fame of his dethe was rore and busines in the [word missing *and gap left*]
> So that of the knowlege of his sure amendment thei were all aferde. [R, fol. 28^r]

If, as Morley's preface claimed, 'the storye in Latten be not to your Maiestie un-knowen', one might imagine Henry reaching testily for the source-text at this point. But the *Lives*' lexicon would have met with readier recognition, as it moved freely between various registers of the court. Morley responds as readily as Wyatt did in 1527, garnishing another Plutarch New Year's gift-translation, to contemporary taste for the proverb: 'So moche often tymes the fury of men for ambicion sterith them to unhappinesse.'[26] Elsewhere he tilts easily towards a more modern courtierspeak, exhibiting Hannibal's wily attempts to deploy the 'signe manuell' captured from the dead body of Marcellus to deceptive effect. And when the action shifts in exile to Asia Minor and the court of Antiochus (R, fols 20^v-23^v), it is hard to separate Morley's vocabulary, which dwells at length on the difficulties of counsel and the 'envy which ever Raignes in grete princes houses' (R, fol. 20^{v}), from that, say, of Sir Francis Bryan translating Guevara's dispraises of the courtier's life. Talking too long to the wrong ambassador (the sort of peril for which David Starkey's lively portraits of Henry's court have taught us to read alertly) is clearly a danger with which Morley can empathise:

wherby his enemyes founde occacion to bacbite him / so that suche suspeccion was had towardes him / that he was clene excluded oute from the princes councell. (R, fol. 21^{r})

What, then, were the lessons such an enlarged Plutarch could offer? As points of general policy in the conduct of war, Morley's translation can hardly be distinguished from the sort of advice on 'The tyme devised convenable to move werre' embedded in mediaeval war-histories translated for Henry and his leading nobles in the 1515-25 years as incitations to a new Crusade. Works like Richard Pynson's *A Lytell Cronycle* (*c.* 1520), dedicated to Edward, Duke of Buckingham, or BL, Royal MS 18 B.XXVI, a unified royal manuscript-set of such histories including the same Hetoum work, now titled *The floure of Histories of the Est*,[27] with their sharp eye for the advantage of ground, the knowledge of one's enemies, or the campaigns that collapse for 'dis-purviaunces' (failures in infrastructure), are not such distant cousins as might first appear to Morley's men of war. Morley's reports of Hannibal's campaign intelligence, of the fierce winter as it struck north African armies 'inclosed in highe hills of the Alps and Apenyne' (R, fol. 8^{v}), or of a battle fought 'so fiersly thre howres that at that tyme being a greate erthquake it was not harde of neither parte' (R, fol. 10^{r}) all speak the same language.

For all that, though, the focus is different. Morley is still within recognizable proximity to the traditional vocabularies of chivalry (so, later, is William Master's 1555 translation of the same Scipio life, now retitled *The ymage of honour and chevalry*). But that language does not wholly occlude a note that is, if faintly, still recognizably more interested in a less feudal and more secular version of character-analysis. The cautious ambition of Morley's Plutarchan lives finds its own place between the range of two commonplaces, both later picked up for expansion by Bacon's essays: *laudando praecipuere* (by praising to instruct, 'Of Praise') and *optimi consilarii mortui* (dead men are the best counsellors, 'Of Counsell'). Among these counselling dead, Plutarch's name, with Cicero's and Seneca's, is that most often found in the first centuries of the Renaissance. It was Plutarch, for example, whom Montaigne mentioned by name 68 times and quoted from more often (398 allegings) than any other author. Nor was the weight of such testimonies necessarily pitched against innovation: it was from Plutarch's own quotations that Copernicus first learnt that ancient authors had been prepared to contemplate a heliocentric cosmos, and (as the holograph of *de Revolutionibus* clearly shows) drew strength to imagine that the world might not be earth-centred. In the epigraph to this essay, it is the 'modern' history of Tacitus or Sallust, joined with the politic wisdom and the composite experience of Plutarch's moral essays and biographies, that Cornwallis contrasts with advantage to the simpler-minded mythic chivalry of popular English romance reading. They might stand, sixty years later than Morley's first Plutarch gift, or Berners' *Huon* or Froissart, for a choice between styles that still confronted the English monarch, when counselled by histories. As Morley's later tilt at Robin Hood suggests, the moral weight of the *auctor* was important for him: the preface to the *Theseus Life* is pitched carefully against the hypothetical objections of 'one who wolde saye that the wrighters of storis [stroris in MS] were but meane parsons and soche as that only for luker wrote that whiche was often fals and untru'. Morley retorts by pointing to real authors, real warriors, real governors: the Julius Caesar of 'Commentaris', Augustus, 'the great Turkes brother'.[28]

Plutarch was not quite in that league as a ruler, though the Suidas lexicon recorded a tradition in which he served as a consul.[29] But his Renaissance Englishers properly insist on his practical experience: for William Master 'Plutarchus' is 'himself as noble a Governour as an excellent learned man and grave Philosopher'.[30] When we come to examine the impact of Plutarch as he was Englished or as his writings lent weight to original English vernacular writings of the sixteenth century, the predominant effect is unmistakably preceptive and consiliar. By the time of Morley's death in 1556, neither of the great Plutarchan collections, the *Vitae Parallelae* or the *Moralia*, had achieved complete translation into English: those tasks were still in store for Thomas North (1579) and Philemon Holland (1600), respectively. The former work was still best known either in epitome or in the composite Latin versions that had reached England from the Venice[31] or Frankfurt presses; the latter collection, as often as not through the medium of Erasmus's Latin, had more quickly begun to press home its lessons on the English, as on the French, scene. The 'excellente clerke and grate philosopher Plutarche', in the words of Hales's 1543 title-page of the *De tuenda sanitate precepta*,[32] was a man one looked to above all for 'ethic and practic' instruction: for the 'governaunce of good helthe', for the 'benefit' to be gotten from reining wrath or considering one's enemies, as a 'president for parentes' in the education of children.[33] These were lessons to be repeated and recontextualized: no surprise that More's Utopians turn out to be very fond of Plutarch.[34] An earlier gift to the monarch (now Cambridge, University Library, Add. MS 6858) from More's friend, the greatest of the modern clerks, had found Erasmus selecting Plutarch's 'How to tell a flatterer from a friend' for presentation and counsel.[35] All these Englishings of Plutarch (some by language, some simply by destined reader) correspond closely to the pragmatic picture of northern Renaissance vernacular humanism recently sketched by Warren Boutcher, with a strong, not to say obvious, emphasis on 'effective/affective conduct' and a concern for the 'private-and-public spaces of court and household politics'.[36]

It was partly in the company and the mind-set of this instructing 'governaunce'[37] that Morley's *'Plutarch' Lives*, too, were to be numbered; but with important differences. His versions were in manuscript not print;[38] and their lessons – though at times they dared hardly call themselves that – were to be learnt at the first remove of a life, or pair of lives, considered, rather than in rules more explicitly and abstractly drawn from the *Moralia*. Nor did Morley suggest that the lives were always easy to 'reduce in to Inglishe'. The *Theseus Life*, in particular, he complained, was 'very obscurely by him sett forthe'. In practice, unfamiliar features of Roman proper names often baffle both scribe[39] and translator: Morley has a particular predilection for leaving place-names in their accusatives (Cannas, Trasimenum, and so on). Nevertheless, for all his professed humilities as a translator,[40] his lives were ostensibly aimed, both by occasion and direction, not at more general didactic purposes, but at one man, one monarch. But did he need them? If Henry – as is stated in the preface to the 'Life of Paulus', Aemilius – *already* 'hathe shewed in the ruling of your mighty empiris suche moderasyon, clemens, pyte and marshall justes that ye may well be compared ... to eny other Gresyan or

Romayn, of what state or dignitie so ever they have been before this daye', what is left to be learnt? The contortion involved in still persisting towards a moral, in bending such lives beyond their own announced redundancy into the rhetoric of exemplarity, is perhaps less artless than appears. It leaves a space for an implied reader who is *not* Henry – or perhaps for a Henry who is not the Henry of these prologues and prefaces:

> Who then he be that doth not knowe what the meane is in soche a case, let him loke uppon the lyfe of this nobyll Romayne Paulus Emilius, and there shall he se as in a glas or myerour the parfect, suer waye howe to govern him with reason in all kynde of prosperite or adversite.

FIERCE AND MILD: LIVES FOR GOVERNORS

Hannibal and Scipio Africanus, the twinned commanders ('Emperours' is his preferred term) that Morley drew from Acciaiuoli (or Plutarch, as he thought) are considered in his text in various aspects. What lessons did he seek to elicit from their lives and deaths? Three sites need inspection: the preface to Henry (Morley's own work), the evident moralizing of *The comparing together* of the heroes that brings the manuscript to a close (R, fols 38^{v}-40^{r}: here the source is Acciaiuoli), and such embedded virtues as the *vitae* themselves choose to bring forward, and from time to time, to moralize. The three are not fundamentally at odds, though the last, inevitably as the longest, offers best hope of light and shade. Each, though, also bears comparison with other, competing versions of the Scipio and Hannibal story in the years during which Morley was working on his lives.

The preface paints the crudest contrast, between the 'gentle Scipio and the fierse Affrican Haniball' (R, fol. 3^{r}). For Morley, the lesson to be learned (the lesson, at least, as mini-packaged in the dedication) is that of a single virtue. His Scipio has many 'giftes of nature', both of body and mind, and to them he adds 'meny vertues', but the greatest of these ('specially that singuler vertue', 'this delectable vertue') is 'mekeness'. Henry, too, is 'gentle and gracious', 'good and gracyous'. Like the king of Persia, pleased with the simplest soldier's gift of water, cupped in the hands, Morley's Henry is said to be 'by his humanitie well pleased with all', even with 'me unworthie'. It's worth recalling in this context how successful such an abjection of the author/translator as royal subject might be. If the contents of this volume as a whole point, by and large, to Morley's limited success by the rising standards of secular Tudor careerism – his failure to win great office or to enrich his family notably by the spoils of the Reformation might be offset against the older yardstick of success in family alliances – yet there is a simpler criterion, survival, by which he might well be judged to have succeeded. One remarkable feature of Morley's record is well picked up by Helen Miller, in her study of Henry VIII and the English nobility: he is the *only* English peer to have done reliable service in all six treason trials of the reign.[41] (Perhaps one can be too successful, though, in keeping one's head down? That neither Alistair Fox's lengthy *Politics and Literature in the Reigns of Henry VII and Henry VIII* (1989) nor Elizabeth Heale's more recent survey *Wyatt, Surrey and Early Tudor Poetry* (1998) has a single entry under 'Parker' or 'Morley' is, in its way, a striking testimony to Morley's 'mekeness'.)

That Scipio is the preferred model of the pairing, Acciaiuoli leaves in no doubt either. When Morley writes at the start of the Scipio life (R, fol. 24^{r}) that 'his vertuous actes shoulde be our teching', he neither adds to nor takes away from his source in Acciaiuoli. Elsewhere in the correspondence, Acciaiuoli elevates Scipio above Caesar as the worthier governor ('quantum enim Scipio Romane libertati consuluerit').[42] Morley's *Life* of Scipio takes all opportunities available to dwell on the affable in his hero, by small but steady acts of adjectival or syntactic preference. Victories are duly reported and praised, but over and above them the text salutes 'This and othere dedes of magnanimitie as well of spirite as of witte' (R, fol. 24^v^); Scipio's 'highe Liberalitie' and 'singuler gentleness' (R, fol. 26^r^) in the famous episode of the Continence; and his generosities 'no lesse liberall than valiaunt' to Massinissa's nephew. In each case any political or diplomatic explanation is subordinated (usually entirely out of view) to the ethic. The contrast seems particularly visible when the *Life* of Hannibal is briefly troubled by a baffling moment of apparently similar clemency. It falls after the rout at Lake Trasimene, when 56,000 Romans were put to the sword; Hannibal, pointedly enough one might have thought, lets the other Italian troops go. The episode calls out an interestingly imbalanced effort from the biographer to resist the imputation of virtue: Hannibal, it is explained, must have acted in this way

> to gett him therby glory and Fame / among theim / to be called meke and liberall which he was farr fromm / for he was of nature cruell and vengeable / as he that from his youthe had loved none humanytie / but batell and burning / and suche other mischiefes / So that he became not only cruell Duke / but also a captaine full of disceite and faldshode / wherby he greatly prevailed for thos that by force he coulde not wynne them he vanquesshed by crafte. (R, fol. 10^r^)

The blackening of character dilates into an irresistible, Mortonian victory of policy: there are moments when Morley's sheeplike charm seems troubled by dreams of Machiavelli. What is probably merely a scribal error at fol. 26^v^ encapsulates this worried meekness perfectly. 'For the ende,' the very sententious sentence reads, 'of [no gap] is victorye/ the fruyte wherof consisteth in liberalitie and clemencye.' Later on, in 1555, William Master will put it into his margin.

The missing word here is WAR, as the Latin makes plain. There are indeed occasionally great generals so modest that they are incapable of explaining their own victories, and by the time of the English Civil Wars, Scipio was used to model them. Thomas, Lord Fairfax's *Short Memorials* is a classic example of a text so strangely apologetic and unaggressive that its author's signal victories seem completely inexplicable. Philip Skippon, too, perhaps inevitably given his name, was another of these Parliamentary Scipios:

> For his great Heart did such a temper show,
> Stout as a rock, yet soft as melting Snow.[43]

But to most Renaissance readers, and certainly most Renaissance monarchs, it was clear enough what Scipio stood for, and Melting Clemency, or even the famed Continency, was not high on the list. Empire was. Scipio was a Worthy, and Worthies fought and won. In 1532, at much the same time as Morley's little *Lives*, Francis I commissioned, to designs by Giulio Romano, the *editio princeps* of *The Story of Scipio* in a magnificent set of twenty-two Brussels tapestries. Twelve were to show major events of the Second Punic War, from the battle of Ticinum to the decisive victory at Zama; the last ten were devoted to scenes of Scipio's triumph, culminating in 'The Banquet', in which victorious commanders were feted.[44] Scipios were still to be found, and cities are waiting to be sacked, such pieces say: Charles V's Tunisian campaign of 1535, culminating in the capture and sack of Tunis itself on 21 July of that year, was a striking case in point. Another set of tapestries inevitably followed, and the message of their cartouches could hardly be clearer: 'prosigue el emp[erad] su viaje e[n] africa'; 'PLUS OULTRE'.[45]

For all the careful softenings, then, of Morley's dedications, with their praises of clemency and 'moderasyon' and their careful peeps at 'both fortunis, that is to saye, the good and the yll fortune',[46] the 'helthe and victorye' that all his Plutarch dedications typically wish their king still need to be heard with something of a drumroll. If such martial music did not speak greatly to the tenor of Morley's own character, and belied to some extent his wish to live a long life as a tortoise of Senecan persuasion, they echoed nevertheless a style in which his monarch had long been accustomed to hear himself praised. The Great Westminster Tournament Roll, commemorating the most expensive tournament of the reign, ends by saluting Henry as a super-Scipio, a finisher and perfecter of the Nine Worthies:

> The noble nyne which was the worthyest
> To thy begynnyng was not comparabyll
> ...
> Why not thow the tenthe.[47]

Why not indeed? For Punic Wars, read Crusades. 'We gird ourselves for this most holy expedition', an excited Henry had responded to the 1519 appeal of Cardinal Campeggio;[48] and Glenn Burger's and Christopher Tyerman's accounts of early Tudor Crusading projects and literature reconstruct some of the diplomatic initiatives from 1510 to at least 1530 that offered English noblemen and London citizens a Moorish or Turkish context against which Scipio and Hannibal could fight their battles over. It is easy to dismiss these flurries of Crusading fervour as mere pageant stuff;[49] but popular images of both North African Moors, in uppity pirate mood after the Granada expulsions, and of the all-conquering Turk were obviously two contexts (though often merged in representations) in which the more stirring scenes from the Punic wars might be re-read by Henrician subjects. Henry continued to prosecute his own claims for Cyprus throughout the 1520s, and as late as 1528 was continuing to send material assistance to the Hospitallers. (News of their new Malta base brought on a big sulk in 1530: the Tenth Worthy had not been consulted. In the end, Charles V, invading Tunis in 1535, was the ruler to take up the mantle of Scipio.)

Would it be impossible, then, to imagine a Morley fired, perhaps, by the ambition of French humanist programmes for *their* Most Christian Majesty into providing for the English monarch (he too, of course, was king of France) a simpler Scipio, notable for his military *success*, an 'Emperour' 'and Tryumpher' (R, fol. 24^r) of his own? Such a reading of *Lives* might point to the Henry who in 1516 had offered 'to go in his own person and be captain of the seas' against the renewed Turkish offensives of Selim I;[50] the Henry whose capture of Tournai had brought into his own realm – however briefly, for the 1518 Treaty of London swiftly ceded it back again – a city larger than any other except London. We tend now to discount almost all of Henry's continental warfare, but that victory was still in the collective English mind at the end of the sixteenth century, up there with Agincourt and Crécy.[51]

Some support for such a 'strong' reading of *Lives* might point to the many other versions of the Scipio-Hannibal lives, or comparison, that were frequently dedicated to European kings and to military commanders in this period, often in circumstances of pointed analogy and aggravated exemplarity. How often the pair were studied in these centuries would be an exhaustive task to catalogue, but their significance for rulers at war or intending it can be illustrated from a short series of selected dedications. Matthias, King of Hungary, was probably the nearest thing 1470s Europe had to a Scipio. His country stood on the borders of unremitting war with an unappeasable aggressor, the Turk. What more natural reading, then, than the Second Punic Wars? Replying to a Pomponio Leto gift in 1471, Matthias explained that now he was at war – and this is a man who fought Turks, and not (like Henry VIII) dressed up as them[52] – he liked to read nothing better than Silius Italicus' account of Hannibal and Scipio. It was in Matthias's famous Corvinian library that not only Silius but the finest manuscript of Acciaiuoli's Plutarch came to rest.[53] Acciaiuoli, too, composing in the 1460s, was demonstrably alert to the Turkish menace: 'Si fuit unquam tempus ullum', he wrote to the Pope in 1463, 'in quo furentes impetus barbarorum reprimendi videantur, nunc manifestissime esse ostenditur, cum illi capta Bizantio, Sinope Trapesuntioque devictis. ...'[54]

Not all the modern Carthaginians lived at that end of the Mediterranean. Back in England, Anthony Cope, urging a composite Hannibal-Scipio pair on Henry VIII in 1543 in another vignette of Punic reading, explained in his *Historie of the most noble capitaines of the worlde* how 'well pondering the tyme of warre to be nowe in hande' (STC 5718 sig. a3) a reading of Scipio and Hannibal would help 'your gracies warres' in view for Ireland. Cope's 1540s reading stands in interesting contrast to Morley's more clerkly account. It offered exactly the *complement* of rulerly virtues that Morley took pains never to make explicit, the heady cocktail of Scipio *and* Hannibal, that gave the comparison edge: the one 'crafty, politike, peynfull and hardy'; the other 'wise, chaste, liberall and continent'. Such a complementary set of values might be differently weighted, of course: Thomas Berthelet's prefatory verses to the same volume make clear that for him at least Scipio is to be *the* hero:

> Lo thus maie menne playnly here beholde
> That wyly wytte, power, guyse, nor policie,
> Coulde Aniball ever styll upholde,
> But by Scipios worthy chevalrie,
> His manhode, vertue, and dedes knyghtly
> He was subdued, there is no more to sayne.

Cope himself is shrewder, and demands they be taken together.

One could go further. Sometimes the monarch counselled is directly averted from Scipio: stanza 63 of William Alexander's early Jacobean *A Paraenesis to Prince Henry*, for example, points a very different moral from Scipio's mildness:

> But as by mildnesse, some great States do gaine,
> By lenity, some lose that which they have ...
> Brave *Scipio's* Army mutini'd in *Spayne*,
> And (by his meeknesse bold) their charge did leave.[55]

How readily such more explicit and hortatory transferences could be worked, and how readily in each direction, emerges by different textual strategies in different Scipionics. William Master's 1555 manuscript translation of Acciaiuoli for the earl of Pembroke makes perhaps for the most direct comparison with Morley's work. Its author, a King's College, Cambridge man, attempts only the Scipio life, seeing no need to go beyond the best:

> For what needed at the First to write of the disdaign of *Cneius Pompeius*, or the ambicion of *Julius Caesar*, of *Alexanders* pride and drunkennes, or of *Annibals* subtilitie, howtynes, and crueltie? specially seing that *Scipio* was not only not spotted with any of thiese blotts, but also adorned with all kind of honour. Vyce hath no place where vertue hath full maistree. (fol. 4^{v})

But he has evidently learned what Morley's education in the household of Lady Margaret Beaufort never taught him: the art of commonplacing. By the time this translator, 'most humble and addict Oratour', comes to pen his dedicatory epistle to the Earl of Pembroke (there can be little doubt that this version of the Life has settled firmly to its role as a textbook for a Marian general), Master's summary overview of the work is capable in brief space of a much more comprehensive, less monocular account of the text than Morley's:

> For therin hath he not left to be conjectured, but pointed out in open woordes to be perceived, that the wisedom of valeant capitaines shuld so evenly counterpeize the balanze of mans britle estate and condicion, that nother shuld they sinke by any storm of ill happ, nor be puft upp with any prosperitie: That it is foly to use force, where devise woll serve: That standing assured in their owne vertues, they use not envie, to hinder, but love, to farthre an other mans glorie: That they repose no trust in the wavering minde of the vulgare people: That if Scipio sought to strengthen his common welth by land with victories, and oversea by confederacies: they shuld refuse no paine nor perill for the welth of theire contrey; That they should follow conquest: be pietifull in forgeving: wise in correcting: liberall in rewarding: diligent in wynnyng: and circumspect in keping. For seldom or never shall it be suerli recovered that was thoroughly lost whether it be in strength or in affection: with forty maters more, and therwithall some fine practisies of warr, woorthie all to be shoonned and abhorred. (Glasgow, UL, Hunterian MS 466, fols 3^{v}-4^{v})

Most of these, however unremittingly general they may sound to the modern ear, reappear in the full sentential dignity of the margin as the text proceeds. This was one version, then, of what it was to read for action, in the phrase Anthony Grafton and Lisa Jardine have made famous.[56] Master offers to teach his own master 'what it may comprehend in iii or iiij houres reading, so many, and those so notable things' (fol. 4^{v}). Three or four hours, forty matters more: the recipe is oddly dispiriting. But action where? Master's marginal glosses (Morley has none) do yet more work, in bringing the analogies and distinctions home. Glossing '*Proconsul*', for example, Master explicates: 'a lieuetenant of the Romanes in a provynce, with lyke authoritie there as a *Consul* had at *Rome*. So that for example we may call Irelond not unfitly a province, and the Deputie there a Proconsul'. (fol. A8^{r})

In other features of the paratext of *The ymage of honour and chevalry* William Master spells out the parallel virtues of its modern patron, William Herbert, earl of Pembroke, even more obligingly. Master's preface, written at London on 30 December 1555, and long title are both at pains to connect the author with the subject: like Scipio, Plutarch himself is 'as noble a Governour as an excellent learned man and grave

Philosopher'.[57] That 'Governour', which re-sounds Thomas Elyot's famous title of 1531, may allow us to bring one more text into play, and one that bears on Morley in the 1530s in particular. Xenophon's *Cyropaedia*, with its portrait of the formation of the model ruler, was for many readers the natural progression from Plutarch: it was the next text Bruni moved on to 'praecipuo quodam amore' after beginning his translations of Plutarch's *Lives*. Cicero's Epistle to Quintus had familiarized readers of a Scipio biography with the tradition that Africanus always carried about with him a copy of Xenophon's *Cyropaedia*. And in Spenser's famous letter to Raleigh, Xenophon's text is specifically preferred to Plato, 'So much more profitable and gracious is doctrine by ensample, then rule'. Xenophon, too, was Morley's unwitting choice of author for the Agesilaus *Life* that he offered Thomas Cromwell. Along the same line of tradition, William Bercher's 1567 *The VIII Bookes of Xenophon* was one of the last books to be dedicated to Master's early patron.[58] Had Morley, too, heard, as Ascham would later, in the opening of Elyot's *The Governour* – 'I late consideringe (most excellent prince ...)' – the careful imitation of Xenophon's first sentence? Whether or not Morley was alert to such echoes, his choice of generals speaks for itself: Scipio and Hannibal were the governour's governours, so to speak, a natural choice for rulers of men and realms. And 'facundyus eloquent Plutarke', his chosen author, had been, he believed, 'maister unto the good emperour Tragyan'.[59]

In approaching Morley's choice of text, then, and considering the ways in which he wished that text to serve, we should allow for various pressures, from the scholarly to the more sharply contextual, to a more cautiously open sense of what it might be to study the different characters of past greatness. The need in question was not merely that of the *exemplum*, the 'Ymage', the 'patterne', the 'comfort' and general incitation: the conviction that (whichever one it was that you preferred) 'There was never founde a better capitayne'.[60] Such convenient, and conveniently distant, praises might bolster the royal valour of an emerging early modern nation-state; but they might equally speak to the important need for such a burgeoning state and its monarch to *overgo* a Scipio. The same volume in which Berthelet expresses his own preference between Scipio and Hannibal goes on to insist to Berthelet's royal master that his own 'gracious warres, in Spayne, Fraunce| Britayne, and Scotland' and 'the triumph therof' are 'much *more* worthy of glorie ... the artillery more perillous, the armour more sure, and the castelles more strong. In so much that the wynnyng of Tirwyn or Morlace, is muche more to be estemed, then the wynnyng of Capua or Carthage'.[61]

The contexts of early Tudor diplomacy afford some – but only some – support, then, for such battle-zone readings of the works his peers presented to Henry VIII. On one view, Berners's Froissart, completed right in the middle of a particularly charged period of Anglo-French relations in 1521-3, offers something of a parallel. Yet this 'active' reading is not the only possibility Berners's text seems to hold in play, and here (as with Morley, as with Acciaiuoli too) there may be room for approaches and readers that are more self-questioning, more inward or simply more *politique*. Rulers like Morley's or Berners's Henry, or Acciaiuoli's Medicis, or Louis XI (to whom the Charlemagne was presented on a diplomatic mission in 1461), had more than one thing on their mind; and a gift-text, however singular its dedication, often needed to be more than single-minded.

Acciaiuoli is a case in point. All his *Lives* seem undeniably ruler-pointed from the moment they left the Florentine man of affairs's workshop, even perhaps while they were still in his notebook. Acciaiuoli wrote with clear parallels in mind between the ancient and modern commonwealths of Rome and Florence, and of the charged role of the overmighty citizen in each. In Donato's Florence, from humanist to ruler was a short step and a natural one: the two-volume version of the Acciaiuoli Latin parallel lives in the Laurentian library boasts a Medici dedication that meets and matches the Piero dedication in the first printed edition. The larger circumstances of Acciaiuoli's composition are also worth attending to. From the first, they give an idea of the interaction between the public duties of governance, the focused dedication of the work to rulers, and an eclectic scholarship that served at once the state and the state servant's own career. Acciaiuoli had studied Greek with Francesco di Castiglione, Carlo Marsuppini, and most significantly Johannes Argyropoulos, from whose instruction Acciaiuoli's notebooks survive. These were later worked up into Acciaiuoli's own commentaries on Aristotle's *Ethics* and *Politics* – themselves works with a textual life over the long sixteenth century – alongside Acciaiuoli's public career in the financial oligarchy of the *Monte Commune* and on a series of diplomatic missions. Acciaiuoli was no general himself: but his state's affairs brought him time and again into the business of government, of diplomatic mission, and of financing the war loans of the Medici. From these conjoint experiences of the *vita activa* and the snatched hours of study his own lives are fashioned, unevenly but not without nuance. In Garin's fine verdict, 'Gli eroi di Plutarco costituiscono non delle "idee", ma le celebrazioni di un'umanità da cui e possibile imparare una forma di vita.'[62]

THE PAINS OF GREATNESS

Though the pragmatic concerns and Florentine civic context of Morley's source-text seem incontestable, then, both Acciaiuoli's and Morley's Hannibal and Scipio have other angles to them, and are shown in aspects that often fight free of too businesslike a reading of their own famous histories. With Polybius just onstream again at the time Acciaiuoli selected and composed his *auctores* (the Morley *Life* of Hannibal checks Polybius in at R, fol. 4^{v}), the main episodes of the two lives were not in dispute: Scipio's early training, father's death, the youthful preferring to office, the relief of Spain, the Continence, the recuperative justice after Roman oppressions in Sicily, the African campaign, and the great victory at Zama; Hannibal's childhood oath, his 'pryvate and as who saith a kindeled hate descending from his Father whiche of all the dukes of Cartage / most hated the Romains' (R, fol. 4^{v}), the Saguntine campaign, the long and arduous years of Italian peninsular warfare and small-state politics, the flight to Asia Minor.

Beyond these, though, what Acciaiuoli and Morley both responded to, what moved them both to pity and dilation, were their heroes's repulses. Both play up the Romans' intense suspicion of the youthful Scipio, their 'skante' consent and 'great mutacyon of mindes in repenting to have graunted him suche rule' (R, fol. 24^{v}), the continuing mistrusts that dogged the Spanish and African campaigns and the eventual repulse from the city he had saved. For Hannibal, the clog is first the faction of the 'some that were miscontented with all' (R, fol. 4^{r}) at Carthage; later, the more bitter experience of his own failure to turn battle-triumphs into enduring victories:

This tryfulling oftymes after warde he sore repented that he had not harde the councell of Maharball the Captaine of his knightes / which woulde that he shoulde furthwith have gone to Rome / and when he saw that he delaide the tyme / said unto him / Haniball thou canste optaine the the victorie / but thou canst not use the victorye. (R, fol. 13^{r})

Hannibal's last years in Asia 'as one exiled' (R, fol. 20^{v}) incite the biographer to a telling picture of the great general, famous for his stratagems, now reduced to the unfamiliar role of a Cassandra, truth-telling but uncredited:

Thus Haniball was well harde and highly praised for his wise councell / rather then folowed / which is greatly to be marveiled ... that his counsell was not accepted ... whose counsell / howbeit that the king folowed not / afterwardes he confessed only Haniballs Councell to be beste and all other worth nought woorthe / for ... he lacked not flaterers ynoughe to bere him so in hande a perpetuall evill aboute kinges which hering gladly that pleaseth them willfully suffer them selves to be begiled. (R, fol. 21^{v})

Acciaiuoli ends the *Life* by reporting three versions of Hannibal's death at the court of Prusias, king of Bithynia: he prefers (understandably, as the only one with a speech attached) Livy's account, with its final curse.

In composing these competing versions of the hero-general and the ungrateful commonwealth, Acciaiuoli looked back not so much to the careful imagination of what Plutarch's missing *Scipio* may have been, but to a Scipio nearer home and his own time – Petrarch's. In the letters, in *De viris illustribus*, above all in the *Africa* and the *Vita Scipionis*, the imagination of the first great humanist had been stirred by many aspects of the story: Scipio's great friendship and love for the poet Ennius; the tantalizing fragments of the first great Roman epic, Ennius's *Annals*; the good man on trial before his own Senate (here Petrarch turned to Livy); the laurel crown (Valerius Maximus) with which the accused hero signals his silent reproach of the envious, 'non minore reus de invidia triumphans quam victor olim de hostibus triumpharat'; the exile.[63] 'Morley's Petrarch' is there in his 'Plutarch' too, its name not Triumph but Mutability: 'And surely this sodaine mutacion ought to be a great example to us of the humain fragilitie whiche often we forgett in prosperous fortune.' (R, fol. 34^{r})

This saddened note in Morley's *Life* is a far cry from *The Story of Scipio*, Francis I's great galumphing, triumphing sequence of Brabant-Brussels tapestries, which the French king ordered to be woven with silver and golden thread. (In 1797, in the war-years after the French Revolution, they were deliberately burned in order to recover their metal content.)[64] The warp of Morley's Scipio is not gold and silver, but the true nobilities exhibited in adversity. His recognition of Scipio's 'humanitye' in all its 'hap', the 'magnanimitie' that was Envy's bane, his salute to Hannibal's 'perseveraunce' that 'could watch / labour and haste when nede was / and suffer all paines That a vallyaunt Emperour might suffer' – these are the Petrarchan threads of Acciaiuoli's *Lives of Scipio and Hannibal*, and in the end give a more plausible sense than Henry's Crusade-dreams of the imagined experiences that impel Morley towards this choice of text for translation. This larger constancy is what singles Morley's heroes out from all the figures that his folio Plutarch offered:

And suerly, most nobyll Prince, there hath bene and is dyvers that can and hathe done grete conquestes, butt there be very fewe that when soche good, prosperows fortunes happen unto them, but that they eyther be to moche prowde thereof, or when yll fortune cums to them, to moche abasshed thereof, so that the best part, whiche is the meane, is quite sett a parte.[65]

The part within Plutarchan lives that is itself set apart for conscious judgment is the *comparatio*. Passages from Livy might thicken his *Vitae*, but in the comparison Donato Acciaiuoli was left to reach his own assessment, to attempt an evener balance than the single if decisive verdict delivered at Zama. His initial strategy is to hold not to difference, but to what both heroes had in common: their personal strength and feats of arms, their valour, the-*ingenium* of their strategy (their 'overcomming by greate witt all difficulties'), the many great battles each won, and won on foreign soil. Hannibal, the worthy recipient of 'highe fame', is met and answered 'as unto Scipio all men gave ... highe commendacion and Well worthie' (R, fols 38^{v}-39^{r}). Slowly the balance tilts, though, as Zama comes into view: 'and laste of all by pure valiance had the better of Haniball in a sett felde'. Here Acciaiuoli's text dwells, and reformulates Scipio's victory more emphatically, more pointedly – 'not by no crafte/ but by plaine and pure valiaunce' (R, fol. 39^{r}) – before gradually turning the *comparatio* into a *separatio*. Again, the effect is poised. Hannibal's masterful control of an army made up of 'so divers nacions' is particularly commended, before the catalogue of shortcomings builds up – the failures to press home the advantages after Trasimene and Cannae, the 'falsnes and crueltye whiche ever was in him' (one can see why Hannibal would do useful service as a figure for Oliver Cromwell at the Restoration).[66] Yet the text leaves space open to ponder the proper place for an intelligently 'wylie and subtill' character, both in war and in diplomacy. 'For Haniball all that he did was muche by pollecy more then by armes': Morley will not commend, but reports coolly that commendation has happened. A quick canter through Scipio's distinctive virtues is easier going:

But Scipio / if we will beleve true writers rather then suche as backebite him was of another fashion sober and pitefull not only in batell but after that victory gentle and treateable/ wherby oftentymes he moevid those that he overcamme to have greate faith and love unto him / and as in conntenaunce and Chastitie adjoined with liberalitie what might be more comended. ... (R, fols 39^{r-v})

After that, the heroes can be reunited in virtues that any writer will agree on: both were 'excellently well lerned and desiring ever to have in companie with them such as was well lettured'. Scipio befriends the poet Ennius, Hannibal holds 'in greate familiaritie' the Spartan Sophilus and is said to have written a *Life* himself. In their eloquence and 'valliauntnesse' both 'seeme to be like'. If Hannibal (whose rooted hatred of the Romans from a childhood oath has been established at the start) in the end is an aggressor, 'the causer of the beginning of the warrs / in the ende to his countries distruction', 'Scipio contrary so defended his comon wealth / so kept it / so increased it' (R, fol. 39^{v}). '*so*' what, we may ask? The turn is characteristic:

so ... that thos that remembre it doubt not to call the Romains unkinde which rather suffered their defendour to go into exile then to punishe suche as falsly accused him / and surely for my parte I cannot call that Citie kinde that so suffered so noble and innocent a prince as Scipio was to have such rebuke.

Morley's version of fidelity is measured, in the end, not by reward for 'valliauntnesse', but by the purer fires of rejection: 'But Scipio being of noble minde thought it better to give place and go exiled from the Citie then by Civile discorde to put it in Jeopardy of perdicion' (R, fol. 40^{r}). Acciaiuoli and Morley close with a chastened hymn to Scipio's 'willing determined', his persistent and irreproachably civic voluntarity.

These pages have tried to suggest some of the values that Morley would have cherished in his understanding of the authorial character of 'Plutarch', some of the choices that informed the real author, Acciaiuoli, of the text Morley chose, and some contrasting contexts and linked texts in or against which these *Lives* of Hannibal and Scipio might be read. There are obvious difficulties in pressing forward to much beyond this still somewhat general picture. For one thing, the problems of dating with anything like exactness these manuscript translations makes it harder now to reflect with much certainty upon the parallels of *occasion*, as compared to person, that their gifts may also cautiously have invoked. And given the need for such cautions, the mere fact of the annual gift, its marker as a ritual moment in the continual anxieties and the hoped-for reciprocities of a client-patron relationship, may in the end far outweigh the local significances of any one of the class that remains.[67] The *nexum* marks proximity, but the proximity itself (as at the moment of Morley's daughter's disgracing and execution) can occasion danger. At such moments, prudence may suggest a particular value and caution in a demonstrable continuity of client practice: but that makes it no easier to read into Morley's 'accustomed' giving of Plutarch a story that interacts neatly or closely either with the supposed rhythms of Henrician policy or with the jagged irregularities of a more faction-led narrative of the reign's events.

There are other interpretative dangers involved in isolating any one author from the larger web of material aggregating around his subject. To read 'Plutarch's' Scipio or Hannibal adrift from the early Tudor period's larger sense of the great Roman/Punic conflict may acknowledge the special status accorded to the author as great clerk or noble governor, but is liable to miss the material (much of it handsomely illustrated) with which a 'Plutarch' Scipio might reasonably expect to be conferred – with Livy above all, or with Nepos, but also with humanist retellings of the war such as Leonardo Bruni's and its own vernacular diffusions.[68] Petrarch's *Vita Scipionis*, too, as I have suggested, continued to exercise its influence. 'Plutarch' on Scipio, in other words, is often the work of, or if it is not often invites conflation with, 'other authores'.[69] Its matter may be considered now as the growth of an empire, now as the tactical conduct of a war; now for the life of a pagan so virtuous that he 'and other soch gentiles' might 'appiere to judge Christian magistrates of government', now as a *contemptus mundi*, in which even the greatest of generals experiences the rejection and mistrust of his *patria*.

Silius Italicus had famously presented in Book I of the longest surviving Latin epic, his *Punica*, a Scipio poised between Virtue and the lighter pleasures of Fortune. Similar choices often confront the Tudor reader of Scipio's or Hannibal's *fortuna*. The later English vernacular of the same pseudo-Plutarchan Scipio text, Master's *The ymage of honour and chevalry*, is more explicit than Morley in offering its reader a choice of readings. One faced the known capacities of a patron and read for the pleasures of action, viewing Scipio as the 'peereles paragon' of 'valeant stomak'. The other proposed a more inward reading of 'proportionate temperature', 'expressing ... that the most notable conquest was, for a man to vanquish himself'.[70] Morley's *Lives*, by holding both generals together still, offer a double version of that choice. There is little doubt which version he privileges and meekly proffers to a prince he must have known was less 'noble and innocent' than the hero of his pages. But that is what examples are for.

ABBREVIATION

R London, British Library, Royal MS 17 D.XI.

NOTES

1 In the preface to the *Somnium Scipionis* translation, Morley describes himself as 'accustomed, allways afore this present tyme, either to send youe sum notable worke concernynge sum christen doctours wrytyng in the Laten tonge, or ells sum of their workes by me translated into our tounge': see below, Appendix 4, p. 241.

2 A modern re-evaluation of Berners is much to be desired; for a brief account of his more generous admission of romance 'unpossybylytees', see D. Gray, *The Oxford Book of Late Medieval Verse and Prose* (Oxford, 1985), pp. 392-3.

3 *Lord Morley's 'Tryumphes'*, ed. by Carnicelli, p. 77.

4 J. K. McConica, *English Humanists and Reformation Politics under Henry VIII and Edward VI* (Oxford, 1965), p. 152.

5 Oxford, Bodleian Library, Laud MS Misc. 684, fol. 2ʳ.

6 'The Structures of Politics in Early Modern England', *Transactions of the Royal Historical Society*, 6th ser., 5 (1995), 59-90 (63).

7 The outlines can be followed from M. Treu, *Zur Gerschichte der Ueberlieferung von Plutarks Moralia* (Breslau, 1884); R. Weiss, 'Lo Studio di Plutarco nel Trecento', *La Parola del Passato* 32 (1953), 321-42; R. R. Bolgar, *The Classical Heritage and its Beneficiaries* (Cambridge, 1954), pp. 485-7; C. Mitchell, *A Fifteenth Century Italian Plutarch (British Museum Add. MS 22318)* (London, 1961); D. Geanakoplos, *Greek Scholars in Venice* (Harvard, 1962); G. Resta, 'Le epitomi di Plutarco nel quattrocento', *Miscellanea erudite* 5 (1962), 1-132; and N. G. Wilson, *From Byzantium to Italy: Greek Studies in the Italian Renaissance* (London, 1992). I am grateful to David McKitterick for two of these references.

8 Wilson, *From Byzantium to Italy*, pp. 46-7.

9 'Donato Acciaiuoli Cittadino Fiorentino', in E. Garin, *Medioevo e Rinascimento: Studi e Ricerche* (Bard, 1954), pp. 211-87; Garin gives further consideration to Acciaiuoli's political philosophy in *La Cultura Filosofica del Rinascimento Italiano: Ricerche e Documenti* (Florence, 1961), pp. 67-71, 102-5.

10 C. B. R. Pelling's edition of *Plutarch: Life of Antony* (Cambridge, 1988), pp. 31-6, offers a sharp account of working methods; see further Pelling, 'Plutarch's method of work in the Roman Lives', *Journal of Hellenic Studies*, 99 (1979), 74-96.

11 D. A. Russell, *Plutarch* (London, 1972), chaps 6-8 (especially at p. 142); Pelling, too, finds the *synkriseis* prone to sink to a level 'uncomfortably trivial after the grandeur of the closing narrative': see his *Antony*, p. 19.

12 Garin, 'Donato Acciaiuoli', pp. 267-71, discusses the Demetrius dedication to Piero de Medici and that of the Charlemagne to Louis XI. On Charlemagne, see further D. Gatti, 'Vita Caroli di Donato Acciaiuoli', *Bullettino dell'Instituto storico italiano per il medioevo e archivio muratoriano*, 84 (1972-3), 223-74.

13 J. Stephens, *The Italian Renaissance: the Origins of Intellectual and Artistic Change before the Reformation* (London, 1990), pp. 177-84, offers a cool overview of a heated historiographical site concerning Sallust and Plutarch.

14 Michael Reeve (to whom I am extremely grateful for this and for the final information of the next note) writes of the epitaph for Scipio near the close of the Life that it 'is given here with circumstantial detail ... apparently absent in the other sources hitherto reported', citing L. Bertalot, *Initia humanistica latina I: Poesie* (Tübingen, 1985), no. 1150.

15 *Epistolae et commentarii Iacobi Picolomini Cardinalis Papiensis* (Milan, 1506), fols 114[r], 168[v]; Garin, 'Donato Acciaiuoli', pp. 274-5.
16 *English Humanists and Reformation Politics* (see n. 4 above), p. 152.
17 *Institutio principis christiani*, ed. by O. Herding, (Amsterdam, 1974), p. 179; discussed by T. Hampton, *Writing from History: the Rhetoric of Exemplarity in Renaissance Literature* (Ithaca & London, 1990), pp. 48-62.
18 R. Aulotte's brief remarks, presented as 'Plutarque et l'humanisme en France et en Italie', in *Les humanistes et l'antiquité grecque*, ed. by M. Ishigami-Iagolitzner (Paris, 1991), pp. 99-104, helpfully review his own magisterial contribution to the Plutarch *fortuna*, most substantially *Amyot et Plutarque: la traduction de 'Moralia' au xvie siècle*, Travaux d'Humanisme et Renaissance, 61 (Geneva, 1965).
19 Aberystwyth, NLW, MS 17038C, fol. 1[v].
20 As they were for those of his French counterpart, Simon Bourgouyn.
21 R. Pfeiffer, *History of classical scholarship from 1300 to 1850* (Oxford, 1976), Appendix I.
22 See above, n. 7.
23 See, for example, R, fol. 25[v], 'of riches of riches' or fol. 28[r], 'At the whiche / at the whiche' and 'oute out' within the same nine lines. I discuss one case of word-omission later in this essay.
24 J. N. H. Lawrance, 'Humanism in the Iberian Peninsula', in *The Impact of Humanism on Western Europe*, ed. by A. Goodman & A. Mackay (London & New York, 1990), pp. 220-58 (222, 230).
25 The 1440s seem to have been the first decade in which the question becomes an issue: both Leonardo Bruni and Alfonso de Cartagena seem to have made a similar, if more determinedly conscious, choice: see Lawrance, 'Humanism', pp. 225-6.
26 R, fol. 28[r]. Wyatt's proverbializing – the reference is to *The Quyete of Minde*, presented to Catherine of Aragon in 1527 – is discussed by E. Heale, '"An Owl in a Sack Troubles No Man": Proverbs, Plainness, and Wyatt', *Renaissance Studies*, 11 (1997), 420-35, and A. N. Brilliant, 'The Style of Wyatt's *The Quyete of Minde*', *Essays and Studies*, 24 (1971), 1-21, (13-15).
27 Both works are discussed in Hetoum, *A Lytell Cronycle: Richard Pynson's Translation (c. 1520) of La fleur des histories de la terre d'Orient (c. 1307)*, ed. by G. Burger (Toronto, 1988), chap. 2 and Appendix.
28 R, fol. 2[v]: he returns to the figure of the Turk in BL, Arundel MS 8, fol. 13[v].
29 Plutarch's *ornamenta consularia* are now read, like the similar award to Quintilian, as a 'mark of academic renown': *Antony*, ed. by Pelling (n. 10 above), p. 3, citing C. P. Jones, *Plutarch and Rome* (Oxford, 1971), p. 56.
30 *The ymage of honour and chevalry*: Glasgow, University Library, Hunterian MS 466, fol. 2[r].
31 Goff P-832-P-835; Resta, 'Le epitomi di Plutarco' (n. 7 above).
32 STC 20062, *The Preceptes of the Excellent Clerke and Graue Philosopher Plutarch for the Preseruacion of Good Healthe*, trans. by J. Hales (London, 1543).
33 STC 20052, 20053, 20056, 20056.7, 20057.5.
34 Plutarch's *Moralia* and the portrait of Sparta in the 'Life of Lycurgus' contribute substantially to More's imaginary commonwealth: for a conservative account, *Utopia*, ed. by E. Surtz, S. J. & J. H. Hexter (New Haven & London, 1965), pp. clx-clxi.
35 Brief discussion in H. W. Garrod, 'Erasmus and his English Patrons', *The Library*, 5th ser., 4 (1949), 8 and C. H. Clough, 'A Presentation Volume for Henry VIII: the Charlecote Park copy of Erasmus's *Institutio Principis Christiani*', *Journal of the Warburg and Courtauld Institutes*, 44 (1981), 199.
36 'Vernacular humanism in the sixteenth century', in *The Cambridge Companion to Renaissance Humanism*, ed. by J. Kraye (Cambridge, 1996), pp. 189-202 (199).

37 From *The Governaunce of Good Helthe* (STC 20061 and 20061.7).

38 For a sense of the permeability of these boundaries, see D. R. Carlson, *English Humanist Books: Writers and Patrons, Manuscript and Print, 1475-1525* (Toronto, 1993); for a strong insistence on their status-differences in Morley's case, W. Boutcher, 'Florio's Montaigne: Translation and Pragmatic Humanism in the Sixteenth Century' (unpublished doctoral dissertation, University of Cambridge, 1991), chap. 2, (especially at p. 47).

39 Lucius Martius appears, for example, as Lucus (frequent), Lucius and Luceius.

40 'The Prolog' to the Paulus Aemilius is perhaps the most explict description of Morley's ambitions: 'I have translatyd owte of the Latin tonge in to ouer maternall tonge rudely, but truly, I trust, according to the sens', quoted in *Forty-six Lives*, ed. by Wright, p. 165.

41 *Henry VIII and the English Nobility* (Oxford, 1986), pp. 44-5.

42 Garin, 'Donato Acciaiuoli' (n. 9 above), p. 271.

43 Katherine Philips, '*Epitaph on my truly honoured* Publius Scipio', ll. 25-6: *The Collected Works of Katherine Philips, The Matchless Orinda: Vol. 1, The Poems*, ed. by P. Thomas (Stump Cross, 1990), pp. 229-30, 387-9. For Fairfax's 'meekness', compare G. Villiers, Duke of Buckingham, 'An Epitaph upon Thomas, Lord Fairfax', *The New Oxford Book of Seventeenth-Century Verse*, ed. by A. Fowler (Oxford, 1991), pp. 666-8.

44 P. Junquera de Vega & C. Herrero Cartero, *Catálogo del Patrimonio Nacional: I. Siglo XVI* (Madrid, 1986), pp. 176-84; illustration of 'Zama' and short discussion in A. Dominguez Ortiz, C. Herrero Cartero, & J. A. Godoy, *Resplendence of the Spanish Monarchy: Renaissance Tapestries and Armor from the Patrimonio Nacional* (New York, 1991), pp. 68-73.

45 H. J. Horn, *Jan Cornelis Vermeyen, Painter of Charles V and His Conquest of Tunis: Paintings, Etchings, Drawings, Cartoons and Tapestries*, 2 vols (Doornspijk, 1989). 'The Review of the Troops' and short discussion in *Resplendence of the Spanish Monarchy*, pp. 74-81.

46 'The Prolog' to Paulus Aemilius: *Forty-six Lives*, ed. by Wright, p. 164.

47 S. Anglo, *The Great Tournament Roll of Westminster: a Collotype Reproduction of the Manuscript*, 2 vols (Oxford, 1968), I, pl. 23.

48 *LP Henry VIII* III.432.

49 A pageant of 1518 begins with 'Turks and drums, and strikes a Universal Peace to see them off', the account of Edward Hall, *The Union of the Two Noble and Illustre Famelies of Lancastre and York*, ed. by H. Ellis (London, 1809), p. 595, is significantly expanded at *CSP* (Venetian), ii.1088. For midsummer shows of the City of London with Moors, wildfire, Castles of War, see *A Lytell Cronycle*, ed. by Burger (n. 27 above), pp. xliv-xlv, n. 26.

50 *LP Henry VIII* II.3874. Lady Margaret Beaufort's similarly spirited offer to go with the Crusaders, and 'wash their clothes, for the love of Jesus' is recalled in John Fisher's 'Mornynge Remembraunce had at the moneth mynde of the noble Prynces Margarete Countesse of Rychemonde and Darbye': *The English Works of John Fisher, part I*, ed. by J. E. B. Mayor, EETS ES 27 (Oxford, 1876), pp. 289-310 (308).

51 In Anthony Nixon's poem *Englandes hope against Irish hate*, for example: Northampton, Northamptonshire Record Office, Westmorland (Apethorpe) MS Misc. vol. 30, fol. 11^{v}, linking 'Cressy', 'Bullen', 'Turny', 'Poictiers'.

52 In the disguising of 1510, Henry and the Earl of Essex had put in a joint appearance 'after Turkey fasshion, in long robes of bawdkin, powdered with gold, hastes on their heddes of Crimosyn Velvet, with great rolles of Gold, girded with two swordes, called Cimiteries': Hall, *The Union*, ed. by Ellis, p. 513.

53 Now Vienna, National Bibliothek, Cod. 23.

54 Garin, 'Donato Acciaiuoli' (n. 9 above), p. 272.

55 *The Poetical Works of Sir William Alexander*, ed. by L. E. Kastner & H. B. Charlton, 2 vols (Edinburgh, 1921-9), II, 381-406 (399).

56 L. Jardine & A. Grafton, '"Studied for Action": How Gabriel Harvey Read His Livy', *Past and Present*, 129 (1990), 30-78.

57 The title runs: 'The ymage of honour /and Chevalry / That is to say, The Lief of/ the most woorthie Capi-/ taine *Scipio Aphricanus*/ the Elder, as it/ was writen by *Plutarchus* be-/ ing himself/ as noble/ a Governour/ as an excellent lear-/ ned man and grave/ Philosopher, translated into/ Englysh by Wyll[ya]m Maister/ Decembre/ 1555', Hunterian MS 466, fol. 12^r^. For Pembroke, see M. Brennan, *Literary Patronage in the English Renaissance: the Pembroke Family* (London, 1988), chap. 2, 'The Rise of a Courtier'.

58 *The School of Cyrus: William Barker's 1567 Translation of Xenophon's Cyropaedia (The Education of Cyrus)*, ed. by J. Tatum (New York & London, 1987), pp. i-iv, 1-8.

59 Dedicatory letter to *The Lyff of the Good Kyng Agesylayus*: NLW., MS 17038C, fol. 3^r^.

60 *The historie of the most noble capitaines ... Anniball and Scipio ... gathered and translated into English, out of Titus livius and other authores*, by Anthonye Cope esquier (London, 1544), sig. a1^v^.

61 *Historie of the Most Noble Capitaines*, sig. a3^v^-a4^v^. (See note 60 above.)

62 Garin, 'Donato Acciaiuoli', p. 282.

63 Petrarch, *Vita di Scipione l'Africano*, ed. by G. Martelotti (Milan & Naples, 1954), p. 158. See also A. S. Bernardo, *Petrarch, Scipio and the 'Africa'* (Baltimore, 1962); and S. T. Velli, 'Scipio's Wounds', *JWCI*, 58 (1995), 216-34, for an admirably full account of the visual topos.

64 J.-J. Guiffrey, 'Destruction des plus belles tentures du mobilier de la Couronne en 1797', *Memoires de la Société de l'Histoire de Paris et de l'Ile-de-France*, 14 (1887), 265-98.

65 'The Prolog' to Paulus Aemilius: *Forty-six Lives*, ed. by Wright, pp. 164-5.

66 T. Ross, *The Second Punick War between Hannibal and the Romanes ... Englished from the Latine of Silius Italicus* (1661), dedicated to Charles II while still in exile, presses home the allegory. The presentation manuscript is BL, Harley MS 4233.

67 For larger perspectives on the anthropology of the gift object, see B. Malinowski, *Argonauts of the Western Pacific: an Account of Native Enterprise and Adventure in the Archipelagoes of Melanesian New Guinea* (New York & London,1922); M. Mauss, *The Gift: Forms and Functions of Exchange in Archaic Societies*, trans. by I. Cunnison (London, 1954); *The Social Life of Things: Commodities in Cultural Perspective*, ed. by A. Appadurai (Cambridge, 1986); C. Muldrew, 'Interpreting the Market: the Ethics of Credit and Community Relations in Early Modern England', *Social History*, 18 (1993), 163-83. For books as sixteenth-century gifts, see N. Z. Davis, 'Beyond the Market: Books as Gifts in Sixteenth-Century France', *Transactions of the Royal Historical Society*, 5th ser., 33 (1983), 69-88; P. Fumerton, *Cultural Aesthetics: Renaissance Literature and the Practice of Social Ornament* (Chicago, 1991); L. Hellinga-Querido, 'Reading an Engraving: William Caxton's Dedication to Margaret of York, Duchess of Burgundy', in *Across the narrow seas*, ed. by S. Roach (London, 1991), pp. 2-15; S. Kettering, 'Gift-giving and Patronage in Early Modern France', *French History*, 2 (1988), 131-51; Jason Scott Warren, 'Sir John Harington as a Giver of Books' (unpublished doctoral dissertation, University of Cambridge, 1996); G. Ziegler, '"More than Feminine Boldness": the Gift Books of Esther Inglis', in *Women, writing, and the reproduction of culture in Tudor and Stuart England*, ed. by M. Burke (forthcoming).

68 Notably the translation by Jean Lebegue: for example in the handsome illustrated version now Brussels, Bibliothèque Royale Albert Ier, MS 10,777; or for an example of the Punic sections of Livy, Glasgow, University Library, Hunterian MS 370 (books XXI-XXX). For a full account of the ancient references to Scipio Africanus, see *Paulys Real-Encyclopaedie der classischen Altertumwissenschaft*, ed. by G. Wissowa, W. Kroll et al. (Stuttgart, n.d.), p. vii, cols 1462-70.

69 The phrase is taken from the long title of STC 5718, *The historie of two the most noble capitaines of the worlde.*
70 Hunterian MS 466, fols *3^{r}-A3^{v}.

MORLEY'S TRANSLATIONS FROM ROMAN PHILOSOPHERS AND ENGLISH COURTIER LITERATURE

DAVID R. CARLSON

MORLEY'S TRANSLATIONS from the Roman philosophers Cicero and Seneca – a translation of the concluding *Somnium Scipionis* section of Cicero's *De re publica* and a translation of passages from a pair of Seneca's *Epistulae morales*, both presented to Mary Tudor before 1553 – were something of a departure from the kind of literary work he had done before. Morley says as much himself in the dedicatory letter he attached to the *Somnium Scipionis* translation. 'Moste noble prynces,' he wrote,

> I do ymagyne that ye wyll sumwhat mervell that I do present this yer to your goode grace this litle worke of Tullius Cicero, of my translation into the Englishe tonge, that was accustomed allways afore this present tyme, either to send youe sum notable worke concernynge sum Christen doctours wrytynge in the Laten tonge, or ells sum of their workes by me translated into our tounge as my rude knowledge coulde do it.[1]

Morley's assertion, that he 'was accustomed allways afore this present tyme' to send different kinds of literary work: 'either to send youe sum notable worke concernynge sum Christen doctours wrytynge in the Laten tonge, or ells sum of their workes by me translated into our tounge', might suggest that the Cicero translation was presented before the other philosophical translation, the Seneca. On the other hand, the forms of entitlement that Morley used in his prefaces suggest otherwise, that the Seneca came first. In the Seneca, Morley calls Mary 'lady' and 'a kinges childe', indicating a date before the death of Henry VIII in 1547, while in the Cicero he calls her 'prynces' and 'suster to oure moste redoubted and victoriouse sovereign lorde kyng Edward the syxt', indicating a date after 1547 and before 1553.[2] There is nothing else in the translations, however, or about the translations (in the prefatory letters attached to them or in the manuscripts), suggesting any narrower a dating for them. They do not appear to have been prompted by particular events in Morley's life, nor in Mary's. In fact, the prefatory letter on the Seneca says that making translations was not more than a habit with Morley, for which he was inclined to apologize: he describes the Seneca as 'my poore translacion, which I nowe, with a loving minde, present unto your grace, as I am wont yerely to do, praing the same well to take it'.[3] Morley translated and made his presentations year after year; without the impetus of special occasion, he was keeping himself busily at his writing.

The two translations from the Roman philosophers have particular import, nevertheless, when it comes to placing Morley in relation to the literary-historical movement of which he was part, to which he contributed: the invention of a distinct courtier-literature in early modern England. Henry VIII was a writer, of verse and prose, in English and Latin, of some accomplishment; with remote though salient exceptions – King Alfred, say, or, on slighter grounds, Richard I – Henry's royal forebearers had not been.[4] Richard II, for example, or Henry V, or Edward IV, or Henry VII, each of whom has been shown to have taken an interest in literature – to have cultivated writers and patronized them, to have built collections of books and shared them – none tried writing. Generally, though there are more exceptions, the same holds true for the aristocrats who frequented the royal court during the reigns of these earlier monarchs: before the reign of Henry VIII, roughly, they were not writers, while during and after it they were. Humfrey, Duke of Gloucester, did not write, though his interest in literature was extraordinary.[5] Henry Howard, Earl of Surrey – a person of similar social elevation a few decades later – did write. Before Surrey's generation, there had been exceptions: in Henry, Duke of Lancaster (d. 1361), John of Gaunt's father-in-law, whose *Livre de seyntz medecines* (1353) is original work; or in the series of noble translators, from French into English, including Edward, duke of York (1373-1415), Shakespeare's Aumerle, who translated *The Master of the Game*; John Tiptoft, Earl of Worcester (1427-70), who translated the *Declamation of Noblesse*; and, most recently, Anthony Woodville, Earl Rivers (*c.* 1442-83), who translated the *Dicts and Sayings of the Philosophers*, among other things; or in the few figures known to have written poetry, including John Montagu, Earl of Salisbury (d. 1400), whose poetry, in French, does not survive, and William de la Pole, Duke of Suffolk (1396-1450), the agent of duke Humfrey's downfall, whose poetry might.[6] During Surrey's literary heyday, in the 1530s and 1540s, active as writers were a greater number of courtiers, Wyatt and Surrey being only the best-known of a group that included also (to mention only poets) Francis Bryan, Edmund Knyvet, George Boleyn, Thomas Vaux, Antony St Leger, George Blage, Antony Lee, Edward and Thomas Seymour, John and Robert Dudley, the elder John Harrington, and others.

The earlier attitude had been that, while writing might be done well or poorly, and, when done well, might be fit for admiration or other reward, it was still a menial or servile occupation, like cooking, say, though less essential, and so not fit for the well-born, who had more consequential jobs to do. This disesteem for writing had a history by the early sixteenth century, which the clerical and monastic traditions of the Middle Ages would have done little to alter. For example, as much in demand as it was, John Lydgate's literary work for hire would not have built esteem for writing as an occupation. Plutarch, arguing that 'He who busies himself in mean occupations produces, in the very pains he takes about things of little or no use, an evidence against himself of his negligence and indisposition to what is really good', includes poetry-writing among 'things of little or no use':

> Nor did any generous and ingenuous young man at the sight of the statue of Jupiter at Pisa, ever desire to be a Phidias, or on seeing that of Juno at Argos, long to be a Polycletus, or feel induced by his pleasure in their poems to be an Anacreon or Philetas, or Archilochus. For it does not necessarily follow, that, if a piece of work please for its gracefulness, he that wrought it deserves our admiration.

Plutarch gives examples that discourage the well-born particularly, arguing that even the expenditure of effort on such trivialities is evidence of base inclinations:

> Nay, many times, on the very contrary, when we are pleased with the work, we slight and set little by the workman or artist himself, as, for instance, in perfumes and purple dyes, we are taken with the things themselves well enough, but do not think dyers and perfumers otherwise

than low and sordid people. It was not said amiss by Antisthenes, when people told him that one Ismenias was an excellent piper. 'It may be so,' said he, 'but he is but a wretched human being, otherwise he would not have been an excellent piper.' And King Philip, to the same purpose, told his son Alexander, who once at a merry-meeting played a piece of music charmingly and skilfully, 'Are you not ashamed, son, to play so well?' For it is enough for a king or prince to find leisure sometimes to hear others sing, and he does the muses quite honour enough when he pleases but to be present, while others engage in such exercise and trials of skill.[7]

Nero's literary and dramatic pretensions supplied moralists the opposite kind of example, evidence of the disapprobation that might adhere to artistry cultivated by the nobly born. His efforts – yielding only 'species ipsa carminum ... non impetu et instinctu nec ore uno fluens' 'a flaccid, uninspired, disjoint sort of poetry', and performances so tedious that, in order to escape the theatre, members of his audiences would feign death and submit to being carried off for burial – brought him 'infamia' 'degradation', in the estimate of Tacitus, and left him with a reputation for monstrous vanity (his dying words reportedly being 'Qualis artifex pereo!' 'Dead! And so great an artist!').[8] 'Quomodo, oro te,' asked Nero's tutor Seneca, 'convenit ut et Diogenen mireris et Daedalum? Uter ex his sapiens tibi videtur?' 'How, I ask you, can you consistently admire both Daedalus and Diogenes? Tell me which of these two you would say was a wise man?'[9] – the proper answer being, not the *artifex*.

This attitude persisted into the sixteenth century, if Richard Pace's caricature is any evidence, of the *generosus* at a dinner – one of those 'qui semper cornu aliquod a tergo pendens gestant, acsi etiam inter prandendum venarentur' 'always wearing a horn at their back, as if they expect to be hunting between courses' – saying, 'Corpus Dei iuro, volo filius meus pendeat potius, quam literis studeat. Decet enim generosorum filios, apte inflare cornu, perite venari, accipitrem pulchre gestare et educare. Studia vero literarum, rusticorum filiis sunt reliquenda' 'I swear I would rather see my son hang than take an interest in literature. For the sons of nobles, winding the horn and hunting expertly, training and using a hawk attractively, these are fit occupations. Interests in literature are to be left to the sons of churls.'[10]

By the time Henry VIII came to be writing his erotic lyrics and more sober *lucubrationes*, however, change had come over the attitude towards literary occupation current among the *generosorum filii*. Likenesses between Henry and Nero eventually became evident; those who objected to Henry's Neronian tyranny, however, did not denigrate his artistry nor his vanity about it, as Nero's opponents did. The difference had not altogether to do with aesthetics.[11] The shift in the noble attitude towards literary occupation begins to become evident in the generation coming of age in the reign of Henry VII. John Bourchier, Lord Berners (1467-1533), who was over forty when Henry VII died, and whose literary work was already mostly done by then, is one example;[12] Morley may be another. Though Morley's translations are later, dating from the 1530s and 1540s, he was of this same senior generation. Morley (b. 1481) was old enough to be Wyatt's (b. 1503) father and Surrey's (b. 1517) grandfather almost. In any case, by the time of Wyatt, Surrey, and the other courtier-writers of the early Tudor period – 'the new company of courtly makers' singled out in the Elizabethan period by Puttenham as the point of departure for all worthy English literary history[13] – writing would appear to have become, far from disesteemed, rather a standard of adornment amongst courtiers and aspirants.

Why this shift should have occurred is hard to say. Foreign models, Italian, Flemish, and especially French ones, would have had an influence, though of course Castiglione had been to England and had sought (unsuccessfully) a place for himself at the court of Henry VII, later praising the English court, before writing *The Courtier*,[14] in such a way as to suggest that the influence may not have run all in one direction. The humanist vogue emanating from Italy and the uses to which humanists were being put as envoys and secretaries and tutors would have built esteem for useful eloquence among the nobility, though the courtiers' applications of eloquence tended to be less useful and civic minded. Henry VIII himself was coached in letter-writing by Erasmus, via William Blount, Lord Mountjoy, having had other less notable humanist tutors in his youth,[15] and some of Henry's work, as of other contemporary aristocratic writers, was in this more sober, humanist vein. Of greatest influence, however, would have been the example of French-speaking continental aristocrats, who favoured lyric-writing as one among other forms of diversion. Notoriously, Henry VIII's minions, including Berners's nephew Francis Bryan, as well as Henry's second wife, acquired dangerous French tastes during sojourns abroad.[16] Earlier had come to England the various noble and royal captives, foreign-born, mostly French, who diverted themselves in part with literary occupations while held hostage in England for extended periods: James I of Scotland, if he did write the so-called *Kingis Quair*, who was captive in England 1406-23, and Charles d'Orléans (1394-1465), taken at the battle of Agincourt in 1415 and held until 1440, part of the time in the keeping of the poet duke of Suffolk. René d'Anjou (1409-80), the storied poet-king of Naples and Sicily, became Henry VI's father-in-law in 1445, by virtue of a marriage arranged in large part by Charles d'Orléans's keeper Suffolk. Erotic poetry, deriving from such medieval French models as the writings of Charles d'Orléans, albeit with more recent influences also at work, was the pre-eminent form of courtier-writing to be associated with the court of Henry VIII.[17]

The underlying cause of the shift in attitude towards writing, however, becoming evident among English aristocrats early in the sixteenth century, would have to be social change, with shifts in the underlying class relations determining cultural epiphenomena.[18] It was not writing or the perception of writing's usefulness or lack thereof that changed among the aristocrats of early modern England, so much as the valuation placed on the activity. The ancient objection had been that writing was trivial – entertaining, and sometimes instructive or inspirational, but not essential, or even very useful, when compared to war-making, say, or other facets of statecraft and resource management. Writers themselves have tended to see things differently, of course, and they have also tended to have the last word, or at least the better, more resonant word, *aere perennius*, in Horace's notorious exaggeration (*Carm.* 3.30.1); but writers' own protestations of the value of writing can hardly be disinterested. In the early sixteenth century, writing did not necessarily become less trivial – certainly not among the courtiers, where, if anything, writing became more trivial. Trivial occupations became proper occupations for nobles, however, as a result of the political developments of the early modern period in England and their social consequences.

Mervyn James[19] has described what happened as 'the emergence of a "civil" society, in which the monopoly of both honour and violence by the state was asserted', out of an historically precedent lineage- or honour-based society, 'characterized above all by a stress on competitive assertiveness' (whence 'arose the uneasiness of the man of honour in relation to authority, seen as liable to cabin, crib and confine' (p. 314)), assuming 'a state of affairs in which resort to violence is natural and justifiable' (pp. 308-9), even to the point of overthrowing monarchs:

Honour therefore implied for those who professed it, a pressure towards the consistency of public (and therefore political) attitude which 'faithfulness' to lords and friends involved. As such it had a natural role in the kind of political conflict in which lords confronted unworthy or tyrannical rulers, and if necessary removed them, with the violence of 'war and battle' as the final sanction by means of which the conflict was resolved. The honour emphasis on will and moral autonomy precluded any sense of unconditional obedience, and provided a motive for resistance when authority, even in the person of the king himself, was felt to have failed the governing class it was expected to lead. ... (p. 343.)

The political culture of the world of honour was essentially pluralist. There was little room for the concepts of sovereignty, or of unconditional obedience, and such other *étatiste* notions. ... Honour societies revered kingship, but the place which will and autonomy occupied in the honour code implied the possibility of changing one's master, if he could no longer be freely and honourably served. Seen in terms of honour, that is in terms of an informal complex of attitudes and modes of behaviour, not to be confused with those of the law, kingship constituted one authority (admittedly the dominant one, whose claim to 'faithfulness' was the widest and most inclusive) among a number. ... It was only gradually, and during the Tudor period, that the realm ... [came to be] presided over by a crown whose sovereign authority constituted the only kind of 'lordship' which effectively survived. (pp. 327-8.)

The 'politics of violent conflict, related to the self-assertiveness and competitve emphasis of the honour code' (p. 344) gave way in the early sixteenth century, in James's analysis, to a noble politics based on 'obedience, consistent political behaviour, and order' (p. 360), in circumstances where 'conformity to law' was 'the likeliest guarantee of political and social stability' and 'obedience' gave 'the best insurance of personal survival' (p. 362): 'Henry VII, having rescued the realm from the "troublous" times of the Wars of the Roses, prepared the way for the "triumphant" reign of Henry VIII. In the latter's person the state emerges in all its grandeur not only as the vehicle of the "order" which was God's will for men, but also as the divinely appointed instrument for the renewal of religion' (p. 364).[20]

Debilitated by the economic consequences of the fourteenth-century plagues and then by their own foreign adventures and the internecine rumbles of the fifteenth century – leaving an aristocracy 'more self-effacing, less sure of their mission to coerce incompetent or high handed rulers, in all but a few misguided instances congenitally wary, convinced of the benefits of passive obedience'[21] – and faced finally with the aggrandizements of the early Tudor monarchs – the centralizing, absolutizing early Tudor monarchs, engaged in the 'double task of reducing all subjects, however great, to obedience to the Crown and of consolidating the realm into one unit under the king's sole jurisdiction'[22] – England's nobles were marginalized in terms of political power. This is not to say that the nobility was powerless or without influence:

The concentration of absolute power in a single person conferred a huge advantage on those who had easy access to that person. High politics came to be dominated by events in the monarch's antechamber (or indeed bedchamber) on the one hand and by cliques and factions on the other, every member of the court gravitating around those with direct access to the king, exchanging personal services along the line of access.[23]

Nevertheless, the courtly scramble for access to the monarch and noble faction-making, by means of which, increasingly, power had to be gained and used, indicate the degree to which power was vested in the monarch. To the members of the aristocracy, whose real influence was thus gradually though thoroughly reduced, trivial occupations were appropriate, the more trivial the better. Hence the 'neo-chivalric' play-acting of Henry VIII's court tournaments, for example, and the bizarre elaborations of armour design, at a time when the useful technology of war-waging had moved on;[24] and hence courtier-literature. These were people often with nothing better to do than to play and to write. These were people for whom doing something more consequential might be dangerous, during the reigns of monarchs, especially Henry VIII, whose displeasure, demonstrably, was fatal.

There is 'a strong point to be taken from the elaborate decorativeness of all court dress, manners and behaviour' in the sixteenth-century, as Lisa Jardine has written: 'That is that decorativeness is a signal of role loss.' More specifically, Jardine has argued, there was a 'close relationship between the growing political impotence of the courtier, and the rise' of literary occupations at court:

> The courtier in the courts of Europe became the latter-day supporter of feudal order and centralised government; but his actual role became increasingly parasitic, and the lack of any real function for him or her is reflected in increased decadence in court dress, increased stylisation in court behaviour, elaborate ceremonial and formalised leisure activities. ... The advantage of such a manual [as 'Castiglione's early-sixteenth-century handbook of humanistic studies for the nobility, *The Courtier*'] lay in the fact that it established even a male courtier's value entirely in terms of his manners and social accomplishments. The ability to dispute elegantly on the finer features of the Latin language: skill in drawing-room accomplishments: ... poetic ability as a natural gift: these are the marks of the true courtier. Financial and political acumen or professional training are apparently of no consequence in the parlour-game atmosphere.[25]

There arose a courtier-literature of protest against this state of affairs, a literature of dissent that represents the monarchy's encroachments and the aristocracy's reduction as spreading tyranny: Wyatt's first satire ('Mine own John Poins') is the best-known example, along with some of the overtly political lyrics he wrote, though Surrey too wrote in this vein and the greatest example is probably Wyatt's cycle of psalm paraphrases.[26] As Colin Burrow has pointed out, the extension of the treason law in 1534, to include treasonous utterance as well as treasonous doing, of which Wyatt was aware, made such writing riskier.[27] The legal development at once confirmed the dissenters' view, that the monarch was tyrannical, while also further encourging an opposite, self-censoring, quiescent literary response, pretending that there was no tyranny, to avoid the increased risks of sanction.

This other literary response among the courtiers was writing that acquiesed in, or even celebrated, aristocratic inconsequence. The same literary-historical development has been said to have occured in France: 'La poésie lyrique des princes, résignés ou désabusés, est vécue comme une rêverie où, avec le libre jeu de l'imagination, la fantasie humanie nie, sans les menacer, l'ordre et les valeurs de la société':

> A la fin du Moyen Age l'aristocratie française s'orientera vers le dillettantisme. Les nobles pratiqueront la ruse en politique, l'amateurisme en art. Choisir de vivre pour l'art, attitude de bien des aristocrates à partir de la Renaissance, ce sera choisir l'évasion hors des conditions réeles

de l'existence, dans le domaine de l'imaginaire. ... Pour eux l'existence aristocratique est donc vouée au rêve.[28]

The love-lyrics of the Henrician courtiers – voluminous, repetitous, sometimes astonishing in their effects, but above all always wholly inconsequential – were best from this perspective. Private religious devotions, too, might be appropriate, to the degree that they too distracted (from other socially or politically oriented occupations). Religious polemic was less appropriate, if it were anti-establisment in orientation, though anti-Papal or anti-Turkish propaganda of the sorts that Morley tried was fine, to the degree that it supported the monarchy's authority rather than subverting it. Historiography had dangers, too, as demonstrated by the use to which Surrey, in foul mood, had put the story of Sardanapalus, for example, though not necessarily, and in this respect Plutarch was especially convenient – the most anti-historical, anti-social of historical writers, who insisted that he was writing not history but studies of character instead, meant to illustrate, not social process and historical context, but idiosyncratic virtues or their defects, for reflection and personal emulation, transhistorically.[29]

The philosophical prose of the Tudor courtiers, however, articulates most clearly the fundamental points about the social purposes that courtier-writing served, to keep courtiers out of trouble. Writing the philosophical prose was a way for courtiers to keep occupied with inconsequential occupations, like some of the other kinds of writing they practised. In addition, the philosophical prose the courtiers produced supplied explanation and justification for their inconsequential occupation, inasmuch as the philosophical writings they produced espoused apathy: tranquility of mind, or, in some form or other, disengagement.

The purpose of courtier-writing generally was to express, albeit implicitly, the courtiers' acquiescence in the state of current affairs. Instead of making big trouble, instead of rebelling at home or turning to international piracy, for example, and instead of agitating against their role loss, though they did grumble from time to time, the courtiers were finding other ways to keep busy, for the most part ways that posed no threat. The courtiers' occupation with translating, as with their other literary occupations, attested to their busyness. Writing the philosophical prose too expressed the courtiers' acquiesence, implicitly, in the state of affairs, while also justifying acquiesence, explicitly, in a way that could not have been made to work as well in other genres of writing. Writing was a way for the courtiers to give evidence of the obviation of the threat that the courtier-class had historically posed the monarchy. Writing the philosophical prose gave the same evidence, while also justifying the obviation: the courtiers were writing instead of rebelling because, from the philosophical perspective articulated in the prose, they ought not to have been occupied with anything more activist or engaged than writing. The prose spells out the fundamental point: from the philosophical perspective, quietude was the right attitude to take towards worldly affairs. Like the lyrics, the courtiers' philosophical prose works are the literary products of a decorative class, also, however, providing an explicit rationale for the class's pre-occupation with decorative activities.

In this respect, too, Wyatt is the most important figure. His prose works – the translation of Plutarch's *Quiet of Mind*, dating from the 1520s, the two letters to his son, from the 1530s, and the *Declaration* and *Defence*, from his 1541 trial – tend to be treated as historical documents now, though Wyatt's contemporaries evidently regarded them as *Kunstprosa* or *bonae litterae*, copying them among Wyatt's poems in literary manuscript collections.[30] In translating and imitating genres of ancient philosophical discourse, the epistolary treatise and the forensic apology, Wyatt's prose established a practice that other courtiers were to emulate. The practice was to choose, for translation or imitation, ancient philosophical writings espousing the position that the wise attitude to adopt towards affairs of state or worldly affairs more generally was one of remove. The Plutarch translation,[31] presented to Queen Catherine at New Year's 1528, established the programme, at its beginning and end:

Sore toos are nat esed with gorgious showes, nor the whitthlowe with a ring, nor the hedach with a crowne. For to what purpose is thuse of money for the eschewyng of the sicknesse of the mynde, or for the easy and sure passage of lyfe? Or wherto serveth the use of glorie, or among courtiers apparence? Onelesse that they to whom these thynges chaunce can wisely use them whan they have them, and agayne whan they want them oversuffre the desyres of them. ... (p. 442.)

So nouther gorgiousnesse of buylding, nor weight of golde, nor noblenesse of kyn, nor greatnesse of empire, nor eloquence and fayre spekyng brinketh so moch clerenesse of lyfe and so plesant quietnes as bringeth a mynde discevered from trouble of busynesse. (p. 462.)

Between this beginning and end, the treatise provides practical advice on how to maintain quiet of mind, faced with prosperity as well as adversity: 'therfore the wise man shuld have the best thinges in his desyre, and loke for the worst, and in the temper of them bothe use of neither parte to moche' (p. 457), 'for so variable, dyvers and reboundable is the tune of this worlde, as of a harpe, nor in mortall thynges is there any thynge that is pure, clere, and symple' (p. 456). Given this circumstance, 'it can no wyse be sayde, "while I lyve, this I wyll nat suffre"; lette it be so. But this I may saye,' anticipating the anaphoric 'I cannot' series of Wyatt's later poem 'Mine Own John Poins',

whyle I lyve, this I wyll nat do: I wyl nat lye, I wyll use no crafty deceites for to compasse men, I wyll nat begyle, I wyll nat disceitfully lye in awayte – this, syns it is in us, it is a great help to them that lyfte themselfe up to the surety of mynde. (p. 461.)

Its best advice is that 'we shulde use thinges present as they come without any blame, and shulde rest with the plesaunt remembraunce of thynges past, and at the last we shulde drawe towarde thynges to come unferefully and assuredly, with sure and gladsome shyning hope' (p. 463).

In his letters to his son,[32] Wyatt espouses this same quiet under the name of honesty ('I have nothing to crye and cal apon you for but honestye, honestye' (p. 41)), which he defines as adherence to 'wisdome, gentlenes, sobrenes, disire to do good, frendlines to get the love of manye, and trougth above all the rest' (p. 38), along with 'the eschewing of the contraries of thes', especially 'manye and crafty falshed, the verie rote of al shame and dishonestye' (p. 39). Wyatt personifies honesty in his own father ('no man more piteful, no man more trew of his word, no man faster to his frend' (p. 39)); if not for his honesty, Wyatt argues,

the chansis of thes troublesome worlde that he was in had long ago ovirwhelmid him. This preservid him in prison from the handes of the tirant [sc. Richard III] that could find it in his hart to see him rakkid, from two yeres and more prisonment in Scotland, in irons and stoks, from the danger of sodeyn changes and commotions divers (p. 40).

Wyatt's forensic orations of 1541[33] espouse the honest, Socratic response to wrongful persecution – 'the danger of sodeyn changes and commotions divers' – as that response was described in Wyatt's translation of Plutarch:

Thus I say, knowing ourselfes of unvyncible minde, fortrusting to ourselfes, it becometh us to be assured agayn thinges to come, and to saye that to fortune that Socrates, fayning, did say by Anitus and Melitus, his accusers: "Truly", quoth he to the juges, "Anitus and Melitus may slee me, but to do me hurt or displeasure they can nat". For tho fortune might overthrow hym with dyvers sicknesses, take from him his riches, or accuse hym to a tyrant or to the people, yet might she nat truely make hym yll or faynt-herted or fearfull or altred of his mynde, or els make hym malicyous; and at a worde she might nat bereve him the right order of the mynde, whiche truely profiteth more to man for the ledyng of the lyf than the craft of sayling for to passe the sees. (*Quyete of Mynde*, p. 459.)

'God knowethe,' Wyatt wrote in his *Declaration*, 'what restles tormente yt hathe byne to me sens my hether commynge to examen myselffe, perusinge all my dedes to my remembraunce' (p. 180); but the product of the scrutiny was a clear conscience: 'I never ... [have] done thing whearin my thought coulde accuse my conscience' (p. 179). Of his accusers, he wrote: 'These men thynkethe yt inoughe to accuse and as all these sclaunderers use for a generall rule —whome thou lovest not, accuse. For tho he hele the wounde, yet the scharre shall remayne' (p. 193); 'Theie strake at me but theie hurte me not' (p. 183).

These same ideas recur in the courtier poetry. 'Quiet of mind' poems have been assigned to Wyatt ('Stonde who list upon the slipper top/ Of courtes estates, and lett me heare rejoyce;/ And use me quyet without lett or stoppe,/ Unknowen in courte, that hath such brackish joyes') and to Surrey ('The thinges for to attayne/ The happy life be thes, I finde:/ The riches left, not got with payne;/ The frutfull grownd; the quyet mynde').[34] The same point comes up in the poetry of other courtiers, as for example in Morley's poem, 'Never was I lesse alone then beyng alone.' Its beginning translates an apothegm associated with Scipio Africanus (who was accustomed to say of himself 'numquam se minus otiosum esse quam cum otiosus, nec minus solum quam cum solus esset'), a figure whose moderation amid a life of military and political occupation lent him special exemplary weight for Morley:

Never was I lesse alone then beyng alone:
Here in this chamber, evell thought had I none,
But allways I thought, to bryng the mynd to reste,
And that thought, off all thoughtes, I juge it the beste.
For yf my coffers hade ben full of perle and golde,
And fortune had favorde me even as that I wolde,
The mynd owt off quyat, so sage Senek sethe,
Itt hade ben no felicitie, but a paynfull dethe.
Love, then, whoo love wyll, to stande in highe degre:
I blame him nott a whitte, so that he followe me
And take his losse as quyatly as when that he doth wyne.
Then Fortune hathe no maistre of that stat he ys in,
But rulys and ys not rulyd, and takis the bettre parte.
O that man ys blessyde that lerns this gentle arte:
This was my felicitie, my pastyme, and my game;
I wisshe all my posteritie the wolde ensew the same.[35]

Even Francis Bryan went in for this sort of thing. A poem beginning 'Who list to lead a quiet life' has been imputed to him, as has also been another, beginning 'To my mishap alas I fynde/ That happy hap is daungerous'; and the collection of versified sentences more securely attributed to him, the so-called 'Proverbs of Solomon', also includes various injunctions against worldly engagement ('He ys like to fall that trust to a rotten stycke' (112), for example, or 'Who trottes on the yse ys like for to slyde' (46)). Bryan (because 'you have a syngler zele and delyte in workes that be pytthy and polytike') attracted a poem and dedication from Robert Whittinton, the grammarian and laureate, accompanying Whittinton's bilingual Latin-English 'Senecan' sentences, *The Myrrour or Glasse of Manners and Wysedome*, which includes, inter alia, 'If thou wylte be ryche and lyve quiet, forcast this: stryve with no man by thy wyll' and 'Take with good wyll, that which is of necessyte. Payne is overcome by paciens'. Bryan is said to have persuaded his uncle Lord Berners to produce an English translation of Antonio de Guevara's *The Golden Boke of Marcus Aurelius* (wherein 'is conteyned certayne ryght high and profounde sentences, and holsom counselles, and mervaylous devyses ageynst thencumbraunce of fortune and right swete consolations for them that are overthrowen by fortune', 'and speciallye princis and governours of the common welth, and mynisters of iustice, with other'), and Bryan himself translated Guevara's sententious *A Dispraise of the Life of the Courtier* ('full every where of olde auncient stories and wyse saiynges of the noble and notable philosophers and clerkes'), urging quiet instead. It begins, for example, arguing the case that 'nothing in this world ought to be called great but that heart whiche estemeth no great thinges': 'as touchyng the riches and honor of this worlde, more is the glorye of him that settes light by theim then he that hath the the [sic] cast for to get theim'.[36]

The courtiers did not distinguish, as professional scholars of ancient philosophy might have done, the *ataraxia* of Democritus, the Epicureans, and the Skeptics, from the *apatheia* of anti-Epicurean Stoics like Seneca and Epictetus (whom Wyatt recommends to his son), or from the *euthumia* of a later Platonist like Plutarch, who wrote diatribes against both Epicureans and Stoics that were known to the early sixteenth century – for the courtiers, the differences between the ancient schools were inconsequential.[37] What was wanted was a philosophy of quietism and acquiesence that still did not cost the courtiers too much, as the more austere philosophies of withdrawal might have. They found the requisite ideas indifferently amongst various ancients, and used what they found as suited.

Morley's philosophical translations are in this vein of courtier-writing, propounding philosophical justifications for apathy, though from this perspective the *Somnium Scipionis* translation is somewhat ambivalent.[38] Competing views of civic involvement are articulated in this piece of Cicero. On the one hand, the treatise establishes that the building and maintenence of states is good: nothing pleases God more, it says, and for civic good works blessedness in the afterlife is the reward (*Som. Scip.* 3.1 and 9.2). On the other hand, the treatise establishes also, the more graphically, that the earth is a tiny place, and anything happening in any corner of it, even at Rome, can hardly be of anything but tiny significance, when viewed from the cosmic vista that the dream-vision opens up (*Som. Scip.* 3.7-7.5). It is as if the piece says, both, civic affairs are important and civic affairs are trivial, that they matter and they do not matter. The history of the reception of this piece of Cicero has been divided along these lines.

Hans Baron showed that only in the Renaissance did the vision's exortations to civic engagement begin to be taken seriously again, when the piece was restored to its proper context in Cicero's life and writings; the medieval tradition, having lost track of the *De republica*, among other things, appreciated only the *Somnium*'s otherworldliness.[39]

Morley's translation cannot be placed in one or the other of these camps. It is a straightforward, literal rendition of the Cicero into English. At a place or two, Morley may not have understood the Latin thoroughly, or he may have failed to convey the point of the Latin effectively in English. He did not rewrite, however. Neither adding nor omitting nor altering, in this case Morley reproduces the ambivalence of the Ciceronian piece. Morley knew of and mentions Cicero's *De republica* (fol. 2ʳ); in other words, he did know something of the *Somnium*'s ancient context. Also, when faced with the two crucial passages on civic engagement, he does not take the route of omission or alteration. On the other hand, setting Morley's versions of passages on civic duty side by side with their Latin originals suggests a wish on Morley's part to mitigate the republican, egalitarian torque of Cicero's remarks, or an inability to do otherwise. In 3.1, for example, one of the two sections of the *Somnium* to speak strongly in favour of civic activism, Morley substitutes instead more hierarchized conceptions, compatible with monarchy (if not with absolutism). Morley renders Cicero's 'harum rectores et conservatores' with 'whois rulers, justly ruling', and 'concilia coetusque hominum *iure sociati*' with 'the councellis and congregacions of men *rightfully and justly governyd*', substituting for Cicero's notions of guardianship, entrustment, and association, among equal members of a community, the different notion of governance, of rulers and ruled:

> For there is nothing more exceptable to that prinsly God selestiall, whiche rulyth all this world, than the councellis and congregacions of men rightfully and justly governyd, whiche commonly we call cities, whois rulers, justly ruling, being departed from this world, revert hither. (fol. 3ᵛ.)

Morley recommends Macrobius's commentary (fol. 2ʳ), promoting thereby also the neo-platonist, otherworldly context in which Cicero's piece was circulated throughout the Middle Ages, and in any case the most striking, most memorable image of the *Somnium*, most developed in the Cicero as in Morley's translation and the Macrobian commentary, is the image of the world as an insignificant spot. There are remarks encouraging civic engagement in the *Somnium*; historically, however, the dominant impression that readers appear to have taken away from it has been its promotion of philosophical disengagement from mere earthly concerns.

Morley's version of the Seneca letters gives more obtrusive evidence of a contribution on his part towards doing the job that the courtiers' philosophical prose did, of providing not only evidence of quiet occupation but also rationales for quietude. Though the translating here too is for the most part straightforward and literal, in the present instance Morley also edited. Some of his choices in translating are significant; Morley omitted passages from the Seneca, repeatedly, in ways that establish patterns; and, most grossly, Morley wedded two separate letters from the Senecan corpus, omitting large sections of each in the process and so creating something distinctive.[40]

The bulk of the piece is Morley's translation of a letter to do with the destruction of Lyons by fire, probably in 64, and an unphilosophical reaction to the disaster on the part of Liberalis, an acquaintence shared by Seneca and Lucillius, the recipient of

Seneca's *Epistulae morales*. This letter is no. 91 in the editions now current, though in the Erasmian edition current in Morley's day it was numbered 92 – fourescore twelve, as Morley put it in the presentation manuscript (fol. 3^{r}). Seneca's letter develops the points that Fortune can and does change everything or anything, at any time, anywhere, and that, in any case, Time will destroy all (91.10); and the letter offers, as its moral counsel, exortations to expect the worst, always, and to suffer whatever comes quietly, apathetically.

In making this letter into his own, Morley left some things out. He abbreviated the section on Time the destroyer (91.11-12), for example, omitting a long depressing passage making the point that, if even the mightiest works of nature are subject to decay and destruction, there can be no hope for merely human constructions like states: 'casurae stant', Seneca says, and in fact all things are doomed ('nihil tutum'):

Vasta vis ignium colles per quos relucebat erosit et quondam altissimos vertices, solacia navigantium ac speculas, ad humile deduxit. Ipsius naturae opera vexantur et ideo aequo animo ferre debemus urbium excidia. Casurae stant; omnis hic exitus manet, sive ventorum interna vis flatusque per clusa violenti pondus sub quo tenentur excusserint, sive torrentium impetus in abdito vastior obstantia effregerit, sive flammarum violentia conpaginem soli ruperit, sive vetustas, a qua nihil tutum est, expugnaverit minutatim, sive gravitas caeli egesserit populos et situs deserta corruperit.

The immense force of volcanic fires that once made the mountain-tops glow has eaten them away and reduced to lowly stature what once were soaring peaks, reassuring beacons to the mariner. The works of nature herself suffer. So it is only right that we should bear the overthrow of cities with resignation. They stand just to fall. Such is the sum total of the end that awaits them, whether it be the blast of subterranean explosion throwing off the restraining weight above it, or the violence of floodwaters increasing to a ponderous degree underground until it breaks down everything in its way, or a volcanic outburst fracturing the earth's crust, or age (to which nothing is immune) overcoming them little by little, or plague carrying off its population and causing the deserted area to decay. (91.11-12.)[41]

Also, Morley abbreviates a frightening remark about what can happen, not to individuals, but to states: Morley puts 'Kingdommes, whiche by straunge nacions coulde not be sobverted, by their own civile debates, thei have come to destruction' (fol. 11^{v}), where Seneca had gone the one step further, saying that even those states that survive invasion and civil strife are still also doomed to fall: 'Quae domesticis bellis steterant regna, quae externis, inpellente nullo ruunt: quota quaeque felicitatem civitas pertulit' 'States which stood firm through civil war as well as wars external collapse without a hand being raised against them. How few nations have made of their prosperity a lasting thing!' (91.7).

Morley's largest-scale alteration, however, was his omission of the letter's conclusion, for which he substituted a section from another of Seneca's letters. By omitting the ending of letter ninety-one, Morley avoids a justification of suicide (91.21) – something he avoids on another occasion as well – and he avoided a derogation of Alexander the Great (91.17-18). Alexander quit his geography lesson, the story goes, as soon as he began to learn how insignificant was even the empire to which he aspired when viewed in proper perspective, *Somnium Scipionis*-like; Alexander could not bear it that the ambitions even of rulers were ridiculous. Morley also thus avoided the consideration that follows from this in Seneca's letter, that death makes equals of all, king and commoner alike: 'The beggar and the lord, in one state then they be' (91.16 and 18-21).[42]

Most significantly, omitting the ending of letter 91 made it possible for Morley to avoid Seneca's passing suggestion that there might be kinds of misfortune to which the proper reaction was, not forebearance, but resistance. One of the appeals of this letter for Morley must have been the fact that it concentrates so on natural disaster: the fire that destroyed Lyons was not a product of human agency and could not have been prevented by human agency, so no person nor group could be held to account. However Boethian Seneca's advice sounds at times, Seneca's advice grew out of a different situation: Boethius's misfortune came about by a tyrant's culpable choice, whereas the misfortune at issue in Seneca's letter was more properly implacable. Morley abandons the letter of Seneca's at the point where Seneca distinguishes, briefly, between the one and the other of these kinds of misfortune: calamities fit to be met with resignation and those fit to be met with resolve. Morley leaves out Seneca's proposal that cases of injustice are different:

Nihil horum [sc. Fortune's impositions] indignandum est: in eum intravimus mundum in quo his legibus vivitur. Placet: pare. Non placet: quacumque vis exi. Indignare si quid in te iniqui proprie constitutum est; sed si haec summos imosque necessitas alligat, in gratiam cum fato revertere, a quo omnia resolvuntur.

There's no ground for resentment in all this. We've entered into a world in which these are the terms life is lived on – if you're satisfied with that, submit to them, if you're not, get out, whatever way you please. Resent a thing by all means if it represents an injustice decreed against yourself personally; but if this same constraint is binding on the lowest and the highest alike, then make your peace again with destiny, the destiny that unravels all ties. (91.15.)

In place of the ending of this letter, Morley substituted a passage from another letter in the same collection, a letter in which Seneca attempts to define the right relationship between the good and the honourable, the point being neither can thrive where both are not present (120.3). This letter is numbered 120 in current editions, though in the Erasmian edition it was numbered 121.[43] The letter delineates the man of perfect virtue (120.10) and contrasts him with the man of evil mind (120.20-2), who seems discomfortingly to recall the ageing Henry VIII.[44] Morley has not used these sections of the letter, however, but a section from the middle of it (120.12-17) in praise of apathy – a fairly innocuous bit, making at greater length a point made briefly in the omitted portion of letter ninety-one as well, that having 'a perfecte soule, sett in the highest place of vertue', is a matter of putting up with unpleasantness:

Hoc puta rerum naturam dicere: 'ista de quibus quereris omnibus eadem sunt; nulli dare faciliora possum, sed quisquis volet sibi ipse illa reddet faciliora'. Quomodo? aequanimitate.

Imagine that nature is saying to you, 'Those things you grumble about are the same for everyone. I can give no one anything easier. But anyone who likes may make them easier for himself.' How? By viewing things with equanimity. (91.18.)

In putting together this piece, what Morley avoided were the political threats: the explicit threat of Seneca's suggestion that there is an obligation to fight back against injustice and tyranny, as well as the threat implicit in Seneca's various observations that even the apparently most mighty of empires must fall and fade, and that time will make all equal in death, though these observations on time's ravages might also have been presented, not as threats, but as general exortations to disengage, as they were presented in Morley's translation of Petrarch's *Triumphs*. What Morley choose to keep and use from Seneca was the praise of apathy – of subservient, deferential, obedient quiet of mind:

> Whiche whosoo hath, whatsoever falleth unto him, he shall never curse Fortune, nor blame, but be it swete or sower, take it well, saying, 'this ys my chaunce; I must and will abide it'. Without doubt, he shewith himself to be of a vertuous minde that mornethe not when he sufferethe evill fortune, nor complayneth not of his desteny. He givethe grete ensaumple to other, and shynes in darkenes, none otherwise then the faier clere light, when he shewith himself patient, pleasaunte, an<d> equall, and obeing as well to Godes will as to mans. Suche a one hath a perfect soule, sett in the highest place of vertue. (fols 16^{r}-17^{r}.)

In the end, Morley's Senecan confection has a clear message – a message as pertinent to Princess Mary's uncertain circumstance as to Morley's – of the dangers of the world and the way to overcome them: bad happens here, always, one way and another; the thing to do, as much as possible, is to avoid. After all, as the *Somnium Scipionis* makes clear, to do otherwise is only vanity. This message might have been meant for other courtiers as well, set round the thunderous thrones of the early Tudor monarchs, in the phrase attributed to Wyatt, though borrowed from elsewhere in Seneca's writings. It is a message that the survivors, like Morley, would have taken to heart:

> Who lyst his welthe and eas retayne
> Hymselffe let hym unknowne contayne;
>   Presse not to Fast in at that gatte
> Wher the retorne standes by desdayne;
>   For sure, circa regna tonat.[45]

The message would also have signified for the monarchy (and its apparatus of order-maintenance), indirectly and in a general way, that Morley understood his situation and would be no trouble. Like other courtier writers, he was keeping himself busy with decorative occupations – in this instance, philosophical translations justifying courtiers' disengagement.

NOTES

1 London, British Library, Royal MS 18 A.LX, fol. 1^{r-v}, here with modernized editorial punctuation and orthography, used also for other quotations in the paper. The whole text of the *Somnium Scipionis* translation is given in Appendix 4 below.

2 BL, Royal MS 17 A.XXX, fol. 1^{r-v} (the whole text of this, the translation of Seneca, being given in Appendix 5 below), and Royal MS 18 A.LX, fol. 1^{r}.

3 BL, Royal MS 17 A.XXX, fol. 2^{v}.

4 Lyrics attributed to Henry VIII survive in BL, Add. MS 31922 ('Henry VIII's MS') and Add. MS 5665 ('Ritson's MS'), edited in John Stevens, *Music and Poetry in the Early Tudor Court*, 2nd edn (Cambridge, 1979), pp. 344-5 and 388-425; on Henry's love-letters, see now Seth Lerer, *Courtly Letters in the Age of Henry VIII* (Cambridge, 1997), pp. 87-121; and on the question of Henry's authorship of the anti-Lutheran *Assertio septem sacramentarum*, see David Carlson, 'Royal Tutors in the Reign of Henry VII', *Sixteenth Century Journal* 22 (1991), 274. On Richard I's literary occupations, see Elizabeth Salter, *English and International*, ed. by Derek Pearsall & Nicolette Zeeman (Cambridge, 1988), p. 30. A poem in French and Occitan versions is attributed to him. Single poems have also been attributed

to his successors Edward II and Edward III, though still more dubiously: see Paul Studer, 'An Anglo-Norman Poem by Edward II, King of England', *Modern Language Review* 16 (1921), 34-46, and, for the poem attributed to Edward III, Kervyn de Lettenhove, *Oeuvres de Froissart: Chroniques*, vol. 1, pt 1 (Bruxelles: Devaux, 1870), 77-80 and 541-53.

5 English royal interest in writing in the fourteenth and fifteenth centuries is surveyed in A. I. Doyle, 'English Books In and Out of Court from Edward III to Henry VII', in *English Court Culture in the Later Middle Ages*, ed. by V. J. Scattergood & J. W. Sherborne (London, 1983), pp. 163-81; Michael J. Bennett, 'The Court of Richard II and the Promotion of Literature', in *Chaucer's England*, ed. by Barbara A. Hanawalt (Minneapolis, 1992), pp. 3-20; Jeanne E. Krochalis, 'The Books and Reading of Henry V and His Circle', *Chaucer Review* 23 (1988), 50-77; Janet Backhouse, 'Founders of the Royal Library: Edward IV and Henry VII as Collectors of Illuminated Manuscripts', in *England in the Fifteenth Century*, ed. by Daniel Williams (Woodbridge, 1987), pp. 23-41; and Gordon Kipling, 'Henry VII and the Origins of Tudor Patronage', in *Patronage in the Renaissance*, ed. by Guy Fitch Lytle & Stephen Orgel (Princeton, 1981), pp. 117-64, esp. 120-34; and see also Richard Firth Green, *Poets and Princepleasers* (Toronto, 1980), pp. 91-9. On the literary interests of Humfrey of Gloucester, see esp. Alfonso Sammut, *Unfredo duca di Gloucester e gli umanisti italiani* (Padua, 1980).

6 On Henry's *Livre de seyntz medecines*, see Dominica Legge, *Anglo-Norman Literature and its Background* (Oxford, 1963), pp. 216-20. The aristocratic translators and their works are listed in H. S. Bennett, *Chaucer and the Fifteenth Century*, corrected edn (Oxford, 1979), pp. 296-7, 314-15, and 317. Montagu's poetry is mentioned in E. Salter, 'Chaucer and Internationalism', *Studies in the Age of Chaucer* 2 (1980), 79, and in Paul Strohm, *Hochon's Arrow* (Princeton, 1992), p. 91, with further evidence printed in A. J. Minnis, *Oxford Guides to Chaucer: the Shorter Poems* (Oxford, 1995), p. 14. On the poetry attributed to Suffolk, see Henry Noble MacCracken, 'An English Friend of Charles of Orléans', *PMLA* 26 (1911), 142-80, and, more recently, J. P. M. Jassen, 'Charles D'Orléans and the Fairfax Poems', *English Studies* 70 (1989), 206-24. These examples are all listed by Green, *Poets and Princepleasers*, p. 109.

7 Plutarch, *Pericles* 1-2, quoted here in the 'Dryden' translation, *Plutarch The Lives of the Noble Grecians and Romans*, ed. by Arthur Hugh Clough (New York, n.d.), pp. 182-3.

8 The chief ancient source is Suetonius, *Nero* 20-5; the references here are to Tacitus, *Annales* 14.14-16 (my translations) and Suetonius, *Nero* 23.2 and 49.1 (trans. by Robert Graves, *Suetonius The Twelve Caesars* (1957; rpt Harmondsworth, 1978), pp. 220, 238). Nero's efforts are reviewed more sympathetically by H. Bardon, 'Les poésies de Néron', *Revue des études latines* 14 (1936), 337-49, and by M. P. Charlesworth, 'Nero: Some Aspects', *Journal of Roman Studies* 40 (1950), 69-71.

9 *Ep.* 90.14. Here and subsequently, for Seneca's letters are used the Latin text of L. D. Reynolds, ed., *L. Annaei Senecae ad Lucilium epistulae morales* (Oxford, 1965), and the modern English translations of Robin Alexander Campbell, *Seneca Letters from a Stoic* (Harmondsworth, 1969), and, where Campbell is out, of Richard M. Gummere in the Loeb edition, *Seneca ad Lucilium Epistolae morales*, 3 vols (London, 1917-25).

10 Richard Pace, *De fructu qui ex doctrina percipitur*, ed. by Frank Manley & Richard S. Sylvester (New York, 1967), p. 22; my translation.

11 Julius Vindex, the earliest of the rebels against Nero, is reported to have taunted him with the inadequacy of his lyre-playing, giving it as the reason for the revolt: Suetonius, *Nero* 41.1. The most widely circulated contemporary indictment of Henry's tyranny may have been Wyatt's poem 'Mine Own John Poins', which does not mention Henry's literary efforts. On the other hand, Chapuys reported that Henry's poetry was mocked by Anne and George Boleyn: see Lerer, *Courtly Letters in the Age of Henry VIII*, pp. 118-19.

12 See N. F. Blake, 'Lord Berners: a Survey', *Medievalia et Humanistica*, n.s. 2 (1971), 119-32.
13 *The Arte of English Poesie by George Puttenham*, ed. by Gladys Doidge Willcock & Alice Walker (Cambridge, 1936), pp. 59-62.
14 See Cecil Clough, esp. 'Baldassare Castiglione's Presentation Manuscript to King Henry VII', *Liverpool Classical Monthly* 3 (1978), 269-72.
15 See Carlson, 'Royal Tutors in the Reign of Henry VII' (n. 4 above), pp. 274-6.
16 See Greg Walker, 'The "Expulsion of the Minions" of 1519 Reconsidered', *Historical Journal* 32 (1989), 13-16, and, for Anne Boleyn's gallicism, inter alia, Retha Warnicke, *The Rise and Fall of Anne Boleyn: Family Politics at the Court of Henry VIII* (Cambridge, 1989), p. 27.
17 A de luxe manuscript comprising mostly poetry of Charles d'Orléans was made for Prince Arthur, Henry's elder brother, and has remained in the Royal collection: BL, Royal MS 16 F.II. On it, see T. D. Hobbs, 'Prosimetrum in *Le Livre dit Grace Entiere sur le fait du gouvernement d'un Prince*, the Governance of a Prince Treatise in British Library MS Royal 16 F.II', in *Littera et Sensus: Essays on Form and Meaning in Medieval French Literature Presented to John Fox*, ed. by D. A. Trotter (Exeter, 1989), esp. pp. 51-4. On James I, see *The Kingis Quair*, ed. by J. Norton-Smith (Oxford, 1971), pp. xix-xxv, and on René d'Anjou, see Daniel Poirion, *Le poète et le prince: L'évolution du lyrisme courtois de Guillaume de Machaut à Charles d'Orléans* (Paris, 1965), esp. pp. 52-4.
18 For this principle, see Raymond Williams, 'Base and Superstructure in Marxist Cultural Theory', *New Left Review* 82 (1973), 3-16.
19 In 'English Politics and the Concept of Honour, 1485-1642' (1978), rpt in his *Society, Politics and Culture: Studies in Early Modern England* (Cambridge, 1986), pp. 308-415. References for subsequent quotations from this paper are supplied parenthetically, following the quotations.
20 The 'obsession with obedience' that characterizes the Henrician religious settlement ('From 1535 onwards, Henry's agenda was the preservation and promotion of his royal supremacy' (p. 894) is discussed further in Richard Rex, 'The Crisis of Obedience: God's Word and Henry's Reformation', *Historical Journal* 39 (1996), 863-94.
21 K. B. MacFarlane, 'The Wars of the Roses', in *England in the Fifteenth Century*, ed. by G. L. Harriss (London, 1981), pp. 259-60: 'Wars kill; they also demoralize. Civil wars are usually the more lethal and the more demoralizing. It is possible that what has given rise to the belief that the old nobility was no longer there after 1487 is that its members had become more self-effacing, less sure of their mission to coerce incompetent or high handed rulers, in all but a few misguided instances congenitally wary, convinced of the benefits of passive obedience. On and off for more than a generation there had been much bloodshed, treachery, and abrupt reversals of fortune. The suspected presence of spies everywhere added to the general sense of insecurity; and so had the failure of those traditional bonds which were meant to give some permanence to the relationship between a man and his lord. The married calm of the medieval policy was rent. ... It is an attractive theory. My main doubt is whether so obvious a lesson still had to be learned in 1450. The magnates had surely been grounded in all its rudiments between 1386 and 1415. ... Even so the Wars of the Roses had hammered the lesson well home. To those in any danger of forgetting it under the first two Tudors it was soon recalled by the practical consequences of the least false step.' Cf. James, 'English Politics and the Concept of Honour', pp. 357, 368.
22 Geoffrey R. Elton, *The Tudor Constitution* (Cambridge, 1960), p. 30; cf. pp. 30-2 and 195-200.
23 Patricia Crone, *Pre-Industrial Societies* (Oxford, 1989) p. 60, quoted in G. W. Bernard, 'The Tudor Nobility in Perspective', in *The Tudor Nobility*, ed. by Bernard (Manchester, 1992), p. 19. See also the cautionary conclusion reached by Steven Gunn, 'The Structures of Politics in Early Tudor England', *Transactions of the Royal Historical Society*, 6th ser., 5 (1995), 90:

'There were strong kings in early Tudor England, making policy, directing councillors who worked effectively with one another and destroying those they judged to have betrayed them; there were also political groups of varying types [sc. kinship groups and affinities, factions and other court parties] working to influence those policies and to advance one another's careers, at times at the expense of their competitors. In early Tudor England as in comparable personal monarchies, the interactions between the king and his servants reflected initiatives taken by each in response to those of the other. As our sources rarely take us into the king's council, more rarely into his privy chamber and never into his head, it may be only right to be a little unsure about the ultimate balance between the king and his factions.'

24 Cf. Steven Gunn, 'Chivalry and the Politics of the Early Tudor Court', in *Chivalry in the Renaissance*, ed. by Sydney Anglo (Woodbridge, 1990), pp. 107-28. The quoted phrase is from Paul N. Siegel, 'Shakespeare and the Neo-Chivalric Cult of Honor', *Centennial Review* 8 (1964), 39-70.

25 Lisa Jardine, *Still Harping on Daughters* (Sussex, 1983), pp. 54-6.

26 On dissent in the courtier poetry, see Colin Burrow, 'Horace at Home and Abroad: Wyatt and Sixteenth-Century Horatianism', in *Horace Made New*, ed. by Charles Martindale & David Hopkins (Cambridge, 1993), esp. pp. 34-7, and Alistair Fox, *Politics and Literature in the Reigns of Henry VII and Henry VIII* (Oxford, 1989), esp. pp. 3-7; also, on particular poems, S. P. Zitner, 'Truth and Mourning in a Sonnet by Surrey', *ELH* 50 (1983), 509-29; Alexandra Halasz, 'Wyatt's David', *Texas Studies in Language and Literature* 30 (1988), 320-44; William A. Sessions, 'Surrey's Wyatt: Autumn 1542 and the New Poet', in *Rethinking the Henrician Era*, ed. by Peter C. Herman (Urbana, 1994), pp. 168-92; and Susan Brigden, 'Henry Howard, Earl of Surrey, and the "Conjured League"', *Historical Journal* 37 (1994), 507-37, and '"The Shadow that You Know": Sir Thomas Wyatt and Sir Francis Bryan at Court and in Embassy', *Historical Journal* 39 (1996), 1-31.

27 Burrow, 'Horace at Home and Abroad', pp. 36-7, and 'Tudor Sanctuaries', *Essays in Criticism* 41 (1991), 57-8. The pertinent sections of the new law are in Elton, *Tudor Constitution*, pp. 61-3. Wyatt's understanding of the law is indicated by remarks in his defence, responding to an accusation that he had uttered treason: 'Reherse here the lawe of wordes. Declare, my lords, I beseke you, the meaninge therof. This includythe that wordes maliciouslie spoken or trayterously agaynste the kynges persone shuld be taken for treasone. Yt is not mente, maisters, of wordes which dyspyse the kynge lyghtly, or which are not all the most reverently spoken of him, as a man shulde judge a chaes agaynste hym at the tennis, whearwith he weare not all the beste contented; but suche wordes as perswade commotions or seditions or suche thynges' (*Defence*, ed. by Kenneth Muir, *Life and Letters of Sir Thomas Wyatt* (Liverpool, 1963), p. 196, and cf. pp. 204-5 and 208).

28 Poirion, *Le poète et le prince* (n. 17 above), p. 95; cf. pp. 95-9.

29 Cf. the remark of Robin Collingwood, quoted in Arnaldo Momigliano, *The Development of Greek Biography* (Cambridge, Mass., 1971), p. 3: 'A biography, for example, however much history it contains, is constructed on principles that are not only non-historical but anti-historical.' Plutarch's chief statement of purpose is in *Alexander* 1.2-3 ('Dryden' trans., p. 801): 'My design is not to write histories, but lives. And the most glorious exploits do not always furnish us with the clearest discoveries of virtue or vice in men; sometimes a matter of less moment, an expression or a jest, informs us better of their characters and inclinations, than the most famous seiges, the greatest armaments, or the bloodiest battles whatsoever. Therefore as portrait-painters are the more exact in the lines and features of the face, in which the character is seen, than in the other parts of the body, so I must be allowed to give my more particular attention to the marks and indications of the souls of men, and while I endeavour by these to portray their lives, may be free to leave more weighty matters and great battles to be treated by others.' Important programmatic remarks also occur in *Pericles* 1.1-

2.4, *Timoleon* Prologue.1-5, and *Cimon* 2.4-5. The Surrey poem in question is 'Th'Assyryans king, in peas with fowle desyre', in *Surrey Poems*, ed. by Emrys Jones (Oxford, 1964), no. 32, p. 29; on such early Tudor uses for history, in general, see D. R. Woolf, 'The Power of the Past: History, Ritual, and Political Authority in Tudor England', in *Political Thought and the Tudor Commonwealth*, ed. by Paul A. Fideler & T. F. Mayer (London, 1992), esp. pp. 25-6.

30 Wyatt's letters to his son were copied in the middle of Wyatt's own manuscript collection of verse, now BL, Egerton MS 2711, fols 71r-73r; see Ewald Flügel, 'Die handschriftliche überlieferung der gedichte von Sir Thomas Wyatt', *Anglia* 19 (1897), 413-19. And Wyatt's *Declaration* (fols 5r-6v) and *Defence* (fols 7r-15r) were copied in a courtier miscellany, likely as early as *c.* 1550, of which only a fragment survives, as part of manuscript assembled by John Stow, now BL, Harley MS 78, along with a number of courtier-poems and Surrey's 1542 prose plea for lenience (fol. 24r-v; see Edwin Casady, *Henry Howard, Earl of Surrey* (New York, 1938), pp. 88-91); of it, H. A. Mason, *Editing Wyatt* (Cambridge, 1972), p. 35, wrote that 'it is a matter for regret' that so little of the collection survives, 'for we might then have learned what an intelligent anthology of Wyatt's poems made by a contemporary would have looked like'. Also, that Surrey, in an epigram addressed to Thomas Radcliffe (*Surrey Poems*, ed. by Jones, no. 34.6, p. 32: 'But Wiat said true, the skarre doth aye endure') may have been quoting from Wyatt's *Defence* (*Life and Letters*, ed. by Muir, p. 193: 'For tho he hele the wounde yet the scharre shall remayne') suggests the wider, non-utilitarian interest that even Wyatt's forensic pieces would have held for contemporaries; but on the phrase, see Joost Daalder, 'Wyatt's Proverbial "Though the wound be healed, yet a scar remains"', *Archiv* 223 (1986), 354-6.

31 *The Quyete of Mynde*, ed. by Kenneth Muir & Patricia Thomson, in *The Collected Poems of Sir Thomas Wyatt* (Liverpool, 1969), pp. 440-63. References for subsequent quotations from this edition of the work are supplied parenthetically, following the quotations. The work is discussed in Thomson, 'Sir Thomas Wyatt: Classical Philosophy and English Humanism', *Huntington Library Quarterly* 25 (1962), 79-88.

32 The letters are in *Life and Letters*, ed. by Muir, pp. 38-41 and 41-3. References for subsequent quotations are supplied parenthetically, following the quotations. They are discussed in Thomson, 'Sir Thomas Wyatt: Classical Philosophy and English Humanism', pp. 88-90, mentioning a thematic continuity from the *Queyte of Mynde* to the letters, p. 90.

33 The *Declaration* and the *Defence* are likewise in *Life and Letters*, ed. by Muir, pp. 178-84 and 187-209. References for subsequent quotations are supplied parenthetically, following the quotations. The Greek origin of this genre is described in Momigliano, *The Development of Greek Biography*, pp. 58ff.

34 The 'Wyatt' poem cited, 'Stonde who list upon the slipper top', is in *The Collected Poems of Sir Thomas Wyatt*, ed. by Muir & Thomson, no. 240, p. 240 (sic); the Surrey poem 'The thinges for to attayne' is in *Surrey Poems*, ed. by Jones, no. 40, p. 34; other examples include the Arundel manuscript poem 'If right be rakt and over ronne' ('Amonge good thinges I prove and fynde / The quyet lyfe doth moste abounde'), sometimes attributed to John Harington the elder, in *The Arundel Harington Manuscript of Tudor Poetry*, ed. by Ruth Hughey (Columbus, 1960), no. 17, pp. 90-1, and the Blage manuscript poem 'Sustayne, abstayne, kep well in your mynd' ('Ffor ye shall therby greate quyetnes ffynd'), in *The Collected Poems of Sir Thomas Wyatt*, ed. by Muir & Thomson, p. 411.

35 The Morley poem is quoted from Oxford, Bodleian Library, Ashmole MS 48, fol. 9v. The manuscript was once the possession of Richard Sheale, the minstrel, active in the mid-sixteenth century, and it includes (fol. 10r) another poem on a similar theme that it also attributes to Morley. The first of these two poems was printed in Agnes Kate Foxwell, *The Poems of Sir Thomas Wiat* (1913; rpt New York, 1964), II, 162-3, incompletely, and the

other in Anthony à Wood, *Athenae Oxonienses*, ed. by Philip Bliss (1813-20; rpt New York, 1967), I, col. 117; both are given in full in Appendix 6 below. On the manuscript, see Andrew Taylor, 'The Sounds of Chivalry: Lute Song and Harp Song for Sir Henry Lee', *Journal of the Lute Society of America* 25 (1992), esp. 15-18. For the Scipionic sentence, see Cicero, *De off.* 3.1.1: 'P. Scipionem, Marce fili, eum, qui primus Africanus appellatus est, dicere solitum scripsit Cato, qui fuit eius fere aequalis, numquam se minus otiosum esse, quam cum otiosus, nec minus solum, quam cum solus esset'; and cf. Edward A. Allen, '"Never Less Alone Than When Alone"', *Modern Language Notes* 24 (1909), 123.

36 For the attribution of 'Who list to lead a quiet life' (no. 286 in Tottel's Miscellany), see *Tottel's Miscellany (1557-1587)*, ed. by Hyder Edward Rollins, rev. edn (Cambridge, Mass., 1965), I, 82-3, n. 1; for the other, see A. Stuart Daley, 'The Uncertain Author of Poem 225, Tottel's *Miscellany*', *Studies in Philology* 47 (1950), 485-93. Both these attributions are implausible. For the 'Proverbs of Solomon', see Robert S. Kinsman, '"The Proverbes of Salmon do Playnly Declare": a Sententious Poem on Wisdom and Governance, Ascribed to Francis Bryan', *Huntington Library Quarterly* 42 (1979), 279-312. The 'rotten sticke' sentence recalls the Wyatt poem 'Farewell Love and all thy lawes for ever' ('Me lusteth no lenger rotten boughes to clyme', in *The Collected Poems of Sir Thomas Wyatt*, ed. by Muir & Thomson, no. 13.14, pp. 12-13) and the 'trottes on yse' sentence is recalled in Wyatt's epistolary satire addressed to Bryan ('to the, therefore, that trottes still up and downe,/ And never restes' (in *The Collected Poems of Sir Thomas Wyatt*, ed. by Muir & Thomson, no. 107.11-12, p. 95) as well as in Wyatt's prose *Declaration*, where he uses similar terms to describe his ambassadorial function: 'I trotted contynually up and downe that hell throughe heat and stinke' (ed. by Muir, *Life and Letters*, p. 181). The quotations from Whittinton's sentences, *The Myrrour or Glasse of Manners* (London, 1547 (STC 17502)), are from sigs. a6^{r}, b3^{r}, and b1^{r} respectively; on Whittinton, see Thomas F. Mayer, *Thomas Starkey and the Commonwealth* (Cambridge:, 1989), pp. 17-26, and Carlson, *English Humanist Books* (Toronto, 1993), pp. 102-22. These sentences were regarded as Seneca's until relatively recently and may in fact derive from Seneca's *De officiis*, otherwise a lost work: see E. Bickel, 'Die Schrift des Martinus von Bracara *Formulae vitae honestae*', *Rheinisches Museum* 60 (1905), 505-51. On the Berners translation of Guevara, see Blake, 'Lord Berners', pp. 128-9; the quotations are from *The Golden Boke* (London, 1535 (STC 12436)), fols 166^{v}-167^{r}. The imputation of motive influence to Bryan is made in the book's colophon ('translated out of frenche into englysshe by John Bourchier knyghte lorde Barners ... at the instant desyre of his nevewe syr Francis Bryan knyghte'), supplied by the publisher Berthelet, though the claim is the sort of selling-point that a publisher might not be trusted with and the ultimate source of the intelligence remains obscure. There is no particular reason to doubt the veracity of the information Berthelet conveys; there is no evidence other than this publisher's blurb, however, and the publisher was not a disinterested party. On Bryan's own translation from Guevara, see Catherine Bates, '"A Mild Admonisher": Sir Thomas Wyatt and Sixteenth-Century Satire', *Huntington Library Quarterly* 56 (1993), 250-3, and Perez Zagorin, 'Sir Thomas Wyatt and the Court of Henry VIII: the Courtier's Ambivalence', *Journal of Medieval and Renaissance Studies* 23 (1993), 113-17; the quotations are from *A Dispraise* (London, 1548 (STC 12431)), sigs. a2^{v} and a7^{v}.

37 Thomson, 'Sir Thomas Wyatt: Classical Philosophy and English Humanism', p. 84, comments on the eclecticism of the Plutarch that Wyatt chose for translating. Wyatt's reference to Epictetus, in the second of his letters to his son, bespeaks familiarity with the physical form of the *Enchiridion*, as if Epictetus was more than a name to Wyatt: 'I wold Senek were your studye and Epictetus, bicaus it is litel to be evir in your bosome' (*Life and Letters*, ed. by Muir, p. 43). Though Epictetus's handbook was not printed in England, in any language, until 1567 (Oldfather no. 360), nor in French until 1544 (Oldfather no. 432), it was very

widely circulated in print in Latin translation beginning even in the fifteenth century; the various editions are listed in W. A. Oldfather, *Contributions toward a Bibliography of Epictetus* (Urbana, 1927). For the fifteenth- and sixteenth-century circulation of Plutarch's philosophical polemics, see the bibliography in Robert Aulotte, *Amyot et Plutarque: La tradition des Moralia au XVIe siècle* (Genève, 1965), pp. 325-51. Erasmus published a translation of the anti-Epicurean *Num recte dictum sit latenter esse vivendum* in 1514.

38 The whole translation is given in Appendix 4 below, quotations from it here being followed by parenthetical references to the folios of the manuscript. For comparison are cited the Latin text of *Ambrosii Theodosii Macrobii Commentarii in Somnium Scipionis*, ed. by James Willis (Leipzig, 1970), pp. 155-63, and the English translation of William Harris Stahl, in *Macrobius Commentary on the Dream of Scipio* (New York, 1952). The *Somnium Scipionis* was in wide circulation in Morley's day, in manuscript and print, especially in separate texts of it, apart from the Macrobian commentary; cf. B. C. Barker-Benfield, in *Texts and Transmission: a Survey of the Latin Classics*, ed. by L. D. Reynolds (Oxford, 1983), pp. 224, and 231, and Bruce Eastwood, 'Manuscripts of Macrobius, *Commentarii in Somnium Scipionis*, before 1500', *Manuscripta* 38 (1994), 138-55. A separate edition in Latin was printed by Redman in London *c.* 1535 (STC 5317.5), for example. In addition, in 1539, Robert Estienne published a collection of ancient and patristic excerpts attesting the *De republica*, including the *Somnium Scipionis* section, thereby giving greater currency to contemporary awareness of the nature of the original Ciceronian context of the *Somnium* – and Morley does mention (fol. 2^{r}) that the *Somnium* comes from the *De republica*. For the contents of Estienne's sixteenth-century *De republica*, see Eberhard Heck, *Die Bezeugung von Ciceros Schrift De re publica* (Hildesheim, 1966), pp. 270-6.

39 Hans Baron, 'Cicero and the Roman Civic Spirit in the Middle Ages and the Early Renaissance', *Bulletin of the John Rylands Library* 22 (1938), 72-97; see also Pierre Courcelle, 'La postérité chrétienne du Songe de Scipion', *Revue des études latines* 36 (1958), esp. 205-9, 215-23, and 229.

40 The whole translation is given in Appendix 5 below, quotations from it here being followed by parenthetical references to the folios of the manuscript. It seems likely that this combination of letters was not original with Morley, though the fact that Morley repeatedly advertises his work of combining (fols 1^{r} and 3^{r}) may suggest proprietary pride. In any event, I have not been able to find an antecedent for the combination and so write here as if Morley did the combining himself, basing his work on something like the Erasmus edition of Seneca's letters in the *Opera L. Annaei Senecae* (Basel, 1529), or one of the several later reprints of this 1529 Erasmian edition, where the numbering of the letters matches Morley's, unlike Erasmus's earlier edition, the *Lucii Annaei Senecae lucubrationes omnes* (Basel, 1515). Both the 1515 and the 1529 editions treat as two letters (nos 48 and 49) something that more recent editions count as one (ed. by Reynolds, no. 48); however, in addition, in the 1515 edition, what appears to have been a simple composing error by the printers resulted in another dislocation of the numerical sequence: the 1515 edition assigns two consecutive letters (nos. 85 and 86 in the Reynolds edition) the same number 86 and continues counting without correction, the sequence from this point in 1515 being: 86 (= 85, ed. Reynolds), 86 (= 86, ed. Reynolds), 87 (= 87, ed. Reynolds), 88 (= 88, ed. Reynolds), etc., while the 1529 edition puts the error right, its sequence from this point being: 86 (= 85, ed. Reynolds), 87 (= 86, ed. Reynolds), 88 (= 87, ed. Reynolds), 89 (= 88, ed. Reynolds), etc., with the result that, after its second letter 86, the sequence in the 1515 edition matches twentieth-century editions while the 1529 edition has a different sequence, matching Morley's numbering. Both the 1515 and 1529 editions add explanatory summary titles to each letter (e.g., 'Quomodo ad omne quod evenire potest, firmandus est animus. Et quod omnia mortalium mortalitate damnata sunt. Ubi non indignatione, sed aequanimitate opus est contra fatum', heading the

first of the letters Morley worked on, no. 91 in 1515, p. 307, no. 92 in 1529, p. 199), so that Morley need not have read all the letters in order to make his selections. For an opportunity to study the copies of these two (and other) Seneca editions in the collections of the Centre for Reformation and Renaissance Studies, Toronto, though my circumstances imposed special difficulties, I thank David Galbraith.

The tradition of Seneca's letters is extensive and is complicated by the wide circulation of various collections of *flores* and other compilations, which Morley might have known. For example, the Erasmian *Flores Lucii Annaei Senecae*, first printed at Antwerp in 1534 and often reprinted, has excerpts from both the letters that Morley used, on fols 49^v^-50^v^ and 71^r^-72^v^, but the excerpts do not match Morley's, are not connected with one another, and are differently numbered. This tradition is surveyed in Winfried Trillitzsch, *Seneca im literarischen Urteil der Antike* (Amsterdam, 1971), pp. 211-21, and cf. Gilles Gerard Meersseman, 'Seneca maestro di spiritualità nei suoi opuscoli apocrifi dal XII al XV secolo', *Italia medioevale e umanistica* 16 (1973), 43-135. On the textual tradition of the letters, see esp. Maddalena Spallone, '"Edizioni" tardoantiche e tradizione medievale dei testi: il caso delle *Epistulae ad Lucilium* di Seneca', in *Formative Stages of Classical Traditions: Latin Texts from Antiquity to the Renaissance*, ed. by Oronzo Pecere & Michael D. Reeve (Spoleto, 1995), pp. 149-96; also Reynolds, *The Medieval Tradition of Seneca's Letters* (Oxford, 1965).

41 This imagery is memorably paralleled ('in se magna ruunt') in Seneca's nephew Lucan's *Pharsalia* 1.72-82; cf. Michael Lapidge, 'Lucan's Imagery of Cosmic Dissolution', *Hermes* 107 (1979), 344-70.

42 'Aequat omnes cinis. Inpares nascimur, pares morimur' (91.16) is Seneca's phrase here; the English quotation is a line from Morley's poem 'All men they do wysshe unto them selfs all good', in Oxford, Bodleian Library, Ashmole MS 48, fol. 10^r^, supplied below, Appendix 3.

43 It is most likely a copyist's error that the letter is called eighteen in the presentation manuscript (fol. 3^r^), though this error has ramified in the secondary literature.

44 *Ep.* 120.20-1: 'Maximum indicium est malae mentis fluctuatio et inter simulationem virtutum amoremque vitiorum adsidua iactatio. ... Modo uxorem vult habere, modo amicam, modo regnare vult, modo id agit ne quis sit officiosior servus, modo dilatat se usque ad invidiam, modo subsidit et contrahitur infra humilitatem vere iacentium, nunc pecuniam spargit, nunc rapit.' 'The greatest proof of an evil mind is unsteadiness, and continued wavering between pretence of virtue and love of vice. ... Now he would have a wife, and now a mistress; now he would be king, and again he strives to conduct himself so that no slave is more cringing; now he puffs himself up until he becomes unpopular; again he shrinks and contracts into greater humility than those who are really unassuming; at one time he scatters money, at another he steals it.'

45 *The Collected Poems of Sir Thomas Wyatt*, ed. by Muir & Thomson, no. 176.1-5, p. 187. The allusion is to a choral section of Seneca's *Phaedra* 1136-40, 'metuens caelo / Iuppiter alto vicina petit. / non capit umquam magnos motus / humilis tecti plebeia domus. / circa regna tonat' 'Vigilant Juppiter strikes what comes near high heaven, while the humbly pitched plebian home never takes such great blows; near his domains rumbles the thunder' (my trans.).

THE SACRIFICE OF LADY ROCHFORD
Henry Parker, Lord Morley's Translation of De claris mulieribus

JAMES SIMPSON

IN CERTAIN OF HIS WORKS the concept of parenthood generates Henry Parker, Lord Morley's symbolic system. In the preface to his translation of Erasmus's *Paean Virgini matri* (dedicated to Mary Tudor), for example, Morley expresses horror at the fact that there are those who would prohibit honour to the Virgin as parent of Christ.[1] 'Onely to thynke,' he says, 'that Mary is mother unto God passith all altitude that either may be thought or spoken.' Despite this, there are 'clerkes in our tyme' who regard praise to the Virgin as lessening the dignity of God, 'and so, fallynge frome oone hereticall opynyone to another, at last deny the honoure due to God hymsellf in the moste holy and dyvyne sacrament of the aulter'. Beginning, then, from a denial of 'pietas' in the classical sense, heretics unravel the entire symbolic system of Christian piety. Morley's next move is to advertise Mary Tudor's sense of filial piety towards her own earthly father, since were it not for him, the cult of divinity itself would be threatened. 'The blessyd stay of our moste victoryouse and moste Chrysten Kynge, youre deare father', he affirms, has prevented what would otherwise certainly have happened: that 'verey Epecurs' would have denied the existence of God, or at least his solicitude for humans.[2]

Henry's earthly paternity as itself worthy of the deepest reverence is the theme of a contemporary preface by Morley addressed directly to the king. Whereas the prefaces (and the works) offered to Mary promote a pietistic Catholicism, prefaces addressed to Henry praise him in distinctively evangelical terms. The most radical of these works (the *Exposition and Declaration*) is more or less contemporary with the *Paean* presented to Mary.[3] The rhetorical strain of reformist panegyric to Henry finds its climax in praise of his paternity. Morley hails the king in appropriately patriarchal and imperial terms: the English, with more cause than the Romans in their praise of the Emperor Augustus, might well call Henry '*Pater patriae*, that is, the father of our countrey, one by whose vertue, lernyng, and noble courage, England is newe borne, newly brought from thraldome to freedome'. The English, freed 'from the captivite Babylonical' as by 'a most natural father', can truly declare this to Henry: 'You are our beautie, you are oure honour, you are our glorie' (p. 232 below). Passages like this unconsciously reveal an awareness that it is precisely Henry's problems as 'a most natural father' that have provoked the break with Rome. The very terms of the embarrassment, that is, are figuratively transformed into the terms of imperial triumph.

Parenthood is used in rhetorically opposite ways in these works: in the first it signals conservatism, while in the second it underwrites the birth of a new order. If the entire symbolic system of traditional Catholic practice depends on reverence for parenthood in the preface to Mary, then in the *Exposition and Declaration* the new-born *imperium* acknowledges its father in adoring terms. The striking discontinuities between these possibly contemporary passages may themselves be accounted for in part by reference to Morley's own parental relations. Elsewhere in this volume, Richard Rex argues that Morley produced the *Exposition and Declaration* in order to distance himself from possibly incriminating familial connections: Morley's son-in law had been George Boleyn, Viscount Rochford, executed on a conviction for treasonous incest in 1536 (after a trial in which Morley as a peer had himself sat in judgement).[4] This was one source of danger for Morley in the fevered atmosphere of late 1538, the other (more pressing) being his connections with the Catholic party as the purge known as the 'Exeter Conspiracy' was taking place. Whatever the motive for his production of this unusual work, it is certainly true that the violent aftermath of Henry's own parental difficulties produced parental crises throughout the remainder of the reign.[5] In the trial of Queen Catherine (Howard) in December 1541, for example, the French ambassador Marillac not only notes with astonishment the particular posture of the Duke of Norfolk towards his condemned niece, but also goes on to elevate his observations into a general rule of English parental cruelty. He notes, as 'une ... chose assez estrange', that the Duke of Norfolk, set in judgement over a matter of dishonour to his own blood, 'examinant ces prisonniers, ne se gardoit de rire comme s'il eust cause de s'en resjouyr'. Surrey (the poet, Norfolk's son) and the brothers of the queen, Marillac goes on, 'se promenoient à cheval par la ville'. And so he concludes with a general rule: 'Telle est la coustume de ce pays, Sire, qu'il convient ceulx de mesme sang se mainctenir ainsi et faire force à nature pour donner à congnoistre qu'ilz ne particippent aux délictz de leurs parens et d'aultant plus son fidelles au roy leur souverain.'[6]

In this article I want to consider Morley's own response to the crisis of Catherine Howard's execution, his translation of Boccaccio's *De claris mulieribus*. For just as the Howards were concerned to 'faire force à nature' in order to demonstrate both their lack of complicity with their guilty relations, and their fidelity to the king, so too is Morley's translation an act of parental severance and sacrifice. If humanists are said to experience an 'historical solitude', then the discursive discontinuities of Morley's textual production, and more especially his translation of Boccaccio, provide an interesting case from which to historicize that solitude.[7] Reflection on the solitude of subjection may also explain (as I shall suggest in my conclusion) why Morley found Petrarch's *Trionfi* such an amenable text.

I

At 9 a.m. on 13 February 1542 Morley's daughter Lady Rochford was beheaded in the Tower of London, preceded by Queen Catherine. She had been convicted of treason and sentenced to death on account of her complicity with Catherine Howard's reputed affairs while she was queen. A statute of 1542, asking that both women be 'convicted and attainted of Highe Treasone', describes Lady Rochford as 'that bawde the Lady Jane Rochford'.[8] The charges laid against the queen's reputed lovers are more specific about Jane Rochford: Thomas Culpepper and Francis Dereham , 'the better to pursue their carnal life ... retained Jane Lady Rochford ... as a go-between to contrive meetings in the Queen's stole chamber and other suspect places; and so the said Jane falsely and traitorously aided and abetted them'.[9]

Morley presented his book of exceptional women to the king almost certainly in New Year 1543, less than a year after the execution of his daughter.[10] In it he closely translates into English prose the first forty-six of the one hundred and four narratives contained in Boccaccio's *De claris mulieribus* (produced, in Latin prose, between 1361 and 1375).[11] The presentation of this work surely stands in significant relation to the execution of Lady Rochford. Morley had attended the House of Lords for each reading of the bill passed in 1542 to attaint his daughter and Queen Catherine.[12] If the act legislates so as to punish both queenly lasciviousness and failure to report it, then the translation enlists humanistic learning to align itself, at a discreet historical distance, with the legislation. The book itself (now Chatsworth, Devonshire Collection MS) is a de-luxe volume, significantly more expensive than any other surviving Morley presentation volumes. New Years' gifts served as part of a system of exchange between monarch and subject,[13] whereby (in Morley's words in his Preface to his translation of Plutarch's lives of Scipio and Hannibal) a subject, 'althoughe he had grevously offendid your Highnes ... he were sure to go from you joyous and mery awaie, so moche of grace resteth in that roiall harte of yours' (*Forty-six Lives*, p. 162). If Morley, the father of a reputedly immoral daughter punished by the king, should present a book largely concerned (as we shall see) with control of women so soon after his daughter's execution, then it is manifestly implausible that there be no significant connection.[14] On the contrary, Morley's humanist translation actively participates in exactly the discursive environment of these executions, by way of implicitly assuring the king of the justice of his daughter's death.

Previous marriages by Henry VIII had provoked works concerned with female instruction and defences of female virtue, notably Elyot's *Defence of Good Women*, published in 1540 on the arrival of Anne of Cleves.[15] The Catherine Howard and Lady Rochford executions raised in an acute form, however, the question of female education and control. In the period leading up to the judgement, the French ambassador Marillac reports to his king that were Henry VIII to 'mettre la main au sang de ses femmes', it would be a great shame, but a greater 'infamye pour elles qui en sont cause, de grant doulleur et regret pour les parens, et générallement de grant scandalle non seulement pour les autres dames d'Angleterre, mais aussi pour tout ce peuple qui s'esmerveille fort et pense plus qu'il n'ose dire'.[16]

In the same period, the Duchess of Norfolk was subject to an interrogation in which she was required to state 'in what sort did she educate and bring up mistress Katherine, and what change of apparel she gave her yearly?; whether she knew Mrs Katherine used to banquet and feast out of her house or in the maidens' chamber, and with whom and how often?', and so on.[17] Similarly, the statute asking that the Queen and Lady Rochford be convicted of treason determines that it would henceforward be an offence not to tell the king of any 'will acte or condicion of lightnes of bodie in her whiche *for the tyme beinge* shalbe Quene of this Realme' (my emphasis).[18] Morley's text contributes to this same concern for female instruction. He explains the instructional strategy in his preface: 'as Bocas wrytethe in hys proheme, he menglyssheth sum not verey chaste emongste the goode, yet hys honeste excuse declarethe that he dyd it to a goode entente, that all ladyes and gentlewomen, seynge the glorye of the goode, may be steryde to folowe theym, and seynge the vyce of sum, to flee theym' (*Forty-six Lives*, p. 3). The terms of this statement of *intentio auctoris* echo *accessus* to Ovid's *Heroides*, in which it is declared that Ovid's intention in that work is to exhibit each species of love, praising the virtuous and damning the immoral.[19] In the case of the wholly amoral *Heroides*, spoken in the voice of betrayed women, that ethical defence is fairly desperate. In the case of Boccaccio's text (and Morley's extremely close translation), on the contrary, the instructional account of the preface sits easily with the actual conduct of the lives themselves, in which feminine sins are often moralized.

There are many accounts of women whose actions are described as immoral by the detached male narrator. The series begins with Eve, and includes the following, each of whom is presented in a wholly negative light, or else partially criticized ('whether it be best for me to lawde or blame theyr wyttes, I cannot well tell' (*Forty-six Lives*, p. 22)): Semiramis, Seres, Venus, Europa, Nyobe, Medea, Arachne, Medusa, Yole, Dianira, Jocasta, Procris, Clytemnestra, Helen, Circes, and Sappho (I cite examples only from the forty-six lives translated by Morley). One way Boccaccio underscores the immorality of many of these women is by insisting on their fallible and mortal status. Throughout the series there runs an undercurrent of euhemeristic comment, the effect of which is to demystify the divine attractions of women. Divinity is denied to all the goddesses to whom a chapter is devoted. About Venus, for example, it is said that 'sum calleth hyr a hevenly woman, commen downe from the lappe of Jupiter to the earthe, and, brifly, all they, blyndyd with theyr oune folyshnes, all though they knewe well ynoughe that she was a mortall woman, yet they affirmede hyr to be an immortall goddesse' (*Forty-six Lives*, p. 30). Euhemerism is so relentless, in fact, that it incurs the possibility of undoing the very project of isolating exceptional women: Boccaccio must have recourse to what the 'poetes have founde ... to feyne' as the premise of his narrative (*Forty-six Lives*, p. 71), but no sooner has he included goddesses on the basis of poetic myth than he strips away the myth to reveal an altogether mortal and fallible woman, whose failures are, in Boccaccio's eyes, rather predictable and *un*exceptional. Thus Venus herself, very much a 'mortall woman', 'coulde not resyste suche fylthynes, thoughe she were accomptyd Jupiters doughter and taken as oone of that moste venerable sorte emonge the best' (*Forty-six Lives*, p. 30). Concluding the narrative of Venus, Boccaccio pursues his demystification as far as it will go: Venus is reported to have been the first person to set up 'these comune baudes houses' (*Forty-six Lives*, p. 32). In what is surely a significant addition to this story of a 'baude' considered with veneration by virtue of her father's status, Morley slightly alters his source in its last words. Whereas Boccaccio ends by lamenting the fact that the lascivious ways instigated by Venus penetrated 'ad Ytalos usque', Morley adds 'and dyvers countres moo' (*Forty-six Lives*, p. 32).

If the goddesses are stripped of their mystique to reveal an altogether less palatable reality, the same is true of many of the women about whose mortality there was never question. The second narrative in the collection, for example, is that of Semiramis, which evokes, possibly, not only the accusations concerning 'bawdes' in the Catherine Howard executions, but also the convictions of incest in the Boleyn scandal. Semiramis, despite being a remarkable queen after her husband's death by 'takynge to hyr mans hert', nevertheless falls prey to an unquenchable lasciviousness 'in usynge hirself moste unhappely in fleshly lustes'. Not only did she act 'more beastly then womanly in the company of corrupte bawdes', but, what is worse, she committed incest with her own son. Morley strengthens his source as he translates Boccaccio's denunciation of incest here: whereas Boccaccio says that the pestilence of incest 'passes among ... the troubled cares of kings' ('inter anxias regum curas ... evolat'), for Morley it becomes a pestilence, 'used emongeste the very courtes of prynces', that 'tryhumphes' (*Forty-six Lives*, p. 15). Boccaccio and Morley are ready to describe feminine success in the public world as the result of women adopting a masculine spirit, but feminine sins remain feminine, proof that women make poor rulers. As Boccaccio says in another narrative, women's pride is intolerable, since they are inclined by nature to pride; those who are not are 'more apte to vertue then to rule' (*Forty-six Lives*, p. 54).

Even in narratives of women whose oppression by men is not in question, Boccaccio (and Morley behind him) distracts attention from the male oppressor and blames the woman for carelessness. The narrative of Europa, accordingly, whose rape by Jupiter is potentially dangerous for presentation to Henry VIII, is reworked in the *De claris mulieribus* to displace blame on to Europa herself. In the Prologue to Chaucer's *Legend of Good Women* (*c.* 1386), the narrator can allude only glancingly at this dangerous legend, saying as he does that the daisy opened on May day

> Agayn the sonne, that roos as red as rose,
> That in the brest was of the beste, that day,
> That Agenores doghtre ladde away. (F.112-14)[20]

The mythical decoding of this elaborate periphrasis would read in this way: the daisy opened '... in response to the sun, which was in the breast of the bull, the form that Jupiter assumed when he raped Europa'. The ostensibly utopian scene of May day is, then, cryptically framed within a scene of tyrannical violence by the king of the Gods, a violence that initiates the founding of Thebes, and the figuring of 'Europe' itself as the product of *raptus* from an Asian shore (*Metamorphoses*, 2.846-3.131). Whereas Chaucer alludes only glancingly at this potent myth of regal sexual violence in the highly charged environment of the *Legend*, Boccaccio and Morley describe Jupiter's rape of Europa in an entirely detached and unsurprised manner. The mythic status of the story is stripped away, and Jupiter is not even a king, merely 'the myghty man' ('potens homo'). And in any case, Boccaccio immediately displaces the blame for the rape on to Europa. Before her abduction Europa is already 'a wanton mayden', who should be tending the flock of her father, but instead pays heed to the blandishments of Jupiter; and so, both writers affirm, 'maydens to stray a broode to wantonly and to gyve lyghte eares to suche as speeke fayre to theym, I do little commende it' (*Forty-six Lives*, p. 37). Morley expands in what is surely a significant way at this point. Boccaccio goes on immediately to say that he has *read* of cases in which 'visible stains have attached themselves to the reputation of such as who act in this way' ('cum contigisse sepe legerim sic agentibus honestati ... notas turpes imprimi'). Morley's censure of feminine laxity is, by contrast, underscored by personal experience: '... I do little commende it, *as by dyvers that I have knowne*, that it hath hapnede to, by such wyldnes to have runne into greate diffamy and sclaundre' [my emphasis] (*Forty-six Lives*, p. 37).

Many of these narratives of famous women are, then, rather narratives of infamous women, whose sins are held up for censure and instruction by a largely detached male narrator. Such a deployment of lives of famous women sits well with the tradition of presenting Ovid's *Heroides* as the occasion for moralization, except that the explicit instruction in this text is to men, warning them to avoid feminine wiles. Boccaccio and Morley often pause to chastise women, but they do so by addressing male readers. In the Medea narrative, for example, Morley pauses for an *exclamatio* addressed to men, by way of declaiming against the destructive power of a woman's gaze: 'What a deede that was, lett a wyse man well considre that with oones lokynge on Jasone she was so taken in love that it folowede to be the ruyne of hyr oune naturall father!' (*Forty-six Lives*, p. 60). (All this translated closely from Boccaccio, except that the last phrase there reads 'opulentissimi regis exterminium'.) In conclusion to the same narrative, both Boccaccio and Morley go further, seeming unconsciously to subvert the entire project of the work by exhorting men not even to look at women:

> I say it is not convenyente to let our eyes to largely go aboute to beholde womene. In lokynge on theym, what do we but drawe our herttes to all concupiscencys, that move us to covetouse. ... If then men were wyse, other they wolde looke upp with their eyes to heven, or elles shett theim and looke downwardes to the erthe; betwyxt bothe is noo sure way (*Forty-six Lives*, pp. 62-3).

The whole point of the *De claris mulieribus* is to 'look at' women; by encouraging male readers of this very text not to do so is to acknowledge the dangers of the project, dangers that are held very firmly in control: the narrator exercises his scholarly propriety over the text at every point (consulting different books for information as he does), and he remains almost wholly detached from cases of female suffering. There are no cases of the rhetorical exclamation of sympathy for feminine suffering of the kind we find in Chaucer's representation of feminine grief,[21] and the perspective from which women are surveyed here is consistently male.

This perspective stands in very sharp contrast with the earlier, mid-fifteenth-century English translation of Boccaccio's text into 256 rhyme-royal stanzas.[22] There the narrator does disrupt the decorous detachment of Boccaccio's narration sympathetically to apostrophize female victims or sinners. This translator's readiness to express sympathy is, furthermore, wholly in keeping with his excisions. He cuts the negative sequences from many of Boccaccio's narratives of fallen women: Semiramis's incest is deleted; there is no criticism of Ceres for having introduced the deceptive attractions of civic life; and he attaches no blame to Europa for wandering by the shore. More astonishingly, he even ventures to defend Venus's introduction of brothels, on the grounds that it is a 'vys convenyent / In avoidyng of more syn' (ll. 815-16). This translator begins by saying that Boccaccio wrote 'unto the laude and fame / Of ladyes noble, in prayse of all wymen' (ll. 19-20); in his translation he goes out of his way (and certainly out of Boccaccio's) to ensure that praise is given wherever possible. Of the twenty-one women whose narratives he reproduces, only Circe and Medea are unavoidably criticized.

In large measure, then, the instruction of Morley's text is directed rather at men than women, and the instruction amounts to little more than 'don't trust women'.[23] Men, the text would have it, must exercise control over the feminine, and Morley's dedicatory moves are more pronounced than Boccaccio's in this respect. Both the earlier English translation of the *De claris mulieribus* and Boccaccio's text are addressed to women:[24] Boccaccio's text is addressed to Countess Andrea Acciaiuoli, and is designed, furthermore, to attract the attention of Joanna, Queen of Naples.[25] Morley, by contrast, offers his translation as a New Year's gift to King Henry, with a suggestion that the king will control its circulation amongst the women of the court:

> And for asmuche as that I thoughte howe that your Hyghnes, of youre accustomede mekenes and pryncely herte, wolde not disdayn it, so dyd I imagyne that if by chaunce it shulde cum to the handes of the ryght renomyde and moste honorable ladyes of your Highnes most tryhumphaunte courte, that it shulde be well acceptyde to theym to se and reede the mervelouse vertue of theyr oune sexe, to the laude perpetuall of theym (*Forty-six Lives*, p. 3).

Books cataloguing famous classical and Biblical heroes and heroines point, by implication, to the present, asking how, and if, they might be continued. Boccaccio's own *De casibus virorum illustrium* (1360), for example, had inspired (if that is the word) Chaucer's *Monk's Tale* ((?)1390s). Boccaccio himself stops on the near horizon of his own modernity (the imprisonment of King John of France in 1350), just as Chaucer also begins at Adam and manages to slip in the spectacular falls of King Pedro of Castile (d. 1369), Pierre de Lusignan, king of Cyprus (d. 1369), and Bernarbò Visconti (d. 1385).[26] Bringing the series right up to the present in mid-sixteenth-century England may be a way of glorifying the present when the catalogue includes, for the most part, those worthy of positive fame, as in the case of John Bale's *Scriptorum illustrium maioris brytannie ... catalogus* (1557-9),[27] but it can be dangerous in the case of catalogues of the infamous. Thus Part II of Wayland's 1554 edition of Lydgate's *Fall of Princes* (a translation of Boccaccio's *De casibus*) was suppressed; Part II was to have been an edition of the *Mirror of Magistrates* (an *aggiornamento* of the *Fall of Princes*).[28] In the case of Morley's translation, the king is being encouraged to continue the historical sequence. So far from it being the case that the series is designed 'to the laude perpetuall' of women, its more pronounced theme is the treacherousness of women and their need of masculine control, a control exercised as much by the text itself as encouraged to its male readers. Boccaccio ends his series with a wholly laudatory life of Joanna, Queen of Naples (a potential patron), but then concludes by saying that it is fitting that he should not proceed further into the present, since 'the number of illustrious [women] is so small'.[29] Morley ends his translation well before he arrives at the one famous contemporary woman, and instead leaves his royal reader to follow the trajectory of infamous classical women into the 'infamous' women of Henry's contemporary experience. One such woman was Morley's own daughter, whose capital punishment Morley's gift of humanist translation implicitly commends to the king.

II

In selecting the *De claris mulieribus*, then, Morley chooses a text that sits well with the discursive environment provoked by the Howard scandal, since it answers to surrounding judicial and statutory anxieties about female education and control. It could be argued, indeed, that this concern for female exemplarity is expressed on the block by the victims themselves. Before being beheaded both Catherine Howard and Jane Rochford, according to different reports, presented themselves as penitent *exempla* of treacherous action. A letter from one Ottwell Johnson reports that the women, 'being justly punished (as they said), by the laws of the realm and Parliament, to die, required

(I say) to take example at them for amendment of their ungodly lives, and gladly obey the king in all things, for whose preservation they did heartily pray, and willed all people so to do'.[30] Not only do the women present themselves by their dying words as negative *exempla*; their dying words also (by the same token) imply the extreme narrowness, if not the disappearance, of discursive space in which to articulate any but the king's interests. The same narrowness of discursive possibility is evident in the statutory context of these executions. Thus the 1542 statute that makes it an offence for anyone not to declare knowledge of the queen's misbehaviour also makes it a crime to bruit such news 'openlye ... abrode', or 'privately [to] whisper it in other folkes eares, wherby a sclaunder myght aryse of her'.[31] Getting the volume of such a report exactly right, then, is in itself quite a tricky business (especially bearing in mind that failure to report such knowledge will incur the same penalty as that of the offender). Added to the challenge of the volume is the danger of interference with an earlier statute of 1534, in which it becomes treasonous 'malicyously [to] will or desyre by wordes or writinge ... any bodely harme to be done or commytted to the kynges most royall personne, the Quenes, or their heires apparaunt'.[32] If in the previous section I have suggested how Morley might pitch his work to speak directly and approvingly to Henry through the ostensibly impersonal act of translation, in this I look to the ways in which he might, in however muted a way, criticize both himself and the king. Just as, however, his doomed daughter and her mistress have no space to express criticism of the king, so too does Morley have very limited resources for anything but commendation of his 'most noble and gratiouse sovereygne lorde' (*Forty-six Lives*, p. 3).

Writing works concerned with female exemplarity to a king is a dangerous matter, if Chaucer's *Legend of Good Women* is anything to go by. In the Prologue to that work Chaucer represents himself as under threat by a censorious king. Cupid's malevolence has been aroused by Chaucer's translation of the *Roman de la Rose* and his writing of *Troilus and Criseyde*. Cupid's threat of a spectacular punishment of Chaucer is averted only by his queen Alceste's intervention, whereby Chaucer is to write, in penance, a series of legends of 'good' women. Chaucer is, I think, consciously modelling himself on Ovid and his banishment by Augustus. According to the *accessus* tradition to which I referred earlier, Ovid's ethical intention is to offer models of different kinds of exemplary love; behind this lies a desire to be recalled by Caesar from exile, having offended the Roman matrons with his earlier work, the *Ars amatoria*:

> Qui positus in exilio vitam in longo tempore ducens, Romanarum mulierum benivolentiam sibi recuperare cupiens, epistolarum librum composuit, in quo castas extollendo et incestas deprimendo ponit, ut earum benivolentia recepta, ad statum pristinum reducatur.[33]
>
> [Ovid], who, having lived for a long time in exile, wished to recover the good-will of the Roman matrons, composed the book of letters, in which he describes the chaste with praise and the unchaste with criticism, in order that (their good-will recovered) he should return to his prior condition.

This, along with other *accessus*, has it that Ovid writes (as Chaucer) in compensation for past works, and that he writes (as Chaucer) to reintegrate himself with both his feminine readership and his imperial male reader.[34] Whereas *Troilus and Criseyde* expands and deepens its source's presentation of a woman, the legends are instead characterised by rhetorical abbreviation and excision, as Chaucer must cut the cloth of his stories to fit the exacting and narrow measurements of his royal patrons. Even if Chaucer promises faithfully to fulfil the penance imposed on him by Alceste and Cupid, however, traces of the difficulty of matching stories to Cupid's rigid demands are visible.[35] Are such traces visible in Morley's translation of the *De claris mulieribus*?

On the face of it, the answer must surely be 'no'. Everything that has been said in the previous section would imply Morley's eagerness to comply with the demands of his royal patron, the '*Pater Patriae*', even in the matter of his own daughter's execution. Translating a printed book produced for an impersonal readership, Morley personalizes his work as a special manuscript gift to Henry, whose initials are inscribed into the first letter of the text, and whose presence as reader continues to be felt from that initiating moment.[36] Morley's whole sense of literary tradition, indeed, is intimately linked with Henry as imperial patron. In the Preface to the Boccaccio translation he accordingly links his source text with Roman imperial power. The height of Latin writing was achieved 'in the greate Augustus days', and continued to decline from that point on, until 'the greate empyre of Rome decayde' over six or seven hundred years, by which time the Romans were 'as barbarouse as the best'. The renovation of letters occurred in Italy, he goes on, in the time of Edward III, who held 'the septre of thys imperiall realme, as your Grace nowe doth'; in this time three Italian writers, Dante, Petrarch, and Boccaccio, restored letters, so that, in the case of Petrarch at least, there is hardly any 'noble prynce in Italy, nor gentle man' who is without a copy of his vernacular works (*Forty-six Lives*, pp. 1-3). This standard recitation of humanist literary ideology quietly insinuates (as it usually does) that Henry is the new Augustus; that cultivation of literature and imperial power are mutually sustaining; and that the renovation of imperial letters is about to begin in England. Certainly Morley makes no reference, here or elsewhere in his *oeuvre*, to a pre-Henrician English literary tradition. At New Year's Day 1538, 1539, 1540 or 1543 he gave a pre-Henrician spiritual work by Richard Rolle (the commentary on the Psalms) to Mary, offering it as 'an olde boke and to the fyrst sythe a cast away', and declaring that he does not know either who wrote this 'rude Psalter' or when it was written. If, however, Morley does recognize a pre-Henrician lineage of English spiritual writing, as one might expect him to do in his conservative prefaces to Mary, he makes no references to an English literary lineage, not even in his translation of Petrarch's *Trionfi*, a work one of whose central themes is poetic fame and tradition. For Morley, as for other Henrician propagandists, the renovation of English letters is phoenix-like, without English parentage.[37] Even the Italian works that he does claim as sources are miracles of nature, denying their lineage: no sooner, in the same Preface, does Morley claim that Dante shaped his 'maternal eloquens' than he neutralizes the maternal reference by claiming that Dante's poetry 'semyd a myracle of nature' (*Forty-six Lives*, p. 2).

Even Morley's practice as a translator implies a subservience to authority, as if he treats his source text as itself possessing an inviolable authority, outside which he dare not move. From the moment that Morley begins to translate Boccaccio's preface, Morley's own voice is lost in that of his authoritative source. Whereas the mid-fifteenth-century version of the *De claris mulieribus* consistently maintains a distinction between the translator's voice and that of 'myn autour John Bochase', Morley's 'I' is Boccaccio. The first-person speaker of the Middle English translation is that of the translator, registering his own historicity in the process of transmission, while Morley disappears from the history of his transmission of Boccaccio. The marked division of discursive jurisdiction in the earlier text is also felt in its striking excisions from Boccaccio's work, especially in the sections blaming women. Morley, by contrast, alters or excises hardly anything: very occasionally we feel the pressure of circumstance by the change of a single phrase or word (as noted above), and very occasionally he will abbreviate a small and insignificant passage from his source.[38] Because they are unmarked, however, his original audience could not be expected to register these private moments as changes to the original. From the perspective of this work, humanist respect for the integrity of the text can be redescribed as the expression of both literary and political subservience. It can also be described as the disappearance of discursive jurisdictions. Lydgate's *Fall of Princes* (1431-8), a translation of Boccaccio's *De casibus virorum illustrium*, is punctuated by Lydgate's inserted apostrophes to his royal and aristocratic readers, apostrophes that both mark off Lydgate's clerical jurisdictions and proclaim his right to speak at, even down to, his aristocratic patrons. Morley, by contrast, is himself both aristocrat and author, and the jurisdiction from within which he writes is already that of the king.

All that having been said, let me end by suggesting some of the ways in which we might perceive critique of Morley and of Henry himself in this signally monologic text. The first such approach is from silence, and therefore constitutes very uncertain evidence. Despite what I have just said about Morley's respect for the integrity of the text and his refusal to excise, we should of course not forget that he did omit no fewer than fifty-eight narratives from Boccaccio's total of one hundred and four. As with both Chaucer's *Legends of Good Women* and the mid-fifteenth-century translation of Boccaccio's *De claris mulieribus*, Morley's account of famous women stops short of its full complement, though, unlike both those works, Morley's translation does not explicitly state its incompletion;[39] on the contrary, the New Years's presentation volume is codicologically a complete book, and never promises a certain number of lives. As to why he cut the remaining narratives, we can only speculate. Such idle speculation might pause to reflect that Morley's wholesale omissions relieve him from the necessity of translating the following lives, for example: Thamyris (no. 47), who effectively sacrifices her own son in her self interest;[40] the courageous prostitute Laeena (no. 48, *Forty-six Lives*, p. 107), whose lax ways are blamed on parental indulgence; Athaliah (no. 49, *Forty-six Lives*, p. 111), whose lust for power provokes her to kill all her kinsmen, and whose actions bring condemnation from Boccaccio of those men or women who do not spare their own family in order to protect their own power; Virginia (no. 56, *Forty-six Lives*, p. 128), stabbed to death by her father to protect her virginity; a young Roman woman (no. 63, *Forty-six Lives*, p. 142) whose filial tenderness towards her condemned mother provokes piety and forgiveness in the Senate; Portia (no. 80, *Forty-six Lives*, p. 181), who commits a noble suicide in solidarity with her husband Brutus; and Mariamne (no. 85, *Forty-six Lives*, p. 189), wife of Herod and executed by him with encouragement from her perfidious mother. All these narratives, it might be suggested, are potentially embarrassing for Morley, either because they attack parents for sacrificing children; or because they blame parents for the lascivious ways of their daughters; or because they praise familial pity towards condemned family members; or, finally, because they recognize courage in the tyrannicide. Morley is also relieved from the necessity of translating Zenobia (no. 98, *Forty-*

six Lives, p. 226), who, it has been plausibly argued, is the virtuous model in Elyot's *Defence of Good Women* for Catherine of Aragon.[41]

What of the narratives Morley does translate? Are there resonances here that might suggest critique of both the king and Morley himself? There are narratives of women who are praised without qualification in the *De claris mulieribus*. Certainly there is intellectual admiration for the founders of sciences and arts: Minerva, the Sibyls, and Carmenta. Some warrior-maidens are praised: the Amazons, Penthesilea, and Camilla. So too does Morley follow Boccaccio's approval of uxorial fidelity in the following narratives: the wives of Mennon, Penelope, Gaia Cirylla, Dido, and Lucrece. With the exception of Dido and Lucrece (to whom I shall return), I am unable to perceive significant changes to, or placing of, these stories that would suggest Morley's particular investment in them. By a small contrast, strains of such an investment are perceptible in the narratives of filial victims. Morley admires filial *pietas* wherever he sees it: 'It is a moste holy thynge, the pyte that children have towardes their parenttes' ('Sanctissima quippe filiorum pietas in parentes est'), he remarks in the narrative of Isiphile (*Forty-six Lives*, p. 56), and so praises her for having 'doone so well to hyr father' (that 'father' being a whisker more specific than Boccaccio's 'parenti'). That narrative may be pitched by way of self-justification by Morley; in the story of Polyxena, by contrast, Morley adjusts the Boccaccio to imply justification of his own sacrificed daughter. Boccaccio describes how Polyxena was led by Neptholemus (i.e. Pyrrhus, son of Achilles) as a sacrifice to the spirits of his father ('in piaculum manium patris'), whereas Morley introduces an entirely new idea, without authority in his source. He exclaims that it was 'agaynste all good ordre ... that so swete a mayden shulde be devowred by the hande of Pyrrus for to satisfye for another womans offence!' (*Forty-six Lives*, p. 106). The 'other woman' to whom Morley refers here is Hecuba, responsible for the murder of Achilles. There are, however, so many potential offences and offenders behind the murder of Polyxena that Morley's choice of 'another woman' is presumably significant in the context of his daughter's fatal involvement with Catherine Howard. With that turn, Morley's praise of Polyxena's constancy under the axe takes on the tone of admiration for his own daughter's constancy 'under the swerde of the victore' (*Forty-six Lives*, p. 106).

If that addition does express Morley's admiration for his daughter, it is admiration for 'good women' of the kind we find promoted by Chaucer's Cupid in the *Legend of Good Women*: the only kind of 'goodness' Cupid is prepared to countenance is that of women prepared to suffer the brutalities of male violence patiently. Even if the narrative of Thisbe does not involve male brutality against women, the same tones of pity toward the innocent female victim colour Morley's translation of that story. 'The passione of Cupido is of immoderate power', and 'a comune evyll which neades we muste suffre' (*Forty-six Lives*, p. 47), he repeats from Boccaccio in conclusion to Thisbe's pitiful death. Stories of catastrophic adolescent love always imply parental shortcoming, and Morley does faithfully translate Boccaccio's tentative criticism of Thisbe's parents: 'The ungraciouse lote or chaunce offendyde, or ells percase their sorowfull fathers and mothers' (*Forty-six Lives*, p. 47). Morley is just slightly more specific than Boccaccio in laying a possible blame on 'fathers and mothers', since Boccaccio reads only 'parentes' at that point. This alteration to accentuate paternal failing is in fact made fairly consistently throughout the whole narrative: whereas, for example, Boccaccio has Thisbe kept at home by her parents ('a parentibus') in order that she be preserved for a future marriage, Morley's accent is slightly different: '... when that Thysbe was mariable, hyr father kept hyr styll at home, to th'entent to mary hyr' (*Forty-six Lives*, p. 43).

For the most part possible criticisms of parental action in these lives of famous women remain extremely muted, as in the story of Thisbe. Such criticism, indeed, is most thoroughly neutralized in the longest narrative of all, that of Dido. Boccaccio's Dido is not Virgil's: here Dido commits suicide as soon as Aeneas arrives, in order to preserve her chastity in memory of her husband Sikkarius. With this revised version of *Aeneid* 4, Boccaccio can somehow preserve the respect for Dido that Virgil's narrative provokes, yet also allow damnation of Virgil's Dido at the same time.[42] Respect for this reimagined Dido, however, depends on her readiness to commit suicide, which action prompts Boccaccio to attack women who remarry. He imagines, and rebuts, various entirely plausible feminine arguments in favour of remarriage in turn: 'my parents are dead' (he imagines a woman saying), 'and I am destitute of help'; 'I am rich, and I want to be able to pass my property on to children'; 'my parents and kinsmen commanded me to remarry'. Boccaccio dismisses each of these justifications, using the example of Dido as the strongest counter-argument. Morley slightly sharpens the paternal focus of these imagined arguments: whereas Boccaccio has the widow arguing that her parents ordered her to remarry ('parentes iusserint'), Morley (as in his translation of Thisbe) gives us an overbearing father: 'My father commaundyde me to it' (*Forty-six Lives*, p. 143). Neither Boccaccio nor Morley, however, take time out to reflect on the brutality of their position, which triumphantly dismisses arguments made by hard-pressed women by complacently pointing to Dido's suicide.[43] Only once, indeed, does Morley attack an overbearing and brutal father, in the story of Hypermnestra. Danaus, who orders each of his fifty daughters to murder their cousin-husbands, is damned by both Boccaccio and Morley for attempting to prolong his 'olde, tremblynge yeres'. Morley privately accentuates Boccaccio's fierce attack on Danaus for casting his virtuous daughter in prison, after she has failed to protect his own abject interests. Boccaccio (with Morley closely following) generalizes the attack on men who commit crimes to prolong 'this breve and shorte lyfe of ours' (*Forty-six Lives*, p. 49). At this point, however, there is a very slight change: Boccaccio points out the gratuitousness of this effort to prolong life, 'since we see others going swiftly to death' ('cum in mortem ire ceteros cursu volucri videamus' (*Forty-six Lives*, p. 49)). In Morley's translation the pressure of imminent death is stronger: '... albe it we see dayly afore oure eyes on all sydes men to goo to deathe' (*Forty-six Lives*, p. 49). Even in this potentially embarrassing attack on vicious old men, however, Morley follows his source to include women in the attack: one aspect of Danaus's crime is that he little thought 'how an evyll example he left to ungraciouse women' (*Forty-six Lives*, p. 50).

If we can perceive any glimmers of reflexive consciousness in Morley's text, they reflect on Morley himself, rather than on the king. I conclude this section simply by pointing out that Morley ends with the narrative of Lucrece. Certainly in pre-Henrician English writing, the political implications and consequences of Tarquin's rape of Lucrece had been powerfully expressed. In Book VII of the Gower's *Confessio Amantis* (1390-3) the Lucrece narrative (VII.4593-5130) occupies a central place in the architecture of that book and of the whole poem, by way of revealing the identities between rapacious territorial and sexual possession. Gower deploys the narrative so as to condemn the sexual and political tyrant, and to celebrate his exile.[44] There is nothing of this extended political consciousness in Morley's version or in Boccaccio's.[45] Only at the very end does Boccaccio allude to a political implication: not only did Lucrece's suicide restore her reputation, but 'Roman liberty followed' also ('sed consecuta sit Romana libertas' (*Forty-six Lives*, p. 159)). Morley accentuates this last point in two ways: not only does he expand on the introduction of liberty, but he also magnifies its significance, since these are the very last words of his text: the act of Tarquin was revenged, 'yet this was not all, but for thys acte of Lucres, Rome, that was in boundage before, by hyr obteynede for ever fredome and lyberty' (*Forty-six Lives*, p. 159).

From the perspective of the *De claris mulieribus*, Morley seems to me ideally placed to be the first translator of Petrarch's *Trionfi* (and especially the *Triumph of Cupid*) into English. So far from being, as is often claimed, a humanist recovery of the past, the *Trionfi* seem to me to mark out history's victims. The narrator's own thraldom to the inscrutable and punishing regime of the boy-emperor Cupid in that poem's present simply replicates the situation of isolated figures from the past, gathered as they are into *tableaux morts*, forever suspended in their own thraldom to absolute power. That enthralled suspension forbids re-entry into the current of history from which they arrive, and so dislocates historical narrative, splintering action into fixed, isolated postures. Morley's whole writing career is a gathering of discontinuous positions, each in thrall to an inscrutable power. And his translation of the *De claris mulieribus* is itself an example of that discontinuity, severing as it does his own familial history and solidarities. Like Surrey in thrall to Cupid, who thinks of 'Agamemnon's daughter's bloode' as part of the successful prosecution of the Trojan War, so too in his gifts to the king will Morley 'never ... repent, / But paynes, contented, stil endure'.[46]

NOTES

I warmly thank James Carley for his scholarly generosity, enthusiasm and patience in the production of this article.

1 The presentations to Mary are difficult to date precisely, but the *Paean* was probably written around 1539. See Carley, 'The Writings of Henry Parker, Lord Morley: A Bibliographical Survey', above, p. 35.
2 Quoted in *Forty-six Lives*, ed. by Wright, p. 171. Subsequent citations of works by Morley, or of the 1487 Louvain printing of Boccaccio's *De claris mulieribus* by Egidius van der Heerstraten (the edition used by Morley, and printed by Wright in parallel text), will be to Wright's edition, and will be cited in the body of the text. All letter-forms have been silently modernized throughout.
3 For the dating of the *Exposition and Declaration of the Psalme, Deus ultionum Dominus*, see Carley, 'The Writings of Henry Parker', p. 42.
4 Rex, 'Morley and the Papacy: Rome, Regime, and Religion', above, pp. 89-90. Morley was the only peer to attend all six trials involving the court of the high steward (convened to try members of the nobility), and sat in judgement on his son-in-law; see Helen Miller, *Henry VIII and the English Nobility* (Oxford, 1986), pp. 44-5, and 58 respectively.
5 The most spectacular example of parental disowning of children was the Howard family. Thomas Howard, Duke of Norfolk, for example, presided in judgement over the trial of his

niece Anne Boleyn; is reported to have expressed mirth at the judgement of his niece Catherine Howard (whose marriage with Henry he had arranged); and disowned his son by way of saving himself in 1547. See E. Casady, *Henry Howard Earl of Surrey* (New York, 1938), pp. 53-4 , 87, 205-6 respectively.

6 Quoted in *Correspondence politique de MM. de Castillon et de Marillac, ambassadeurs de France en Angleterre, 1537-42*, ed. by J. Kaulek (Paris, 1885), no. 380 (December, 1541), p. 371. In another letter to Francis I, Marillac wrote that the Duke of Norfolk hoped to gain from the confiscations arising from Catherine Howard's execution, 'yet the times are such that he dare not show that the affair touches him, but approves of all that is done'. Quoted in *LP Henry VIII*, XVI.100, p. 44.

7 For the notion of 'historical solitude', see T. M. Greene, *The Light in Troy: Imitation and Discovery in Renaissance Poetry* (New Haven, 1982), ch.1.

8 *Statutes of the Realm*, 11 vols (London, 1810-28), 33 Henry VIII, c.21, art. 1, III, p. 857.

9 *LP Henry VIII*, XVI.1395, p. 646.

10 For the dating, see Carley, 'The Writings of Henry Parker', pp. 42-3. The essential points of Carley's argument are as follows: the work must have been presented after 1541, since Henry is addressed in the Prologue as King of Ireland; it is certainly a New Year's Gift, since Morley describes it as such. Although no record of New Year's gifts survives for 1543, 1542 is hardly credible, since the scandal concerning his daughter was at its height across the New Year period 1541/2. There is no reference to a queen in the salutation in Chatsworth and so it is unlikely that it dates to the period after Henry's marriage to Catherine Parr in July 1543. There are three other post-1541 New Year's gifts, none of which is as ornate as the Chatsworth manuscript; New Year 1543, when Morley's relations with the king needed careful attention, remains the most probable occasion for such an expensive gift.

11 For the placing of Boccaccio's *De claris mulieribus* in the pattern of his career as a whole, see V. Branca, *Boccaccio, The Man and His Works*, trans. by R. Monges (New York, 1976), especially p. 110.

12 Miller, *Henry VIII*, p. 157.

13 For the importance of presentation manuscripts in this period, see D. R. Carlson, *English Humanist Books: Writers and Patrons, Manuscript and Print, 1475-1525* (Toronto, 1993), pp. 8-12. For an account of a New Year's gift giving, see *Henry VIII: a European Court in England*, ed. by D. Starkey (London, 1991), pp. 126-8.

14 This is the argument of Carley, 'The Writings of Henry Parker', pp. 42-3.

15 For which see P. Benson, *The Invention of the Renaissance Woman: the Challenge of Female Independence in the Literature and Thought of Italy and England* (University Park, Pa., 1992), ch. 7. See also G. Walker, *Persuasive Fictions: Faction, Faith and Political Culture in the Reign of Henry VIII* (Aldershot, Hants., 1996), ch. 8; see especially pp. 186-92 for questions of dating, and p. 196 for other tracts relevant to female instruction published in 1540.

16 *Correspondence politique*, ed. by Kaulek, no. 376 (22 November 1541), p. 367.

17 *LP Henry VIII*, XVI.1409, p. 656.

18 *Statutes of the Realm*, 33 Henry VIII, c. 21, art. 7, III, p. 859.

19 There are many examples of this kind of *accessus*; for a set of examples, see J. Simpson, *Sciences and the Self in Medieval Poetry: Alan of Lille's 'Anticlaudianus' and John Gower's 'Confessio amantis'* (Cambridge, 1995), p. 175, n. 9.

20 *The Riverside Chaucer*, gen. ed. L. D. Benson, 3rd edn (Oxford, 1987), p. 591. Subsequent quotations are from the same edition.

21 The measured sympathy for Thisbe (pp. 46-7) is a partial exception.

22 *Die Mittelenglische Umdichtung von Boccaccio's 'De claris mulieribus'*, ed. by G. Schleich (Leipzig, 1924). The text survives in a single manuscript, BL, Add. MS 10304. Richard Beadle

kindly informs me that the date of the manuscript is mid-fifteenth century.

23 For a lucid and persuasive argument that Boccaccio's practice in the *De claris mulieribus* is more complicated than his statement of intention, see C. Jordan, 'Boccaccio's In-famous Women: Gender and Civic Virtue in the *De mulieribus claris*', in *Ambiguous Realities: Women in the Middle Ages and Renaissance*, ed. by C. Levin & J. Watson (Detroit, 1987), pp. 25-47: 'Throughout the *De mulieribus* he [Boccaccio] has ostensibly praised but actually made suspect the woman who gains *claritas* by participating in public activities; he has commended her for virile qualities while at the same time demonstrating how dangerous these qualities cause her to become' (p. 42).

24 *Die Mittelenglische Umdichtung*, ed. by Schleich, ll. 25-6: 'Without grete ayde of sum noble pryncess / All in veyne shuld be my besyness' (p. 4).

25 See the dedication to Boccaccio's text, in *Giovanni Boccaccio, Concerning Famous Women*, trans. by G. A. Guarino (New Brunswick, 1963), p. xxxiii.

26 For the updating and its point, see D. Wallace, *Chaucerian Polity: Absolutist Lineages and Associational Forms in England and Italy* (Stanford, 1997), ch. 11.

27 John Bale, *Scriptorum illustrium maioris Brytannie, quam nunc Angliam et Scotiam Vocant, catalogus* (Basel, 1559) (both the 1557 and 1559 volumes are printed in this book). For recent discussion of this book, see A. Hudson, '*Visio Baleii*: an Early Literary Historian', in *The Long Fifteenth Century: Essays for Douglas Gray*, ed. by H. Cooper & S. Mapstone (Oxford, 1997), pp. 313-29, and J. Simpson, 'Ageism: Leland, Bale and the Laborious Start of English Literary History, 1350-1550', *New Medieval Literatures*, 1 (1997), 213-35.

28 See W. A. Jackson, 'Wayland's Edition of *The Mirror of Magistrates*', *The Library*, 4th ser. 13 (1932-3), 155-7; also A. S. G. Edwards, 'The Influence of Lydgate's *Fall of Princes*: a Survey', *Medieval Studies*, 39 (1977), 424-39.

29 For Boccaccio's exclusion of modern women, and their possible re-entry, see Benson, *The Invention of the Renaissance Woman* (n. 15 above), pp. 30-1.

30 *LP Henry VIII*, XVII.106, p. 45. The French ambassador Marillac reports much the same to Francis I: 'The Queen was so weak, that she could hardly speak, but confessed in few words that she had merited a hundred deaths for so offending the king who had so graciously treated her. The lady of Rochfort said as much in a long discourse of several faults which she had committed in her life' (*LP Henry VIII*, XVII.100, p. 44).

31 *Statutes of the Realm*, 33 Henry VIII, c. 21, art. 7, III, p. 859.

32 *Statutes of the Realm*, 26 Henry VIII, c. 13, art. 1, III, p. 508.

33 Text cited from F. Ghisalberti, 'Medieval Biographies of Ovid', *Journal of the Warburg and Courtauld Institutes*, 9 (1946), 10-59 (p. 38, n. 3). The manuscript from which the citation is taken dates from the fourteenth century. See also Ghisalberti, 'Medieval Biographies', Appendix B, p. 44. The tradition of Ovid writing the *Heroides* in order to placate Augustus is also found in the twelfth-century *accessus* discussed in R. J. Hexter, *Ovid and Medieval Schooling: Studies in Medieval School Commentaries on Ovid's 'Ars Amatoria', 'Epistulae ex Ponto', and 'Epistulae Heroidum'* (Munich, 1986), p. 161.

34 A point made by R. Copeland, *Rhetoric, Hermeneutics and Translation in the Middle Ages: Academic Traditions and Vernacular Texts* (Cambridge, 1991), p. 188.

35 I argue this fully in my article, 'Ethics and Interpretation: Reading Wills in Chaucer's *Legend of Good Women*', *Studies in the Age of Chaucer*, 20 (1998), 73-100.

36 The opening page of Morley's text (fol. 1a) is reproduced as the frontispiece to Wright's edition.

37 Compare Leland's description of Wyatt as a phoenix; see *Wyatt: the Critical Heritage*, ed. by P. Thompson (London, 1974), p. 25. I consider the strategies of 'renaissance' literary history in my article, 'Breaking the Vacuum: Ricardian and Henrician Ovidianism', *JMEMS*, 29 (1999), 325-55.

38 He omits, for example, Boccaccio's brief account of Minerva as the source of military science (*Forty-six Lives*, p. 27).

39 For the intended scope of the *Legend* as larger than the form in which it has survived, see *Riverside Chaucer*, gen. ed. Benson, p. 1060. The incompletion of the *Legend* is apparent from within the poem itself, since Alceste's commission requires that Chaucer devote most of his time, 'while that thou lyvest', to composition of the *Legend* (l. 481). The mid-fifteenth-century version of the *De claris mulieribus* ends in an amusingly provisional way (ll. 1786-92, p. 92):

> If it fortune to be acceptable
> And please the herers, forth I wyll procede
> To the residue of ladyes notable;
> But fyrste of all, to se howe this shall spede,
> I will take counsell, er it go on brede,
> Leste that I eyre the bareyn se-banke
> And gete me more of laboure than of thanke.

40 *Concerning Famous Women*, trans. by Guarino, p. 104. Subsequent references to Guarino's translation will be made in the body of the text.

41 The scholarly history of this question is rehearsed and evaluated by Walker, *Persuasive Fictions* (n. 15 above), ch. 8.

42 Compare the praise of this Dido with implicit criticism of Virgil's Dido in Petrarch's *Triumph of Chastity*, as translated by Morley:

> I sawe hyr of muche hyghe state and degree
> That for hyr husbande was content to dye –
> And not for Eneas, so affyrme I.
> (Let the vulgar people then holde theyr peace!)
> It is that Dydo that I do here rehearse,
> That honest love broughte unto an ende,
> And not vayne wanton love that dyd her offende.
> (*Lord Morley's 'Tryumphes'*, ed. by Carnicelli, p. 115).

43 The bland and frankly brutal complacency of this position is mirrored in the treatment by twentieth-century historians, who also fail to make any attempt to read into the situation of a woman in the position of Lady Rochford. Take, for example, L. B. Smith, *A Tudor Tragedy: the Life and Times of Catherine Howard* (London, 1961). Smith describes Lady Rochford as 'a pathological meddler, with most of the instincts of a procuress who achieves a vicarious pleasure from arranging assignations' (p. 167); as he describes the night before the execution, he says 'Lady Rochford went mad under the strain of disclosure and ceaseless interrogation, and perhaps it is charitable to believe that she was insane from the start' (p. 170). In *LP Henry VIII* X.1010 , p. 416, we find hints of what might generate an alternative narrative: in May 1536, after her husband's execution, she petitions Cromwell to obtain the plate and 'stuff' of her husband, since she is allotted only 100 marks per annum from her jointure, 'which is very hard for me to shift the world withal'. The Earl of Wilshire (who controlled Lady Rochford's income) grudgingly agreed in July 1536 to raise her allowance, but asked Cromwell 'to inform the king that I do this alonely for his pleasure' (*LP Henry VIII* XI.17, p. 13). I am grateful to James Carley for these references.

44 See Simpson, *Sciences and the Self* (n. 19 above), pp. 213-15. See also the powerfully political, twice told account of Lucrece in Lydgate's *Fall of Princes*, Books 2 and 3.

45 For the connections between Lucrece's suicide and the practice of philology, see S. H. Jed, *Chaste Thinking: the Rape of Lucretia and the Birth of Humanism* (Bloomington, Ind.,

1989), especially pp. 39-40. For the Lucretia story more generally as a 'myth of revolution', see I. Donaldson, *The Rapes of Lucretia: a Myth and its Transformations* (Oxford, 1982), ch. 6.

46 Cited from *Henry Howard, Earl of Surrey: Poems*, ed. by E. Jones, (Oxford, 1964), no. 1, ll. 10, and 25-6 (pp. 1-2).

LORD MORLEY'S *TRYUMPHES OF FRAUNCES PETRARCKE*

Reading Spectacles

MARIE AXTON

SIR PHILIP SIDNEY'S funeral procession was the first English spectacle of which the record was published for sale. Theodore de Bry's thirty engravings after Thomas Lant's drawings, known as *Lant's Roll* are however rightly placed by art historians within the context of Dutch or other continental printing tradition, rather than at the beginning of an English one.[1] Continental custom reserved such funeral publications for commemorating royalty, so that the English frieze draws attention to the fact that Sir Philip was given a mourning procession considerably above his degree: seven (rather than five) mourners and the 'Great Banner' due to a baron of the realm.[2] In Sidney's funeral roll, pictures alternate with an explanatory text recording the names and rank of those seven hundred people who marched, or rode on horseback, accompanying the coffin to its last resting place in St Paul's Cathedral on 16 February 1586/87. The entire series of engravings could be mounted on cloth for display sequentially and 'turned upon two pinnes, that turning one of them made the figures march all in order', as John Aubrey records in his memoirs.[3]

In Lant's publishing venture text and pictures depend on each other and correspond exactly. Even on the Continent, where technical mastery of woodcut and metal engraving surpassed English craftsmanship, relatively few printed books had purpose-made illustrations. 'Reading' an illustrated procession such as the *Triumphes of Maximilian* or, conversely, visualizing a written procession in the mind's eye is tricky, and positively hazardous for a translator.

When Henry Parker, Lord Morley, chose the *Trionfi* he undertook to translate Petrarch's most widely read vernacular work. In Italy it was read in manuscript as a continuation or culmination of Petrarch's *Canzoniere* – as part of the same work. Italian printers continued this practice, producing composite, sometimes companion volumes. Both vernacular works attracted illumination and illustrations: the *Canzoniere* in the 1380s and the *Trionfi* a few years later. Both, too, acquired learned commentaries in the manner of the Ovide Moralisé. Artistic conventions depicting classical myths – Apollo and Phaeton, Apollo and Daphne, together with pre-existing Christian iconography from the pilgrimage of the soul and the ages of man *topoi* – migrated easily into the margins of the *Canzoniere*, and into full-page illustrations of the *Trionfi*. A very few Italian artists transferred Petrarch's own imagery into their manuscript miniatures.[4]

In his *Trionfi* Petrarch created a memorable series of images expressing love's progress to eternity as a sequence of victorious encounters, each victory turned into subsequent defeat by the next challenger. But the allegory is unlike that of Everyman or the lover of the *Roman de la Rose*, which show 'the way of the world'. Petrarch's story is personal and idiosyncratic. Love does not triumph over Chastity. On the contrary, Petrarch's Cupid, or Love, rides in a chariot triumphant over Jove and other gods but is powerless against Chastity. So, too, Chastity meets Death; Death Fame; Fame Time; and Time finally falls to Divinity, also termed Eternity. Although Love's 'chayre' may derive from public triumphs of classical Rome, Petrarch transmutes the public triumph and its conventions to represent a psychomachia, an internal allegorical conflict in which human rites of passage are formalized as sequential epiphanies.[5] However, where Petrarch envisaged only one conventional 'pageant' (Love's) for his entire series, illustrators of the *Trionfi* imagined five more triumphal chariots, adding one each for Chastity, Death, Fame, Time, and Divinity. The five subsequent pageants are not authorized in Petrarch's narrative, where varying modes of 'triumph' in turn embody rather the quality and meaning of each central personification.

Those who have assessed Lord Morley's achievement as first English translator of Petrarch's *Trionfi* conclude that he was influenced by more than Petrarch's bare text. Each triumph confronted Morley with accretions from the civic traditions of several European countries where different customs governed who rode, who was carried and who walked. At the Field of the Cloth of Gold, for instance, it was agreed that when the English Queen and the French Queen met to see the kings jousting on 11 June 1520 they would both be carried 'in richly covered litters, their ladies on palfreys and their servants in waggons'.[6]

'Tryumphe', in Morley's 'maternall tongue', might refer to any celebration of military victory and, by extension, to a moral or spiritual victory, or defeat. Dante in *Purgatorio* XXIX had imagined a Christian procession of the sacrament as a triumph.[7] In the civic life of pre-Reformation Europe the Host was honoured by being borne in procession under a canopy. Royalty entering a city were similarly honoured and protected, whether riding on horseback or carried in a litter, a horse-drawn 'chariot', or a hearse. Petrarch drew on civic traditions of Rome and the rest of contemporary Italy, being steeped in the literary traditions of both. In turn, the success and wide dissemination of his book influenced and re-defined the triumphal spectacles created by Petrarch's own contemporaries and literary successors in Italy, France, and England. In Italy there was the *Hypnerotomachia*, or *Strife of Love in a Dream* as it was later Englished; in England there were Lydgate's *Danse Macabre*; Thomas More's *Nine Pageants* of the Ages of Man; Stephen Hawes's Time and Eternity in his *Pastime Of Pleasure*; John Skelton's mock-heroic tapestries of the triumphs of Cupid and Fame in *Colin Clout*.[8] From these we can begin to reconstruct a context, and something of Morley's intentions and expectations. Morley conceived his translation as a text for royalty, a king's book. Although Petrarch's *Trionfi* was a vernacular poem, Morley accords it the prestige of a Latin or Greek text. Its status as a candidate for humanistic translation and dedication to a royal patron had been prepared by the reception of Petrarch's most popular Latin work, *De Remediis Utriusque Fortunae*. This was translated by Jean Daudin in 1378 into French at the request of King Charles V.[9] Although Morley eventually saw his translation in print, he began the enterprise firmly within the spirit and conventions of manuscript translation and transmission. His Epistle is condescending towards the printed book. He feels that his English Petrarch needs defence against his countrymen because:

Even so there be a nomber of that sorte, that percase when they shall eyther heare redde, or them selfe reade this excellent tryumphes, of this famous clercke Petrarcha, shall lytle set by them, and peradventure caste it from them, desyrynge rather to have a tale prynted of Robyn Hoode, or some other dongehyll matter. ... (Epistle, sig. A2^{v})[10]

In rating the vernacular *Trionfi* second only to 'the devine workes', Morley nevertheless honours its close link to the *Canzoniere* and praises Petrarch, both for love poetry so 'wonderfull made' and for the many-layered copiousness of his thought:

the devine workes set aparte, there was never in any vulgar speche or language, so notable a worke, so clerckely done as this his worke. And albeit that he setteth forth these syxte wonderfull made triumphes all to the laude of hys Ladye Laura, by whome he made so many a swete sonnet, that never yet no poete nor gentleman could amend, nor make the lyke, yet who that doth understande them, shall se in them comprehended al morall vertue, all Phylosophye, all storyall matters, and briefely manye devyne sentences theologicall secretes declared. (Epistle, sig. A2^{v})

Morley's inspiration for his formidable task was a French translation of the *Trionfi* belonging to King Francis I. Its translator had been handsomely rewarded by his king; versifying did not go wholly unrewarded at Henry's court. As Puttenham reminds us 'king Henry the 8 ... for a few Psalmes of David turned into English meetre by Sternhold, made him groome of his privy chamber & gave him many other good gifts' (*The Art of English Poesie*, Bk I, ch. viii, p. 17). That King Francis had a verse translation can be inferred by Morley's own choice of verse, and his emulous 'an Englyshe man myght do aswell as the Frenche man':

one of late dayes that was grome of the chaumber with that renowmed and valyaunte Pryce of hyghe memorye, Fraunces the Frenche kynge, whose name I have forgotten, that dydde translate these tryumphes to that sayde kynge, whyche he toke so thankefully, that he gave to hym for hys paynes an hundred crounes, to hym and to his heyres of inheritaunce to enjoye to that value in lande for ever, and toke suche pleasure in it, that wheresoever he wente amonge hys precyous Jewelles, that booke was alwayes caryed with hym for his pastyme to loke upon, and as muche estemed by hym, as the rychest Diamonde he hadde: whiche sayde booke, when I sawe the coppye of it, I thoughte in my mynde, howe I beynge an Englyshe man, myght do aswell as the Frenche man, dyd translate this sayde worke into our maternall tounge, and after much debatyng with my selfe, dyd as your Lordshyppe doth se, translate the sayde booke to that moost worthy kynge our late soveraygne Lorde of perpetuall memorye kynge Henrye theyghte. ...

(Epistle, sig. A3^{r})

'When I sawe the coppye of it' suggests both that Morley actually perused the French king's book and that the French translation conveyed the *copiousness* of Petrarch's original work. His odd construction, 'I thoughte ... howe I ... dyd translate ... dyd ... translate' (if it is not a case of printer's eye-skip) can be interpreted as distinguishing thought and action. The first use of the modal auxiliary 'dyd translate' may be taken as indicating 'that I was going to translate'.[11] He is confident that an English man could do as well as a French man, and that 'our maternall tounge' could convey Petrarch's layered meanings. 'Much debatyng' need not have taken much time. Once the project had been conceived, Morley says he worked quickly and consequently made errors:

one thynge is, that I dyd it in suche hast, that doubtles in many places (yf it were agayne in my handes) I thynke I coulde well amende it, albeit that I professe, I have not erred moche from the letter, but in the ryme, whiche is not possible for me to folow in the translation, nor touche the least poynt of the elegancy that this elegant Poete hath set forth in his owne maternall tongue. (Epistle, sig. A3v)

His reluctance to correct appears to come from a reluctance to allow that any copy of his translation should be more accurate than the one manuscript he presented to the king.[12]

Morley gave his translation to Henry VIII, probably as a New Year's gift. Official New Year's gift lists for Henry's reign before 1528 are not extant.[13] However, we can see from the New Year gifts given by Bernard André to the king from 1509 that seasonal exchange was customary and certainly preceded these surviving Tudor records.[14] The chronological parameters for Morley's gift books have been calculated by James Carley in this volume, most often based on the titles by which Morley addressed his royal recipient.[15] For the *Tryumphes* Morley records the king's surprise and delight at his skill in Italian, a response wholly appropriate if the gift were in fact his first ever translation from Petrarch in that language.

merveylynge muche howe I coulde do it, and thynkynge verelye I hadde not doone it, wythoute helpe of some other, better knowynge the Italyan tounge then I. (Epistle, sig. A3r)

Morley does not know what Henry did with the manuscript. Like the rest of his books it is not recorded in inventories of the royal library. His printed *Epistle* (*c.* 1554) revives the *Tryumphes* for another Henry: Henry Fitzalan, Lord Maltravers, son of the 12th Earl of Arundel. The young patron is asked to defend this imperfect English book for the sake of its excellent Italian original.

I shall, praye you (mooste noble younge Lorde) the very myrroure of al the yonge noble gentelmen of this realme in vertue, in learnynge, and in all other feates appertayning to such a Lorde as you be, to defende it a [sic] agaynst those that will more by envy the*n* by knowledge deprave it. (Epistle, sig. A3v)

That this was Morley's first Italian translation for the king seems certain, from his own words. But we still do not know when Morley gave this gift to Henry. The original dedication (by which rough chronologies of Morley's other gifts have been established) was lost with its manuscript. Nevertheless James Carley argues both that the *Tryumphes* was Morley's first gift and that it 'must have been a product of the late 1520s or very early 153s'.[16]

There are circumstances which suggest to me, however, that both Morley's first 'Plutarch' translation 'Scipio and Hannibal' and his Petrarch translation may have been made and offered to the king earlier in his reign than has been hitherto suggested. It is understood, of course, that even when we do have a date, of dedication or of gift, neither gives us a certain date of translation. If we begin by acknowledging that our chronology for composition is necessarily provisional, two phrases in Morley's 'Scipio and Hannibal' dedication suggest that this gift was particularly appropriate in 1520 and 1521. Henry Parker was of noble blood, but his right to the Morley title was tenuous. In his 'Scipio and Hannibal' dedication to Henry VIII the translator styles himself 'Henry (by your goodnesse) Lord Morlei'. This is a phrase which does not occur in any of Morley's other dedications. Direct thanks to Henry for his own ennoblement is unique to the 'Scipio and Hannibal'. The phrase alludes to a period of uncertainty beginning with the death in 1518 of Parker's mother (in whom the title was vested by the death of her brother).[17] This uncertainty was apparently resolved by 1520 when Parker was summoned to the Field of the Cloth of Gold as Lord Morley.[18] 1520 is too early for the dedication of 'Scipio and Hannibal' in which Henry VIII is addressed by his title 'defensor fidei'. A date soon after October 1521 would be appropriate, such as New Year 1521/2. Further support for an early date might be found in the comparisons Morley draws between his king and heroic Scipio. He praises both as conquerors, who in triumph, uniquely possess the virtue of meekness. As Jeremy Maule points out, this praise is more appropriate to the Henry who first captured (1513) and then ceded back (1518) Tournai, and who in the first decade of his reign aspired to lead a crusade to the Holy Land.[19]

If the first 'Plutarch' translation could be as early as 1522, what about Morley's first Italian translation? We can unravel a very few Henrician threads from the later printed Marian *Epistle*. An unwarranted impediment was created by Morley's editors who, in their search for his sources of inspiration, confined their field to printed texts of Petrarch. This, for a time, seems to have discouraged further investigation of Morley's place among early English translators of Petrarch. Because Carnicelli did not choose first editions, and seems not to have seriously considered the evidence of manuscript texts, he claims that Morley's source of inspiration, must have been a printed French edition of either 1536 and 1538. With this limited evidence he concludes that the *Tryumphes* were a work of Morley's old age.

This hypothesis, shared by Wright and Carnicelli, is based on two clear errors: the 1536 prose translation they cite is a late reprint of Vérard's edition of 1514. Morley could have read it 22 years earlier. Their verse translation – by Jean de Meynier, Baron d'Oppède – is the second, not the first, complete French verse translation of Petrarch's *Trionfi*. Moreover, it is unlikely to be the royal version mentioned by Morley, since Meynier dedicates his translation to Constable Anne de Montmorency, both in the text published in Paris by Denis Janot in 1538 (sig. A2^{v}-A7^{r}) and in the manuscript draft which, as Simone has shown, precedes the printed edition.[20]

James Carley's identification of Morley's 'grome of the chaumber' as Simon Bourgouyn re-opens the question of dating Morley's *Tryumphes*. This French poet, whose datable work spans the period 1508-29, is the first translator of the complete *Trionfi* into French verse. His translation was not printed. It survives in four manuscripts; all were illustrated.[21] Once Bourgouyn's place in the early French reception of Petrarch is clear, the sources (and complexity) of Morley's inspiration may be better appreciated. Reconsideration of manuscript evidence suggests that an early date for any one of Bourgouyn's *Triumphes* manuscripts could place Morley's own translation in the first, or early in the second decade of Henry's reign rather than in the turbulent final years; that is before Wyatt's and Surrey's experiments with Petrarchan verse forms.

It is undoubtedly true, as Carnicelli suggests, that all three English poets knew the influential Italian edition of 1525 with commentary by Allessandro Velutello. However, even 1525 need not be the *terminus a quo* for Morley's translation, since the text Velutello glosses is that of the 1501 Aldine edition prepared by Pietro Bembo; nor was Velutello's own commentary new. It is a refinement of the work of Bernardo Illicino first published in 1475.[22] Even Morley's understanding of the text need not be confined to either Illicino's or Velutello's words, since Illicino's amplifications of the narrative of love and loss in the *Trionfi* and his identifications of the allusively nameless followers of Love and Fame had already inspired artists and were expressed both in independent pictorial traditions (tapestries, stained-glass windows, and wall-paintings) as well as in those pictures which expanded and adorned even plain unglossed texts of the *Trionfi*.

Once we release Morley from sole dependence on specific printed texts his eclectic enterprise can be appreciated more fully. He remains close to Petrarch's own text and imagery; his occasional debts to the glossators and illustrators are concisely worked into his verse. Morley's choice of couplets and 'riding rhyme' expresses the seriousness of his Italian text whose 'elegancy' and terza rima he does not attempt. What is unusual, but seldom remarked, is the simplicity of the physical presentation of Morley's text, the clear white margins of John Cawood's edition. Its large historiated initials apart, the small book's spareness stands out in comparison both to Vérard's amplified and richly illustrated prose edition of 1514, and to the illustrated manuscripts of Bourgouyn.

Morley was inspired by the success of Bourgouyn's French verse to test the poetic sinews of English. But this does not imply that he had continuing access to Bourgouyn's translation, or even that this was his first introduction to Petrarch's *Triumphes*. There are great blanks in the records. His early bookishness in the circle of Lady Margaret Beaufort is better documented than his time at Oxford, or at court.[23] Morley's previous editors seem to have been guessing when they identified his Italian and French sources. What does seem certain is that, by comparison to the gentlemen translators patronized by Louis XII and Francis I whose manuscripts and source material remain in the French royal library, Morley worked in virtual isolation and without much recognition. After the death of Lady Margaret in 1509, for a decade he had neither a secure claim to the family title nor a powerful patron. Perhaps these precarious conditions partially explain his dogged adherence and devotion to the monarch who re-instated him in the barony of his treason-tainted family, but who must have severely tried his loyalty in the latter half of his reign.

Even a bare outline of Morley's unspectacular career shows however that there were early opportunities for contact with the French court. If Morley was born in 1481, as James Carley suggests,[24] he would have been 33 in 1514, the year Vérard printed the French prose *Triumphes*. That was a year of much diplomatic to-ing and fro-ing between London and Paris and much gift exchange between the two courts. In October the king's sister Mary and her entourage went to Paris for her marriage to Louis XII and were greeted with elaborate street pageants. In January 1514/15 Charles Brandon was sent to Paris to congratulate Francis I on his accession. Morley would have been 39 in 1520 when, together with his wife, he was in the king's retinue at the Field of the Cloth of Gold.[25] It seems likely that during the fourteen days of reciprocal visiting and display some of the treasures of the young French monarch were shown to the English, perhaps during a reading such as the one commemorated in a miniature of 1534: Francis beneath his cloth of state listens to a reading by Macault of his translation of Diodorus Siculus.[26] Morley, himself, had participated in such after-dinner readings in the household of Lady Margaret Beaufort. Two years earlier Francis's travelling library chest was said to contain a manuscript translation 'Triumphes de Petrarch'.[27] There is no doubt that *Trionfi* was a favourite book. Any attempt to identify which text the king carried in 1520, however, must reckon with the richness of his library and with the fact that Francis continually up-dated his travelling collection. In the last decade of his reign his portable *Trionfi* was the octavo 1533 Aldine *Il Petrarca* which was bound (for help with difficult phrases) with G. B. Castiglione's *Il luoghi difficili del Petrarcha* (Venice, 1532).[28]

The continuity of Italian and French illustrations of Petrarch is most readily studied in the still-extant libraries of the French kings Charles VIII, Louis XII, and Francis I. Each king, returning with spoils from an Italian campaign, brought artists, manuscripts, and art treasures. In the libraries of Blois and Fontainebleau: 'France ... took the lead, with large and lavish manuscripts, not only of the *Trionfi* but also of the *De remediis* – both of them in French translation – illustrated by the artists of the School of Rouen, by Jean Pichore and by Godefroy le Batave.'[29] When in 1517 the Cardinal of Aragon and his chaplain Antonio de Beatis were shown the treasures of the library at Blois established by Louis XII they saw: 'books all of parchment, handwritten in beautiful lettering and bound in silk of various colors, with elaborate locks and clasps of gilded silver. We were shown the *Triumphs* of Petrarch illustrated by a Flemish artist with quite excellent illuminations, the *Remedium contra adversam fortunam* also by Messer Francesco.'[30]

Petrarch's fame in France was first as a Latin author. At Blois there were at least three copies of the Latin text of *De Remediis Utriusque Fortunae* and two further copies in French. Jean Daudin's hundred-and-fifty-year-old translation of *De Remediis* (*c.* 1376-7) was printed in Paris by Galliot du Pré in 1524.[31] Petrarch's treatise was re-translated *c.* 1503 for Louis XII (BN, f. fr. 225), and a smaller copy was dedicated to Louise de Savoie (BN, f. fr. 224). Interesting for the present argument is the certainty that the dialogue of 'a king without a son' in Book II (BN, f. fr. 225) was given particular political point in the fourteen full-page coloured miniatures exemplifying occasions of good and bad Fortune. The king, subject to the wheel of Fortune, stands clearly indicating his wife and daughter: the particular ill-fortune of Louis XII.[32] In the smaller manuscript (BN, f. fr. 224), bearing Louise's arms (Orléans and Savoie), the alternating occupants of the chair of Fortune show that she and her son Francis may be the good fortune France needs.

Whether Catherine of Aragon's request for an English translation of the *De Remediis Utriusque Fortunae* may echo the same plight is a matter of speculation. It was diplomatic of Thomas Wyatt, England's best poet since Chaucer, to refuse his queen's request by pleading the inadequacy of English. In his preface to Plutarch's *Quiet of Mind* (dated 31 December 1527) he explains to Queen Catherine why in this his New Year's gift to her he abandoned Petrarch for Plutarch.

> The boke of Fraunces Petrarch / of the remedy of yll fortune / at the commaundement of your highnesse / I assayd / as my power wolde serue me / to make into our englysshe. And after I had made a profe of nyne or ten Dialogues / the labour began to seme tedious / by superfluous often rehersyng of one thyng, which tho peraventure in the latyn shalbe laudable / by plentuous diversitie of the spekyng of it (for I wyll nat that my iugement shall disalowe in any thyng so aproved an auctour) yet for lacke of suche diversyte in our tong / it shulde want a great dele of the grace.[33]

This seems to be the only work of Wyatt published in his lifetime. His Plutarch was brought out by Richard Pynson 'printer to the king's most noble grace'.

Francis inherited Louis XII's early French Petrarchs; he also retained the services of some of the *clercs* and artists who created these treasures. As they began with *De Remediis*, so they continued to receive Petrarch in the manner of that moral Latin dialogue. Although an old tradition that Bourgouyn was *valet de chambre* to Louis XII has been reiterated as recently as 1997, this appointment has so far only been verified by payments made under Francis I.[34] Whether he was formally in service as a groom of the chamber at the time, it is likely that all but one of his *Triumphes* manuscripts can be dated to the period 1512-14.[35]

This mixture of old and new courtiers can be seen in the description of the king's first entry into Paris in 1515 after his coronation. Some of the *gens du roi* in the procession wore the late king's badge of the crowned porcupine, others Francis's salamander and motto. In the place of honour, near the end, Francis, dressed in white and silver, accompanied by his *valets* and *gentilshommes* and riding a white horse, bounded clear of the canopy which decorum required to be held over him.[36]

The offices of *gentilhomme* and *valet* were redefined under Francis I.[37] If Bourgouyn were a *valet de chambre* to Louis he would have shared this title with noblemen; after 1518 in Francis I's household *valet* was the appellation of other painters and poets: Jean Clouet, the portraitist, Jean Pérréal, and Jean Bourdichon, artists who served both kings.[38] As the biographer of Jean Clouet concludes: 'these accounts are incomplete and the lack of documents does not preclude the possibility of his having worked for Louis XII'. So, too, we might say of Bourgouyn. It is enough to know that his translation was in manuscript by 1514, and that it may be earlier.

The fullest version of Bourgouyn's translation is the folio manuscript which bears his name, BN, f. fr. 12423. Each triumph is introduced by Latin verse summaries, which Simone has shown originate with an anonymous fifteenth-century French writer.[39] Such verses were known in France during the early fifteenth century as '*Triumphes de Petrarch*', and were perhaps meant to accompany sets of tapestries, or paintings. Bourgouyn's original French verses follow on, descanting on the Latin summaries; both accompany each section of the text. Each triumph is ended alternately with an explicit '*Sens moral*' and '*Sens historique*'.

The layout of Bourgouyn's folio translation gives visual expression to the *copia* ('the coppye') which Lord Morley admiringly describes in his Epistle. That richness of gloss and imitation was the culmination of a century-and-a-half's reception of Petrarch's text. The anonymous Latin verse summaries first found in French fifteenth-century manuscripts may have been inspired by early Italian illustrations of the *Trionfi*; in turn they inspired independent French illustrations.

In the later fifteenth century these Latin lines prompted vernacular French imitations in various verse forms which at their best aspire to imitate the diversity of Petrarch's verse.[40] These were the work of courtier/administrators. Jean Robertet, friend of Charles d'Orléans and *valet de chambre* to Charles VIII, is the first of the named vernacular versifiers.[41] In a collection made by his son François, Jean Robertet's *Triumphes* in French octosyllabics take pride of place in the profusely illustrated pages of BN, f. fr. 24461, a lightly didactic manuscript with portraits of the pagan gods, illustrated proverbs, and '*dicts moraux*' of the Bourbonnais poet Henri Baude (unusually set in landscapes). François himself wrote *Les Triumphes de Pétrarque en roundeaulx* preserved in BN, f. fr. 1721. Another such manuscript is BN, f. fr. 1717 entitled 'Dictz moraux pour tapis ou verrieres de fenestres'. Simone argues that these paraphrases demonstrate 'an alert and specific interest in the original work of Petrarque', primarily in the moral content of the *Trionfi*.[42] His claims for the seriousness of these French adaptations of the *Trionfi* are borne out in the fine illustrations. This moral interest is apparent in the anonymous Cambridge, Fitzwilliam Museum, MS Marlay 3 where a French *Triumphes* manuscript (laid out for illustration) is bound in a contemporary vellum binding with a Latin Book of Hours. Several of Petrarch's own images are captured, but the text is selective. This section on Death moralizes an illustration at several removes from Petrarch's own verse.

> En ung car tout couvert de noir
> Alloit puis la mort qua veoir
> Estoit tres laide et tres obscure
> Et son car tiroyent pour voir
> Fragilite. ce vous asseure
> Qu'en travail vit et si na l[u]xure
> Certaine a vivre longuement.
> Terme et declin qui bien peu dure
> O fin tu vient pareillement.
>
> sus ung viel sercueil tout po*r*ry
> Se soit la mort qui nourry
> Et en sa char mainte vermine.
> Et avecques main tien marcy
> Haulsoit une faux faisant signe
> de tout abattre en brief termine
> Et son car cheminoit tousjours
> Ou quel na Roue qui ne pigne
> Quoy qu'arrousees soye*nt* de plours
> Dessoubz soy helas Japparceuz
> La chastete Ruee iuz
> Toute pale et descoulouree
> La mort la pics avoit dessuz
> Sa gente poictrine serree
> Telle rudess Reparee
> Ne sera jamais comme croy
> Car de vertus estoit paree
> dont cest pitie dung tel desroy (fol. 76^{r-v})

In France it was in this manner that the *Trionfi* was first welcomed, not as a conclusion to the lyrical *Canzoniere*, but primarily as an extension of *De Remediis*. The 'new' French poets Jean Robertet, François Robertet, Jean Molinet, Simon Bourgouyn, shared a common interest in native verse forms. Yet (mysteriously) they continued to work willingly through the anonymous Latin verse summaries, even after Pietro Bembo's Aldine edition (1501) had made it cheaply and abundantly clear that these Latin verses were not written by Petrarch.

Simone's comprehensive study shows that in France the poetic confidence to versify Petrarch was built up by a strong tradition of vernacular descanting. England lacked such a vigorous tradition. Morley, who responds to the stimulus of the French verse *Triumphes* with 'an Englyshe man myght do aswell as the Frenche man', immediately distinguishes his enterprise from that of Bernard André whose political allegory of envy and avarice, the *Twelve Triumphes of Henry VII*, versifies the labours of Hercules with no trace of visual or textual influence from Petrarch.[43] Nor does Morley follow Skelton whose essay in the genre of 'triumphs' seems to have been undertaken in a quite different spirit. It is generally recognized that his *Colin Clout* (*c.* 1523) was tilting at Wolsey's emulation of the glory of Henry VIII and Francis I: the magnificent building plans, the garnering of art treasures. In the context of Simone's work it seems possible that Skelton is deriding not just Wolsey's taste for Petrarchan tapestries but a whole school of 'rhetoriqueurs' with their inventories of mythological figures and 'goodly chares Conveyed by olyphantes'. Not much of the seriousness or elegance of the 'Dictz moraux pour tapis' survives his skeltering rhyme:

Wyth dame Dyana naked
How lusty Venus quaked
And howe Cupyde shaked
His darte, and bente hys bowe
For to shote a Crowe
At her tyrly tyrlowe
And howe Parys of Troye
Daunced a lege de moy
Made lustye sporte and joy
With dame Helyn the Queene
With such storyes by deen
Their chambres wel be seen
With triumphes of Cesar
And of Pompeius war
Of renowne and of fame
By them to get a name

Nowe all the worlde stares
How they ryde in goodly chares
Conveyed by Olyphantes
With Lauriat garlantes
And by unycornes
With their semely hornes
Upon these beastes ridyng
Naked boyes striding
With wanton wenches winkyng.[44]

In early French versified *Triumphes* the lyrics for Laura seldom keep company.[45] In sharp contrast Italian scribes and printers present the *Trionfi* as the culmination of the Laura lyrics. In early Italian manuscripts in recognition of this close association, in which *Trionfi* renders the lyric sequence of love and loss in a more narrative mode, illustrations surprising in the *Trionfi* can sometimes be explained as cross-fertilization from the sparse but powerful illustrations of the first and last of the 'sonetti in morte' (CCLXIV 'I'vo pensando');[46] I am thinking here of Bartolomeo Sanvito's death image of Laura hurtling, like Phaeton, from her runaway horse-drawn car;[47] of CCCLXVI 'Vergina bella'; and of CCCXXIII 'Standomi un giorno solo'.[48] In his creation of a personal mythology Petrarch returns again and again to a few poetic and conceptual nuclei. This intertextuality of the *Canzoniere* and *Trionfi* is sometimes expressed by the interchange of imagery.[49] Laura's apocryphal chariot in *Trionfi* is such a case.

Italian illustrations of the clash of triumphators, both in manuscript and in print, seldom correspond to Petrarch's text. Looking only at printed illustrations which Morley could have seen, the Triumph of Death in the Venetian editions of Petrus de Plasiis and Matteo Capcasa wholly ignores Petrarch's initial peaceful mise-en-scène, preferring instead a confrontation of four-wheeled open wagons. The figure of Chastity atop a chariot is drawn by unicorns and might well be a statue; her challenger, naked skeletal Death with sickle, and similarly perched, is drawn by oxen. As his car rolls over corpses, devils in the sky behind the procession pitch the damned into perdition and angels carry tiny souls to heaven.[50]

A welcome exception comes from a manuscript written in Rome *c.* 1508.[51] Here, as in Petrarch's text, Chastity walks carrying her ermine pennon, surrounded by her ladies; Death wrapped in black (but without the Petrarchan banner) advances on an ox-drawn waggon, wielding in her arm an un-Petrarchan scythe; in the foreground Laura and the poet sit beneath a laurel exchanging their last words, as they do at the end of the Triumph of Death cap. 2.

One of the tantalizing curiosities of the French manuscript reception of the *Trionfi* may be seen in Jean Robertet's exquisitely illustrated 'Mors vincit pudicitiam'. Here again, the Latin and French verses are only distantly related to Petrarch's text, but the picture is both innovative and much closer: Death is feminine and the triumphal image is completely without chariots. Seven lines of Latin above frame Chastity prostrate beneath the feet of the three Fates. While Atropos and Clotho are decidedly matronly, the beauty of Laura/Chastity is reflected in the central face of a youthful Lachesis. Below the picture Robertet's eight-line French poem concludes with a Latin tribute to the time worn fatal sisters.[52]

> Combien que lomme soit chaste et tout pudicque
> Les seurs fatalles par leur lor auctentique
> Tranchent les nerfz et filletz de la vie
> A ce la mort tous les vivans convie
> Le chaste au fort plus sa manent peult vivre
> Qui ce treuue de arans vices delivre
> Mais en la fin il ny a roy ne pape
> Grant ne petit qui de ses las eschappe. (fol. 4^{r})

Throughout the Robertet sequence there is not a single chariot. The usual French illustration for Death, however, is an image probably derived from the Venetian editions of Capcasa: skeletal Death riding upon *his* car straddles or stands on the corpse of Laura/Chastity.[53]

How did Morley read his Petrarch? Probably with the lyrics since he makes a point of praising them: 'these syxte wonderful made triumphes [were] all to the laude of hys Ladye Laura, by whome he made so many a swete sonnet' (Epistle, sig. A2^{v}). In composite volume or in the two-volume sets these vernacular works were, as we have seen, available in Italian printed editions.[54]

Petrarch did not give his *Trionfi* a final form. There are consequently four families of manuscripts which preserve different orders and division of the fourteen *capitoli*;

these families are perpetuated in the printed texts, with occasional merging and shifting of sequence. Carnicelli rightly places Morley's text in Wilkins's 'family D': with four *capitoli* for Love, one for Chastity, two for Death, three for Fame, one for Time and one for Divinity/Eternity. However, Morley's *Tryumphes* shares one salient feature of families A-C: his text is not glossed. Perhaps the most useful literary conclusion one can draw from this complex stemma is that Morley could well be working with partly corrupted text and that he might first be given the benefit of the doubt when one of his readings is blurred or when it diverges from the twentieth-century printed texts his editor has chosen for him. Particular details are tantalizing. For instance, Morley's source for glossing the names of classical heroes and heroines as he pads out a half-line or places a rhyme has been attributed by Carnicelli to Velutello (1525). But Morley's 'storyall' and philosophical readings might equally come from a manuscript or printed book whose plain text remained close to Petrarch's but was accompanied by 'visual glossing' of its illustrations. In this case the identity of the mysterious figures accompanying Love is openly proclaimed in a pictorial procession where 'Julius Caesar' or 'Ypolite' is inscribed on a tunic.[55] Even Bourgouyn's text reads differently, illustrated in the French images (BN, f. fr. 12423) or in Italianate manner (Paris, Arsenal MS 6480).[56]

Since Petrarch's *Trionfi* in the D stemma was considered so rich in meanings that Italian and French readers in the early sixteenth century were seldom offered a plain text, Morley's enterprise seems bold, as is his confidence in his 'maternall tongue'. Eschewing gloss or commentary, he does not reach outside his verse for clarification. This was presumably the method attempted in the anonymous Vérard prose translation, but the prolix amplifications swamp tiny islands of paraphrase recognizable as Petrarch's original. It is not surprising, then, that Morley's translation expands Petrarch. But sparingly he incorporates a gloss or identification in a half-line, occasionally fulfilling the need to complete a couplet.

Carnicelli is critical of Morley who 'expanded the 1953 lines of the original to 2750'.[57] His helpful edition is full of monitory knuckle-rapping; school-masterly notes of 'expansion', 'blurring', 'misreading', 'added by Morley', as Carnicelli closely compares a modern critical edition of the Italian text with Morley's English. This is no doubt true. However, against this view of Morley's diffuseness as translator there is a case to make for the coherence and resourcefulness of his visual imagination. This gift is particularly evident in the *capitoli* of Death. He has an ability, too, for rendering what one might call Petrarch's filmic effects, the gradual merging and replacement of one picture by another. He can coherently relocate Petrarch's imagery in England. When Love's procession comes to the isle of Cythera, the god arrives at a triumphal arch. Morley omits this Roman artifact and keeps our eyes on Love high in his 'chayre' around which vices gather:

> Nowe for to declare this matter by and by
> This Goddes chayre, where that they sat on hye,
> There was about it errour and dreames
> And glosynge ymages of all nations and realmes;
> False opynion was entrynge the gate
> And slypper hope stode by theyr ate
> Wery rest, and rest with wo and payne
> The more hygher he clam the lesse he dyd obtayn (Love, IV, sig. E3^{v})

When Petrarch next mentions the arch, Morley sustains the image from his own culture. The press thrusting around Love's chayre and 'gate' enter a prison which smoothly becomes a castle (sig. E4^r). Morley's chayre and scaffold and castle-gate/prison have the quality of stage furniture, familiar in the mummings and devices of the Henrician court. The energy of his thought passes through and past the couplet rhyme to achieve the scene:

> Holden and tyed and kept by forse
> Crying for mercy tyll that he be horse
> In this castell syghynge for Sorga and Arno
> Was I prysoner many a longe daye so
> That by my wytte, I coulde no meanes fynde
> Oute for to gette there I was so blynde. (Love, IV, sig. E4^r)

The strength of Morley's simplicity shows to best advantage in his treatment of Laura/Chastity. From the evidence of the Epistle, it is clear that he is familiar with the four levels of meaning favoured by the glossators ('all moral vertue, all Phylosophye ...') yet he resists making Laura into an abstraction. Familiar personifications in the tradition of the *Roman de la Rose* accompany Laura when, leaving Love bound in the Temple of Chastity, she returns from Rome on foot surrounded by a little band of virtuous companions:

> Honestie and shamefastnesse they went before ...
> Wyt and sobernes folowed the trace
> Well set in hyr harte without arrace ...
> And beuty lacked not, with a chast clene thoughte
> All these agaynst love my Lady broughte (Chastitie, I, sig. f3^r)

There is not the faintest rumble of a chariot wheel here in the movement of 'this felowshyp' of ladies. Morley makes Petrarch's sharp contrast between the visual signs of male power in Love's military conquest and those which express Laura's particular womanly strengths which, having defeated Love, go on to transform Death.

Again, in the Triumph of Death Petrarch's Laura walks with her companions; her power is not expressed by command of a triumphal car. The exhilaration of victory is lightly touched in the modest demeanour of women on foot in a little troop or squadron. 'Un bel drappelletto'[58] can mean both ensign or banner as well as a band or company of men or women. The first French prose, and first verse, translations respond to this new diminutive as a challenge to the copiousness of their vernacular. Jean Meynier, Baron d'Oppède, simply cuts out the troublesome line.[59] In Morley's translation (as in all other texts) Laura and her troop are given their authentic standard: a white ermine on a green field (ll. 25-6). He goes on to interpret *drappelletto*, with a sense of English social decorum, as 'canapye'. The word is used as early as 1380 by Wycliffe to mean 'covering or hangings suspended over a throne, or held over a person walking in a procession' (*OED*). It is used in 1513 to mean 'a special covering held over a shrine or over the Host borne in procession':

> This noble Lady with hyr company then
> Turned (as sayde is) from that hygh victory
> All together going under a fayre canapye (Death, I, sig. g1^v)

Fig. 1. 'All together going under a fayre canapye,' Morley, 'Death', I, sig. g1^{v}, BN, f. fr. 594, fol. 134^{v}. By kind permission of the Bibliothèque Nationale de France, Paris.

Morley does not take his 'canapye' from Velutello's gloss: 'In un bel drapelletto, cio è in un bel raccolto & insieme unito numero' (sig. d6^{r}). He may have adapted '*drap d'or*' from Vérard's prose text of 1514. Or Morley, too, may have seen what evidently inspired Vérard's anonymous translator. In Louis XII's *Triumphes* manuscript (BN, f. fr. 594, fol. 134^{v}) (Fig. 1) Laura/Chastity returns from her triumph. On her right and walking ahead of her wagon is Lucrece, bearing Laura's ermine banner, accompanied by other named chaste ladies of Antiquity; to Laura's left, and slightly behind her in the next plane, walk her Virtues. Two angels hover over these Virtues holding above them a white cloth of honour. Morley sees with contemporary decorum. His cloth unites, even as it honours, Laura's multiple meanings: Laura and her attendant Virtues 'going' together under a canapy. The cloth here covering many is appropriate to one: to a king or to the Host. As this unusual triumph begins, Morley's 'canapye' prepares his reader visually for Laura's final calm response to her challenger, when she says Death will have no power over her chaste companions:

> In these chast companyes this is true & playne)
> Thou hast no reason nor yet noo power. (Death, sig. g2^{v})

In Morley's *Tryumphes* no tapestry juggernaut destroys the scene which Petrarch created for the eye of the mind. He insists *io vidi* (Velutello, sig. d6^{v}), a phrase Morley avoids. But, as Laura and her company turn, so Morley withdraws in a parenthesis of perfect tact ('as sayde is') to let the reader's imagination take over.

The poetic power in the two *capitoli* of Death depends on almost imperceptible transitions of vision. Petrarch's Death appears abruptly, unannounced, as a dark banner; then we see the awesome woman in black who halts the small, merry troop of virgins returning simply and on foot from Rome. It is crucial to this triumph that Death should appear as a lone, yet terrifying, *woman*, her power and status announced only by her 'Banner'.[60]

> Quand' io vidi una insegna oscura et trista:
> Et una donna involta in veste negra. (Velutello, sig. d6^{v})

Morley again eschews the authority and immediacy of 'io vidi' but keeps the power of surprise:

> When that all sodenly there dyd appeare
> A sadde blacke baner that approched nere
> And a woman wrapped all in blacke. (Death, I, sig. g2^{r})

In Morley's translation the black banner challenges the small troop with its ermine ensign. We see only the banner and the lone woman 'all in black'. However, in Vérard's edition menace and mystery of banner and lone woman are dispersed by glossing adjectives which now inhabit the main text: 'le regard si atropiste', and 'cerbericque femme'. In keeping with one of the most popular pictorial traditions Vérard's *text* gives a scythe to the woman in black ('une grande et mortelle faulx ague', sig. g4^{r}), instead of Petrarch's *spada*. In confirmation, opposite and facing this text, skeletal death wields *his* scythe in a full-page illustration of *his* triumphal cart (sig. g3^{v}).

Despite Morley's admirable restraint and his preference for the literal sense, neither he nor the two later sixteenth-century English translators quite catch the exquisite simplicity of Petrarch's closure of *capitolo* I.[61] But Morley's refusal of the military clichés, and the dance of death skeleton show him working closer to the text, preserving the meaning of Laura's transmutation of terror by peaceful acceptance of mortality. Her triumph continues as we observe a literal encounter of woman and woman. As we watch, little by little, the black hag is transformed by Laura's serene faith, in some of the most beautiful poetry of the book:

> Even as a swete lyght that commeth to decay
> Lytle and lytle consumynge awaye
> When that the byrth lycoure is past and gone
> The flame extincte then lyght is there none
> Not pale she laye but whyter then the snow
> That the wynde agaynst the hyl doth blowe
> As he that wery is, and woulde have rest
> So she laye when death had hyr oppreste
> And as one that slepeth softe and quietlye,
> So myght they all then and there espye
> Dreadful death that fooles have in disgrace
> Fayre and beautifull in that swetest face. (Death, I, sig. G4v-H1r)

The *imprecision* of 'that fooles have in disgrace' may be forgiven in the precision of images and the gentle movement of the verse as it comes to a tender close.

> Non come fiamma, che per forza è spenta;
> Ma che per se medesma si consume;
> Se n'ando in pace l'anima contenta:
> A guisa d'un soaue et chiaro lume,
> Cui nutrimento a poco a poco manca;
> Tenendo al fin il suo usato costume.
> Pallida no; ma piu che neue bianca,
> Che senza uento in un bel colle fiocchi;
> Parea posar, come persona stanca.
> Quasi un dolce dormir ne suoi begliocchi
> Essendo'l spirto gia da lei diuiso
> Era quel; che morir chiaman gli sciocchi.
> Morte bella parea nel suo bel uiso. (Velutello, sig. e1r)

Mary Sidney, tied by her much more difficult *terza rima*, stays literally closer to Petrarch but her accurately rendered 'did seeme' is fastidious beside Morley's spare wording

> Dreadful death ...
> Fayre and beutifull in that swetest face. (Death, I, sig. H1r)

He knows not 'seems'. But Mary Sidney achieves a fine visual clarity in spite of her more self-conscious artifice:

> Right lyke unto som lamp of cleerest light,
> Little and little wanting nutriture,
> Houlding to end a neuer-changing plight.
> Pale? no, but whitelie; and more whitelie pure,
> Then snowe on wyndless hill, that flaking falles:
> As one, whom labor did to rest allure.

And when that heauenlie guest those mortall walles
Had leaft: it nought but sweetelie sleeping was
In hir faire eyes, what follie dying calles
Death faire did seeme to be in hir faire face. (Death, I, 163-72, p. 277)

Laura, returning to the poet in a dream in *capitolo* II, confesses what could not be guessed by the reader of the *Canzoniere*: that their love was mutual. She explains her long silence in gentle reproof of his songs to the world. Their last parting is thus even more poignant and comes with the arrival of dawn. Laura answers the poet's final question, gently revealing that he has many years to live before they will at last be united. At the prospect of Laura's departure to heaven the French editions have their wagons ready. Driven by the pun on Laura / *l'aurora*, the quasi-divinity of Illicino's gloss and, perhaps, by pictorial amplification of sonnet 264 (the first *in morte* where Laura plunges like Phaeton from the car of the sun) these French editions turn sunrise into a golden chariot in which Laura ascends to heaven:

Lacteur: Ap*res* celles parolles je vy ceste belle dame monter q*ui* pour sen aller mo*n*ta en ung / celestin chariot dor do*n*t je demenay gra*n*t dueil car ses doulces p*ar*olles me furent trop briefves. Helas jestoye en gra*n*t pensee a scavoir si tost ou tard je la suyvroye.[62] (sig. h2^{v})

Vérard's printer has set the exchange as a dialogue on his page with speakers' parts for which the probable Petrarchan precedent is *De Remediis*, but he has completely lost the actual words exchanged in farewell.

Vedi l'aurora de l'aurato letto
Rimenar a mortali il giorno; e'l sole
Gia for de l'oceano in fin al petto.
Questa vien per partira; onde mi dole:
S'a dir hai altro; studia d'esse breve,
Et col tempo dispensa le parole.

Quant'io soffersi mai, soave & leve
Dissi,m'ha fatto il parlar dolce & pio:
Ma'l'viver sanza voi m'è duro et greve:
Però saper vorrei Madonna, s'io
Son per tardi sequirui, o se per tempo:
Ella gia mossa disse, al creder mio
Tu stari'n terra senza me gran tempo. (Velutello, sig. e4^{r-v})

Morley's version of the final parting of the lovers at dawn does not attempt the language of the *aubade* or the elegancy of Petrarch's Laura / *l'aurora*. Morley's Laura speaks simply, no aureate diction mitigates the pain of her parting words, a parting not visualized. The distance between mortal and immortal is kept in the pronouns *thou* / *you*. Formulaic phrases supply, as ever, Morley's couplet rhymes. But the urgency of their final questions and answers presses past these expected rhymes into the next line for meaning. Laura's parting and the punishment of her lover's solitary long life are understood, not seen.

Mary Sidney misses the sun lifting *his* breast above the sea; she captures the quiet last exchange, but perhaps the mutual grief is too formal:

See from hir golden bed Aurora bright
To mortall eyes returning sunne and daye
Breast-high above the Ocean bare to sight.
Shee to my sorrowe, calles me hence awaie,
Therfore thy words in times short limits binde,
And saie in-brief, if more thow haue to saie.
Ladie (quoth I) yor words most sweetlie kinde
Have easie made, what ever erst I bare,
But what is left of yow to live behinde.
Therfore to knowe this is my onelie care,
If sloe or swift shall com our meeting-daye.
She parting saide, As my conjectures are,
Thow without me long time on earth shalt staie.
(Death, II, 178-90, p. 282)

Morley dispenses with personified Dawn and her bed, and ignores the Sun breasting the sea. Always slightly awkward in his phrasing (the reverse 'you ensue') he nevertheless stays true to the tenderness and intimacy of the scene and the sober grief of parting:

The nyght is past now commeth the bryght daye
Yf that to me thou wylt more saye swete hart
Be short I byd the for I must hence departe
O sayde I, myne owne swete Lady dere
For al the sorowe and payne I have had here
In lovinge you these wordes so fayre and swete
Doth recompence my love and makes all mete
But from you thus for to be seperate playne
Is unto me a deadly mortall payne
But one thynge nowe to me you must declare
Or that ye from my wofull presence fare
Shall I lyve longe tell me after you
Or shortly as I woulde O Lady you ensue
She aunswered gently as farre as she coulde tell
Longe after hyr on earth here should I dwell. (Death, II, sig. $H4^v$-I^r)

Finally Morley in his Triumph of Divinity continues to visualize and connect. While Petrarch analytically distinguishes the three aspects of Time (past, present, and future) before these dissolve in Eternity, Morley's pictorial concision depends upon superimposition of triads based on the structural pun of sun and son, as do some Italian woodcuts for the Triumph of Divinity: tripartite time, and the three-fold universe 'sonne, firmament and the skye' merge and are transfigured in a final tableau of the Trinity, stable at last, on the single foot of the cross: 'Stand fyrme on one fote sure stable and faste'(sig. $M3^v$). Morley may be recalling a miniature or a woodcut, since in his lifetime an unillustrated Italian *Trionfi* was the exception. His 'wordish picture' is vivid and belongs to an iconography manifest in a Florentine 'broad-manner' engraving dated by A. M. Hind *c.* 1470-90. Sometimes mounted on a car, sometimes not, this Christ on the cross is held in the arms of God, surmounted by the Holy Spirit, and pulled by the Gospel creatures or the human figures of Matthew, Mark, Luke, and John walking simply toward the reader (Fig. 2).[63]

Fig. 2. 'Stand fyrme on one fote sure stable and faste,' Morley, 'Eternity', Vérard (Paris, 1514), sig. Q2r. By kind permission of the British Library Board.

Questo pensaua: et mentre piu s'interna
La mente mia; ueder mi parue un mondo
Nouo in etate immobile et eterna;
E'l sole, et tutto' l ciel disfare a tendo
Con le sue stelle; anchor la terra, e'l mare;
Et rifarne un piu bello et piu giocondo.
Qual merauiglia hebb'io, quando restare
Vidi in un pie colui, che mai non stette;
Ma discorrendo suol tutto cangiare?
Et le tre parti sue uidi ristrette
Ad una sola, et quell'una esser ferma;
Si che, come solea piu non s'affrette. (Velutello, sig. g7^{r-v})

And as that I was solitarie in this meditatione
It semed to me I sawe a wonderfull facion
A newe fayre worlde stable and eterne
And this olde world that semeth so ferme
The sonne and the stares and the heaven rounde
And the great se also with the earth and ground
To vanyshe clene awaye & in theyr rome & place
A newe merier world made by godes grace
What great trowe ye, then admiracion had I
When I sawe the sonne firmament and the skye
Stand fyrme on one fote sure stable and faste
That with his swyft course runnyng at the laste
Changed all thinges mortall and then restrained,
His thre partes brought to one part unfayned
And then no distinction no difference of them at al. (Divinitie, sig. M3^{v})

Five copies of Morley's small printed quarto survive, re-dedicated to Henry Fitzalan, Lord Maltravers. Morley's undated quarto was not a hugger-mugger affair. The *Tryumphes* were printed by John Cawood, Queen Mary's official printer. The Epistle offers Maltravers a book fit and once fitted for a king. In the event, Morley's hopes were disappointed and the youthful protector of his Epistle died in August 1556, just four months before Morley himself. Morley's *Tryumphes* is now an exceedingly rare book. It is likely that Maltravers's copy was lodged in the Arundel library; a copy of Morley's translation was still there at the time of the Lumley inventory.[64]

It is striking, though, that although only five copies of the unique edition survive, four of them were bound as if they were supplementary to the 1579 edition of Petrarch's *De Remediis Fortunae*, translated by Thomas Twyne as *Phisicke against Fortune, aswell prosperous, as adverse*.[65] Twyne's *Phisicke* and Morley's *Tryumphes* are bare texts, not set forth with marginal commentary as are many of their Italian and French brothers. To some extent the continental marginal commentaries pre-empt the reader's eye from the discoveries of Petrarch's own mastery of spectacle. In the first Triumph of Love continental commentary barges in from the margins naming the subtly described individual heroes and heroines enslaved by love, quite vitiating the role of the dreamer's shadow friend, who draws the dreamer into the procession and gradually introduces Amor's nameless entourage. Nor are these English texts illustrated. Both quartos sport as their only decoration woodcut compartments for the

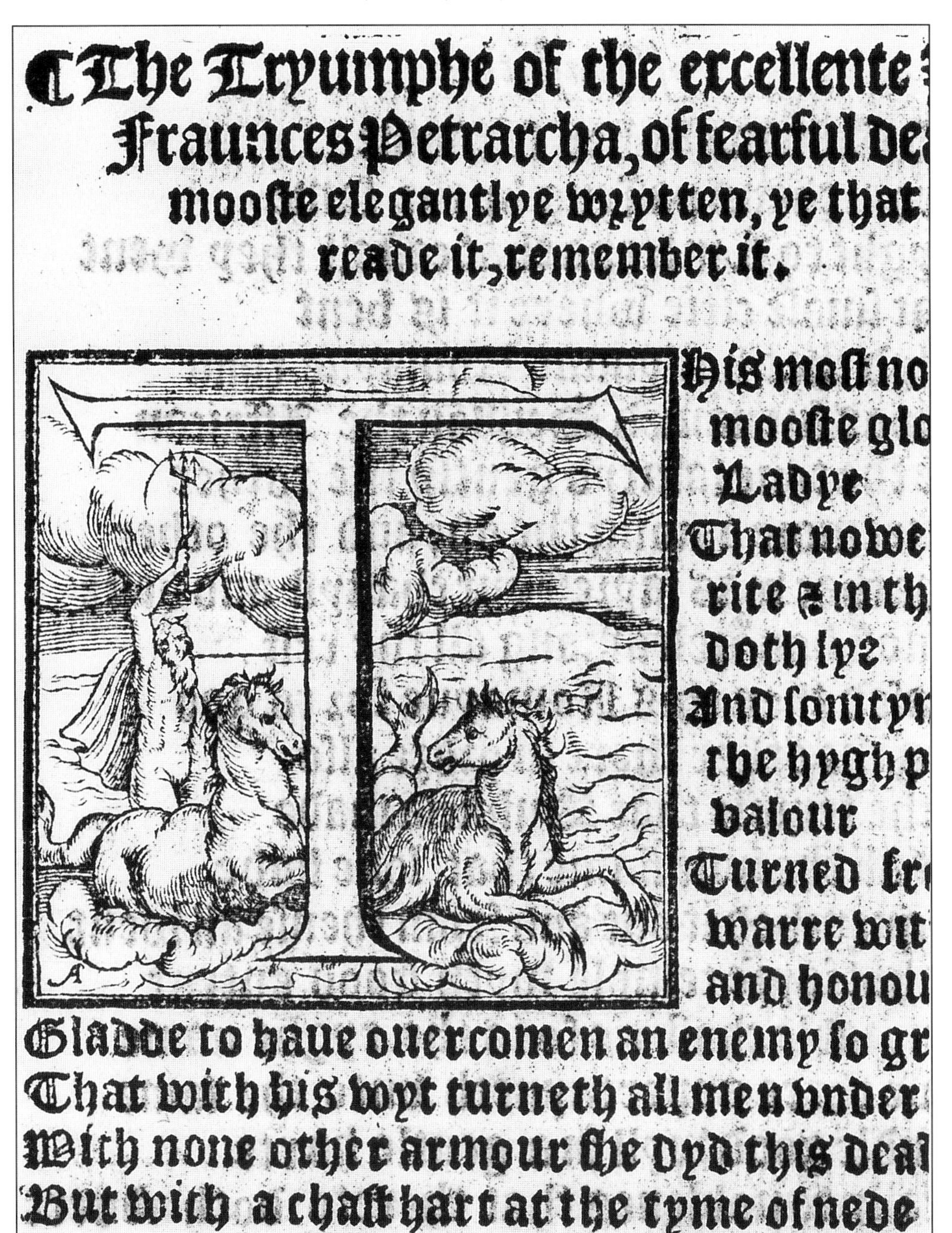

¶ The Tryumphe of the excellente
Fraunces Petrarcha, of fearful de
mooſte elegantlye wrytten, ye that
reade it, remember it.

This moſt no
mooſte glo
Ladye
That nowe
rite & in th
doth lye
And ſomtym
the hygh p
valour
Turned fr
warre wit
and honou
Gladde to haue ouercomen an enemy ſo gr
That with his wyt turneth all men vnder
With none other armour ſhe dyd this dea
But with a chaſt hart at the tyme of nede

Fig. 3. Arnold Nicholai's mark *Lord Morley's 'Tryumphes'*, 'Death', STC 19811, sig. G1^{v}. Original 56 × 56 mm. By kind permission of the Bodleian Library, Oxford.

title-page, and historiated woodcut capitals whose subject matter seems to bear little or at best tangential connection with the text.[66] Physically they thus bypass both the glories and the contradictions of the continental illustrated editions. Yet the larger historiated initials which signal each new triumph were by a master craftsman, Arnold Nicolai, engraver and block-cutter of Antwerp. Despite their elegance they were not, I think, purpose made for the *Tryumphes* (Fig. 3)[67]

I strongly suspect from the records of partnership in the Stationers' Register that Cawood's unsold sheets of the *Tryumphes* reached the later Elizabethan printer Richard Watkyns by the following route. Upon the accession of Elizabeth I, Cawood, who printed 'at the signe of the Holy Ghost' in St Paul's Churchyard, was reconfirmed in his patent as royal printer but yoked in that office to the reliably Protestant Richard Jugge, whose books issued from the sign of the Bible, also in Paul's Churchyard. Together they printed the Bishops' Bible of 1568 and many other staunchly reformed texts.[68]

The more obvious gravity of the *Remedia* may have prevented Morley's translation being swept away. But from the perspective of the renaissance of English poetry which blazed out so brilliantly in 1579, it looks rather as if Morley's *Tryumphes* was reissued wrapped in a fifteenth-century shroud. Also published in 1579 was *The Shepheardes Calender*, in which Spenser anonymously addresses not only Petrarch but also Petrarch's best-known Italian and French imitators. By 1579, too, Philip Sidney's imitations of Petrarch's verse must have been well under way. Within ten years Mary Sidney was to make her translation of the Triumph of Death, possibly as a response to the recent deaths of her daughter, her parents, and her brother, Philip. Wyatt's and Surrey's Petrarchan imitations had been printed in 1557 in *Songes and Sonettes* by Richard Tottel (and reprinted at least seven times). These more familiar achievements of the high Elizabethan age make it hard for modern readers to do justice to Morley, whose verse has more of C. S. Lewis's 'drab' than his 'golden'. But the lack of appreciation has also to do with the date of publication and with modern perceptions of Morley's *Tryumphes* in literary history. If, as I have argued, his translation is no later than the early 1520s, then Morley deserves to be seen not as the follower of fashion but as its maker, and the modern reader, like Morley's patron Henry VIII, should be 'more pleased therewith than he was before'.

ABBREVIATIONS

Allegory and Spectacle	*Petrarch's Triumphs: Allegory and Spectacle*, ed. by Konrad Eisenbichler & Amilcare A. Iannucci (Ottawa, 1990)
Les Manuscrits à Peintures	F. Avril, N. Reynaud, *Les Manuscrits à Peintures en France 1440-1520* (Paris, 1993)
Carley, 'Presentation Manuscripts'	J. P. Carley, 'Presentation Manuscripts from the Collection of Henry VIII: the case of Henry Parker, Lord Morley', in *Order and Connexion*, ed. by R. C. Alston (Cambridge, 1997), pp. 159-99
Carley, 'Writings'	'The Writings of Henry Parker, Lord Morley: a Bibliographical Survey' (above, pp. 27-68)
f. fr.	fonds français

Orth, 'Triumphs' — M. D. Orth, 'The Triumphs of Petrarch Illuminated by Godefroy Le Batave', *Gazette des Beaux-Arts*, VIe periode 104 (Dec. 1984), pp. 197-206

Orth, 'Godefroy Le Batave' — M. D. Orth, 'Godefroy Le Batave Illuminator to the French Royal Family 1516-1526', in *Manuscripts in the Fifty Years after the Invention of Printing*, ed. by J. B. Trapp (London, 1983), pp. 50-61.

Pellegrin, *Manuscrits de Pétrarque* — E. Pellegrin, *Manuscrits de Pétrarque dans les Bibliothèques de France* (Padua, 1966)

Simone, *French Renaissance* — F. Simone, *Il Rinascimento Francese* (Turin, 1961); trans. as *The French Renaissance* by H. Gaston Hall (London, 1969)

Trapp, 'Iconography' — J. B. Trapp, 'The Iconography of Petrarch in the Age of Humanism', *Quaderni Petrarcheschi*, IX-X (1992-3)

Wilkins, *Making* — E. H. Wilkins, *The Making of the 'Canzoniere' and other Petrarchan Studies*, Storia e Letteratura (Rome, 1951)

NOTES

I am grateful to Richard Axton, James Carley, and Jeremy Maule for advice and inspiration at every stage of this essay's development – from conference to book. To J. B. Trapp I owe special thanks for guidance in a field which is new to me.

1 A. M. Hind, *Engraving in England in the Sixteenth and Seventeenth Centuries*, I *The Tudor Period*, 3 vols (Cambridge, 1952-64), pp. 132-7. S. Bos, M. Lange-Meyers, & J. Six, 'Sidney's Funeral Portrayed', in *Sir Philip Sidney: 1586 and the Creation of a Legend*, ed. by J. Van Dorsten, D. Baker-Smith, & A. R. Kinney (Leiden, 1985), pp. 38-61 (p. 47). *Lant's Roll* or: *Sequitur celebritas & pompa funeris quemadmodum Clarencio Armorum et Insignium rege institute est* (STC 15224: London, 1587-8).

2 Bos, Lange-Meyers, & Six, p. 51. See also J. Landwehr, *Splendid Ceremonies: State Entries and Royal Funerals in the Low Countries 1515-1791, a bibliography* (Leiden, 1975). J. F. R. Day gathers together recent pertinent arguments on this subject in his 'Death be very Proud: Sidney and ... Elizabethan Heraldic Funerals', in *Tudor Political Culture*, ed. by D. Hoak (Cambridge, 1995), pp. 179-203.

3 J. Aubrey, *Brief Lives*, ed. by R. Barber (London, 1975), p. 280.

4 The first comprehensive study of illustrations of Petrarch is that of V. Masséna, Prince d'Essling, and E. Müntz, *Pétrarque: Ses études d'art, son influence sur les artistes, ses portraits et ceux de Laure, l'illustration de ses écrits* (Paris, 1902). Essential analysis and reproduction of the printed Italian illustrations are provided by A. M. Hind, *Early Italian Engraving*, 7 vols (London, 1938-48). See also A. Venturi, 'Les Triumphes de Petrarque dans l'art Représentatif', *Revue de l'Art Ancien et Modèrne*, 20 (1906), 81-93, 209-21.

J. B. Trapp's 'Iconography' (pp. 11-73) is an indispensable re-assessment and overview of the illustration of Petrarch's vernacular and Latin works (see esp. pp. 26, 28, 42).

For recent work on the Commentaries see G. C. Alessio, 'The *lectura* of the *Trionfi* in the Fifteenth Century' in *Allegory and Spectacle*, pp. 269-90.

5 For recent studies of the influence of classical and early Italian civic triumphs on the *Trionfi* and Petrarch's influence on subsequent spectacles see: A. A. Iannucci, 'Petrarch's Intertextual Strategies in the *Triumphs*'; R. Monti, 'Petrarch's *Trionfi*, Ovid and Vergil'; and K. Eisenbichler, 'Political Posturing in some "Triumphs of Love" in Quattrocento Florence', in *Allegory and Spectacle*, pp. 3-10; 11-32; 369-82.

6 R. J. Knecht, *Renaissance Warrior and Patron: the Reign of Francis I* (Cambridge, 1994), p. 174.

7 *The Divine Comedy* II, *Purgatorio*, trans. and commentary by J. D. Sinclair (Oxford, 1971), p. 416.

8 In *Les Douze Triomphes de Henry VII* (*c.* 1497: BL, Royal MS 16 E.xvii, ed. and trans. by J. Gairdner, *Memorials of Henry VII*, Rolls Series 10 (London, 1858), pp. 307-27), attributed to Bernard André, Petrarchan influence is minimal, as its Englished title makes clear: 'Here follow twelve exploits performed by Hercules, figured under twelve triumphs achieved by the very illustrious and puissant King Henry Seventh of the name, King of England.' The thinly allegorized labours celebrate victories which secured the Tudor succession.

9 Simone, *French Renaissance*, p. 186. There is an anonymous English translation of part of *De Remediis*: 'A dialogue between Reason and Adversity' in Cambridge, University Library, MS Ii 6.39, fols 177[v]-188[v]. It is written in an early-fifteenth-century hand. See N. Mann, 'Manuscripts of Petrarch's "De Remediis": a checklist', in *Italia Medioevale e Umanistica*, 14 (1971), 57-90.

10 Citations and quotations from STC 19811 are taken from the BL copy, G. 10713: *The Tryumphes of Fraunces Petrarcke, translated out of Italian into English by Henrye Parker knyght, Lorde Morley* (J[ohn] C[awood]: London, n.d.). The earliest dated use of the book's title-page compartment by John Cawood is 18 Dec. 1554: no. 83 in R. B. McKerrow & F. S. Ferguson, *Title-page Borders in England and Scotland 1485-1640* (London, 1932).

In accordance with the conventions of this volume u/v, i/j have been altered to modern usage.

11 Could Morley have meant 'and translate'?

12 James Carley in 'Presentation Manuscripts' (p. 174) suggests that 'Morley viewed the presentation copy as something inviolate, as a master-copy in a certain sense, and that he was unwilling to tamper with subsequent versions, unless he could make the same changes in the original'.

13 Carley, 'Presentation Manuscripts', pp. 159-76 (170); Carley, 'Writings', above, p. 42.

14 See D. R. Carlson, 'The Writings of Bernard André (*c.* 1450-*c.* 1522)', *Renaissance Studies*, 12.2 (1998), 229-50. The Account books of John Heron record gifts from Henry VII to André; the earliest New Year gift recorded is in 1501 (PRO E101/415/3, fol. 41[r]). New Year gifts from André to Henry VIII survive for 1510 (p. 241), 1515 (p. 242), 1520 (p. 244). André wrote New Year's orations for Henry VIII, and poems on the English victories of Flodden and Thérouanne in 1513 (p. 230). This reference was kindly supplied by Jeremy Maule when we first discussed whether the Triumphes and Scipio and Hannibal translations might be as early as 1521.

15 Carley, 'Writings', pp. 41-5.

16 Carley, 'Writings', p. 42.

17 R. Axton, 'Lord Morley's Funeral', below, p. 221.

18 Oxford, Bodleian Library, Ashmole MS 1116 records the English courtiers who accompanied King Henry to the Field of the Cloth of Gold. Morley and his wife are both listed. As a baron Morley was permitted an entourage of 2 chaplains, 2 gentlemen, 28 servants, 12 horses; Lady Morley was allowed 2 women, 3 manservants, 6 horses. See J. G. Russell, *The Field of Cloth of Gold* (London, 1969), pp. 201-2.

19 J. Maule, 'What did Morley give when he gave a "Plutarch" Life?', above, p. 118.

20 H. G. Wright assumes that King Francis's book 'must have been *Les Triumphes Petrarque traduictes de langue Tuscane en Rhime francoyse par le Baron d'Opède* (Paris, 1538)': see *Forty-six Lives*, p. ci n. 1.

Simone (*French Renaissance*, pp. 263-4) has shown that BN, f. fr. 20020 is an early draft of Baron d'Oppède's printed book. Both manuscript and printed book are dedicated to Anne de Montmorency, as Constable of France, a title he received in 1538. Pellegrin (*Manuscrits de Pétrarque*, pp. 468-9) describes this manuscript.

Carnicelli in *Lord Morley's 'Tryumphes'* (p. 33) assumes that this anonymous printed prose translation (attributed in the eighteenth century to George de la Forge), *Les Triumphes Messire Francoys Petrarcque* (Paris, 1536), is a first edition. It is however a reprint of Barthélemy Vérard's publication (Paris, 23 May 1514), *Les Triumphes messire Francoys Petracque* (*sic*).

After mentioning Jean Meynier, Baron d'Oppède (p. 178, n. 27), presumably as a possible groom of the chamber, and his edition of 1538, Carnicelli (p. 33) concludes: 'We know for certain that Morley had seen at least one of these translations and that it had inspired him to translate the *Trionfi* into English.'

However, extant manuscript versions of this prose translation may well be earlier than Vérard's edition. E. Pellegrin (*Manuscrits de Pétrarque*) identifies several early undated and anonymous French manuscripts which transmit the same text as the printed prose translation ('dit La Forge'): BN, f. fr. 1119 (p. 444); BN, Nouvelle Acquisition fr. 10867 (p. 481); St Genevieve 1125 (p. 481). She traces (pp. 418-19) the attribution of this prose translation to 'George de La Forge' to an eighteenth-century entry in Paris, Arsenal MS 3086, an ascription known to Simone (*French Renaissance*, pp. 257, 263). The printed edition of 1514 and these early manuscript versions are all anonymous texts. She doubts, as does Simone (p. 315, n. 53), that these manuscripts derive from the printed text (a suggestion which had been made by E. Golenistcheff-Koutouzoff in 'La Premier Traduction des *Triomphes* de Petrarque en France', in *Mélanges Hauvette* (Paris, 1934), pp. 107-12.

21 Carley, 'Writings', p. 42.

P. Chavy calls Simone Bourgouyn a valet de chambre of Louis XII in *Traducteurs d'Autrefois Moyen âge et Renaissance: Dictionnaire des traducteurs et de la littérature traduite en ancien et moyen français (842-1600)*, 2 vols (Paris & Geneva, 1988), I, 1093, repeating the appellation made by Hélène Harvitt in 1922 'Les Triomphes de P[etrarch] traduit en vers français par Simon Bougouyn, (*sic*) valet de chambre de Louis XII', *Revue de Littérature Comparée* (1922), pp. 85-9. He is followed by E. König & G. Bartz, *Boccaccio und Petrarch in Paris* (Munich, 1997), pp. 279-309, who discuss and offer an early date for the Bourgouyn manuscript now belonging to the firm Heribert Tenschert.

22 'Velutello is not mentioned by Morley, but it is very likely that he knew Velutello's work' (*Lord Morley's 'Tryumphes'*, ed. by Carnicelli, p. 31). Bernardo Illicino was first printed in Bologna in 1475 by [Hannibal Malpiglius] for Sigismundus de Libris (Goff P-380).

23 M. K. Jones & M. G. Underwood, *The King's Mother* (Cambridge, 1992), p. 165, cite Cambridge, St John's College, MS D91.19, pp. 80, 92 for their statement: 'She had paid for his schooling at Oxford.'

24 Carley, 'Writings', p. 30.

25 The original accounts of the French preparations are in BN, f. fr. 10383.

26 P. Mellen, *Jean Clouet* (London, 1971), plate xxxx.

27 The inventory of books at Blois made in 1518 lists eighteen books carried in the king's mobile library: E. Quentin-Bouchart, *La bibliothèque de Fontainebleau, 1515-1589* (Paris, 1891), pp. 8-9. See also Carley, 'Writings', p. 41.

28 T. Kimball Brooker, 'Bindings Commissioned for Francis I's "Italian Library" ... dating from the late 1530s-1540', *Bulletin du Bibliophile*, 1 (1997), 33-91 (43-5).

29 Trapp,'Iconography', p. 40. See pp. 40-1, n. 131 and p. 48, n. 157 for concise analysis of the French manuscript families: the earliest prose, and two earliest verse translations, and for discussion of the continuity of their French illustrations which, regardless of text, were indebted for their content to Bernardo Illicino's commentary. Professor Trapp has shared some of his recent work in a private communication and points out that in Bourgouyn's early

manuscript (BN, f. fr. 12423) the illustrations 'are based upon the woodcuts of Capcasa's Venetian printing of 1492-3' (Matteo Capcasa (Venice, 1492/93: Goff P-388)).

For a detailed account of the layout and contents of these manuscripts see Pellegrin, *Manuscrits de Pétrarque*. The three Bourgouyn manuscripts still in Paris are dealt with on pp. 424-8, 453-6, 458-61.

30 *The Travel Journal of Antonio de Beatis*, trans. by J. R. Hale & J. M. Lindon, ed. by J. R. Hale, *Hakluyt Society*, series 2, no. 150 (London, 1979), pp. 133, 191.

31 Simone, *French Renaissance*, pp. 188, 194; B. Moreau, *Inventaire chronologique des éditions parisiennes du xvie siècle*, 4 vols (Abbeville, 1972-92, III, no. 726 (p. 228).

32 F. Avril, & N. Reynaud, *Les Manuscrits à Peintures en France 1440-1520 Bibliothèque Nationale* (Paris, 1993), p. 414. A.-M. Lecoq also discusses the explicitness of this visual identification in *François I Imaginaire* (Paris, 1987), pp. 25-38.

33 STC 20058.5, *Tho. Wyatis Translatyon of Plutarckes Boke, of the Quyete of Mynde* (R. Pynson: n.d. [?1528]), sig. a2[r].

34 For Bourgouyn's place among these royal servants see Carley, 'Writings', p. 41.

35 In helpful comments on an earlier version of this essay Professor Trapp, while cautioning the unwary in this minefield, suggested that the illustrations to Bourgouyn's text place two of the four manuscripts *c.* 1512-14, the end of the reign of Louis XII and the beginning of Francis I: BN, f. fr. 12423, and the Tenschert MS; only Paris, Bibliothèque de l'Arsenal, MS 6480 is later. For further work on Arsenal MS 6480 see: Myra D. Orth, 'Triumphs', p. 205, who dates it *c.* 1524, and Simone, *French Renaissance*, p. 218, who dates it 'around 1530'.

36 Knecht, *Renaissance Warrior* (n. 6 above), p. 48; Lecoq, *François I*, pp. 173-4, also cites *La Mer des Hystoires,* Bk IV (Paris, 1518).

37 *Valet* (originally equivalent to *seigneur*) was the term used by Charles VIII and Louis XII for their intimate companions, but it was not acceptable to the noblemen who served Francis. Under the new style *gentilshommes de la chambre* the king's titled friends retained the same intimate duties; they might also be chosen as special envoys to other monarchs. Such was Guillaume du Bellay, seigneur of Langey, diplomat, soldier, administrator. See Knecht, *Renaissance Warrior*, pp. 121-2. See Glenn Richardson, 'The Privy Chamber of Henry VIII and Anglo-French Relations, 1515-1520', in *The Court Historian* 4.2 (August, 1999), pp. 119-40 (pp. 123, 127).

38 Both artists appear in the Royal Accounts of Francis I 1516-49 (BN, f. fr. 21449 and 21450). Francis retained the artists of Louis XII. In 1516 both painters earn 180 livres. The next year Bourdichon receives 240 livres, a fee he retains until he disappears from the accounts in 1522 (presumably the year of his death). Sometime between 1517 and 1519 Perréal, Nicolas Belin, and Barthélemy Guety 'were advanced from *varlets de garderobe to varlets de garderobe extraordinaires*'. By 1519 Clouet had moved up the list from 14th to 6th and was called 'Jamet Clouet peintre'. By 1526 all the artists appeared under the title of *Peintre et Gens de Mestier*. Mellen, Jean Clouet, pp. 12-13.

39 Simone, *French Renaissance* (pp. 218-19), gives credit for discerning this independent tradition to L. E. Kastner, 'A propos une prétendue traduction française des *Triomphes* de Pétrarque', *Zeitschrift für Romanische Philologie*, 30 (1906), 574-7.

40 Simone, *French Renaissance*, p. 245.

41 Jean Robertet was son of Pierre Robertet, secretary to the Duke of Bourbon, although his date of birth is not known. He served both Louis XI and Charles VIII and from 1492 was *valet de chambre* to the latter. By the time Charles VIII made his Italian campaign in 1494 Robertet had retired from court; he died *c.* 1503-4. M. Zsuppán, *Jean Robertet: Oeuvres* (Geneva, 1970), pp. 9-10: see pp. 74-5 for her assessment of his debt to Petrarch.

42 The scribe is identified as François Robertet; Jean Robertet's verses are dated *c.* 1476, and the manuscript BN, f. fr. 24461 in which they are recorded is described and dated 'vers 1500-

1505' by Avril and Reynaud, *Les Manuscrits à Peintures*, pp. 354-5. See also Simone, *French Renaissance*, p. 222.

43 *Memorials of Henry VII*, trans. by James Gairdner (n. 8 above), pp. 307-27.

44 John Skelton, *The Boke of Colin Clout*, in *Pithy, Pleasant and Profitable Works* (London, 1568), sig. Q6.

45 E. H. Wilkins explains that in Italy: 'Throughout the Manuscript period the *Triumphs* were markedly more popular than the *Canzoniere*: of 213 fourteenth- and fifteenth-century manuscripts listed by Narducci as containing one or both of the two works, some 85 contain the Triumphs alone, some 79 contain both the Triumphs and *Canzoniere*, and only some 49 contain the *Canzoniere* alone.' See his 'The *Quattrocento* Editions of the *Canzoniere* and the Triumphs', in *Making*, pp. 379-403 (p. 379).

46 Castlevetro in 1582 seems to be the first critic to argue for a through-composed unity of the two works. *Lord Morley's 'Tryumphes'*, ed. by Carnicelli, p. 35.

47 See S. Samek-Ludovici, *Petrarca, I Trionfi illustrati nella miniatura da codici precedecti del seculo XIII al seculo XIV Studio con note esplicativi del poema* (Rome, 1978), Plate 79, from S. Daniele del Friuli, Biblioteca Guarneriana, MS 139, fol. 107^{v}.

Other versions of this illustration cited by J. B. Trapp in 'Iconography' (pp. 37-8) are London, Victoria and Albert Museum, MS L101-1647, fol. 106^{r} and Madrid, Biblioteca Nacional, MS 611, fol. 97^{r}, where Laura's funerary altar stands in the foreground and below its inscription the death of Laura is delicately figured in gold as the Fall of Phaethon from the chariot of Apollo'.

48 This poem of six visions of the death of Laura had an independent fame in the sixteenth century as 'The Visions of Petrarch'.

49 S. Sturm-Maddox, '*Arbor vittoriosa triunfale*: allegory and spectacle in the *Rime* and *Trionfi*', in *Allegory and Spectacle*, pp. 98-113, traces relationships between the *Trionfi* and the less obviously triumphal design of the *Rime*. She argues for the consistency of allegorical personification in the *Rime* and notes that the last additions (*c*. 1373-4) to both works were poems glorifying Laura in triumphal imagery.

50 J. B. Trapp, 'Iconography', pp. 53-4, discusses Florentine manuscripts whose wheeling cars first inspired an anonymous Florentine copper-engraver, and subsequently the engravers employed by the Venetian publishers of the *Trionfi*: Petrus di Plasiis, Venice, 1490; Goff P-386, and Giovanni Capcasa, Venice, 1492/3; Goff-P388.

The Florentine engraving 'six subjects on one plate' is reproduced in A. M. Hind, *Early Italian Engraving*, 7 vols (London, 1938-1948), I, pt. 1, pl. 24. Later examples are de Plasiis, sig. $e2^{v}$, $f5^{v}$ and Capcasa, sig. $e1^{v}$, $f4^{v}$.

51 Madrid, Bibliotheca Nacional, MS Vit. 22-3, fol. 16^{r}; Trapp, 'Iconography', pl. XXXIII.

52 *Les six triomphes de Pétrarcque*, BN, f. fr. 24461, fol. 4^{r}. See *Lord Morley's 'Tryumphes'*, ed. by Carnicelli, pl. 15; Trapp, 'Iconography', p. 43.

53 This version is found in BN, f. fr. 594, fol. 134^{v} in the Tenschert MS and Arsenal MS 6480 (illustrating Bourgouyn's text), in Vérard's printed *Les Triumphes messire Francoys Petracque of 1514* and subsequent editions based on this prose text.

54 See Wilkins, '*Quattrocento* Editions', in *Making*, pp. 379-401 (p. 379): 'The printing of the *Triumphs* and the *Canzoniere* began in 1470. Within the period 1470-1500 there were printed at least twenty-five editions containing both works and nine separate editions of the Triumphs.'

55 BN, f. fr. 594, a manuscript made for Louis XII, retains on fol. 3^{r} its allusive worthies marching beside Love's car; by fols 7^{v}-8^{r} gold letters on garments name illustrious lovers in the troop.

56 M. Orth shows that the miniatures of Paris, Arsenal MS 6480, which she dates *c*. 1524, are stylistically indebted to the Italian illustrations of BN, fonds italian 548, the Sinbaldi *Trionfi*

(at that time in the library at Blois), yet in some visual details of content are closer to earlier French 'Italianate' illustrations than to Petrarch's text. Orth, 'Triumphs', pp. 197-206; Orth, 'Godefroy Le Batave', pp. 50-61 (p. 56).

57 'The original' for the purposes of his edition is *Francesco Petrarca: Trionfi*, ed. by C. Calcaterra (Turin, 1927); Carnicelli's authority for translation, when not his own, is *The Triumphs of Petrarch*, trans. by E. H. Wilkins (Chicago, 1963), pp. 73-4, 165, 173. Wilkins's translation is based on the text of *Le Rime Sparse e i Trionfi*, ed. by E. Chiòrboli (Bari, 1930).

58 *Lord Morley's 'Tryumphes'*, ed. by Carnicelli (p. 212), gives the line as: 'in un bel drappelletto ivan ristrette': went together in a small group. Velutello, whose illustration is a skeleton driving a two-wheeled open cart, gives this reading and glosses the line: 'cio è in un bel raccolto & insieme unito numero'; see *Le Volgari Opere del Petrarcha con la Espositione di Allessandro Vellutello da Lucca* (Venice, 1525), sig. d6r. Wilkins's 'troop' and 'glory' are lightly, but not visually, military: 'Together made a troop that was but small – / The glory that is true is ever rare', *The Triumphs of Petrarch*, trans. by E. H. Wilkins (Chicago, 1962), p. 53.

59 When Mary Sidney translated the two *capitoli* she invented a diminutive 'squadronet': London, Inner Temple, MS Petyt 538, vol. 43, fol. 286r.

Bourgouyn adapts the Italian noun: 'ung beau drappelet serres', Paris, Arsenal MS 6480, BN, f. fr. 12423. I thank James Carley for verifying these readings. Simone commends Bourgouyn who 'learned how to apply himself to the exploration of all the diminutives the language provides in seeking to render the grace of certain Italian lines,' *French Renaissance*, pp. 253, 316, n. 62.

The printed French prose translations follow Vérard's 1514 text; the walking ladies are covered with a cloth of gold, a visual detail which deflects attention from Petrarch's small ermine *insegna*. The ladies are: 'joinctes et ensemble couvertes et encourtinees soubz ung beau et riche drap d'or' (sig. g4r).

Baron d'Oppède writes:

En tel estat ceste divine dame
Plein de los, de vertu & de fame,
Qui ne fut oncq par nul effort pollue
Avecques soy sa compaignie eslue,
S'en retournoient victorieusement
De la bataille & pacificqeuement,
Bien peu estoient en cestuy nombre, car
De CHASTETE la gloire on trouve à tard,
Et peu de gens a present la possessent (sig. G8r)

60 In the London musters described by Henry Machyn: 'The distinction of the Banner, Standard, and Guydon may be observed. Only one great Banner appeared, that of the king ... At funerals banners and bannerolls seem to have been allowed to all peers and their ladies; standards but not banners, to all knights and their ladies; penons, but not standards to esquires. Mere gentleman had no penons, but only scocheons of arms'. 'Note upon Funerals', in *The Diary of Henry Machyn*, ed. by J. G. Nichols (London, 1848), p. xxvii.

61 The modern translation by Wilkins is the best:

Not pale, but whiter than the whitest snow
Quietly falling on a gentle hill,
She seemed to be aweary and at rest.
And that which is called 'death' by foolish folk
Was a sweet sleep upon her lovely eyes,
Now that her body held her soul no more;
And even death seemed fair in her fair face. (p. 60)

For William Fowler see *The Works of William Fowler*, ed. by H. W. Meikle, Scottish Text Society, 2 vols (Edinburgh, 1914); for the Countess of Pembroke see *The Triumph of Death by Francis Petrarch*, in *Collected Works of Mary Sidney Herbert, Countess of Pembroke*, ed. by M. P. Hannay, H. J. Kinnemon, & M. G. Brennan, 2 vols (Oxford, 1998), I, 273-87 (pp. 277, 282).

It is perhaps just possible that Vérard honours this woman to woman epiphany with a small woodcut (sig. g5^{v}): a crudely cut figure in long gown, holding two darts sits facing a woman in a bed.

62 Vérard, *Les Triumphes messire Francoys Petracque* (Paris, 1514).

63 A. M. Hind, *Early Italian Engraving*, III, B. II, pl. 196. As Professor Trapp has noted, this illustration of Eternity/Divinity was influential; it is followed in the Venetian editions of Petrus de Plasiis of 22 April 1490, sig. Q7^{v}; and of Giovanni Capcasa 12 January 1492/3, sig. Q6^{v}. See above n. 29, n. 50. An undated Florentine miniature may possibly precede these engravings; it is reproduced in Samek-Ludovici, *Petrarca*, II, pl. 20 from Florence, Biblioteca Nazionale Centrale, MS Pal. 192, fol. 47^{r}.

64 'In quarto [no.] 1778: Francis Petrarkes triumphes englished by Henrie Parker lorde Morley, anglice', *The Lumley Library: the Catalogue of 1609*, ed. by S. Jayne & F. R. Johnson (London, 1956), p. 209. The cataloguer arranges his books by format: folio, quarto, octavo, and is careful to note 'manuscript' beside entries which are not printed books. For links between Morley and the Earl of Arundel see K. R. Bartlett, 'The Occasion of Lord Morley's Translation of the *Trionfi*: the Triumph of Chastity over Politics', in *Allegory and Spectacle*, pp. 325-34.

65 The British Library and Bodleian Libraries have composite copies. STC 19811 in Sion College's composite volume (given to the College by the widow of a seventeenth-century London printer) eluded Pollard & Redgrave's first *Short-Title Catalogue*. It was bound after *The Phisicke* and entered in the College's eighteenth-century catalogue not under Petrarch but as 'Henry Parker's Triumphs'. Sion Library sold their STC 19811 at Sothebys: Lot 50 on 13 June 1977 (*Catalogue ... of Books and Manuscripts the Property of Sion College*, p. 54). They retained their less valuable *Physicke* (ARC K. 12.5.P.44P), now at Lambeth Palace Library. The Huntington Library copy was also bound with *Physicke*; see Carley, 'Writings', pp. 58-9, n. 50.

66 The title-page compartment of Cawood's edition of STC 19811 (McKerrow & Ferguson 83) is still in an early state. See above, n. 10. Subsequent wear and tear can be seen in its later use by Cawood and Jugge in *The Bible in English* (1569) and other serious religious works.

67 Ruth Luborsky has kindly shared with me before publication material from her book written in collaboration with E. M. Ingram, *A Guide to English Illustrated Books 1536-1603* (Tempe, Arizona, 1999). She identified the signature of Arnold Nicolai of Antwerp from my description of the engraver's mark: a swash italic *A*, common to the large historiated initials of Lord Morley's *Tryumphes*. For his continental work see A. J. Delen, *Histoire de la Gravure dans les Anciens Pays Bas ... provinces Belges, des origins jusqu'à la fin du dixhuitième siècle* (Brussels, 1920), pp. 85-123.

Arnold Nicholai worked in England early in his career before returning to join Plantin *c.* 1555. He did bespoke work for Richard Jugge and later for John Cawood. His '*A*' is found on Richard Jugge's Pelican device (McKerrow, no. 125, p. 45) which appears for the first time on his profusely illustrated 1552 edition of Tyndale's *New Testament* (STC 2867). Nicholai's mark appears, too, on its fine frontispiece portrait of Edward VI (sig. *1^{r}). Jugge's printing was known in the trade for fine initials. He may have met Nicholai through the Antwerp printer S. Mierdman, who printed a 16mo Tyndale *New Testament* for Jugge in 1548 (STC 2852). Nicholai provides more evidence for an early association between Jugge and Cawood, whose device he cut (McKerrow 129); it appears on the 1555 Statutes of 2, 3 Philip and Mary.

68 After Cawood died in 1572 Jugge may have retained the remaining *Tryumphes*. Certain it is that Jugge names his son-in-law Richard Watkyns, the printer of Petrarch's *Phisicke against Fortune*, as one of his beneficiaries when he died in 1577. See H. R. Plommer, *Abstracts from the Wills of English Printers and Stationers from 1492 to 1630* (London, 1903), p. 24.

By 1579 Watkyns places Jugge's device and monogram in works printed in his own name. He sets McKerrow & Ferguson 123 in *Of Ghosts and Spirits Walking by Night*. McKerrow & Ferguson 181, used by Jugge in William Patten's *Calendar of Scripture* 1575, is chosen by Watkyns for the colophon of his *Phisicke against Fortune*.

LORD MORLEY'S 'RYDING RYME' AND THE ORIGINS OF MODERN ENGLISH VERSIFICATION

SUSANNE WOODS

HENRY PARKER, Lord Morley's translation of Petrarch's *Trionfi* both followed and helped to create the Henrican fashion for continental letters,[1] offering at the same time a topic that appealed both to the medieval taste for discourse on the world's vanity and to a new fondness for heightened pageantry.[2] The work's versification, however, looks backward rather than forward. Though he claims to offer a close translation, Morley acknowledges his inability to manage the graceful terza rima of the original: 'I professe, I have not erred moche from the letter, but in the ryme, which is not possible for me to folow in the translation, nor touche the least poynt of elegancy that this elegant Poete hath set forth in his owne maternall tongue.'[3] His choice in place of terza rima is the Chaucerian couplet which George Gascoigne a generation later labeled 'ryding ryme'.[4]

Just slightly later than the period when Morley was translating the *Trionfi* into his version of Chaucerian couplets, Henry Howard, Earl of Surrey, was translating two books of Virgil's *Aeneid* into the first decasyllabic blank verse in English that has a right to be called 'iambic pentameter'.[5] The differences between the two kinds of verse are immediately apparent when one juxtaposes the first several lines of their openings. First Morley:

In the tyme of the Renewinge of my suspyres
By the swete remembraunce of my lovely desyres
That was the begynnynge of soo longe a payne
The fayre Phebus the Bull dyd attayne
And warmyd had the tone and tother horne
Wherby the colde wynter stormes were worne
And Tytans chylde with her frostye face
Ran from the heate to her auunciente place
Love, grefe, and complaynt, oute of reason
Had brought me in such a case that season
That myne eyes closed, and I fell to reste
The very Remedye to such as be oppreste. (sig. A4^r)

The syllabification ranges from twelve (in lines 1, 2, 12) to nine (in lines 4, 6, 7, 8, 9, and 11, though some of these may be read as decasyllabic by pronouncing a final 'e'). Accentuation can be equally variable, with, for example, six in line 12, five in line 5, and four in lines 1-2 (in what we would describe as an anapestic movement).

By contrast, Surrey's translation of the *Aeneid* Book II maintains a decasyllabic norm that most readily falls into iambic pentameter movement:

They whisted all, with fixed face intent,
When prince Aeneas from the royal seat
Thus gan to speak: 'O Quene! it is thy wil

> I should renew a woe cannot be told,
> How that the Grekes did spoile and overthrow
> The Phrygian wealth and wailful realm of Troy:
> Those ruthfull things that I my self beheld,
> And whereof no small part fel to my share.
> Which to expresse, who could refrain from teres:
> What Myrmidon? or yet what Dolopes?
> What stern Ulysses waged soldiar?
> And loe! moist night now from the welkin falles;
> And sterres declining counsel us to rest.' (ll. 1-13)

It was by no means clear in the 1530s and 1540s that Surrey had developed the line of English verse that would serve as the base for serious English poetry for more than four hundred years. In retrospect, his decasyllabic line with its usual pause after the fourth syllable, promoting an iambic pattern, and his blank verse made possible Marlowe, Shakespeare, Milton, and even Robert Browning. It would also be Surrey's sonnet form, with its three quatrains and couplet, that would solve the problem of English having fewer riming words than romance languages (probably one of Morley's problems with *terza rima*) and create multiple structural possibilities: the traditional 8/6 rhetorical organization, or 12/2, or 4/4/4/2. Shakespeare's genius gave the form its name, 'Shakespearean sonnet', but Surrey invented it.

Surrey's were among many experiments a Henrican courtier might admire and might or might not follow. For a courtier seeking to translate great classical or continental achievements into English, John Lydgate, the 'Monk of Bury' (*c.* 1370-*c.* 1450) remained the primary English model.[6] Lydgate's principal verse form (ababbcc) was what Gascoigne designated 'Rythme royall [which] is fittest for grave discourse',[7] and Lydgate believed himself to be following Chaucer's line rhythms. Sixteenth-century poets saw in Chaucer's (more-or-less) decasyllabic line not the smooth forerunner of a clear iambic pentameter, but an often rough line that, in the couplets of the *Canterbury Tales*, charged forward to its rime. Gascoigne describes this couplet verse almost as an afterthought: 'I had forgotten a notable kinde of ryme, called ryding rime, and that is suche as our Mayster and Father *Chaucer* used in his Canterburie Tales, and in divers other delectable and light enterprises ... this ryding rime serveth most aptly to wryte a merie tale.'[8] To our ear Lydgate's lines are rougher and less elegant than Chaucer's, but to Gascoigne, and probably to Morley and his contemporaries, Lydgate's prosaic complexity was considered more artful and serious than Chaucer's greater accessibility.

Lydgate's *Troy Book* and *Fall of Princes* were popular well into the century, but his versification, with its inconsistent number of syllables and accents, was a difficult model. The poets of the the generation before Morley, Stephen Hawes (fl. 1506-17) and John Skelton (*c.* 1460-1529), and his near contemporary, Alexander Barclay (*c.* 1475-1552), acknowledged Lydgate as their master and apparently did seek to imitate his versification as well as his topics.[9]

Morley probably knew Lydgate's two principal works in Chaucerian couplets, the *Troy Book* and the *Siege of Thebes*. Morley's patron, Lady Margaret Beaufort, left to Henry VIII in her will Lydgate's *Siege of Troy*.[10] The *Troy Book* is Lydgate's most extended effort in this meter, and can be read as decasyllabic only by a more liberal reading of extra-syllabic final e's than Chaucer allowed:

And thus Priam for every maister sent:
For eche kerver and passyng joignour
To make knottis with many corious flour,
To sette on crestis withinne and withoute
Upon the wal the cite round aboute;
Or who that wer excellyng in practik
Of any arte callyd mekanik
Or had a name flouryng or famus
Was after sent to come to Priamus.[11]

Lydgate's sixteenth-century reputation, however, rested largely on the aureate permutations of his rime royal stanzas. Morley had in his possession portions of the *Fall of Princes*, a work so popular it was to provoke one of the most reprinted and imitated sixteenth-century publications, the collaborative *Mirror for Magistrates*.[12] Typical of Lydgate's *Fall* is this stanza on Fortune as a rose with thorns:

Bi exaumple, as there is no rose
Spryngyng in gardeyns, but ther be sum thorn,
Nor fairer blosme than Nature list dispose,
Than may ther beute, as men ha[ve] seyn toforn,
With bittir wyndes be fro ther braunchis born,
Nor noon so hih in his estat contune
Fre fro thawaityng & daunger of Fortune.[13]

In the sixteenth century Lydgate was primarily associated with aureate diction and rime royal, Chaucer with stories and couplets.

By choosing couplets rather than stanzas for his own serious verse, Morley may have been nodding to Chaucer, and looking to find a way beyond the scarcely accessible complexity of Lydgate. He may even have seen in the model of the *Canterbury Tales* the seriousness that Gascoigne missed. The couplets of Morley's *Tryumphes*, however, remain fifteenth-century in their internal rhythms, while Surrey was producing the first recognizably modern English versification, and even the more problematic Sir Thomas Wyatt was moving toward firmer syllabification and greater consistency of accent.

Morley's innovation, then, is to revive the Lydgate line in couplets – 'ryding rime' for serious purposes – with his internal rhythms remaining more like Lydgate's than Chaucer's. Because Morley was an aristocratic poet circulating his verse in the 1530s and 1540, when English versification was undergoing an important transition, his conservative production provides an important benchmark against which the contemporary practices of Wyatt and Surrey can be better understood. Further, for Morley to have been using the Lydgate line at so late a juncture for what was considered heroic verse may say something about his traditionalist approach to Englishing the classical and continental models of humanism which he worked so hard to import and distribute. I want first to situate the larger picture of English versification in Morley's time, and then say more about where his practice fits in.

English versification is a hybrid of Germanic, romance, and classical models. Its success depends nonetheless on its ability to represent the English speaking voice in pleasing ways both predictable and unpredictable: predictable, since all meter is an abstraction and regularization of patterns inherent in a particular language, and unpredictable, since verse artistry depends on variation as well as regularity, variation that gains its force from the expectation of regularity. Versification is the art of creating expectations which are fulfilled or surprised.

Scholars of the history of English versification have long agreed that the first four decades of the sixteenth century are the most difficult and crucial for the development of poetic form in Modern English, particularly the English iambic pentameter line. Wyatt has typically been the focus of attention on this issue, with his early imitations of Petrarch in lines that range from eight to twelve syllables but seem to be moving mostly in iambic patterns. Is he trying to write what we think of as iambic pentameter, or something else? If versification begins with creating expectations, just what expectations was Wyatt trying to create? I have argued elsewhere that Wyatt and Surrey were part of an effort to find and define an English heroic line, a subset of the general effort to signal the right of English to join Italian and French in creating a linguistic culture as grand as the classical models revived by renaissance humanism.[14] Only in retrospect was Surrey's blank verse the answer, with Morley's Lydgatian line and Wyatt's hybrid equally serious alternatives.[15]

The problem confronted by the poets of the early sixteenth century, articulated in modern terms, is this: by what should a line of English verse be measured? Old English verse had been measured by the number of heavily stressed accents (four) divided into two half-lines (hemistiches) by a clear prosodic pause, connected by some alliterative device.[16] This verse did not use end-rime, although elegant patterns of assonance and consonace support the basic metrical pattern.

Romance verse, including medieval Latin verse, measured lines by the number of syllables, often with conventions of elision, syncope, and acope adding to the complexity of the measure. End-rime signalled line endings and added resonance, with complex riming structures one of the characteristics of European lyric verse of the middle ages. Probably through the model of the French-speaking court, English lyrics began to take on these characteristics by the twelfth century, though with some lingering uncertainty as to what could be legitimately considered a convention of elision.[17] Musical accompaniment and short lines made it relatively easy to generate ballads and songs with regular accentuation and a more-or-less regular count of syllables in medieval English lyrics.

Difficulty came with the effort to produce an English heroic line, a longer line in imitation of the classical French Alexandrine or, more directly, the Latin hexameter. Petrarch's adept handling of the Italian hendecasyllabic line made it a model for others, including Chaucer, as early as the fourteenth century, and it transferred successfully to Scottish verse by the end of the fifteenth century.[18] But Lydgate and his followers, such as Thomas Hoccleve and, later, Hawes and Barclay, appeared to find the relative regularity of the English decasyllabic line not artful enough, and they also seemed uncertain as to how best to distribute the traditional English accentuation, and where to place a mid-line pause. The result is a more-or-less decasyllabic verse that moves into the sixteenth century crediting the 'monk of Bury', as here in the modesty *topos* that begins Hawes's *Pastime of Pleasure* (1509):

> Your noble grace / and excellent hyenes
> For to accept / I beseche ryght humbly
> This lytell boke / opprest with rudenes
> Without rethorycke / or colour crafty

Nothynge I am / experte in poetry
As the monke of Bury / floure of eloquence
Which was in tyme / of grete excellence.[19]

Because English is a stress-accent language, the pattern of accents will always be important in English versification. In the Lydgate line, the tendency is to revert to the four-beat romp among 8-12 syllables that underlies Gascoigne's label 'ryding rime'. Spenser would use a version of 'ryding rime' in some of the eclogues of the *Shepheardes Calendar* as late as 1579 (e.g., in the 'February' eclogue), but it is already a deliberate archaism. It is curious that Morley is attempting the Lydgate line as an English heroic line as late as the 1520s or 1530s. The two questions that remain are why he used it at all in the face of the experimentation by Wyatt and Surrey that was leading away from it, and whether he used it effectively.

For the first, one can only surmise. Morley's conservatism may have been part of his nationalism, or what Kenneth Bartlett notes as his 'English particularism'.[20] He is bringing Petrarch to England, but he is also Englishing Petrarch. For the second, I find Morley's use of this old and soon discredited line to be readable and sometimes quite effective, and his handling of the couplet remarkably sophisticated.

Consider, for example, ten lines from 'The Tryumphe of Love, III', which contain a typically Petrarchan description of the lover's distress:

He that is a lover ful well knowes this
How that the hart from the bodye departed is
How nowe he is in warre, and forthwith in peace
Howe when his love doth shewe ungentlenes
5 He wyll not be aknowen, but his malady hyde
Thoughe that it prycke hym both backe and syde
This evell feele I, and yet more thereto
When with my love I have to do
The bloude for feare renneth to my harte
10 And streyght abroade in my vaynes doth starte.[21] (sig. D4^{r})

Although these lines purport to translate Petrarch's hendecasyllabic tercets, syllabification is not the controlling measure of the line. Of these ten lines, line 8 has eight syllables, lines 6, 9, and 10 have nine syllables, lines 1, 4, and 7 have ten syllables, line 3 has eleven syllables, and lines 2 and 5 have twelve syllables (10-12-11-10-12-9-10-8-9-9). What keeps the measure is a very traditional sense of four strong stresses in each line:

/ / / /
He that is a lover ful well knowes this
/ / / /
How that the hart from the bodye departed is
/ / / /
How nowe he is in warre, and forthwith in peace
/ / / /
Howe when his love doth shewe ungentlenes
/ / / /
5 He wyll not be aknowen, but his malady hyde,
/ / / /
Thoughe that it prycke hym both backe and syde
/ / / /
This evell feele I, and yet more thereto

When with my love I have to do
The bloude for feare renneth to my harte
10 And streyght abroade in my vaynes doth starte.

Lines 2 and 4 could easily be read as five-stress lines as well, but the metre – the rhythmic expectation abstracted from the stress-accent feature of the language – consists of couplets in which each line carries four strongly accented syllables. Any given performance of the line might smooth out the strength of the accented syllables, or dispute which four in a given line are meant to carry the heavy stress, but the basic pattern is clear enough. Syllabification is highly variable, but does not easily extend beyond twelve syllables or below eight, since stress-accent is always measured in relation to relatively unaccented syllables, and too many syllables might tend to produce additional stressed syllables (as in lines 2 and 4 above), while too few would confuse the reading by making the context of unstressed syllables too sparse to guide the movement of the line.

Though in a narrative and contemplative mode rather than the lyric intensity of a sonnet conceit, the topic of these lines is similar to Petrarch's *Rime* CXL, where the lady's appearance rushes the lover's blood to his face, and her displeasure sends it back to his heart. Since both Wyatt and Surrey wrote versions of *Rime* CXL, we can see something of how their experimentation contrasts with Morley's 'ryding rime'.

Wyatt's version of Petrarch's sonnet keeps a careful decasyllabic count, but experiments both with placement of the cesura and with the number of accented syllables, although the norm is five (e.g., ll. 1-3 have five clear accents, ll. 4-5 have four, and l. 6 can be counted as four or five, depending on whether the generative '-is' in 'lustis' is pronounced as a full syllable):

The longe love that in my thought doth harbar
and in myn hert doeth kepe his residence
into my face preseth with bold pretence
and therin campeth spreding his baner
5 She that me lerneth to love & suffre
and will that my trust and lust[is] negligence
be rayned by reason shame and reverence
with his hardines taketh displeasur
Wherewithall unto the hertes forrest he fleith
10 leving his entreprise with payn & cry
and ther him hideth & not appereth
What may I do when my maister fereth
but in the feld with him to lyve and dye
for good is the liff ending faithfully

This seems less a struggle toward iambic pentameter as we know it than an effort to keep a decasyllabic norm in imitation of Petrarch's hendecasyllabic model. The result is more lines in which five relatively-stressed and therefore accented syllables seem inevitable. The relation of relatively stressed to relatively unstressed syllables in each line is more regular than in Morley, though not altogether predictable and sometimes completely elusive. One reason may be Wyatt's tendency to place his cesura in the middle, after the fifth syllable, as in ll. 5-8 and 11. This may be an effort to imitate the old mid-line cesura of the earliest English verse, or it may be an experimental effort to test the felicity of varying mid-line pauses. In any case, it militates against iambic movement by breaking up the pattern of syllabic pairing on which iambic movement depends.

Surrey, like Wyatt, keeps a consistent decasyllabic line in his version of Petrarch's sonnet CXL. Unlike Wyatt, he controls accentuation by placing the cesura regularly after the fourth syllable, occasionally after the sixth, thereby keeping the syllabic pairs that tend to promote an iambic reading (I have indicated the cesuras):

Love that doth raine and live within my thought,
And buylt his seat within my captyve brest,
Clad in the armes wherein with me he fowght,
Oft in my face he doth his banner rest.
5 But she that tawght me love and suffre paine,
My doubtful hope & eke my hote desire
With shamfast looke to shadoo and refrayne,
Her smyling grace convertyth streight to yre.
And cowarde Love, then, to the hart apace
10 Taketh his flight, where he doth lurke and playne
His purpose lost, and dare not shew his face.
For my lordes gilt thus fawtles byde I payine;
Yet from my lorde shall not my foote remove:
Sweet is the death that taketh end by love.

This is the experimental direction that would be successful for the future of English poetry, although both Wyatt and Surrey, and many mid-century poets, also pursued the artificial long line of poulters measure and fourteeners – couplets of twelve and fourteen, or fourteen and fourteen lines. 'Poulters measure' and 'fourteeners', as they were called, extended the old three- and four-accent ballad measures (3-3-4-3), and for a time they eclipsed the promise of Surrey's iambic pentameter in the English search for a native heroic line.[22] Morley seems to have avoided that distracting fad.

Of these three passages on the lover's dilemma, Morley's translation of Petrarch's verse is the most traditionally English. It harkens back to the Old English four-beat line and it varies syllabification in ways associated with Lydgate. If it sometimes suggests elevating a fifth accent, that was permitted in the range of variation allowed in the Lydgatian tradition. If Morley's verses appear archaic and difficult to read now, particularly in the context of Wyatt and Surrey's more successful strategies for the English heroic line, they nonetheless retain a power not obvious from Gascoigne's dismissive comments of 'ryding rime'.

The final section of 'The Tryumphe of Love' (IV) presents a vision of Love's power that lies behind other English depictions, including the Castle of Busirane episode in Spenser's *Faerie Queene,* III.xi:

Nowe for to declare this matter by and by
This Goddes chayre, where that he sat on hye
There was about it errour and dreames
And glosynge ymages of all nations and realmes
False opynion was entrynge the gate

And slypper hope stode by theyr ate
Wery rest, and rest with wo and payne
The more hygher he clam, the lesse he dyd obtayn
Damnable lucre was not wanting there
Nore profitable hurte always in fere
Cleare dishonoure, and glory obscure and darke
False lealtie lefte not there to warke
Nor beguyldynge fayth, nor furious busynes
Nor slowe reason lacked not in the presse. (sig. E3^{v}-E4^{r})

The mimetic rhythms of 'The more hygher he clam, the lesse he dyd obtayn' with its pointless busyness, or of 'slowe reason', virtually immovable in the line, give the verse much more than just a quaint lurching after rime. This is conscious versifying, tumbling its lists in a variety of syllabic number. As the passage moves into the confines of Love's dungeon, so the rhythms take on a steadier beat, the syllabification becoming more regular:

A prison open, entre who woulde
When he was in gotten oute he ne coulde
Within trouble, confusion, and mysery
A sure sorowe, a myrth uncertaynly.
Lyppary nor Ischa nor Volcan boyls not so
Stronglie and Mongebell put therto
As boyled the place where the castell was
And briefly whosoever thyther dyd pas
Is there bounde in hote and in colde
In darknesse everlastynge in that hold
Holden and tyed and kept by forse
Crying for mercy tyll that he be horse. (sig. E4^{r})

The following 'Tryumphes' of chastity, death, fame, time and divinity also show Morley skilled in pacing his rough couplets. Petrarch's chaste 'Lady that I love best' (sig. F1^{r}) easily deflects Cupid's arrow in 'The Exellent Tryumphe of Chastitie', sending an army of virtues and virtuous ladies against the terrors of the god of Love: 'O what a gloryouse bande there was/ That agaynst love with hyr dyd passe!' (sig. F3^{r}). The Lady's virtuous thoughts contain the tumult confronting her, as Morley's balanced monosyllables show his attention to line movement mimetic of statement:

Olde wyse thoughtes in a yonge tender age
And gratiouse concorde all fury to asswage,
And Beuty lacked not, with a chast clene thoughte. (sig. F3^{r})

While Chastity's lines tend to be balanced and end-stopped, Death hurtles even the greatest across the barriers of time and verse:

I am the same importune cruell best
Callyd death fearefull that doth arrest
All creatures wyth my great force and myght
Or the daye ende makyng it the nyght
It is I that hath quite and cleane wastyd
The great grekes nation and also hastyd

The noble Troyans unto theyr declyne
And last of all have made to ende and fyne
The Romaynes glory wyth this blade kene
That pycketh and cutteth all away cleane. (sig. G2^{v})

The last line shows that Morley also knows how to wield a phonemic knife.

Chastity knows that death can destroy her body, but not her virtue (119) nor her fame. Ultimately, though, all is subject to time and divine decree, as the *Tryumphes* move to their final vision. Like Death, the levelling apocalypse hurries forward with run-on lines:

What great (trowe ye then) admiracion had I
When I sawe the sonne, firmament, and the skye
Stand fyrme on one fote sure stable and faste
That with his swift course runnyng at the laste
Changed all thinges mortall and then restrained
His thre partes brought to one part unfayned
And then no distinction, no difference of them at al
But the herbe and grasse and flowers with all
All bareyne and bare before and behynde,
Which variacion doth naturally bekynde
Much bitter sorowe to our nature frayle
All at ones together then and there to fayle. (sig. M3^{v})

The tumultuous running and lurching of 'ryding rime' is here as effective as it is anywhere, as effective, one could argue, as many of the smoother measures in Surrey.

Lord Morley's verse represents an accessible and often clearly artful use of an old, soon discredited English versification. It offers not only an early-sixteenth-century reading of Petrarch's *Trionfi* but also an understanding of the continuing potential of the fifteenth-century English line. A closer look at the *Tryumphes* may well give us a better handle on what fifteenth and early sixteenth-century poets and readers admired about Lydgate and Hoccleve, and perhaps help us develop a better ear for fifteenth-century verse generally.

Morley's versification rests on its own, however, as skillful and generally effective in the difficult task of Englishing the great Italian humanist model. It is to his credit that he sought to bring Petrarch's genius home to a native verse, but it is also his misfortune that his younger contemporaries were experimenting in a direction that was to sever the old line irrevocably from a general English readership.

NOTES

1 *Lord Morley's 'Tryumphes'*, ed. by Carnicelli, pp. 9-19. Carnicelli supposes that Morley did his original translation, a gift to Henry VIII, in the late 1530s, though the print version was published between 1553 and 1556 (*Tryumphes*, pp. 10-11). Both James Carley and Marie Axton would date it earlier than Carnicelli: see Carley, 'The Writings of Henry Parker, Lord Morley', above, pp. 40-3; Axton, 'Lord Morley's *Tryumphes of Fraunces Petrarcke*', above, pp. 174-5, making it clear that Morley thought this effort should be particularly valued. All quotations from the *Tryumphes* are from lightly punctuated STC 19811 and are cited by sigla.

2 Thomas More's 'Pageant Verses,' connected to tapestry illustrations which More presumably designed, provide an earlier example of this tradition (*English Sixteenth-Century Verse*, ed. by Richard S. Sylvester (New York, 1974), pp. 119-24. As Carnicelli notes (pp. 64-5), pageantry in the tradition of the *Trionfi* underlies several of Spenser's allegorical set pieces in *The Faerie Queene*. Spenser's early interest in 'Visions' and 'Complaints', with their iconographies of fame and vanity may be added to this tradition (*A Theatre for Worldlings*, trans. from Jan Van Der Noodt, 1569, and the 1591 collection, *Complaints: Containing sundrie small Poemes of the Worlds Vanitie*, in *The Works of Edmund Spenser: a Variorum Edition 10 vols*, ed. by Edwin Greenlaw et al., vol. 8, *The Minor Poems: Part Two* (Baltimore, 1947), pp. 5-188).

3 In the dedicatory letter to Lord Maltravers, Carnicelli, p. 78. 'Ryme' in this period generally meant both verse form and rime scheme, since both 'rime' and 'rhythm' had the same origin. Throughout this essay I use 'rime' to refer specifically to patterns of like-sounding words, and 'verse' to refer to the more general configurations of poetic form.

4 'Certayne Notes of Instruction Concerning the Making of Verse or Ryme in English,' 1575, in *Elizabethan Critical Essays*, ed. by G. Gregory Smith, 2 vols (Oxford, 1904), 1, 56.

5 Surrey was executed in January, 1547 and apparently did his translations after 1540; Book 4 was published by John Day in 1554, Books 2 and 4 together by Richard Tottel in 1557. See the discussion of their dating in *The Poems of Henry Howard, Earl of Surrey*, ed. by Frederick M. Padelford (Seattle, 1928), pp. 233-4. All citations from Surrey's verse are from this edition. See also William A. Sessions, *Henry Howard, Earl of Surrey* (Boston, 1986), pp. 134-6.

6 Alain Renoir, *The Poetry of John Lydgate* (London, 1967), pp. 1-5.

7 Gascoigne, vol. 1, 56.

8 Ibid.

9 Hawes' *Pastime of Pleasure* is a long dream allegory about courtly education, written in 46 chapters of rime royal stanzas (ababbcc). It was first presented to Henry VII in 1506, then published by Wynkyn de Worde in 1509 and 1517. It was republished in 1554 and 1555. Skelton is best known for his short riming lines ('Skeltonics'), but his satiric 'Bowge of Court' is in rime royal, and the longer line appears in other works as well (e.g., 'On the Death of ... Edward the Fourth' and his allegorical court interlude, *Magnificence*). Barclay's *Ship of Fools* and his pastoral *Certain Eglogues* were written and circulated in Henry's reign, and were influential in Elizabeth's through a 1570 publication.

10 Lady Margaret left to John St John a copy of the *Canterbury Tales*, and to Parker's wife a copy of Gower (see M. G. Underwood & M. K. Jones, *The King's Mother* (Cambridge, 1992), p. 241). Gower's *Confessio Amantis* is in tetrameter couplets, and looks backward towards earlier English practice, such as the anonymous early-thirteenth-century English rendering of the French *Kyng Alisaunder* (originally in Alexandrines, the source of the term). This and other medieval English narratives stayed with a four-beat line whose origins were likely in the Old English alliterative line, although rime generally replaced alliteration by the twelfth century. See, for example, *Early Middle English Verse and Prose*, ed. by J. A. W. Bennett & G. V. Smithers (Oxford, 1968, 2d edn), pp. 1-51.

11 From 'The Rebuilding of Troy,' *Troy Book*, II, 523-31, in *John Lydgate Poems*, ed. by John Norton-Smith (Oxford, 1966), p. 15. I have regularized the orthographic symbols.

12 Leiden Voss.Q 9. (I am grateful to James Carley for this reference.) The *Fall of Princes*, based on Boccaccio's Latin prose work *De casibus virorum illustrium* (*c.* 1360), has been described as 'his most comprehensive work', notable for the 'sonorous solemnity' of its stanzaic verse (Walter F. Schirmer, *John Lydgate: a Study of the Culture of the XVth Century*, trans. by Ann E. Keep ([Berkeley and Los Angeles, 1961]), p. 206). For its influence in the sixteenth century, and particularly on the *Mirror for Magistrates*, see C. S. Lewis, *English Literature in the*

Sixteenth Century (Oxford, 1954), p. 240, and *The Mirror for Magistrates*, ed. by Lily B. Campbell (Cambridge, 1938), pp. 9, 45.

13 *Lydgate's Fall of Princes*, ed. by Henry Bergen, 4 vols (Washington, D.C., 1923-7), 'Prologue', ll. 57-63, vol. I, 2-3. See Bergen's outline of the complexities of Lydgate's meter, vol. I, xxviii-xlvi. See also Derek Pearsall, *John Lydgate* (Charlottesville, 1970) for the most thorough modern analysis of Lydgate's work (e.g., pp. 223-54 on *The Fall of Princes*). For the principal Lydgate manuscripts, see Derek Pearsall, *John Lydgate (1371-1449): a Bio-Bibliography* (Victoria, *English Literary Studies*, Monograph Series 71, 1997), pp. 68-84.

14 Susanne Woods, *Natural Emphasis: English Versification from Chaucer to Dryden* (San Marino, 1985), pp. 69-103.

15 Woods, pp. 89-91; see also *The Aeneid of Henry Howard, Earl of Surrey*, ed. by Florence Ridley (Berkeley:, 1964),p. 4. For the timing on the Surrey and Morley translations, see Sessions, p. 135, and Carnicelli, pp. 10-11. All quotations from Wyatt are from the Egerton Manuscript as transcribed by Richard Harrier in *The Canon of Sir Thomas Wyatt's Poetry* (Cambridge, 1975).

16 E.g., 'The Battle of Brunanburh' (*c.* 930), ll. 1-5:

> Her **Ae**thelstan king   **E**orla drichten
> **B**eorna **b**eaggiffa   and hys **b**rother eac
> **E**dmund **A**theling   **ea**ldorlangne tir
> Geslogan aet sake   sweorda eccgum
> Embe Brunanburh   ...

17 So this famous thirteenth-century *reverdie* keeps a strong sense of accentuation, although it has rime and some general fidelity to the 8/6 (or 7/5) syllabic patterns common to French *reverdies*:

> Sumer is icumen in –
> Lhude sing! cuccu.
> Groweth sed and blweth med
> And springeth the wude nu –
> Sing! cuccu.

(*Medieval English Lyrics*, ed. by R. T. Davies [London, 1963], p. 52.)

18 Including a version of the *Aeneid* rendered into Chaucerian couplets by Gavin Douglas, completed in 1513.

19 Huntington Library copy, 1554 edition. For a summary of these issues, see Derek Pearsall, *Old English and Middle English Poetry* (London, 1977), pp. 197-204, and Woods, pp. 46-56.

20 Kenneth R. Bartlett, 'The Occasion of Lord Morley's Translation of the *Trionfi*: the Triumph of Chastity over Politics', in *Petrarch's Triumphs: Allegory and Spectacle*, ed. by Konrad Eisenbichler & Amilcare A. Iannucci (Ottawa, 1990), pp. 325-34.

21 Cf. Francesco Petrarca, *Trionfi*, ed. by Guido Bezzola (Milan, 1984), p. 49 (III.151-6):

> Or so come da se 'l cor si disgiunge,
> e come sa far pace, guerra e tregua,
> e coprir suo dolor quand'altri il punge;
> e so come in un punto si dilegua
> e poi si sparge per le guance il sangue,
> se paura o vergogna aven ch 'l segua.

22 Woods, pp. 115-17.

LORD MORLEY'S FUNERAL

Richard Axton

HENRY PARKER, Lord Morley, died on 25 November 1556, three years into the reign of Queen Mary, and anything but a traditional Catholic funeral would have been very unlikely. The occasion was important enough to interest Henry Machyn, a merchant taylor in London with a keen eye for all forms of pageantry, and he chronicled it in his now fragmentary *Diary*:

> The iij day of Desember was bered in Essex my lord Morley, weith iij harolds, master Garter and odur [heralds, a] standard and a banur of ys armes, and iiij baners [rolls], and iiij baners of emages, and elmett, and cott[-armour,] targett and sword, and viij dosen of skochyons ... dosen of torchys, and ij whytt branchys, and [many] mornars, and after the masse a grett dener.[1]

Machyn's interest is in the public spectacle, though this was probably not an event he saw with his own eyes, since it happened outside London. Morley was buried in the parish church at Great Hallingbury in Essex, where the manor of Hallingbury Morley had come to him, like his title, through his mother Alice Lovel.[2]

Machyn's account is almost entirely a list of the heraldic features of the funeral. This chivalric aspect of the burial of the eighth baron Morley is highlighted by the very next entry in Machyn's *Diary*, which relates the funeral of Robert Downes, Master of the London Ironmongers:

> The sam day at after-non in London [at saint] Mare Colchyrche in Chepe, on master Robart downes the master of the Yrmongers with xij torchys, [ij white] branchys, and iiij grett tapurs; and vj pore men [did bear] hym to the chyrche, and all theys pore men had gownes, xxij gowns; and he had [a] tombe m[ade], in the] tombe a caffen of led, and when that he cam to the grayff he was taken out of one of wood, and putt in-to that of lede; and the morow ij (masses) song, and a godly sermon, and after a grett dener; and ther wher mony blake gownes gyffyn to men and women.[3]

Here the emphasis is civic charity, appropriate piety – note the 'godly sermon' which may indicate the Reformed sympathies of Downes's faith – and material comforts. It would be wrong to suppose that Lord Morley's mourners went home dinnerless or that the poor of his parish did not receive the traditional dole. But it is probably safe to assume that the mortal remains of Master Robert Downes went to their rest without the assistance of heralds of arms. By contrast, the death of a baron of the realm, closely connected with the royal household, made a breach in the ranks of the aristocracy which could be healed only by the ceremonial ritual of a full heraldic funeral. However, Machyn's account reveals nothing about Morley's religious convictions.

A much fuller account of Morley's last rites, hitherto unpublished and unknown to the College of Arms, survives in a heraldic miscellany among the Finch-Hatton manuscripts at Northamptonshire Record Office.[4] The modest purpose of this essay is to present the text and to consider it briefly as evidence of Morley's social status and his religious position.

Finch-Hatton 2 is listed, following the legend on the spine of the volume, as

'Marriages, Christenings & Funerals of Princes, ending with Regulations of Henry VII for the Palace of Westminster xvi c'.[5] The remembrances of noble funerals which occupy the heart of the collection range from 2 to 20 pages; they have a standard form, like chapters, with book-hand headings in larger characters to set off different sections of the ceremonies. Many of the texts, including this one, show a diagram of the arrangement of mourners and pallbearers round the coffin, and indicate the 'rayles' of the hearse that enclose the coffin on its bier on the church floor. The more elaborate of these sketches are in the shape of a flag of St George.

The narrative of Morley's funeral (A72) occupies two folios (four complete sides), preceded by a blank folio. The scribe typically makes an ornamental pen rest after final 's' and 'd' (these might be mistaken for a final 'e' except that the hand is so clear). The text begins on fol. 141^r and is transcribed here line for line, including catchwords, and with original punctuation.

The enterement of the right hon-
norable Sir Henry Perker knight
lorde Morley.

In the yeare of our Lorde God, A Thowsande
five houndred and syxe and fyftye on wensday the
xxvth day of November aboute x of the clocke in
the Evenynge departed out of this transitory world
att his howse of Hannyngbery Morley the right
hon*or*able S*i*r Henry Perker Knight Lord Morley who
made his Executor the Right honnorable S*i*r Henry
Perker knight, now Lord Morleye.

The said Lord Morley being dep*ar*ted out of this
world preparac*i*on was made for his buryall in Right
honnorable order as hereafter followeth.

Firste the body of the said defuncte was sered
and coffered, and that being donne was brought out
of his chamber, and for that there was noe chappell
the said corps was sett in a convenient place; where
there was said every day service and light burninge both daye and night from the said xxvth day of
November unto Thursday the third daye of decemb*er*
that all things were in a Redynes for his Enterrment
vizt.

Then there was prepared in the p*ar*ishe churche a Rayle
hanged w*i*th blacke clothe and garnished w*i*th scochins
of his Armes, and w*i*thin that Rayle a place p*re*pared
for to sett the said corpes ov*er* hanged w*i*th blacke
clothe, alsoe the Quere of the said churche was
hanged w*i*th blacke clothe and garnished w*i*th scochins
of his Armes / All things in aredynes the daye
was appoynted for his buryall w*i*ch was Thursday
in the forenoone, the third daye of december.

The order in procedinge to the Churche from the howse of Hanyngbery with the said Corsse.

Firste

[fol. 141v]
First, the Porter as conductor.
Then the crosse, and on eche side a clerke in a Surplesse with a whyte Braunche in his hande.
Then all Prestes and clerkes singinge.
Then the Standart borne by Arthur Waterhowse.
Then all Gentelmen.
Then the Banner of his Armes borne by Thomas Parker, my Lords brother that now is.
Then the healme and creste borne by Portculleye
Then the Targett borne by Rougecrux.
Then the cote of Armes borne by Garter Principall Kinge att Armes hee weareing the Quenes cote.

Then the Corpes borne by vi. yomen in blacke cotes.

The banner of St George borne by John Dogett

On eche side vi.yoomen in gownes and hoodes over theire hedds with torches.

The Banner of our Lady borne by Nycholas Wright.

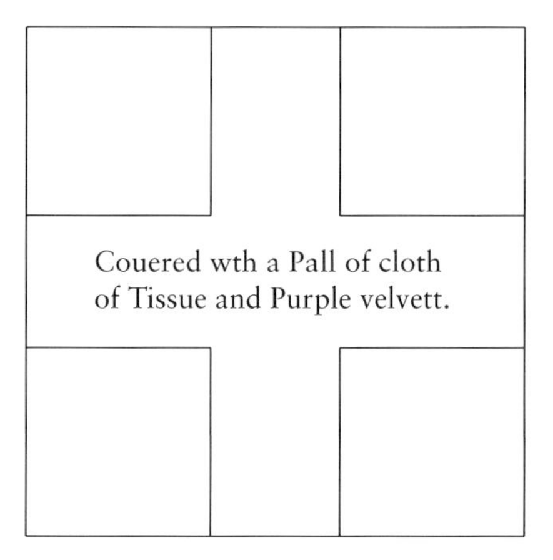
Couered wth a Pall of cloth of Tissue and Purple velvett.

The Banner of King Henry the saint borne by Edmond Brysseley

on eche side ii. bannerrolles of his descents borne by other of his servaunts

The Banner of the Trynitie borne by John St.John.

Then the morners in theire gownes with theire hoodes on theire heddes. The Lord Morley cheife.

Mr. George Browne.
Mr. Thomas Barington.
Mr. Charles Parker my Lords Brother.
Mr. Edward Senethrope.
Then all yomen in blacke cotes and thus proceeded

[in

[fol. 142r]
in order to the churche, in att the Weste dore, where as hee was receaved with holly water, and sen-

sed according to the order of holy churche by the
curate of the said churche.

Then the corps being placed in the place
appoynted w*i*thin the Rayles beganne dirge songe
by Note solemply by the Preistes and clerkes
and Masse of the Holly Goste there being done,
beganne Masse of Requiem songe by Note in
lyke sorte w*i*th deaken and subdeacon proceeded to thend.

The Order of the Offeringe

First the morners conducted by Garter principall Kinge of Armes, offered the cheife morner
firste assisted by the reste, then they came downe
and the cheife morner stode styll w*i*thin the Rayles
and the rest offerred the hatchments in this
manner.
The cote of Armes firste offerred by George
Browne and Thomas Barington.
Then the sworde offerred by Cherles Perker
my Lordes brother and Edward Senethrope.
Then the Targatt offerred by the ij. firste
Then the healme and creste offered by the ij.
other Charles Parker and Edward Senethrope
havinge allwayes going before them Garter principall Kinge of Armes / Then the chefe morner
offerred for himselfe / then the other iiij. morners
money either one for them selves, and then
offerred all Gentylmen, After them all yomen
and all that woulde offer for the sowle of the Lord
dep*ar*ted.
Then offering donne the Masse proceeded to
thend, and att *verbum caro factum est,* the

[Morn*ers*

[fol. 142^{v}]
Morners dep*ar*ted out of the cherche to the Place
to dynner, but att the tyme of the said wordes, before
the dep*ar*tuer of the Morners the standard and
Banner of his Armes were offerred, by Arthur
Waterhowse and Thomas Parker.
Masse donne the said Dicken *[deacon]* w*i*th the reste of
the Quere came downe to the Rayles *[and censed]* the corsse
iij. tymes, and att every carielussion *[kyrie eleison]* the Beddes
was bidd by Roug*e* croix in this sorte -

Of your charitye praye for the sowle of the Right
honnorable S*ir* Henry Parker knight late lord
Morley. Pater noster etc.
And when that the corpes was censed, and
all prayers done and sayde that aught to be saide
before the Buryall then the pall was turned

upp, and the corpes borne to the grave by the
vj. yomen having the iiij. Banners of Saints borne
at the iiij. corners, and on eche side ij. bann*er*rolles
of his dissents, and thus when that all prayers
was saide, hee was putt into the Tome for him
appointed, whereas other of his Auncienters lay.
By his said yomen all this done, the mynisters
of the churche repared home to the howse of
the said defuncte to dynner whereas was prepared for them a good dynner / And also there was
given att the dore a dole the same day, notw*ith*standing the dole w*i*ch had bene given there afore.
Dynner done, every man was contented for his
paynes. And thus ended the seremonye of the
enterement of the right honnorable S*ir* Henry
Parker knight late Lord Morley. *On whose
Sowle God have mercy.*
Amen.

This account shows that Morley's last rites were perfectly conventional in both chivalric and Catholic senses. Almost every feature of the account can be matched in one or other of its companion texts. The funeral of Sir John Bruges, Lord Chandos on 12 April 1556 (A71) is a very close Marian parallel. Contrast with two Edwardian funerals included in the collection is striking: the Earl of Southampton, who died 30 July 1550 (A56); and Lord Wentworth, who was interred on 5 March 1551 (A77). Both these funerals have distinctly Reformed features and are simpler than Morley's, despite the Earl of Southampton's higher rank.[6] Morley's standing as a peer put him on a footing with Wentworth, the King's Chamberlain.[7] The two men were among the peers who tried Anne Boleyn in 1536, and at Wentworth's trial in 1550 Morley was his prosecutor.[8] Their funeral rites, however, differed in a number of liturgical and ceremonial features.

There were nine days between Morley's death and burial. Such delays, normal in pre-Reformation England, were occasioned by the need for elaborate funeral preparations by the heralds – the making of mourning gowns and hoods, banners, and painting of paper-paste armour and scutcheons; consequently the body had to be embalmed.[9] Reformed burials were much brisker; both Wentworth and Southampton were buried within four days. During the nine days that Morley's corpse lay in state 'there was said every day service and light burninge both day and night'.

Morley's corpse was taken from house to church in a procession (apparently on foot, despite being over half a mile) conducted by a porter; a cross was carried, flanked by two clerks in surplices, each bearing a 'whyte braunche' (candlestick, *OED branch* 2d, 1552) singing priests and clerks are specifically mentioned; then the armorial procession of mourners in proper precedence. Neither of the Edwardian funeral accounts mentions a porter or cross; both diligently record 'syngynge in the English tongue the Psalmes therunto appoynted'. At the West door of Morley's parish church 'hee was receaved with holly water, and sensed according to the order of holy churche'. 'Hee' is here spoken of as if Morley were still one of the living congregation. The use of candles and crosses, 'fetching' the corpse to church and 'the minister meeting them at churche stile with surplesse, with a company of greedy clarkes' are among the supersitions complained of in the 1572 Admonitions to Parliament, impatient at the conservatism of Elizabethan funerary practice.[10]

The procession into church bears the same form in the Edwardian and in the Marian funerals in Finch-Hatton 2, testifying to the conservative power of heraldic protocol. Following the standard-bearer come gentlemen in mourning gowns and hoods, then the heir with the deceased's banner of arms.[11] Then come the three heralds bearing the hatchments ('achievements': square, lozenge-shaped tablets exhibiting the armorial bearings), the helm and crest, the target (small, round shield); finally the coat of arms is borne by the highest-ranking herald, Garter King of Arms. In each of the funerals discussed the corpse was carried by six yeomen in black coats and the coffin is flanked by bannerols (*OED banderole*: 'banner about a yard square, borne at the funerals of great men, and placed over the tomb') of descent, two on each side. Both the Reformed funerals displayed the descent of the deceased's wife, an indication, perhaps, of Protestant emphasis on the dignity of marriage itself.

Morley's pall 'of cloth of Tissue and purple veluett' was a more sumptuous and expensive material than the black velvet used for Southampton and Wentworth. Notably, too, the banners of the saints borne at the four corners of the hearse are not found in the smaller and simpler Edwardian arrangements; in the accounts of these the sixteenth- and seventeenth-century scribes are content with a plain square. This may indicate that the hearse structure was either much smaller and simpler or, possibly, dispensed with altogether. Heralds' directions from the middle of the sixteenth-century 'At the funeralle of a Barron' give the dimensions of the timber hearse as 14 feet high, 12 feet long, and 9 feet broad.[12] The timber was to be wrapped with 120 yards of baize. The upper and nether valences each were to be of 14 yards of velvet, with fringes of black and gold 'halfe a quarter and a nayle depe'. A regular pall contained 30 yards of black velvet.

The bannners carried for Morley by four of the chief mourners were (anticlockwise): St George, Our Lady, the Trinity, and King Henry the Saint (Henry VI). The same configuration had been used for the funeral of Lord Chandos (A71) eight months before, the only difference being in the patron saint: St John the Baptist for Sir John Gage, Lord Chandos where Morley has King Henry the Saint, with whose name he was christened. The particular practice of including the banner of an 'advourer' (patron saint) had been laid down in 'The Ordering of a Funerall for a Noble Person in Hen.7. time':

Item, to be hadde A banere of the Trinitie, A baner of oure Lady, A bannere of Seint george, A baner of the Seynt that was his advoure, And a Baner of his Armes.[13]

The liturgical forms mentioned in Morley's funeral are traditionally Roman: dirge (the antiphon '*Dirige, Domine, Deus meus*' which begins the Office of the Dead) and 'Masse of the Holly Ghost'. Both this and the 'Masse of Requiem' which follows are 'songe by Note' – i.e. in plainchant. The latter is sung through by deacon and subdeacon.

At Lord Wentworth's funeral, by contrast, the text says simply: 'And for the sarvyce begann, and att the endynge of the Gospell the pryncipall morners offerred.' Since the chief mourner here was Lord Edward Seymour, son of the Duke of Somerset, the Protestant emphasis is not surprising. Immediately after Southampton's corpse was set in its hearse in the church of St Andrew, Holborn:

> the sermon began wich was made by Dr Roper whose Antheme *[i.e. text]* was *[the scribe leaves a blank space]*. The sermon being ended, then began the communyon songe very melodiously and so procedid to the offerynge (A56).

A sermon seems to have been optional in the Catholic funerals recorded in Finch-Hatton 2, but at Lord Wentworth's funeral there was also preaching – by no less than Myles Coverdale, translator of the first complete English bible in 1535 and an ardent Protestant, made Bishop of Exeter in 1551. It did not take place until after the visual high-point of the service – the offering:

> the hatchments sett upon the Table, by the hands of Gartier who receaved them, And thereupon the sermon beganne, wich was made by Myles Coverdalle. Then the deane proceeded with the communyon and all the mourners receaved yt (A77).

The most dramatic part of all noble funerals was the offering; this was in two parts, having respectively secular and spiritual significance: the mourners' offering of hatchments or arms of the deceased, and the offering of money for his soul (in Protestant practice this was done 'in commemoration of the defunct').[14]

The first offering emphasizes the honour of the public person, the second his humility *in propria persona*. The heraldic pomp is sandwiched within the devotional rite; as always strict attention is paid to rank. At Morley's offering, the chief herald, Garter Principal King of Arms, conducted the chief mourner, grandson and heir of the deceased, from the hearse to the altar. The young Henry Parker returned to stand within the rails, now symbolically invested with the honour of the deceased. Garter then conducted the mourners in pairs as they carried Morley's arms to the altar. The coat of arms was carried by Thomas Barrington (Morley's son-in-law) and George Browne.[15] The sword was carried, point-down, by Charles Parker, brother to the heir, and Edward Senethorpe; the target was offered by the first pair; finally, the helm and crest by the second. Clare Gittings has written: 'The whole ritual of the heraldic funeral revolved around the legitimate transfer of titles and power; the private persona counted for very little indeed.'[16] Moreover, it was a symbolic transference of power authorized by the Crown in the person of Garter King of Arms, 'hee weareing the Queenes cote'.

As was customary, the chief mourner then offered money 'for himselfe' followed by the other four 'money either one for themselves'. Offering by all gentlemen and all yeomen followed and by 'all that woulde offer for the sowle of the Lord departed'. The writer's phrase states clearly the central Catholic doctrine of the community of living and dead, and the power of charity, prayer, and alms, to effect change in the state of the dead. Prayers for the dead emphasizing this community, 'they with us and we with them', are included in the Edwardian 1549 Prayer Book. But by 1552 there was a decisive shift in liturgical emphasis, as Eamon Duffy has argued:

> In the world of the 1552 book the dead were no longer with us. They could neither be spoken to nor even about, in any way that affected their well-being. The dead had gone beyond the reach of human contact, even of human prayer. There was nothing which could even be mistaken for prayer for the dead in the 1552 funeral rite. The service was no longer a rite of intercession

on behalf of the dead, but an exortation to faith on the part of the living. Indeed, it is not too much to say that the oddest feature of the 1552 burial rite is the disappearance of the corpse from it.[17]

Morley's rites are serenely untouched by any such theology.

After the offering the Latin Mass proceeded to '*Verbum caro factum est*'. At these words Morley's standard and banner of arms were offered by Arthur Waterhouse and Thomas Parker, brother of the new Lord Morley. The last vestiges of Morley's honour having been offered up on the altar, the mourners left the church and went to dinner. It is likely that, as in Wentworth's funeral, 'Garter brought home the said morners', since the next heraldic intervention is by Rouge Croix.

This startling departure of 'family' from the ceremony seems to have been usual in the funerals of Catholic nobility. It leaves the clergy and heralds to perform the office of burial. The deacon and choir process down into the nave of the church singing *Kyrie eleison* thrice. But it is a herald who calls out the bidding prayer, 'half prayer, half declaration' which 'marks the official demise of the public person of the deceased'.[18] At each *Kyrie* Rouge Croix cries out, 'Of your charity praye for the sowle of the Right honnorable Sir Henry Parker knight late lord Morley. *Pater noster etc.*'

The burial itself was attended with considerable further ceremonial. Morley's corpse was again censed and carried to the grave by the six yeomen. The banners of the saints were carried at the four corners and bannerols of descents displayed at the sides. Finally, 'hee was putt into the Tomb for him appointed, whereas other of his Auncienters lay'. The coffin was then censed a second time and the pall turned up.

The ministers (and presumably the yeomen) proceeded to Hallingbury Morley for 'a good dynner'. There was a dole – a handout of coin and food to the poor people of the parish – at the door. That this was additional to an earlier dole emphasizes the largesse of the new Lord Morley, though it gives no indication of the scale of the expenditure.[19] From the point of view of the Reformed Church such charitable funeral doles were yet another form of superstition.[20]

The thoroughly traditional and Catholic nature of Morley's actual burial contrasts strongly with the concluding events of the Edwardian funerals just five years earlier. Lord Wentworth's corpse appears to have been set down in the choir before the 'table' (altar), thus breaking down the mystique of priestly space. After Garter left with the mourners:

> the rest of the officers of Armes remayned behynde, then began the Sarvyce for the buryall, and the Corps was brought out of the Quyre into the Chapell and there buryed in Vaute, which was prepared for him (A77).

Mourners, knights, gentlemen, and servants proceeded to Lord Edward Seymour's house for a 'greate dynner'. At the Earl of Southampton's funeral the mourners departed similarly after the offering, led out by Garter King of Arms, who shed his coat at the church door. The remembrance notes that 'the Executours remayned in the quyer to see the Body buryed' (A56). Both these Reformed funerals conclude with 'a great dynner', but there is no mention of a dole.

The final concerns of Wentworth's funeral narrative are with payments ('every man was contented for his paynes'), though the heralds' fees and material costs of the 'seremonye' are not detailed, as they are in some of the accounts in Finch-Hatton 2.

The expense of Morley's funeral can only be guessed at. At a time when a nobleman's funeral could cost £1000 it was not particularly lavish. The standard cost of making and draping a hearse in the mid-sixteenth century was £80.[21] Using as a guide the expenses for the funerals of Lord Wentworth (1550), King's Chamberlain, and Lord Chandos (1556), it seems likely that heralds' fees came to about £20 and that a similar sum would have been spent on painters' work. The size of the dinner and dole could easily be ten times that.[22]

Everything about Morley's funeral tallies with what is otherwise known of him: it was doctrinally conservative and, within the prescription of heraldic funerals, modestly sumptuous.

He died at a time when the heralds had just consolidated their powers, particularly over funerals of the nobility, had established a permanent home for their library, and had gained renewed royal patronage.[23] From the time of Henry VII there existed a protocol for heraldic funerals, '*The manner of the orderyng of the settyng forth of a corps, of what estate that he be*', which laid down the appropriate dress and hood materials for each estate and the number of mourners: fifteen for an emperor, thirteen for a king, eleven for a duke, nine for a marquess or earl, seven for a viscount or baron, five for a knight banneret or bachelor, three for an esquire or gentleman.[24] This protocol is copied into Finch Hatton MS 2 (A123, p.179). It was a tradition that made irrelevant any consideration of the individuality of the person in death.

One detail is puzzling: Morley had only five mourners, as befitted a Knight of the Garter, rather than seven as befitted the dignity of Baron. It is as if there was something precarious, something not quite full-blooded about his barony: dormant in the female line since the death of his Yorkist uncle Henry Lovel, shadowed in his mother by her Yorkist husband William Parker, standard-bearer to Richard III, threatened by her second marriage until the decisive intervention of Lady Margaret Beaufort, the king's mother, and finally resurrected 'by instrument unknown'. There is another parallel here with Lord Wentworth, who also had only five mourners at his funeral and whose instrument of elevation (in 1529) is also unknown.[25]

Morley's own thoughts on death – however they were shaped by his reading of Petrarch – would have been sharpened by the death of his wife, Alice St John, in December 1552, aged 66. She was buried in the church at Great Hallingbury, with the inscription 'regio sanguine prognata'. As she died during Edward VI's reign and after the appearance of the new Prayer Book, it is possible that the funeral rites given her were to some extent 'reformed'. At the least, her husband would have felt a pressure to conform. Morley was also predeceased by his only son Henry in December 1553, a few months after Mary's accession.[26]

In view of the discussions earlier in this volume, there are no longer any grounds for thinking Henry Parker, eighth Lord Morley, anything but a staunch Catholic. Alice's funeral would have made him acutely aware of the way in which those changes affected the burial of the dead, and Morley would have presented his heirs with a dilemma had he died four years sooner. To some extent the heraldic paraphernalia of noble funerals served to mask alterations in official doctrine and liturgical style. Yet the carefully chosen words of the sources indicate that these heraldic chroniclers were aware how important were the issues at stake in these ceremonies. Comparison of Morley's rites with those of his Edwardian peers shows how much changed and changed back within six years. The timing of one's death was crucial. Morley was fortunate in the end that he died securely within the reign of his beloved Queen Mary and that he could be buried in the manner of his ancestors.

NOTES

1 *The Diary of Henry Machyn*, ed. by J. G. Nicols (London, 1848), p. 120. This remains the standard edition of a very fragmentary manuscript; conjectured readings are given [thus] by Nichols.

2 A brief account of Hallingbury and of the Morleys is given by H. M. E. M. Cocks, *The Great House of Hallingbury: its Place in History* (Great Hallingbury, 1988). Morley's arms are reproduced from an unidentified heraldic manuscript on p. 12. Alice, Lady Morley is considered to have inherited the right to the title on the death of her brother Henry Lovel, Lord Morley in 1489. Her husband William Parker died and she married Sir Edward Howard before January 1506. Howard was slain at Brest on 25 April 1513. Alice died on 23 December 1518 and her will was proved on 22 February 1519. In 1520 her son Henry Parker was at the Field of Cloth of Gold as 'Lord Morley'. His name appears in a College of Arms list of peers present in the Parliament which first met on 15 April 1523. G. E. Cockayne, *The Complete Peerage of England, Scotland, Ireland, Great Britain and the United Kingdom*, ed. by V. Gibbs et al., 13 vols in 14 (London, 1910-59), 9, 220-2, where it is noted that this list in Dugdale's *Summonses*, pp. 492-3, 'is a fabrication based on the Heralds' record of attendance' and that 'the writs for this Parl. have not been found' (p. 222n). Since neither of Alice's husbands was summoned to Parliament, and since Henry Parker was known as Lord Morley before any writs of summons were issued to him, it is probable that the barony lapsed on the death of Henry Lovel and was restored to Henry Parker (with limitation in tail male) by investiture or by some instrument of creation which has not yet been discovered (p. 221n).

By her remarriage to Sir Edward Howard, Parker's mother, Lady Morley, jeopardized her son's title. It was entirely owing to the generosity and shrewdness of Lady Margaret Beaufort, in whose household young Henry Parker was cup-bearer and personal attendant, that 'master Parker's lands' and title were secured for him. (Michael K. Jones & Malcolm G. Underwood, *The King's Mother* (Cambridge, 1992), pp. 114, 280). In the dedication to his translation of Plutarch's Lives of Scipio and Hannibal, BL, Royal MS 17 D.xi), Morley refers to himself as 'Henry (by your goodnesse) Lord Morlei', which may support the notion that Morley's peerage was fortunate, a direct act of royal favour.

3 *The Diary of Henry Machyn*, ed. by Nichols, p. 120.

4 I am grateful to the Archivist, Mr Robert Yorke, for confirmation of this. London, College of Arms MSS I.10 and I.11 are sixteenth-century collections of contemporary accounts of heraldic funerals, many of which were apparently copied by the scribes of Finch-Hatton 2. See below, n. 6.

5 'A List of the Hatton Manuscripts', compiled by C. W. Foster MA FSA; it is found in Lists Box 18. In the Revised Catalogue (a folder of handwritten sheets calendaring contents of MSS 1-50) FH2 is described as: 'A very thick volume, not foliated, various hands, boards, paper cover much decayed.'

Two early-seventeenth-century scribes appear to be responsible for the contents of the collection and their items have been numbered in modern pencil A1, B2 and so on, at the top of the page. Several items are marked in pencil 'Dugdale'. There is no continuous pagination, but the feet of the pages on which new items begin sometimes carry small inked numbers in seventeenth-century hand; these possibly refer to earlier gatherings of A and B separately.

Scribe A writes an upright secretary hand of the early seventeeth century and is responsible for the majority of entries. A16-A106 are remembrances of the interments of English royalty and nobles. From A108 on are accounts of the obsequies of foreign royalty. Scribe B contributes fewer entries; he writes a sloping, cursive hand with a strong italic element. After item 124 there is a summary list of Burials in a third hand, occupying 5 pages, and grouping the events according to rank of the deceased: Kings, Queens, King's Children, Earls, Viscounts, Churchmen, Barons, Noblewomen, Knights of the Garter, Knights, Esquires; the last two categories are Months Minds and Obsequies.

Principles of hierarchy and chronology vie in the ordering of the entries. In the latter part of the volume are copies of regulations from the time of Henry VII: 'The sitting or goying at interement. ... Reformacion of Apparell for grete Astats of women in tyme of mornyng. ... Fees apperteyning to the officers att armes att the enterement of any noble persone' (A121) and 'Certaine articles appoynted by the king or soveraigne lord King Henry VIIth att his pallace of Westm*inster*' [31 Dec 9HVII] (A126).

The text of the volume begins: 'The promise of the French kinge touchinge the matrimony of my Lord Dalphin and my Lady Elizabeth the Kings Eldest Daughter' [1475] (pencil f.1a). It ends: 'For an homage ... successorum suorum in futuro' (unpaginated). The earliest occasion recorded appears to be 1466 and the latest 1633.

6 Earlier accounts of both these Edwardian funerals follow one another in College of Arms, MS I.11, fols 111-116. 'The enterement of the noble and puyssant lord Wryothesley' differs only in the diagram of the hearse and banner bearers; below a sketch of what seems to be an upright sword and the word 'ducis', a rectangular box contains the words, 'no*n* portabat*ur* q*u*ia spectat solu*m* ad regem sed fuit om*ni*a suspe*n*sa cum aliis insigniis honoris supra tumulu*m* in dicta ecclesia'.

7 Both Finch-Hatton 2 and College of Arms I.11 refer to 'The Enterement of Thomas Lorde Wentforde' but this is clearly the same man, Treasurer and Lord Chamberlain. His paternal aunt was Margaret Wentworth who married Sir John Seymour and was mother to the Duke of Somerset, Lord Seymour of Sudeley, and Jane, third wife of Henry VIII. In the contemporary record of his part in putting down Kett's rebellion he is refered to as 'the old Lord Weinford'. See Cockayne, *The Complete Peerage*, 12.2, 497-498n. He was admitted to the House of Lords on 2 December 1529, but it is not known whether by writ or patent or *par parole*. He resembles Morley in this respect, too.

The only other Edwardian funeral in Finch-Hatton 2 appears to be that of John Wallop Knight in July 1551 (A91).

8 Cockayne, *The Complete Peerage*, 9, 224.

9 The body of Francis Talbot, Earl of Shrewsbury, had to wait 24 days in preparation for interment in 1560. See Clare Gittings, *Death, Burial, and the Individual in Early Modern England* (London, 1984), p. 166.

10 See Eamon Duffy, *The Stripping of the Altars* (New Haven & London, 1992), p. 578; Gittings, p. 44.

11 Thomas Hawley, Clarenceaux Herald who visited Essex in 1553 to enroll rights to arms in that county, would have been familiar with Morley arms. BL Add. MS 7098 contains what purport to be copies of entries made at a Visitation by Hawley in Essex and elswhere during 1552 and 1553. See 'Quartered coates of the nobility and gentry of Essex' by John Morley: BL, Lansdowne MS 865, fol. 188^{r}. George Gatfield, *Guide to the Printed Books and Manuscripts Relating to English and Foreign Heraldry and Genealogy* (London, 1892), p. 136.

12 College of Arms, MS I.14, fol. 178^{r}. Pictures of three baronial hearses from heraldic manuscripts of the later sixteenth century are given by J. F. R. Day, 'Death Be Very Proud: Sidney, subversion and Elizabethan heraldic funerals', in *Tudor Political Culture*, ed. by Dale Hoak (Cambridge, 1995), pp. 179-203, pl. 48-50.

13 BL, Cotton MSS, Julius B.XII, fol. 7[v], printed in *Queene Elizabethes Achademy (by Sir Humphrey Gilbert): A Booke of Precedence*, ed. by F. J. Furnivall, EETS ES 8 (London, 1869), p.29. Among funerals in Finch-Hatton 2, John Earl of Bedford 1554 (A57) had St John; Henry Earl of Sussex 1556 (A58), King Henry the Saint; Stephen Gardiner Bishop of Winchester 1555 (A66), St Stephen.
14 Gittings, pp. 176-7.
15 I am grateful to Miss Marion Colthorpe for identifying Thomas Barrington of Hatfield Broad Oak, Essex (1530-81) as husband of Morley's daughter Alice. She suggests that George Browne is possibly of White Roding, named in the 1581 will of his son Wistan Browne of Abbess Roding, Essex. John St John, bearer of the banner of the Trinity, is presumably a relative, perhaps nephew of Morley's deceased wife Alice St John. Nycholas Wryght may be related to the John Wright of Hatfield Broad Oak who flourished *c.* 1538 (*The Victoria History of the County of Essex*, vol. 2, ed. by W. Page & J. H. Round, London, 1907, pp. 109-10). It has not been possible to identify the other mourners.
16 Gittings, p. 178.
17 Duffy, p. 475.
18 Gittings, p. 178.
19 At the Earl of Shrewsbury's funeral 6000 poor each received 4*d.*, a loaf, and beef. Day, 'Death be very proud', p. 183n.
20 The Admonition of Parliament of 1572 complained in scorn, 'that breade must be given to the poore, and offerynges in buryall time used, and cakes sent abrode to frendes' (Duffy, p. 578).
21 College of Arms, MS I.14, fol. 178[r]-178[v].
22 Lord Chandos's funeral at Sudeley was a more lavish affair in several respects: there were 30 poor men (one for each year of his age), the Bishop of Gloucester officiated, the heralds were in attendance 14 days and had considerable travel expenses, and there were 'poore people about v or vi thowsant' who received 2*d.* apiece (Finch-Hatton 2, A71).
23 Credit for securing the charter from King Philip and Queen Mary, dated 18 July 1553, which made them into a corporation, is usually given to Thomas Howard, Duke of Norfolk, who became Earl Marshall in 1554. See Sir Anthony Wagner, *Heralds of England* (London, 1967), pp. 176-82.
24 College of Arms, MS L12 fol. 64b cited by Wagner, p. 106; College of Arms, MS I.15, fol. 153b: 'the nomber of mourners after the degre of the deffunct'.
25 See above, n. 7.
26 Young Sir Henry Parker was made Knight of the Bath at the coronation of Anne Boleyn in 1533; he was Groom of the Privy Chamber attending on Anne of Cleves in Calais in 1539.

TEXTS

In the texts which follow abbreviations have been silently expanded. Punctuation and capitalization is editorial; 'i' and 'j', 'u' and 'v' have been normalized in accordance with modern usage. Double 'ff' at the beginning of words has been treated as a single capital.

1. Additions on the writing line are indicated by / \; additions between the lines by \ /; additions in the margin by \\ //.
2. Suppressions by crossing out are indicated by [-].
3. Substitutions are indicated by [/].
4. Accidental loss is indicated by [[ ]].
5. < > show editorial insertions.

APPENDIX I

a Dedicatory Letter to Cromwell prefacing the Lyff of the Good Kyng Agesylayus. b The Comparcuyon of ... Kyng Henry to this Agesylayus

Written on paper between 1537 and 1540, probably for presentation on New Year's Day 1538. The manuscript went from Cromwell to the royal library. It was later removed by Roland Kenrick and was given to Edward La Zouche in 1602.

Aberystwyth, NLW, MS 17038C, fol. 1v

The Lyff of the good Kyng Agesylayus wretten by the famus clerke Plutarke in the Greke tounge and traunslatyd out of Greke into Latyn by Anthony Tudartyn and drawen out off Latyn into Englysche by me Henry Lord Morley and dedycat unto the right honorable Baron the Lorde Croumwell Lord Pryvy Seall.

fol. 2r The aunsyent and famylyar acqueyntaunse whiche my speciall good Lord I have had with youe meny a day, and if there were no more occasyons but that yet schuld compel me always possible to schew that of my part I schuld not be neclygent to kepe and ourly to renew hit, lest in my so doing youe might rightfully blame me and ley unto me the dyshonest vise of forgetfulnes whiche – as Seneke writtith – where it hathe place it is a evident argument that there was no perfect love and amytie byfore, and so by one offens lose not only my aunsyent frend but allso the self same vertu of frendschip which Cycero, Senek, Quyntillyan and Plutarke with all the facundyous court of orators so eloquently commendes. God deffend my good and syngular good Lord that I schuld fol. 2v so do / to youe in especiall that hath and dothe ourly teche me by youre goodnes schewid unto me what it becomyth me to do agayne to youe. And albeit that the goodnes of God and the tender favor of oure most gracyos soverayngne lord and king hath now brought youe by youre wyse discressyon to that fortune that littell it nedith youe any frendschip that I ame abill or in power to schew you, yet youre goodnes I dought not is suche with youre humanytie but that youe will nothing so moche accept in me as myself which I with no lesse good hart do geve unto youe than dyd Eschynes to his maister Plato, that seing he had nothing in ryches as other had to reward his good maister, withall he gave his maister his owne self praing him to take that gyfte well in fol. 3r worth, for if he / had had better he schuld. And albeit that the wyse philozofer had resayvyd of other meny gret rewardes, yet toke he the wordes of this his discyple with his good will adjoynyd ther unto above the gyftes of the others. All I then hoping of the same do present unto youe this New Yers Day myselff with the very loving hart that may be thought a pore frend may geve youe and farther more pray youe with that to resayve this littell boke of the lyff of the most nobill king Agesylayus wrytton in the Grek tong by the facundyus eloquent Plutarke, maister unto the good emperoure Tragyan, and translatyd out of Greke into Latyn by Antony Tu[b/d]ertyne and out of Latyn into Inglysch by me Henry Morley, not without sum labor, for as it is trewth that in all fol. 3v his boke intytulyd the / lyves of Plutarke he semes not to have taken more payne then in the commending of this vertuus prynce, even ther after he hath inforsyd himsellf in the straungnes of the stille whiche the same hathe so foloyd in the traunslacyon, that to convert the same into oure tong I say as for my part, that littill have of cunnyng to do hit, but for a eloquent orator it schuld be moche to do. Youre lordschip may then with good reasun say unto me that I was not well advysyd to take upon me to translat that thing the which was to hard for me to do. Unto that my speciall good lord I schall aunsser unto youe that where there lakith connyng there lakyd no good will, and farther thowghe that I have not foloyd word by word, which Oras sayth a 4^{r} translator is not bound to do, yet I trust I have not / arryd far from the sens. And here it is to be notyd that Plutarke, which wrote not only of this good kyng but of dyvers other as well of Romayns as of Grecyans, when he tellith off twayne which there lyves were sumwhat like, at the later ende of the toue of there lyves he confarrith a Romayne and a Grecyan together, but in comending of this king he adjoynithe no few unto him as me thynkith because that he thought none so moche prayse worthy as he, and of sewertie if this kyng being a panyme, as not only Plutarke but all other wryters of storys tellithe, was so good, so vertuus, so meke, so hardy as this Agesylayus, I can not thinke whome we myght compare so well unto him as oure most dere, 4^{v} most naturall and most gracyous soverayne lord Kynge / Henry, for as moche as there may be found in this royall persun all and as moche as may be requyryd in a chrysten kyng – clemens, justyce, pytie, relygyon, wysdom and constaunce – and wold to Chryst Jhesu my speciall good lord that I had that scyens, that eloquens that was in this Grecyan to confar these kynges together, then I wold not dought but that he schuld well say that this Grecyan the panyme schuld esely geve place to oure most Chrysten kyng. But for as moche as that I ame far frome suche knoledge, though cunyng lake, the treuth (which nedes never no payntyd eloquens) schall helpe me to confar oure Henry to this Agesylayus, whiche breffly at the ende of thys worke I schall 5^{r} declare, praying youre good lordschip that under your / protectyon it may be schadoud and that if there be any that wold other in the translacyon or other wyse fynde fault or inpungne it that you will in this worke as well as you have bene in other urgent causys of myne a schyld inexpungnable and I schall alwayes pray to God that ye may long serve our dere prynce to Godes and to his plesure and to the comon welthe of us all. Amen....

fol. 31^{r}
The comparcuyon of oure most dere and gratyous soverayne lord Kyng Henry to this Agesylayus kyng of the Lacydymones.

Now here restith namore my speciall good lorde but that according as I promysyd in my prolog that I confar oure most dere and gratyous soverayne kyng Henry with this most vertuus and 31^{v} nobill Agesylayus. If then the / lyff of thys panym kyng be well understand ye schall fynd that he began his rayne moche about the age of eightene yers and that imedyatly upon the same he passyd frome his owne cuntry into Asya with a good and just cause to war upon the Persyans. As to there agys it is playne that nyghe unto that same yers oure good Kyng Henry toke upon him by just title of right to governe the empyere of Ingland and that schortly after he passid with his puyssaunt army to make war upon the Frenchemen. Where in like case as Agesylayus was often by just promes cyrcumventyd, he always keping his promes fast and sure, even so oure Henry what double promesse so ever the Frenchmen made oure prynce kept his faithe that he ons promysyd unvyolat as well word as writting. And Agesylayus gat with his wyse coundyt / 32^{r} dyvers riche cuntryes, no les dyd our Henry get too royall strong towns Torwyne and Torney. It foloithe Agesylayus dyd overcum the Persyans in a sett battayle. Dyd not oure Henry so to at the battayle of Esperons overcum the Frenchmen by valyauntnes and by the wyse governans of his owne royall parson? Agesylayus with his [-straunge] humanytie made all straunge nacyons glad to be confederat with him and to assyst him with horsys and men of war. Evyn in lyke fachion oure Henry by his pytie, his liberalitie and nobilnes drew to him the emperoure Maxymyllyan with his Germayns, the gret lordes of Flaunders with the Flemynges and dyvers other of all cuntrys to do him servys. Then Agesylayus cummyng home toward his cuntry was assautyd wyth dyvers Grecyans as Thebeans, Boecyans and suche other. Was not oure prynce in like wyse with 32^{v} the unjust Skotes whiche // being in legg with him all faithe set apart invadyd oure Henry's empyer? And as Agesylayus by his prefect overcame all his enemys, evyn so dyd oure Henry by his leueten\a/ntes overcum the Skotes, the kyng hymsellf slayne and innumerable of his lordes and subjectes. Agesylayus when he was retornyd was always redy to socor and defend those his neybours that were confederat unto him. Who can say nay but oure Henry hathe alwayes socoryd Flaunders, Frauns and Skotlande so that when any of thes hathe bene like to be oppressyd having his ayde they have bene relevyd agayne so that justly it may be sayd by oure Henry whome that he clevithe unto dothe prosper? Hyther unto I thinke, my good lord Cromwell, there can no man deny but this whiche I have sayd in the lawde of this oure most fol. 33r Crysten kyng, but that all a sectyon set apart I have decl (*sic*) / declaryd nothing but the treuthe.

Now to make an end, as Plutarke wryttithe of the vertus of Agesylayus, so intend I to wryt of the vertus in oure Henry and thereafter to confar them together. Wher that Agesylayus observyd so hyghly his faithe whiche is the best relygyon that can be in such wyse that often his enemys dred not upon his promes to cum into his campe and elleswhere, what may be les sayd of oure good kyng that hathe kept his promes in suche wyse that Charles as well affore as after that he was elect Emperoure dred not to passe the sees with a few in nomber and so put him sellf into oure Henrys handes? What schuld I say off Francis the Frenche kyng that seing the just faithe of oure prynce doutyd not to cume into oure kyngs strong toune of Calys? I pas over Chrysternus fol. 33v kyng of Denmarke and other inferyor lordes whiche at this present day withoute / drede only upon the trust of oure kyng abyde and taryed his will and plesure. Now where that Agesylayus is praysyd for his temperans, who is more temperat in all thinges, in eting, in drinkyng and in other voluptyose plesurs then oure Henry?[1] Agesylayus is comendyd for his wysdome, that he so rulyd his cuntry that bothe they lovyd him and feryd him. Wher was there ever any kyng better belovyd then our kyng Henry, more feryd then he, that by his highe wysdome when he schuld schew grace and when he schuld with justyce correct offenders? Now where Agesylayus is praysyd for loving, maynteynyng and avaunsyng of suche as truly servyd him, in this the worle[s/d] may see how moche oure prynce passis Agesylayus, whiche a multytude as well grett fol. 34r as small for lyttell labors enhaunsyd to grett dingn (*sic*) / dingnyties. Now wher Agesylayus did study to save his subjectes from harme and countid hit more better to defend his owne trew subjectes then to overcum ten thousand enemys, who hathe I pray youe more better savid his subjectes then oure kyng that in thirty yers which wellnere he hathe most happely rulyd without any invasyon or blodsched by any enemys were the<y> never so puyssaunt? Hathe he not farid as well in battayle as other wyse his dere subjectes, so that rightfully he may be callyd the father of the cuntry? Then to conclude, Agesylayus had this wyse maners that he chose not those to be of his councell that were most myghtyst but those that were most best. And in this oure Henry is no les to be commendyd then a councellor of God himsellf, that studithe for nothing so moche fol. 34v as all power, all dingnytie set apart, as to take to his counsell / suche as be good and vertuus in wyt and resun wherby the good lyve in quyet and the evyll be punyschid. Now last of all, where Plutarke breffly praysys Agesylayus for obsserving religyon, what laude schall and may all Chrystendome geve unto kyng Henry that, where treuth was taken away and error bare rule by usurping of the spyrytuall bysschop of Rome, hathe and dothe dayly by devyne wysdome as a most chrysten relygyus prynce reforme the same by worde whiche is groundyd by the worde of God, by dede in schewing hymsellf the very trew mynster of God to se the worde of God mayntaynyd? This is his lyffe. This is his vertuus wayes, which althoughe as Plutarke wryttithe that Agesylayus were olde yet his excellent spryt semyd to be young, evyn so oure Henry entering fol. 35r into welfavord age schewith that by his nobill dedes / what is the offyce of a kyng by exalting the good and suppressing the evill, wherby as Agesylayus is now at this day frome so meny worldes past a quyke rememberauns, so schall oure gracyous and dere soverayne kyng a thousand yers to cum be a lyvely rememberans whiche schall never be extyncte but always more and more better then this Agesylayus had with all wrytters in perpetuall memory.

Amen.

NOTE

1 In *Of the Knowledge Which Maketh a Wise Man* (1533) Sir Thomas Elyot characterized Dionysius as 'a man of quicke & subtile wit, but therwith he was wonderfull sensuall, unstable, & wandring in sondrye affections. Delyting sometyme in voluptuous pleasures, and other tyme in gatheryng of great tresure and rychesse. ...' Quoted in F. W. Conrad, 'A Preservative Against Tyranny: the Political Theology of Sir Thomas Elyot' (unpublished Ph.D. dissertation, Johns Hopkins Univ., 1988, pp. 145-6). Conrad suggests that Elyot had Henry in mind in this description. Concerning Morley's description of Henry, Sir Geoffrey Elton has observed (private communication): 'I am sure you had to say these things about the great Henry, and I am reasonably sure that when he read them Cromwell sneered.'

APPENDIX 2

Letter of Henry Parker, Lord Morley, to Thomas Cromwell

Written on paper, 13 February 1537(?)

London: Public Record Office SP 1/143, fol. 74

My synguler good Lord after my most harty recommendacion unto youe, so do I send youe by my trusty servaunt this bringer, to pas the tyme with all in the Italyun toung, a Boke of the Cronykle of the Florantyns. The Auctor of hyt as yt apperythe in the Boke wrote yt to Clement the seventhe late Bysschop of Rome. Youre lordschip will marvell moche when ye do reade yt how he durst be so bolde to present suche a warke unto hym; For he so declaryth theyer petygrew that yf one schulde reade a hundrethe bokes he myght lake to know of theyere usurpacion whiche he schall fynde aparant in his fyrst Boke. So consequently he prosedythe to the begynyng of the Augmentaccion of the Cyte of Florans. And in the tellyng of theyre Jestes he tellythe frome the great Charlamayne whiche new redyfyed Florans most part all the Jestes of the italyans. Youre lordschip I have oftentymes harde you say hath bene conversant among them. Sene theyere factyons and maners. And so was I never. But yf they use suche fraudes, Myscheves, Treasuns, and conspyrasys, as he wryttyth that they do, I do not skant account them worthy to be nomberyd amongest Chrysten men. And forbecause that as I say sythens the great Charles the Bysschop of Rome hathe wythe all the prynces medlyd and bene now in lege with them and somtyme otherwise at war and stryf, now cursyng now blessyng, which they lyttell pas upon he so acountyth the myschef that they have usyd to mayntene theyer usurpyd power and dingnyty, that I do knowe very well youre lordship will affyrme to have redd no suche thing. At the last in the viiith boke he declaryth of the warre which the florantyns hadd agaynst the bisschop of Rome, And Farnando that tyme kyng of Naples. I think yt passys lyttell fyfty yeres sythens that war was. And how unjustly he usyd them. And forbycause the Kyng Oure Soueraigne Lordes cause and theyers be sumwhat lyke. For asmoche as agaynst all reason he dothe what in hym ys agaynst the kyng aswell by cursyng as by sowyng off devysyon with all nacyons agaynst the kyngs Magestie and the Realme. I do exort youre Lordschip to note well what the Florantyns did agaynst the Romyssche Bysschop. And how lyttle they reputyd his cursynges, what schamfull abusyons they leyde to his charge. Howe to maynteyne theyre righteus cause they callyd a Counsell of all the Bysschopes of Tuskan and causyd the prystes wyll they nyll they to do as they commandyd them. And appeled utterly frome his evyll dysposyd Court unto the generall Counsell. And this one example ys for oure Prynce so great a Declaracion of his rightfull defens, that I woold to God that not only all Inglysche men but all other nacyons hadd redd the same therby to see whyther a Cytie may resyst in theyre right the wrongs done to them by a Bysschop better than one of the most nobelyst Kynges of Crystendome. And my most especyall good Lord I most hartely pray youe to schew the very wordes unto the Kynge. For I do thynke his Majestie shall take great pleasure to see them. In conclution bycause my Letter schuld not be to tedyous to youe, in suche places as the Auctor touches any thing consernyng the Bysschop of Rome, I have notyd it with a hand or with wordes in the marjant to the intent it schuld be in a redynes to youe at all tymes in the redyng. And Farthermore this Boke off Machiavelle de principe ys surely a very speciall good thing for youre Lordschip whiche are so ny abought oure Soveraigne Lorde in Counsell to loke upon for many causys, as I suppose youre self schall judge when ye have sene the same. Praing youre Lordschip to accepte yt wythe no les good wyll then my mynde is to wyll to youe and all yours helth and honor. And when youre Lordschip schalbe at convenyent leasor I pray youe to be so good Lord unto me as to tender me in suche things as Maister Rycharde Croumwell schall sew to youre Lordschip for me. And thus I comyt youre good Lordschip to God. From Halingbury Morley, the xiii day off February.

Al your Lordschypps to commande

Harry Morley

APPENDIX 3

The Exposition and Declaration of the Psalme, Deus Ultionum Dominus, made by Syr Henry Parker knight, Lord Morley, dedicated to the Kynges Highnes

Printed in London in 1539 by Thomas Berthelet, the King's Printer, this work survives in three identical copies on paper, all in modern binding: BL, 292.a.33(2); Lambeth Palace 1553.07(3); Oxford, Bodleian Library, Mason CC.37. None of them is the presentation copy. This text follows the British Library copy.

sig. A2^r To the most high and myghty prynce, HENRY the VIII, kynge of Englande and of Fraunce, defendour of the faithe, lorde of Irelande, and in erthe supreme heed immediatly under Christe of the church of Englande, his most humble subject, Henry Parker knight, lorde Morley, wyssheth all welth and prosperitie.

If I had, most Christyan prynce, and my most dere and graciouse soveraygne lord, as Virgil saythe, an hundred mouthes, with as many tounges, and therewith as moche swete eloquence, as had the Grecian Demosthenes, or the Romayn Cicero, yet coulde not I expresse halfe the vertue, sig. A2^v halfe the rightuousnes, that is in your most royal / majestie, as in a perfecte arke of all princely goodnes and honour. For where as unto this presente tyme of your most happy reigne, this youre Empire mooste triumphant, hath ben wrongfully kept, as tributarie unto the Babylonicall seate of the Romyshe byshop, your moste sage and polytike wisedome hath benne suche, that as it maye be well thoughte, by divine inspiration, ye have taken a very kynges harte, whiche seketh, as it ought, to rule, and nat to be ruled. And hath set the Englysshe nation at fredoome and lybertie. What worthy thankes for so noble a dede, and so beneficial an acte, can your mooste bounden subjectes render unto your high majestie? We may moche better say to you, than ever sig. A3^r might the Romans unto the most / noble Emperour Augustus, that ye are not onely the noblest kynge that ever reigned over the English nation, but also *Pater patriae*, that is, the father of our countrey, one by whose vertue, lernyng, and noble courage, England is newe borne, newly brought from thraldome to freedome. For where as there is nothing more swete than libertie, nothynge more bytter than bondage, in so moche that death hath ofte ben chosen to advoyde servitude. What owe we unto you most gracious soveraigne lorde, which ar by you, as by a most natural father, the bondes broken, set out of danger, from the captivite Babylonical, so that we may say plainly as the Jewes dydde to Judith: You are our beautie, you are oure honour, you are sig. A3^v our glorie. Sci-/-pio the Affrican dyd moche for the Romayns, Codrus for the Atheniens, Epaminondas moche for the Thebans, Themistocles moch for the Grecians, Cirus moche for the Persians, Salandine moche for the Egyptians, and yet all these compared with your hyghnes, may seme almost to have done nothing at al. I therfore, most Christen king beinge a parttaker of all your inestimable benefites, have and shal always study, whyche wayes, and howe I maye, to the uttermoste of my litel and moste feble puissance, give thankes to your highnes for the same. And for as moche as I knowe my selfe unmete to do any bodily service, condigne to so vertuous and excellent a prince, yet at the least I shal gyve unto your hyghnes that thing which aswel the feble, sig. A4^r / as the stronge maye gyve, that is to saye, hartye prayers to God, for the preservation of so just, so mercyfull, and so faythefull a kynge. I than offer unto your hyghnesse this newe yere, dere and dred soveraygne lorde, this psalme of king David, *Deus ultionum dominus*, with a briefe declaration of the same, moste humbly praienge your high accustomed goodnes, to accepte it in gree, and not to regarde the rudenes, but rather the faithfulnes of me your subject, that wylleth with the very harte, as he writeth, goodnes, and all goodnesse to you: And to youre ennemye the 4v Babylonicall byshoppe of Rome, reproufe, shame, and utter ruine. /

Deus ultionum dominus, deus ultionum libere egit.

O Lorde God almighty, that haste made with thy worde, heven and erthe, with all the beaultie thereof, and doest with the same, fede all kynde of beastes, in tyme requisite,[1] and haste put under mannes subjection, beastes in the erthe, byrdes in the ayre, and fyshe in the see, so that he is lytell lesse in dignite than angelles, and at the last crowned hym with glorie and honour,[2] as thou hast done our moste victorious prince, makynge hym thyn annointed king to rule under the, 5r the Empyre of Englande,[3] whiche hathe, doothe, / and intendeth alwayes to defende thy worde: We pray the, with devoute hartes, to assist hym, in suppressynge the prowde heed of the poluted citie of Babylon, the Romysshe bysshop. *Deus ultionum dominus*, that is to say, thou that woldest we shulde committe al vengynge to the, revenge us ageynst this serpent, that wolde, to maynteyne his power, devoure thy holy worde, if his myght were as great as his malyce.

Exaltare qui iudicas terram, redde retributionem superbis.

It is not to me unknowen, my savyor and redemptor Jesu, that whan thy holy wyll is, in lyke maner as thou diddest defende the people of Israel, by thy duke and leader Moyses, from the 5v prowd and obstinate / Pharao, Josua from the XXXI kinges, Gedeon from the Amolytes, Sampson from the Phylistiens, David frome Golyas, Ezechias from the Assirians, Asa frome the Ethiopians, Judas Machabeus from Antiochus and Nycaor,[4] Constantine from Maxentius, Theodosius from Eugenius, the noble Henry the Fyfte frome the Frenche men, the wyse Henry the Seventh from the tyrant kynge Rycharde, with infinite mo: all be it they semed to be inferior to the innumerable multitude of their adversaries, yet thou overthrewest them, in exaltyng thy power. Gyve than my lorde, and my helper, power to our prince, to thruste downe this byshop of Rome, not only his adversarie, but chiefe ennemy to thy glorie, which seketh by tyrannous / 6r presumption, to bryng in his subjection, all pryncis of the worlde. I cry to the good lorde, *Exaltare, qui iudicas terram*, that is to saye, Be thou lyfte up on hygh, and ascende up to thy seate, that arte the judge of the universall erthe, and render to the proude bysshop as he hathe deserved.

Usquequo peccatores domine, usquequo peccatores gloriabuntur?

All be it mercyfulle Jesu, thou dost permytte by thy secrete jugement, evyll persons to prosper, I my lorde and God, that knowe not, but as man knoweth, saye to the, O good God, howe longe shalte thou suffre, I say from the botom of my hart, howe longe wylt thou suffre this seate of 6v Sathan, to glorifie it selfe in evill doinge? What / great damage to al Christendom, and what great mischief wrought Honorius agaynst Frederike the good emperour in his journey ageynste the Turkes? This wycked bysshoppe sente letters to the Soudan, shewynge hym whyche wayes he myght distroy the Chrysten armye. What shulde I say of Bonifacius the Third, of Alysander the VI, of Julius the Seconde, the greatte thefe of the worlde, of Leo the Tenthe, of Clemens, and nowe of Paule, that dyvellyshlye alway go about to set one Christen prynce agaynst an other, onely to maynteyne theyr usurped and tyrannous estate? *Usquequo peccatores domine, usquequo peccatores gloriabuntur?* How long shal such proude prelates prosper? Howe longe 7r tyme wolte thou suf-/-fre theym?

Effabuntur et loquentur iniquitatem, loquentur omnes: quia operantur iniustitiam.

Those that be adherentes to his cursed courte, they murmure, they grudge, and do that in them is, to resyste the holy zele, whiche our kinge hath, to set forth the holy worde of God.[5] But our prynce, that hath Goddis worde fervently and moste constantly fyxed in his hart, wyll with his assistens, persever agaynst all them, that wolde ought do to the contrary. And as the royal kyng David, although he were rebuked of his father, his bretherne, and his frendes, let not to go naked, to fyght against gret Golyas: even so let them saye all, that do evyll, what they wyll, our prince woll not cesse to resyst with / all his power, the obstinate wylle and usurped authorite of the proude byshop of Rome.

sig. A7v

Populum tuum domine humiliaverunt: et haereditatem tuam vexaverunt.

And not withoute cause oure prince dothe and woll withstande the malycious power of this synfulle seate of Rome. For sythens the tyme that Sylvester chalenged by gyfte that that Constantyne never gave hym,[6] he and his successours, enjoyenge temporall possessions, felle frome thy holye faithe, whiche before was spredde by thy apostelles througheout the unyversall worlde. And as it had great successe, and dayly increased in all countreyes more and more, as longe as they that were in the / apostels place, folowed theyr humilitie, povertie, and obedience: so by the pride, covetousnes, and tyranny of this Babylonicall monster, it hath lefte Asia and Affrike, and scasely remaineth in Europa, a small corner of the world. Wherfore this may be well sayde, They have put downe thyn electe people, and they have vexed thyn inheritance. Who ought not with al his hole hart, to bewaile this piteous decaye? Or who wylle not be glad to resyst the malyce of those that be the causers therof?

sig. A8r

Viduam et advenam interfecerunt, et pupillos occiderunt.

As this decayer of the monarchye of Christendome is for the moste parte occupied in greattest mischeves, as in stryvynge ayenst / truthe and Goddis gospell, in vanysshynge true religyon, and settynge up hypocrisy and ydolatry: in hurlynge downe al good order, and obedience, soo sometyme that all men and women to, maye have juste cause to hate hym, he commeth from the grettist to the smal, and falleth to the spoylyng of wydowes, to the slaughter of straungers, to the murder of orphanes. And as he and his somtime sturre up themperour ayenst the French kynge, somtyme the Frenche men ayenst the Imperyals, brefely eche kingdome in other neckes, so somtyme they come to lower matters, and sette one private man to poyson an other, one cytezen to murder an other. In so moch that men thynke, fewer Chrysten men to be alive at this day, than they, for the / maynteynynge of their quarelle, have caused to dye by fyre, swerde, hunger, and pestilence.

sig. A8v

sig. B1r

Et dixerunt, non videbit dominus, nec intelliget deus Iacob.

They perceiving, that al thing came to passe as they wolde have it, and that the blynde worlde beleved, they might pull out of heven, and throwe into helle, whom they lusted, handeled the mattier in suche sorte, that who soo ever sayde the contrarie, had all princis in his toppe, redy with the swerd, to take theyre parte. Anone they were exalted in such pride, that as Lucyfer dydde, they presumed to pitche their trone equal with God,[7] and letted not to boste, to bragge, and to say: God shall nat see oure abusion, the God of Jacob shall / nat perceyve wheraboute we go.[8]

sig. B1v

Intelligite insipientes in populo, et stulti aliquando sapite.

But our prynce, most mercyful savior Jesu, whiche is thy Christ, that is to say, thyn annoynted kyng, even as his regal majesty, requireth of hym, ceasseth nat to warne all people, specially those, that be symple and unlettred, to gyve them monition by the worde of God, to be wyse, to take hede, howe they have fallen into extreme darknes, in gyvynge credite to his erronious doctrine, and fals traditions, in leanyng to moche to his lawes, and commaundementes: and wisheth all men to trust in God, whiche woll the deathe of no synner, but all menne to be saved/[9]

B2r And yf they do not this, they fall clene from / God, unto a frayle temporal mans arme, whiche is but fleshe, and shall come to duste.

Qui plantavit aurem, non audiet, aut qui finxit oculum, non considerat?

He that consydereth welle with hym selfe, the wonderfull workes of God, must nedes see, that he is alone almighty. He that marketh howe faythfull he hath bene in all his promyses, can not but thynke, that he alone is to be trusted? He that seeth what power he hath given to other thynges, must nedes graunt, that he hym selfe hath all power. He created all thynges, he made the eares to hear, and the eyes to see, now, is it lyke, that he, whiche sette eares uppon youre B2v hedes, and gave you power to here / can be deafe, and here nothynge hym selfe: And if he be any thing quycke of herynge, shall nat the voice of the innocentes bloud, shed by your crueltie, which crieth still, at the laste come up to his eares? Can they lament styll, and never be herde? Shall he that hath set eies in your forheades, and gyven you power to see, not se the great abuses, the fals wrestynge of his holy worde, the wycked desyre that this papisticall sort hath, to maynteine theyr pompe, pride, and tyranny? Shal he here them, and se al these your mischevous intentes, and not see you one day punyshed?

Qui corripuit gentes non arguet, qui docet hominem scientiam.

B3r Shal nat he, that chaungeth all worldly monarches, and dothe / transpose, as Daniel the prophete saythe, realmes, countreyes, and empires,[10] nowe to rule, nowe to be ruled, shall not he hurle downe this seate of Sathanas? He changed the dominion of the Assirians, and gave it to the Medes, frome the Medes to the Persians, from the Persians unto the Greekes, frome the Grekes unto the Romaines, and wolle not he brynge the proude and usurped estate of these, that ought to serve, from the noughty, to naughte at all? or to saye, as it oughte to be, restore it rightfully to theym, that a longe season have ben wrongfully kepte from it? Thou arte styll that same selfe God, that taughtest Paul thyne apostell, the secrete hyd science of scripture. Thou art he that B3v dydste soo illuminate the mynde of thyne / electe and tenderly beloved disciple John, that he, whyche before was a fyssher man, utterly unlerned, nowe excellynge the reste of the Evangelistes, uttered manye hygh mysteries, and suche as the other thre left untouched, writing that wonderfulle piece of worke, *In principio erat verbum.*[11] No mervail, if thou that taughtest the unlerned suche hygh mysteries, teache the lerned at length, to knowe the false doctrine, the wylye wayes, the abhomynable hypocrysye, the detestable ydolatrye of this wycked monster of Rome. Can he that teacheth the hethen to folow thinges juste and righte in the face of the lawe, suffre the Christians, stil to blonder, styll to be in blyndnes, styll to be seduced by this Babylonycall B4r strompette? /

Dominus scit cogitationes hominum, quoniam vanae sunt.

I myght greatly mervayle, ye and more then mervayl, how this chaire of pestilence[12] coulde so long stande in honour, savynge that I knowe verye welle, bothe to what folyes the vayne cogytations of men bryng them, and howe lyghtly the people are illuded by superstition, and colour of religion.

The Jewes sometyme thyn electe people, not withstandynge they sawe with theyr eyes the red sees devyded, to gyve theym passage, water sprynge oute of the harde stoone to quenche theyr extreme thurste, meate descende downe from heaven to fede them whan they were full hungrye, B4v yet whyle Moyses was in the mount Sinai, / they forgettynge al these myracles and benefites of God set up a calf, and toke it for their God.[13] I myght mervayle, and greatly mervayle, that the Christen people coulde be so fonde, to leave the word of God, and his hevenly doctrine, and folow this wicked byshop of Rome, and his dyvellyshe dreames. But as this is not the fyrst evyl change, that foolyshe man hath made, soo let us assure our selfes, that vayn cogitations dure nat ever, the seduced tourne ageyne, whan good guydes shewe them the way.

Beatus homo, quem tu erudieris domine, et de lege tua docueris eum.

Blessed mayste thou be callyd, moste Christen kyng[14] HENRY the VIII supreme heed of the sig. B5r churche / of Englande. Blessed arte thou, whome God hath taught, to espie out the peryllous doctryne of the byshop of Rome, wherby the people of Englande ar brought from darkenes to lyght, from errour to the hygh way of righte knowlege, from daunger of dethe eternall, to life that never endeth, to be shorte, even from hel to heven. By the, O sage kynge, the worde of God, that in tyme paste was cloked and hyd to the elders of thy realme, is now manyfest to chylderne, that ceasse not to prayse with their mouthes God, and his holy worde. For the mayntenance wherof, most royall kynge, thy prayse shall styll continue uppon erthe, and than depart, whan all menne have taken theyr leave of it. Happy, happy is that man, good lorde, whom thou sig. B5v tea-/-chest, happy whom thou endewest with thy doctrine.

Ut mitiges ei a diebus malis, donec fodiatur peccatori fovea.

Albeit O lorde, thou hast long forborne, and suffred this greatte deceyvour of the worlde, this Romayne bysshop, to reygne after a cruell sorte, proudely commaundynge all princis, all estates to obeye his lustes, yet thy goodnesse be ever praysed, thou haste at the last reysed up a prince, and by him digged a pytte, to hurle this wycked wretche in, where bothe he, his false doctrine, his hypocrisye, and idolatrie, shall as oure truste is, be buried for ever. This pitte hath ofte bene sig. B6r a makynge, many have dygged and lefte of, er ever the pytte hath ben fully made. /

Noble HENRY the Eyght is he whom, we trust, thou wolt always ayde and presorve, not only untyll all popyshe power be brought into the diche here in Englande, but also untylle all Christian nations shall have soo covered this dyche, that Romish power be never able to ryse ageyne.

Quia non repellet dominus plebem suam: et haereditatem suam non derelinquet.

Let England I say, put other nations in memorie, of the great falle, that the estate of Christendome toke, whan kynges began to obey the lewde doctrine of priestis, whan pristes presumptuously toke upon theym to rule Goddis worde after theyr fantasyes, and not theyr sig. B6v lustes accordyng to his / lawes. Let fortunate Englande whiche nowe, in spyte of tyrantes tethe, hathe recovered her inheritaunce, be an exaumple to the reste of Christendom, that Goddis wyll is not to forsake his people, to see their right inheritance wrongfully kept from them. God hateth all suche as usurpe upon his anoynted kynges. Awake Christen kynges awake, Englande blowethe the trompe, and sheweth you all, how ye may avoyde bondage, and howe, accordinge to your title and name, ye may as kynges rule and reygne. God chose not you his kynges, for to be reuled, but to rule.[15] Ye maye have offycers under you, as many as you wyll: beynge kynges, sig. B7r you oughte to have none above you. /

Quoadusque iustitia convertatur in iuditium, et qui iuxta illa omnes qui recto sunt corde.

God a longe season suffered Pharao, to vexe his people, to heape affliction uppon affliction, and yet at the laste he mette with hym, and in a day was even with hym for all the injuries he hadde done to his people. He forbare a great whyle, and yet a tyme came that he wolde suffer no longer, but converted justyce to judgement, and rightuously executed suche sentence ayenst him, as he had long before differred. The tyme is at hande, that Christe shall for their great abhomination se these tyrantes at Rome turned out of their triumphant thrones, wherin they syt sig. B7v as gods, treadinge downe the lawes of Christ, / settynge up theyr decrees and decretals, as rules, or rather misrules, to disordre almooste all that God had welle ordred before.[16] The tyme is at hande, that they shalbe brought from pride to mekenesse, from superfluities to honeste povertie, from voluptuous luste to sober and chaste lyfe, from haute and imperious commaundementes to humble and lowely obedience, from feined holynes and hypocrisie to godlynes and ryghte religion, and than shall we have good cause to saye, as Saynt John sayde in the Apocalyps, *Cecidit Babylon, cecidit Babylon civitas magna*, that is, the greatte Babylon, the greatte citie of Babylon is fallen downe, she is fallen, that made al nations dronke with the wyne of her hooryshe fornication.[17] /

Quis consurget mihi adversus malignantes? aut quis stabit mecum adversus operantes iniquitatem?

Lyke as the excellente kynge and prophete David, greatly mervaylynge, dydde demaunde, who shulde ryse with hym to subdewe evyll doers, workers of wyckednesse, so may our moste noble and Christen kynge saye, who ought not to rise with me, to the vanquishyng of this monstruous hydra, considering the innumerable mischeves, the civile discord, the cruel warres, the effusion of Christian bloudde, that hath bene shedde by the practises of these Romayn bishops? Who hath not harde, how these good prelates, have set princis subjectes ayenst their soverai-/-nes, moch contrarie to the doctrine of Peter and Paul, which expressely commaunde, and woll all subjectes to obeye their pryncis, under peyne of perpetuall damnation.[18]

They ceasse not to encomber all pryncis realmes with Sedytion, where they perceyve any thyng in hande, touchynge their refourmation, and wol kynges styl suffer such sowers of hatrede and mischiefe, styll to have to do in their realms? Ought they not rather to give ere to our moste noble prince, sayenge with David, *Quis consurget mihi adversus malignantes? aut quis stabit mecum adversus operantes iniquitatem?* Who wolle ryse with me ayenst these wicked men? what prince wolle folowe, to take parte with me, ageinst these moste / ungodly persons.

Nisi quia dominus adiuvit me, paulominus habitasset in inferno anima mea.

If there were none that wolde folowe the godly wayes, and further the vertuous procedynges of the most worthy Henry our kyng, yet God, that ever doth assiste and exalte the good, resyste and withstande the proude,[19] shall under the shadowe of his holy wynges defende all rightuous causes. They that seke rightuousnes may ofte be broughte into manye straytes, moch trouble, great distresses, but yet if the confidence and trust, that they oughte to have in God, fayle theym nat, they are ever sure to escape. Davyd was broughte into many dangers, and yet evermore / delyvered. And who knoweth nat what jeopardies the kinges highnes hath escaped only by the helpe of God?[20]

Si dicebam motus est pes meus misericordia tua domine adiuvabat me.

The kynges hyghnesse maye say, as wel as ever David might, when so ever I said to the, my fote slypped, or fayled me, my frendis or subjectis, whom I entierly trusted and loved, were not as I toke them, thy mercy, good lord, alwayes did helpe me, and kepte me evermore from fallynge. The bysshoppe of Rome hath sought many wayes, to make his gracis feete slyppe: but God be thanked, his highnesse standethe everye daye more surer than other, every daye more faster / than other.[21]

Secundum multitudinem dolorum meorum in corde meo consolationes tuae laetificarent animam meam.

It is not to be douted, but his highnesse moste tender and gentil harte, felte great dolour, whan he sawe suche to have intended hym moste hygh displeasure, whom he toke to be his trustiest servauntes,[22] and as the dolours were greatte, soo muste his gracis gladnesse be greatter, to see the wakynge eye of God, so redy to undo his enemies, so prest to preserve and defend his highnes. His wysedome, hath devoured a great multitude of peynes, folowyng the fervent studye and desyre he hathe to maynteyne the word of God, ayenst the proud / Babylonicall byshop, and yet the consolation and comfortes, which he taketh by the overthrowe of soo intollerable a monster, of suche an ennemy to truthe and Goddis honour, is farre greatter than ever were his peynes.

Nunquid adhaeret tibi sedes iniquitatis? quia fingis laborem in praecepto.

Can the seate of wyckednesse, be joyned with the good lorde? Is it to be thought, that thou chosest hym to thy vycar, whiche worketh all thinges in maner contrary to thy wylle and pleasure? Wolt nat thou declare one daye in other realmes, as well as thou haste done in this noble realme of England, that thy wyll is, the bysshoppe of Rome, which abuseth the pretense / of thy commaundementes, to the settynge forthe of his abhomynable doctryne, be taken to be as he is, thyne ennemye, a deceyvour of as many as truste hym? He hathe seditiousely swarved frome that state, and degree, whiche thou settest hym in. He is made of an humble sheparde, an ymage for pryncis to kisse his shoes, wol nothing move the good God, that thou styl with suche pacience suffereth hym thus to abuse thy pacience? Moyses coulde hurle Chore, Dathan, and Abiron into helle, for disseveryng them selves from his governance.[23] And shall not other princis brynge this runnagate, this strayeng byshop, under the yocke of obedience, as Henry the Eyght hath done? Helpe them, good lorde, as thou haste holpen hym, open their / eyes, as thou haste doone his, the popysshe power is utterlye confounded.[24]

sig. C3r

sig. C3v

Captabunt animam iusti, et sanguinem innocentem condemnabunt.

He and his never cesse to seke the distruction of the rightuous, styll condemnyng the innocentes blod. Here if a man wolde but reherse, howe many they have condemned by fals processe, chargynge theym with errors, that died for truthes sake, he shuld find a great slaughter, a great quantitie of innocentes bloud drawen by these bloud suckers. But he that lusteth to put in writynge, what bloudde hathe ben shedde, what a noumber of men have dyed at suche tymes, as these have set Christen princis one / against an other, he shulde be able to justifie, that gret mylles myght be driven with bloude, if that that hath ben shedde coulde runne together. A piteouse case, that the innocent shoulde be taken for the gyltie, a worlde to be lamented, that the wycked shoulde sende the godly to be slayn, even as lambes in the fleshambles. Our lorde be thanked, Englande is nowe oute of that case, and none slayn, in especiall by proces and judgemente, but suche as are unworthy to lyve.[25]

sig. C4r

Et factus est mihi dominus in refugium, et deus meus in adiutorium spei mei.

Men knowe, what wayes this byshop and his adherentes, have sought and dayly seke, to hurt noble Henry the VIII. Men se, howe / his hyghnesse maye stylle saye, as David sayde, The lord is he, that I fly unto for helpe, he is the comforte of my hope, he is myn hoole truste and shote anker. If he continue his aide and succour toward me, I woll nothynge doubte, but as I have passed over the Babylonycall walles: that soo one day, other princis woll come to the sackynge of this harlot, that hath so longe deluded them, I truste every byrde woll take his fether, and that the prowde crowe of Esope, beinge ones naked, shal make the worlde to laughe, whiche a longe season hath made it to wayle.

sig. C4v

Et reddet illis iniquitatem ipsorum, et in malitia eorum disperdet eos, disperdet illos dominus deus noster. /

sig. C5r

He hath played the tyraunte to many yeres, prowdely vexynge whome he lusted, sparyng neither kynge ne keysar. God, styrred by the synnes of the people, and angry with the ygnorance of princis, hath suffered hym thus to reygne and rage over them both, a longe[26] season, and yet sufferethe him to rule in many nations, both as moche as ever he dydde, and to as moche their losse and damage, as he and his pyrates, I wolde have sayde prelates, can devyse.

God is a God fulle of compassion, and one that longe suffreth, stylle lookynge for and desyrynge amendement. But where he seeth no hope of redresse, he payeth in one houre all dettes. Assuredly, yf we woll use, the knowlege, which God hath sent us, to his honoure, / the time is come, that he intendeth to execute his ryghtuouse sentence ayenst this sect of Sathan,

sig. C5v

ageinst this dronken strompette, soused in the bloudde of sayntes and martyrs. All the worlde shall crye out, and saye, Woo woo to the, thou greatte Cytie of Babylon, thou myghty stronge citie, soo buylded uppe with blyndenesse of people: the houre is come, thy judgement is given, though yet not executed.[27] They that have bene enryched by the, shal stande afarre of, wepyng and wailinge. The kynges of the erthe shal nowe lament, that ever they medlyd with thy marchaundyse: lamente, that ever they toke thy parte: lamente, that they consented with the, to
C6ʳ the vexation, trouble, prisonment, banyshynge, spoylynge, and sleing of innocent-/-tes. They shall nowe stande afar of: they wolle noo longer favour thy wycked doinges. They woll sorowe, that they soo longe have suffred the, and be moche aferde, leste God be lykewyse angrye with them. And so thou lefte alone, forsaken of all princys, hated of all the godly and good men, shalt wofully come to a myserable ende. The lord our God hym selfe shall brynge the to shame, sorowe, ruine, and utter confusion. /

C7ʳ Londini in aedibus Thomae Bertheleti typis impress.
Cum privilegio ad imprimendum solum.

ANNO M.D.XXXIX

NOTES

1 A reminiscence of Ps. 144:15-16, 'Oculi omnium in te sperant et tu das escam illorum in tempore oportnuo. Aperis manum tuam et imples omne animal benedictione', which was perhaps more familiar to Morley through its frequent use as a grace before meals.

2 Ps. 8:6-9 (cf. Hebrews 2:6-8, though the reference to beasts, birds, and fish shows that Morley is citing the psalm).

3 An obvious allusion to the 'imperial theme' of Henrician propaganda, sounded most famously in the opening of the Act of Appeals, that 'this realm of England is an empire'. 24 Henry VIII, c. 12, in e.g. *The Tudor Constitution*, ed. by G. R. Elton, 2nd edn (Cambridge, 1982), p. 353.

4 See Exodus 3-15 (Moses), Joshua 12:7-24 (the 31 kings), Judges 7 (Gideon), Judges 15-16 (Samson), 1 Sam. 17 (David and Goliath), 2 Kings 19 (Hezekiah and the Assyrians), 2 Paralipomenon [Chronicles] 14:12 (Asa), and 2 Machabees 8-9 (Judas Machabeus).

5 The 'word of God' was a slogan which featured prominently in the propaganda of the 1530s, alluding not only to Henry VIII's express promise and eventual delivery of an officially sanctioned vernacular Bible to his people, but also to the frequently stated view that this word of God served to endorse the royal claim to ecclesiastical supremacy. For further discussion of this point, see Richard Rex, 'The Crisis of Obedience: God's Word and Henry's Reformation', *Historical Journal* 39 (1996), pp. 863-94 (pp. 889-93).

6 The Donation of Constantine, a document which purported to record the gift to Pope Sylvester I by the Emperor Constantine of jurisdiction over a large swathe of the western Roman empire, although occasionally challenged in the Middle Ages on grounds of its invalidity according to Roman Law, nevertheless retained a good deal of credence until the time of the Renaissance. Its invalidity was conclusively demonstrated by the great fifteenth-century humanist Lorenzo Valla on legal, historical, and philological grounds. His exposé of the Donation was translated into English and published by William Marshall in 1534, apparently with Thomas Cromwell's encouragement, and thus played its part in the general English campaign against the papacy in the 1530s. See *A treatyse of the donation or gyfte and endowment of possessyons gyven and graunted unto Sylvester pope of Rhome by Constantyne emperour of Rome* (London, n.d [1534], STC 5641). Morley is obviously aware of Marshall's translation, although his insinuation that the forgery was the work of Sylvester himself, which adds an edge to his argument, is inconsistent with Valla's identification of anachronisms in the text.

7 Isaiah 14:12-13.

8 This is the substance of the claim that the papacy was Antichrist, although Morley avoids the explicit identification here. The identification of the papacy as Antichrist was often made in Henrician propaganda, and was privately made by Henry himself, but was by no means the virtual dogma of the Church of England that it became under Elizabeth and James I.

9 Ezechiel 18:23. This was a major text in the theological controversies of the sixteenth century, the crux of Erasmus's defence of free will against Luther, and thenceforward the basis of most attacks on the harsher doctrines of double predestination formulated by some varieties of the Reformation.
10 Daniel 2:21.
11 John 1.1.
12 An allusion to the 'cathedra pestilentiae' in which, according to Ps. 1:1 (Septuagint tradition), the blessed do not sit.
13 Exodus 14:15-29 (Red Sea), 17:6-7 (water from the rock), 16 (manna from heaven), and 32 (golden calf).
14 'Rex Christianissimus' was the traditional appellation of the kings of France. Henry had sought for its transferral to the English crown by the papacy, and indeed Julius II had conditionally granted his wish in 1512. See J. J. Scarisbrick, *Henry VIII* (London, 1968), p. 33. Morley also hints at English ambitions on this title in the *Miracles of the Sacrament*. See below, Appendix 7.
15 Compare Richard Morison, *An Invective ayenste the Great andDetestable Vice, Treason* (London, 1539; STC 18111-3), sig. D5r: 'God hathe made hym, as al his noble progenitours of right ought to have ben, a fulle kynge, that is, a ruler, and nat ruled in his owne kyngedome, as other were.' This is the work which is bound together with Morley's in BL, 292.a.33.
16 This again is the doctrine of the 'papal antichrist', albeit still stopping just short of the explicit appellation.
17 Apocalypse [Revelation] 18:2.
18 1 Peter 2:13-17 and Romans 13, the twin pillars of obedience doctrine, almost invariably cited or quoted in Henrician propaganda.
19 James 4:6.
20 This seems to allude to the so-called 'Exeter conspiracy' of late 1538, the aftermath of which was characterized by such indefinite invocations of untold dangers narrowly and providentially escaped.
21 The reference to the machinations of the pope seems to allude either to the papal role in the Franco-Imperial peace of 1538 or to the proceedings which commenced in Rome in autumn that year and culminated in the papal excommunication of Henry.
22 Probably an allusion to those members of the Privy Chamber and others implicated in the so-called 'Exeter plot' in the winter of 1538-9.
23 Numbers 16. Morison appeals to the same example, *Invective*, sig. C5r.
24 Morison expresses similar hopes that other princes will imitate Henry in repudiating papal authority. See his *Invective*, sig. D6r.
25 The difficulty of the argument here is apparent to the author himself. The discussion of 'false process', of death for the sake of truth, and bloodshed threatens to remind readers of things perhaps best forgotten: Fisher, More, the Carthusians, and perhaps even his, Morley's, own son-in-law, George Boleyn.
26 The phrase 'a longe' is doubled in the original.
27 Apocalypse [Revelation] 18:10.

APPENDIX 4

Morley's Translation of the *Somnium Scipionis*

Written by the scribe of Chatsworth, Devonshire Collection MS, and presented between 1548 and 1553.

London, British Library, Royal MS 18.A.LX, fol. 1r

To the ryght highe and exellent prynces, the lady Mary, suster to oure moste redoubted and victoriouse sovereign lorde, \Kyng/ Edwarde the syxt, your humble oratoure Henry Parcar, knyght, lorde Morley, wyssheth to your grace all prosperouse fortune, with encreasce of vertue.

Moste noble prynces, I do ymagyne that ye wyll sumwhat mervell that I do present this yer to your goode grace this litle worke of Tullius Cicero, of my translation into the Englishe tonge, that was accustomed, allways afore this present tyme, either to send youe sum notable worke concernynge sum christen doctours wrytynge in the Laten tonge, or ells sum of their workes by me / [. 1v] translated into \our/ tounge, as my rude knowledge coulde do it. To this, with your patience, moste gentle prynces, if ye so mervell, I wyll aforehande, with all humble reverence, excuse me why that, as saide is, I present to your vertuouse handes thys Tullius Cicero worke, intitled in the Laten *Somnium Scipionis*, in Englishe, *The Dreame of Scipion*, surely to this ententt: yf parcace that, when your goode grace had at your pleasure redde it, as I thynke that in the Laten ye have allredy seene yt, that the booke myght be seene of sum of those that by their lyfe shew theymselfes rather to be of Epicurs secte, then of Tullius secte, whiche proveth many ways and with wonderfull wordes the soule of man to be immortall and after this lyfe, lyvynge vertuously, that ther is a place in heaven, sure and certeyn, where ther is beatitude eternall. And I do professe, noble lady, that I, that am a Christen man, am muche worthy of blame, that seynge a paynymme that knew not Chryste nor his blessed religion to folow vertue so as Tully dyd, and I, taught by Chrystes wordes, so often fall from vertue into vyce. But allthoughe I confesse me so to do, and have done, yett I thank that eternall God I never had in my hert, nor wyll have, any false Faith to thynke otherwyse, but that, to theym that beleve well and in tyme amende their faltes, but that suche shall have joy eternall, and contrary, that beleve otherwyse, payne in hell everlastynge, as to my poore understandyng this moste eloquent paynyme playnly declareth. Then, exellente prynces, this is not for youe to looke uppon, that so passys your honorable days, and with suche vertue, that fame telleth it frome the easte to the west, but for theym that muche commende vertue and folow it nothynge at all. And I am not ignoraunt but the wordes of Cicero ar so wonderfull, and the sense in many places so diffuse, that it passeth my learnynge or capacyte to put it in oure speache, as it shulde be; but brifly, if your goode grace be pleased with it, whome [. 2r] my studye is allwais, next our moste gratiouse leage lorde the kynge, your deare brother, / above all other ladyes in the worlde to please, that no persones ells wylbe offended therwith. Forasmuche as I have doone in the translatynge the best I can and woll gladly have don it better, to that entent that all those that be the kynges your brother subjectes myght not onely heere it, but also folowe and understand it, as well as the noble Romayne Macrobius that dyd expounde it. For to conclude, I doubte not but that yow, noble and vertuous prynces, shall ryghte well accepte my goode hert and wyll, and excuse in this my faultes. And I shall pray to Cryste continually to preserve your vertuouse lyfe to Nestor lyfe,[1] and after this transitory and troubleouse sea to brynge youe to the courte celestiall for youre merytes. Amen.

Appendix 4

The dreme of Sypyon, taken owt of the syxte boke of Cicero, intytlyd *De republyca*.

<1.1> When that I was cume into Africa, then Anlio Manlio consul and I being trubyn of the fol. 2v Forth Legion, ther was nothing that more delightid me then to go se the kyng Masinissa, to owre famyly by just cawse / a sure and a most loving frind.

<1.2> To whom whan I was cume, the olde man embrasid me whith weping teres and, within a litle spase, after lifting up his ies to heven, said, 'I thanke the high sonn and all the feloship celestiall that, or I pas from this lyfe, I do se with these ies Publius Cornelius Scipio, whois name to here rejoyshith my hart and shall, forasmouche as ought of my remembraunce shall never slyde the goodnes of that most invicte gentilman.' And this donne, I demaundid hym of the state of his kyngdome, and he me, of the state of owre commonwelthe; and thus, mouch wordes said, as well of his part as of myne, we consumyd the daye.

<1.3> And after the regall preparement of soper, we continuid owre talking most part of the night, and alwayes the olde man speking of the valiant Affrican in souche wise that, not only his wordes but also his dedes, he remembrid them all. Afterward, when we went to rest, the wery jurney that I had and the long wache withall cawsid me to slepe faster than I was accustomyd to do.

<1.4> Then to me, as I beleve by the means of the communycacion that we had togyther that night, I do imagyn that the mynd thereof and the talkyng came to souche effect that it pretendid sume thing lyke to that whiche Ennius writh of Omer, which was accustomid, that he spake of, being awakid, in his slepe he spake of the sam dreming.[2] In like maner, Scipion Affrican shewid hymselfe to me, in that forme that, by his image, whiche I knew passingly well, I did parceyve in very dede that it was the selfe same parson. And the sight of hym sumwhat made me afraid and abasshid, untill that tyme that he bade me cumme unto hym and \not/ to drede hym, but willid me to kepe well in memory his sayinges and wordes, all whiche wordes ar thes.

fol. 3r <2.1> 'Seist thow not', sayes he, 'yender citie, whiche, being constraynid by me to obey the people of Rome, how it begynnys and / anewe to stere warre and battayle agayne, and will not be in quiet and in rest?' And thus saying, me thought he shewid me from a high <and> a noble plase, full of rutilant starres, the citie of Cartage. 'Whiche sayid citie, thow, being but a yong captayne, or two yeres be passid, shall fynially overtorne and deface, whereby that surname shal be gyven to the, as itt were by inerytaunce from me, to be namyd Scipio Affrycan, and whan thow hast vanquyshid Cartage and triumfyd therefore, and by common consent of the people of Rome creatid sensor and electid legate to Egipte, to Syria, to Asia, and to Grecia, and afterward being chosen agayne consull, shall bring a most dangerus battayle to good successe and vanquiche the strong town of Numancy.

<2.2> 'And for thes great enterprisis, shalt be carriid triumphantly in a chariet into Rome. Yet for all this thy glory, thow shalt fynd, by the parswasion of thy nevyes, the commonwelth in gret troble and vexasion. In whiche sayd troble, my Scipio, thow must shew thy light of thy mynd and thy excellent wit and counsell, albeit that I do well see that tyme to be doughtfull and, as it were, predestinate. Yet no<t>withstondyng, when thine age shall cumme by the course of the sunne to eight tymes seven, whiche makyth in nomber fyftey and syx yeres complete, a tyme for the predestynat, the hole state of the citey shall rest in thy governaunce, as in that man in whome the hole commonwelth shall depend; and to this thow shalt be electid dictator, and deme and dispose all thinges at thy pleasure, provydid that it be thy chaunce to scape the wykyd handes of thine adversaries and enymys.'

<2.3> Now when that Lelyus, with thes wordes, had made a gret owghtcrye, with other that fol. 3v were there also present, Scipio, as me thought, soberly smylyng, prayid them not to / awake me ought of my dreme, but willid me and them to here the rest what he wolde saye, whiche was this.

<3.1> 'To the entent,' sayes he, 'thow mayst be the more prone and glade to defende the commonwelthe of thy countre, know it is sure and serten, for thos \that have prosperid there commonwele/, there is a plase in heven ordeynyd, where shouche blessid parsons have

everlasting beatitude. For there is nothing more exceptable to that prinsly God selestiall, whiche rulyth all this world, than the councellis and congregacions of men rightfully and justly governyd, whiche commonly we call cities, whois rulers, justly ruling, being departed from this world, revert hither.'

<3.2> With thes wordes, I myselfe, albeit that I was aferde, as well for daunger of dethe, as also of the false conspiracy of them that were co<n>versant abought me, yet I axid hym whether he or my father Pallus lyvyd, ye or naye, whiche we that lyve in the world thinke that they be clene extynct. Whereunto he aunserd and saide that, for truth, they lyvid and were paste from the bandes of their bodies, yeven as from and (*sic*) obscure and darke preson, and he saide also that owre lyfe, which we call a lyfe, was non other but a very deth, and, 'for becawse thow shouldes credit me, lo, behold where thy father Pallus commyth to the'.

<3.3> Which, as sone as I sawe hym, there fell from my ies a flud of teres, but he, imbrasing me and kyssyng, forbed me to wepe ony more. And I than, as sone as I had oppressid my lamentacion and might speke to hym, sayd in this wise. 'I pray the, most best and most holy father, if it be so as I do here Sipion Affrican tell, whi do I tary here on the erthe and not rather hast me to cumme where that ye be?'

<3.4> 'Not so', sayde he, 'it behovyth the to do, for onles that he, who is the lorde of this 4[r] temple / and all that thow doist se, do delyver the from the bandes of this thy body, it is impossible for the to enter this plase. For men were creatid by this condycion and law, for to defend and kepe that globe, which thow seist in the myddyst of this temple, that is namyd the erthe, and to this is gyven a soll, of thos everlasting fyers whiche you name planettes and starris, which, being round and globus, anymatid with devyne myndes, accomplysshe there sircuitis and compasis with a selerite marvalus.

<3.5> 'For whiche reason and cawse, as well thow, Publius, as all other good men also must kepe there sollis in the custody of there bodies, and to not enfors it by vyolens from the body, withowt his commaundement, which gave it them, lest we should seme unwittyly to forsake the office of man gyven us of God. But so, my Scipio, as thi father and grandfather have donne, so occupy thow trew justice and pytie, whiche, if it be mouche commendable to do it to thi parentes and kynsfolke, so to do it specially to thy countrey is the grettyst laude that may be.

<3.6> 'And \so/ to do, and to lyve, is a right way to heven and to that companey of them whiche allredy have lyvid and now, being losid from the body, do inhabite that plase whiche thow seist.' Now the place whiche I saw was a most bright syrkle, rutilant and shining, as a bright, flaming fyre, whiche, as youe takyth it of the Grecyans, call it *orbem lacteum*, that is to meane, the mylke-white waye.

<3.7> And I than, whiche stedfastly beheld it, myght well thinke that al thing I saw was excellent, bewtius, and marveleus. For there were sterres whiche I had never synne in this world before, and of shouche gretnes that I wolde not have thought them so grete, of whom the least 4[v] of them / his globe or quantite was gretter than the hole erthe, so that the erthe we lyve apon semid so small and lytill, and owre dominion or empyre also no gretter then the poynt in the mydis of a syrkle is to be comparid to the cyrcumferens abute it.

<4.1> Whiche said cyrkle, when I beheld it studiusly, Paulus sayd unto me, 'how long, I praye the, shall thy mynd be fyxid apone shouche erthly thinges? Dust thow not behold in the temple, syns thow camyst hither, what is in it, and how with nyne globys, or rather cyrkles, all thes thinges are joynyd togyhter? Of whom the outtermust is celestiall, that imbrasis the rest, being that high God eternall that gydes them all, as well thoes that moves as thos that standes fast, by an order sempyternall.

<4.2> To the whiche globe ar subject other seven, turnyng with movyng contrary to the fyrst of the said globes. Onne of them possessith that plase that on the erthe ye call Satorn; and after hym, that fortunat and wholsum sterre to mankynd, who is namid Jubiter; and after Jubiter, that rutilant and tyrrible sterre callid Mars; and so under hym, in the myddell region, the sunne hath

his plas, the duke and prince and moderator of the rest, the mynd of the world, and the temperer of all thinges, who is of shouche gretnes that it fulfyllith and gladith all creatures to accumpaney this said sun. Foloith Venus and Marcury, and in the loist orbikle or cyrkle the mone hath hyr course, receyvyng her light att the beames of the sun.

<4.3> 'And underneth the said mone, there is nothing but that which is frayle and transitory, excepte only the soll of man, gyven by the goodnes of God to mankynd; and, to conclude, above the mone all thinges be eterne and imortall. And as for the erth, being the nynth cyrkle and constitute in the mydes of all, movyth not, and unto hit al thinges havyng weyght ar carrid with there mosion.'

fol. 5r <5.1> Then, when I had well markid all this, / I was gretly asstunyd; but being commen at the last to myselfe, I demaundid hym, 'what sound is this, so swete, that I do here?' 'This is', sayde he, 'that armoney that, by unequall partes conjoynid but yet by reason distinguid, is made by impulse of thos orbis or sirkles and, tempering the treblis withe basis, dothe make this armony tunably. For it cannot be that so gret movynges should be made with silence, and nature berith it well that the extreme should sound, on the onne side a base and on the other side a treble.

<5.2> 'For whiche cawse, that most high starry course, the conversion whereof is veement, is and must nedes be movid with a sharpe and swete sonde; and this inferior, where the mone is, with a base sound. For the erthe, whiche removyth not, is alwayes adherent to the loo plasis, complecting the middell part of the world. And the same eight coursis, in which is the selfe same mesure of sound, make seven distincte soundes betwixte them, whiche nomber in al thinges is the very knot wherby thos, that have byn excellent by tewnynges of stringes and setting of songes, have found the sience of musike and have openyd a pathe to themselves to cum to this place, as other high wittis have donne, in there daies, that have gyven themselves to devine studies.

<5.3> 'And note it well, if men should have there eres full off that upper sound that I have spoken of, it should make them deffe, for there is no duller \sens/ than is your hering, a<s> i<t> doth apere by the river of Nile, where it runnyth at a plase callid Catadupa. For there it dissendis from high mountaynes, whereby the people there inhabiting, for the gretnes of the sonde, ar deprivid of there hering. So than, as I have tolde the before, by the veement course of the planettes, there is made so great a sound that it were imp\o/ssible mortall mennys eres should fol. 5v abide it, no more than a man may abide to loke derecly agaynst / the sonne, whiche, by his bright beames, dimmithe the sens of youre sight and takyth it clene awaye.' Now, when I hard thes wordes, I marvaylid mouche at them, and, lokyng styll downeward to the erthe,

<6.1> Scipion spake to me and saide, 'Mewse not so of this litill spot of ground, but behold upwarde and loke apon the thing celestiall, and contemme and dissp\i/se thes humayne thinges, and call to thy minde what thow shalt wyn by the glory of men or get by yt. For thow maist se that, in the rare plasis where ye dwell, great and mighti wastes and desartis, and the inhabitantes on the erthe so disparsid that the onne may not attayne to cumme to the other. For some dwell sideward, sume overthwart, and sume under the erthe, directly agaynst ye, of whome it is impossible ye shoulde obtayne renowne or glory.

<6.2> 'And thow maist se the erthe cumpasid and as it were gyrdid with gyrdellis, the reason whereof, the too cyrkles farthest devidid, the onne from the other, be not abitable, the onne by extreme colde, the other by farvent hete of the sonne.

<6.3> 'And too plasis only abitable, of wich the south partes hathe there fete contrary to youres, nothing towardes your kynd, and this other part, of the north, where youe dwell, I praye youe saye how lytill a part partaynyth unto youe. And for conclusion, all the erthe whiche is inhabitid of youe[3] is no better but a lytill ile, compasid with that see wh<i>che ye call the occean. See, low, that whiche ye put so great a name unto, how small and lytyll a thyng it is!

<6.4> 'And to speke of thes groundes that be knowen and laborid, where is there onne of us or of our name that coulde pas Caucasus, whiche thow seist, \or/ rowe over the ryver of Ganges?

Or the farthest part of the orient, or the lowest part of the occident, or in the partes of Auster or
6[r] Aquilo, tell / of thy progenitors actes or thy name?[4] Certes not. Of all whiche partes taken awaye, thow mast well se in how narrow a corner your glory is delatid, and thos that now speke of us, how long shall they speke of us?

<7.1> 'And parcas thow wilt saye that owre children, that be to cumm, shall tell the actys or dedes of your aunsient progenytors, yet for unmesurable fluddes and sackyng and burnyng of countres, whiche of necesyte sumtyme do fall, I saye not only that ye shall not obtayne etarnall glory, but I saye also your glory shall indure but a small tyme and season.

<7.2> 'And what skyllis it yf thy p\o/sterite talke of the, when none of them that were borne afore the hath harde of the, whiche were as good men as thiselfe, or parcase better than thiselfe, specialy when, of them whiche owre name may be hard of, there memory cannot cumme to onne yeres remembraunce?

<7.3> 'Men do reken the yere by the circute only of the sonne, that is to saye, onne planet; but for veri truith, when all the sterres cum to onne point, that may truly and wel be callid a yere, whiche is so long a tyme that scant I dare saye how mayny multitude of yeres that yere comprehendes, or it cum to that poynt.

<7.4> 'For as sumtyme it semid the light of the sonne to be clene extinct, when that the gost of Romulus entrid this temple, even \so/ at that same tyme when that revolucion shall cum, that the sonne shall so be darkid, and all the signes and sterris shal be redusid to there fy<r>st state, whiche as yet we ar not cumme to by the twenty part, when that shal be cumme, then reken thow that tyme is to be accomptid onne hole yere.

<7.5> 'Wherefor, if thow disspayre that thow shalt comme into this \place/, in the whiche all
6[v] thes noble men be, how lytill is to be exstemid that glory / that scant can attayne to onne porcion of that yere? Therfore, my Scipio, loke upward to heven and the etarnall howse. Thinke of it, and credit not the opinion of the vulgar people, nor trust not to the vayne promes of men nor to thine owne substaunce and goodes. For by there miseres, it is necessary that vertu lede the to the trew bewtie and glory.[5] And what other men will saye of the, though thow deservit not, who can let them? Yet will they speke and talke at large. And for all there talke, doust thow not remember in how narow a corner as the erth is thow art spoken of? Therefor, it is impossible that the memory of ony mortall man may last ever, but that by deth or by the course of tyme, as well thiselfe as all other, there glory shal be extinguissed and put in oblivion.'

<8.1> When, then, he hadde thus said, I aunserd hym in this wise. 'I shall, Scipio, do what I can, sithens I do parceyve that to do well is, as it were, a pathe to cumme to heven; study, as I have donne from my childode, to folow your excellent doinges, in shouche wise that your glory by me shall not be apayrid; and I will so labor, so mouche the more, for the reward whiche ye saye I shall by well doing obtayne.'

<8.2> Then sayd he to me, 'Labor so busily to do, I exort the, and thinke suerly that there is nothing mortall of the but this thy fraile body. For thi minde or soll is not that thing whiche thi forme dothe declare, but it is a thing which onne cannot, as who should saye, poynt it with his fynger. But think thiselfe to be a very god, for he is a god that lyvith ever, and hath all his senses ever, and remembryth ever, and so governyth his body, which he rulith as that high prince, God all myghty, rulith this world. And as this saide world is in part mortall, and God the ruler /
7[r] thereof immortall, in like maner, though the body dy, the soll movith and lyvith.

<8.3> 'For take it for truith that that thing, that movyth alwayes, must nedes be eterne forever; but that thing, that gyvith moving to ony other thing and takyth itselfe moving from ony other thing, when that the said moving commith to an ende, of verry necessite than commith the thing itselfe thereby to an ende of life. Wherefor that thing alone, that movith itselfe becawse it never forsakith itselfe, it doth never sease to be movid, and that thing also is the orig\i/nall and beginning of all thinges that ar movid.

<8.4> 'But the beginning itselfe hath none originall, for al thinges prosede of the beginning.

But the beginning itselfe prosedith not of ony other thing, for that cannot ryghtly be callid the begynning which is ingenderid of another thing. And verily, that that hath no beginning hath no ending. For the beginning, being extingusshid, it can nether be regeneratid and renewid by ony other thing, nor can itselfe procreat any other thing, for of necessite al thinges must prosede of the beginning.

<8.5> 'Thus, therefor, it is concludid that the beginning of moving risith therof that a thing movith itselfe, but that beginning can nether have beginning; yea, and it must nedes be that nature itselfe must stand hole and stable, and that it be not forsid from the fyrst course by ony violence.

<9.1> 'Wherefore, seing it is evydent that that thing is everlasting which is movid of itselfe, what is he that will deney this same nature to be geven to the soll of man? Agayne, everything that is movid with an owtwarde violens is withowt lyfe, for the thing that is induid with lyfe is[6] movid with an inward / violence, which is of hymselfe, and this is the proper and peculier nature and force of the soll. Whiche, becawse it only movith itselfe, it is serten that itt never had beginning and that it is eternall.

fol. 7^{v}

<9.2> 'Loke, therefor, that thow occupie this thy soll and minde abought thos thinges that ar best, that is to saye, about the prosperite of thi countrey. For sartenly thi minde, being occupiid therew<i>th, shall fle the swiftlyer into this glorius steate and mansion. Yea, and that so mouche the more spedily, if whan as yet it is shut in the bodey, it will prease forthe, beholding the thinges that are abrode and vehemently contending to withdraw itselfe \from the body/.

<9.3> 'For as towching the sollis of those parsons, that have gyven themselves to the volupte pleasures of the body and have byn mynysters to the same, and for there carnall appitites have violated both Goddis law and mannis, they be tormoylid abought the erthe, after there departure from there bodies, and coum not to this hevenly place before they have byn turmentid many hundrides of yeres.' Thus he departid, and I awakid owte of slepe.

NOTES

1 *Nestor lyfe*: most likely a copyist's error (repeating 'life' from the previous phrase) for the cliché 'Nestor's age'.

2 Morley's phrase 'that whiche Ennius writh of Omer which was accustomid that he spake of being awakid in his slepe he spake of the sam dreming' appears to represent a misapprehension of Cicero's (admittedly compressed) Latin phrase 'quale de Homero scribit Ennius de quo videlicet saepissime vigilans solebat cogitare et loqui' 'in the manner of Ennius's report[ed experience]s of Homer of whom he used to think and speak very often in his waking hours'. Ennius's dreams of Homer are reported, e.g., in Cicero *Academica* 2.51.

3 Morley omits to translate a brief phrase following this one: 'angusta verticibus lateribus latior' 'narrow at the top and broad at the sides'.

4 'tell of thy progenitors actes or thy name': this appears simply to mistranslate 'tuum nomen audiet'.

5 'credit not the opinion of the vulgar people nor trust not to the vayne promes of men nor to thine owne substaunce and goodes. For by there miseres it is necessary that vertu lede the to the trew bewtie and glory': the Latin corresponding to these phrases reads rather differently 'neque te sermonibus vulgi dedideris nec in praemiis humanis spem posueris rerum tuarum. Suis te oportet inlecebris ipsa virtus trahat ad verum decus' 'you will no longer give heed to the gossip of the common herd, nor look for your reward in human things. Let Virtue, as is fitting, draw you with her own attractions to the true glory.'

6 The manuscript reads 'that is' at this point.

APPENDIX 5

Morley's Translations from Seneca's *Epistles* (91 and 120)

London, British Library, Royal MS 17.A.xxx, fol. 1r

I shall most humbly praie unto you, moste noble and vertuous Ladye Mary, to accept as for this
tyme the translacion <of> thies two Epistles of Senecke joyned in oon. Which althoughe thei be
1v but short, yet for the grete goodnesse that maie be noted in them, thei ar no lesse worthey to / be
loked upon then a fayer dyamonde or saphyre, whiche in value farr surmountethe an huge rocke
of stone. Not that the matier of them anything apperteynethe unto you, being so gratious, so
mightye, and so victorious a kinges childe as ye be, and, by his favour and love, in most highe
2r felicitye, / but for other, whiche harde Fortune blowith here and there, into so soundry daungires,
that when they wene to have escaped from Sylla, that most perilous monstre, they furthewith fall
into Caribdis, a farre worse confusion. They, then, that be so wrapped in suche dysease, lett them
2v loke, / tha<t> can knowe the Latyne tong, o<n> this golden epistle of this vertuous Sen<e>cke;
thos that can but rede the mother tong, to loke on this, my poore translacion, which I nowe, with
a loving minde, present unto your grace, as I am wont yerely to do, praing the same well to take
3r it. And I shall praie unto God to sende / youre gentle harte contynuaunce in vertue unto the laste
houre. Amen.

The foure-score twelfth Epistle of Senecke, joyned to the same parte of the eighteenth Epistle of
3v the said auctour, translated into Englishe by / Henry Parker, knight, lorde Morley, as folowythe./

4r <91.1> Thy frende and myn, Lucillus, Liberalis ys nowe wonderous sorye of the newes that Lions
in Gales ys brent by fyre. This chaunce percace might moeve every man, specially one that hathe
4v a sincere and pure love to his countrey, as he hathe, whiche nowe makethe him to / serche by
divers wayes the constancye of his minde, thinking that whyche unnethe he thought coulde not
have chaunced and happen unto him. This unloked for evill, and well nere suche an evill as hathe
not ben harde of heretofore, yt ys no wonder thoughe men doubt no suche chaunce, forasmoche
5r / as it was without example. I meane forbicause there hathe not ben seen no suche sodain a
destruction. For fyre hathe often vexed many cyties, but not so that it hathe utterley taken all
awaie. For where enemyes have put fyre in a town everywhere, yet some placys have ben fre;
5v and / thoughe thei begann a newe again to put fyre to yt, yet seldomme the violens was never so
greate but that something was lefte therof. Nor there hathe not ben so sore an erthe-quake, that
yt sub<v>erted all the towne up-so-doun. And breiflye, there was never so terrible a rage but that
yt left some parte standing where it went./

6r <91.2> But this soo faire a worke and soo noble a citie, whiche was to other a spectacle of
beaultie, one shorte night hathe overthrowen it, and in soo greate a peax and tranquylitie
chaunced this, whiche coulde not have ben doubted in tyme \of warre/, who shall beleve this,
everywhere batailles and warre being ceased, and thorowe the worlde no distention nor de= /
6v bate? Lyons, that was late seen in Galles, ys nowe sought for where it ys, certainly. Fortune,
whosoever she hath openly troubled, hath given theym tyme to feare that whiche thei shoulde
after suffre. Nor ther was never no great ruyne, but in the same, it had some space of tyme or it
7r fyll. But in this most greatest citie, and in the ruyne therof, was no / space, but one sillye nighte.

And for conclusion, I tarie lenger to tell the the ruyne therof then the tyme of perishing of it was in dede.

<91.3> All thies thinges moevethe and enclynethe thaffection and mynde of Liberalis, althoughe he seme to have an upright remembraunce to be thoughtfull, and not without a cause. (fol. 7v) For thinges / not loked grevethe so moche the more. A newe souldain mysfortune gyeveth the sadd mynd a newe waight, to oppresse a man into more sorowe. Nor ther ys no mortall man, but that whiche gyeveth him more cause to marveill at, ys cause whye that he \the/ more lamentethe that yt shoulde so sodainly and so merveilously happen unto him.[1]

(fol. 8r) <91.4> For / whiche cause ther shoulde happen to no man nothing unwares, but that the mynde shoulde be warned to thinke, not onely that whiche ys wont, but that whiche maie be, maie chaunce unto us. For what thing ys that, but Fortune, when she lyst florishe yt, nor shyne (fol. 8v) it never so prosperously, but that she will overtorne, and / specially the more faire and exellent that it ys? What ys to her to harde to bring to passe?

<91.5> Sometyme, we happen to hurte \with/ our own handes our own self. Sometyme, using her own power, shee bringeth us in perell, and we do not knowe whiche waye nor by whom. And (fol. 9r) there is no tyme of this, except in our most pleasant pastymes riseth / up causes of sorowes. Bataile in the mydes of peax, and where we thinke to have most sure aide and helpe, often that self hope turneth into feare. Our frendes turnethe to be our foo, our felowe to be our enemye. Thus, when we most thinke to be in most tranquylitye, as yt were in a fayer sommer, in a moment (fol. 9v) it tornethe / unto the vyolent and stormy wynter, so that we seme to have enemyes without enemyes, and unknowen causes to lament, and yf all this shoulde lacke, overmoche fely<ci>tie doth finde it. Sycknes dothe invade them that be most temperate. Thos that be of most strongest (fol. 10r) complexion, ther cometh to them tysys,[2] whiche ys to meane a con- / sumption; to the innocent, pain and torment; to the most secrettiste, busines and vexacion. Thus Fortune faynethe ever some newe matier to suche as seme to forgett her, to put them to busynes.

<91.6> So that, that thing whiche by a longe seryous labour, travaile, and coste hathe ben (fol. 10v) brought to passe and buylte, in one / small shorte daie, destroyeth yt quyte and clene. He giveth to moche tyme that saithe a daie ys but an houre, when one ungratious an<d> infortunate houre ys ynoughe to subvert a[-n] grete and mightye empire. Certainly, we shoulde have some cause of (fol. 11r) comforte, yf yt might be possible to repayr all thinges assone, / that ys destroied, as that thyng that maie destroye. But thincrease of thinges goo slowely to worke; the decaie goith on apace.

<91.7> So that yt maie be said that nether private thinges nor yet common thinges endure but a while; asswell cities as men be subverted by desteny. Where there ys most quyet, ther lac- / (fol. 11v) kethe no drede nor feare but that alwaies where we loke lest for busines and vexacion, there most [-most] it cometh unto us. Kingdommes, whiche by straunge nacions coulde not be sobverted, by their own civile debates, thei have come to destruction.[3] Thies thinges, then, ought often (fol. 12r) to be had in remembraunce: not / present thinges, but suche thinges as maie fortune unto us, that is,

<91.8> exile, tormentes, bataile, sickenes, drowening, and suche infynite evilles, redy at the hande. Chaunce maie \take/ thy country, and the awaie from thy country. And thow maist, (fol. 12v) dwelling in a citie, be drevin to dwell in wildernes, and wher as thou seist this / throng of people, there percace thou shalt see a place inhabitable. Let, then, all the condicion of myserable mankind be put afore our eyes and, not that whiche often dothe fall, but that whiche for the more parte dothe fall, have in our thought, as a straunge newe thing.

(fol. 13r) <91.9> Howe many cyties in Achaia, howe many townes in Asia, with one / erthe-quake have ben overthrowen? And, not onely in thies countries, but in Sula,[4] in Cipres and Paphus, this plage haith chaunced unto them. And we, whiche comenly do heare thies newes, what ar we in nombre to be compared to them? Let us then ryse and make us strong against all mysfortunes, (fol. 13v) and whatsoever chaunce, / let \us/ ymagyne that it is nothing so great as the fame that goeth therof.

<91.10> A riche and excellent cytye ys burnt, that was the beaulty of all the hole countrye where it was sett. But thinke again therto, that all the other, that nowe \thou/ hearest to be noble and of great magnificens, tyme shall consume them, so that, where they were, unnethe shal be / 4[r] any remembraunce. Doist thou not se that in Achaia the foundacion of divers noble and riche townes be quyte and clere so subverted that men cannot perceive where thei stode?

<91.11> Not \onely/ all thinges made by mannes handes decaie, but great mountaines go in 4[v] sonder, and regions where men dwelt in, the salt sees have quyte and clene / eaten them up.[5]

<91.12> Breifly, to nombre all the waies of Fortune, yt were to long. One thing I knowe well, that all the workes of mortall men ar by mortalytie dampned and ended.

<91.13> This manner of consolacion do I use to give to our friende Liberalis, morning for 5[r] thincredible love that he have to his country, / whiche peradventure was burnt to that intent, that it shoulde be better reedyfyed again then ever it was. Many thinges have fallen down to ryse again the higher. An enemy to the cytie of Rome,[6] when he sawe it burne, said that nothing 5[v] greved him so moche as that he knewe very well yt shoulde be better made / then ever it was before.

<91.14> And faierly, yt is not unlyke but that every man shall do their diligence to do this in like maner. I praie to God it maie so be, and that yt maie with better fortune contynewe lenger. For this citie of Lions, it hath not had the age of an hundred yeres, whiche ys \the/ extreme age 6[r] skant of mans liff, and / yet many times hath suffered many harde chaunces.

<91.15> Let therfore stable our mindes with patiens. For aswell to to (*sic*) the citie dwellers, as to the self cities, falleth mysfortunes whiche cann never be resisted, but by vertue.[7]

<120.12> Whiche whosoo hath, whatsoever falleth unto him, he shall never curse Fortune, 6[v] nor blame, / but be it swete or sower, take it well, saying, 'this ys my chaunce; I must and will abide it'.

<120.13> Without doubt, he shewith himself to be of a vertuous minde that mornethe not when he sufferethe evill fortune, nor complayneth not of his desteny. He givethe grete ensaumple 7[r] to other, and shynes in darkenes, none / otherwise then the faier clere light, when he shewith himself patient, pleasaunte, an<d> equall, and obeing as well to Godes will as to mans.

<120.14> Suche a one hath a perfect soule, sett in the highest place of vertue, above whiche there ys nothing but the minde of God whereof he hath parte; and specially never more then 7[v] when he / remembreth his own mortalitie, and thinketh that he was borne to dye, and that his body ys no house stable to tarry in, but a lodging, and a wonderous shorte lodging, whiche he must depart from, when he hath ben a gest long ynough.[8]

8[r] <120.15> Doist thou not se, my Lucilius, howe many inconvenyences moeveth us / to this good rememberaunce?

<120.16> Nowe we complain of our belly, nowe of our stomach, nowe of our hedd, nowe of our chekes. Sometyme our synewes, sometyme our feete greveth us, somety\me/ to grosse, sometyme to feble, and nowe we have to moche blodde, and forthewith we have to litle.

8[v] <120.17> And yet we, having in our / custody so feble a body, we hope ever of tomorowe, and thinke never to dye untill thextreme age, never satisfied with money, nor with coveting to be greate. What extreme madnes ys this? What more folly or folyshenes maie be then this? 9[r] Thies thinges, my Lucillius, yf they be wysely called to rememberaunce, shall cause / not onely Liberalis, our dere frende, but also all men to suffre all evill fortune that maie fall.

Finis.

NOTES

1 The Latin of this sentence is gnomic in a way that appears to have caused Morley difficulties: 'nec quisquam mortalium non magis quod etiam miratus est doluit' 'every mortal feels the greater pain as a result of that which also brings surprise'.

2 'Tysys': *phthisis*, Grk., in the Latin letter in the Greek form; also occuring in EME as 'tyssyke': e.g., Skelton, *Mag.* 555, 'Can you remedy for a tysyke?'

3 To this sentence of Morley's 'Kingdommes, whiche by straunge nacions coulde not be sobverted by their own civile debates, thei haue come to destruction' corresponds a pair of phrases in the Latin letter the one of which Morley omitted and the other of which he altered: 'Quae domesticis bellis steterant regna quae externis inpellente nullo ruunt: quota quaeque felicitatem civitas pertulit' 'Thrones which have stood the shock of civil and foreign wars crash to the ground though no one sets them tottering. How few the states which haue carried their good fortune through to the end!'

4 *Sula*: the Latin reads 'Syria'.

5 Morley omits to translate a fairly lengthy passage of four sentences that follows at this point in the Latin, the concluding portion of 91.11 and the opening of 91.12: 'Vasta vis ignium colles per quos relucebat erosit et quondam altissimos vertices solacia navigantium ac speculas ad humile deduxit. Ipsius naturae opera vexantur et ideo aequo animo ferre debemus urbium excidia. Casurae stant; omnis hic exitus manet sive ventorum interna vis flatusque per clusa violenti pondus sub quo tenentur excusserint sive torrentium impetus in abdito vastior obstantia effregerit sive flammarum violentia conpaginem soli ruperit sive vetustas a qua nihil tutum est expugnaverit minutatim sive gravitas caeli egesserit populos et situs deserta corruperit.' Moreover Morley's translation of Seneca's conclusion is, 'One thing I knowe well that all the workes of mortall men ar by mortalytie dampned and ended', in place of 'Hoc unum scio: omnia mortalium opera damnata sunt inter peritura vivimus.'

6 Recovery of the identification of this 'enemy' as Timagenes is a development of the textual and editorial tradition that post-dates the Erasmian edition of Seneca that Morley would most likely have used.

7 Of 91.15 Morley abbreviates the first sentence (the phrase he omitted is italicized): 'Itaque formetur animus ad intellectum patientiamque sortis suae et sciat nihil inausum esse fortunae *adversus imperia illam idem habere iuris quod adversus imperantis* adversus urbes idem posse quod adversus homines' and he omits the rest. Moreover he leaves *Ep.* 91 here altogether, omitting a concluding section (91.16-91.21) that amounts to about one-quarter of the letter. For the rest Morley translates a portion of *Ep.* 120.12-120.17 (beginning 'Quicquid inciderat non tamquam malum' and ending 'quid stultius potest') amounting to about one-sixth of that letter.

8 Morley omits to translate the two sentences following this one in the Latin, the first sentences of 120.15 which justify suicide: 'Maximum inquam mi Lucili argumentum est animi ab altiori sede venientis si haec in quibus versatur humilia iudicat et angusta si exire non metuit; scit enim quo exiturus sit qui unde venerit meminit.'

APPENDIX 6

Two Poems by Morley

Oxford, Bodleian Library, Ashmole MS 48, fol. 9^v

Henry, Lorde Mo\r/ley, to his posteritye

Never was I lesse alone then beyng alone:
Here in this chamber, evell thought had I none,
But allways I thought to bryng the mynd to reste,
And that thought, off all thoughtes, I juge it the beste.
For yf my coffers hade ben full of perle and golde,
And fortune had favorde me even as that I wolde,
The mynd owt off quyat, so sage Senek sethe,
Itt hade ben no felicitie, but a paynfull dethe.
Love, then, whoo love wyll, to stande in highe degre:
I blame him nott a whitte, so that he followe me
And take his losse as quyatly as when that he doth wyne.
Then Fortune hathe no maistre of that stat he ys in,
But rulys and ys not rulyd, and takis the bettre parte.
O that man ys blessyde that lerns this gentle arte:
This was my felicitie, my pastyme, and my game;
I wisshe all my posteritie the wolde ensew the same

Si ita Deo placet, ita fiat.

Wrytten over a chambar dore wher he was wont to ly at Hollenbury

10^r Henry, Lord Morlay

All men the do wysshe unto themselffe all goode,
And he that wold wisshe othar[-way]\wyse/, I cont him wors than woode.
And what that good shulde be, fewe can tell or non;
And off that wantone sorte, I knowe myselffe am oone
That often ha[-th]\ve/ desyryde that thyng hath done me harme,
Tyll Reasone rulyde fantasye and my fond wyte dyde charme
And teld me, yf that good I dyde intende to have,
Yt neathar was in dignitye nor in muche gold to save,
But to refus both twayne, to hold myselffe contente,
Not with my fond desyars, but that which Gode hath lente:
Wysdome and experience to knowe that all delyght
Doth pas as doth the day that passith to the nyghte.
A soden wynd doth ryse, and when that Gode wyll call,
Wher ys then your dygnitye? Go, tak your leve off all.
The beggar and the lord, in one state then the be.
Thus Reasone doth remembre and sayth, 'Go, lerne off me:
Thowe woldeste have this and that, and in thy fond desyre
The very stable good, thow throwist it in the myar.'

I sayd unto myselffe, Reasone the truthe doth tell,
And to insewe that way I was contentyde well,
And wisshe to wyn that good unfaynede with my harte,
And wold that all my frenddes off that wissh shuld have parte.

Si ita Deo placet, ita fiat.

APPENDIX 7

Morley's Account of the Miracles of the Sacrament

Written on vellum, probably for presentation on New Year's Day 1556. It is not known when it left the royal collection, but it was bought back into the British Museum collection from Thomas Butler in 1841.

London, British Library, Add. MS 12060, fol. 1r

To the most high, most excellent and most most mighty Princesse, the Lady Mary, by the grace of God Quene of Inglonde, of Fraunce, Naples, Jerusalem, and Irelond, Defendoresse of the Faythe, Pryncesse of Spayne and Cecyle, Archduches of Austriche, Duches of Mylayne, Burgundy and Brabaunt, Countesse of Haspurge, Flaunders and Tyrole.[1] Your humble subject Henry Parker Knyght, Lorde Morley, prayeth unto Cryst Jesu and to his blessyd mother to prosper your magestye and your dere husband, our lorde and king, longe to raigne togyther in perpetuall honour and felycytie.

The Prologe
Claudyan the excellent poete, most gracyous soveraigne lady and maistres, that was in his flowers in the good Emperour Theodosius time, albeyt that he was no Cristen man, yet doth he write many notable versys, well worthy to be had in mynde with kinges and quenes and governers of contrees and common welthes. And among other his manifolde wise versys, this one
. 1v / may well be comparyd to your excellent magestie, which is this:

Regis ad exemplum totus componitur orbis.[2]

The sence, as I do take yt, is this, that as the prynce or princesse gyveth example of vertue or otherwise unto ther subjectes, even after that sort folowith the people, other to vertue or to vyce. And suerly in my pore judgement his sayenge ys most true. For when the headis doth ensue the happy way to vertue, maintayneth religion, shewith pitye to the pore and miserable, resysteth the proude, exalteth the meke, and causith true justyce to be ministred to ther subjectes without parcialytie, remembrith that ther dignytie is no better then a Maye floure that today shewith fayre and tomorow is withered and drye, and the beauty therof past, and finally, thinketh in ther hartes that death shall devoure the greatest as well as the porest creature under ther subjectyon, oh, such governers or headis as gyveth such example of life to the worlde must of necessytie be the occasyon and in maner a clere light to all the worlde to folowe that waye. As you, my most
l. 2r deare and gracious lady and maistres, hath done and doth from your tender / infancy unto this present day of your most prosperous raigne.

For which well doing God shall kepe you, preserve you, and blysse you to the laste age and all worldes shall say and wryte of you laude and commendatyons and that you alone above all other Cristen quenes are worthy to have that honorable name to be the Defendoresse of the Faythe. And although that by your <right> of inheritaunce and by the righte of your puissaunt husband, our gracyous soveraigne lord and king, ye have betwixt you two [[ ]] have the greatest parte of Cristendome under your subjectyon, yet this one tytle <you> have deservyd by your fact, to have <the nam>e of the Defendoresse of the Faithe, s<urpass>yth all the rest of your tytles and croun<es and i>s the very precyous gemme, shinyng e<ver stron>gly in your forehead, never to be darkyd <in thi>s life nor in the lyfe to come.

For wher that of late <dayes> this your most noble realme was brought <to> that barbarous estate that ther was in the <he>adis of the people as many dyvers ar<gu>mentes as ther hath ben fol. 2v heretyckes synce Christes Churche began, by reason wherof the vulgar was so / amased that many thought ther was no religion at all but to do as Epicure or vile Sardanapaulus dyd that folowed so his vityous life that unto this day he is despised of all, lernyd and unlernid. Even in lyke maner this your realme was brought to that sedytion that first they denyed the head of the Church, the popes holynes, next wolde have no saintes honored but threwe vile matter at the crucifyx, and adding mischeife to myscheife, denyed the sevyn sacramentes of the Church, some of them willing to have but thre, some none at all. And by their desertes fyll into so reprobable a will that they not only expulsed the name of the precyous Mary, mother to Christ, out of ther common prayers but therunto wolde not the Ave Maria to be sayde.

This was greatly to be lamentyd but this that folowith moche more, for the most devine holy sacrament of the aulter, the very sancta sanctorum, which all Cristen realmes hath belevyd to be really the very body of Christ, these heretyckes without sence or wytt, more abhomynable then Machomet the false prophete, hath so despised yt and handlyd yt, and in such an herytycall sorte fol. 3r that as the / excellent Maro sayeth to tell yt

Animus meminisse orret luctuque refugit[3]

and by ther false doctryne as moche as in them was, hath condemnyd all the kinges in Cristendome and ther progenitours with ther subjectes to be no better then idolaters, for which sayd offence of idolatrye and for false heritycall opynions all Cristen realmes hath ben scourged, eradycate and subvertyd.

And here, with your gentle pacyence most Cristen Quene, I wyll somwhat dyvert from my pore oratyon and declare what hurt hathe come by heresyes, what murder, what penurye, to these contryes folowing, that is to say, to the Jewes, to the Grecyans, to the Italyans, to the Egiptians, to the Affricanes, to the Bohemes, to the Spanyardes, to the Britaignes, somtyme rulers of this realme, and last to the empyre of Germany, and to this your realme at this present day.

I say therfore that yt is manifest to them that have readde the Byble that from the creatyon of the worlde unto ther perpetuall ruyne the Jewes were for the most parte evermore idolaters, for fol. 3v which offence God gave them somtyme / into the handes of the Philistines, somtyme to the Assirians and in processe of tyme they were scourged by Nabuchodonazer, who toke ther kynge and brought hym and his people captyve unto Babylon. This punishment might well have ben the cause to have made them left ther idolatrye and yet ther cytye reedifyed againe by the favour of God and by the graunt of Syrus, king of Persia, they lefte not ther olde wayes, tyll that by malyce they had put to death the savyour of the world, Christ Jesu, and in his tyme had thre dyvers sectes among them, that is, the Pharasyes, the Saduces and the Essayes.[4] What divers opinyons they had *Historia ecclesiastica* declareth and therfore for brevitye I let yt passe.[5] One thing is sure, that Christ blamed them and reprovyd them for ther inconstancy in manye places of the holy gospell and declaryd unto them how ther perpetuall destructyon was at hande, which folowed in very dede, by Titus Vaspasianus, who lefte not one stone of their cytye stonding upon another and slewe innumerable of them by famyne and sworde, the rest solde lyke beastes and fol. 4r now are slaves and despised people throughout the universall worlde, / living in captyvytie and under trybute. Thus farre, most excellent lady, is sayd of the Jewes.

It folowith of the Grecyans. Our savyour Crist havyng suffred passyon for our redemptyon, commaunding his apostles to preach in his name, that all that belevyd and were baptised shulde have the kingdome of glory, innumerable by fayth were cristenyd. But this faythe lasted not longe among the Cristen men, but that some fyll to heritycall opinyons and so disturbed Cristes people, that many that wolde have ben Cristen men, seynge such devisyon of Cristians among themselfes, utterly forsoke that name, and contynued paynymmes styll as they were before. But yet Christ, that promised to Peter that his faith shuld never fayle, although that the Manatistes[6] and Donatistes and other tyrauntes did impugne the truthe, yet the more they so dyd to Christes religyon, the more yt florished, but not without the persecutyon and bloudshedding of innumerable saintes, tyll at the last the great Constantyne, being a Britaine borne in this your

Fig. 1. Cambridge University Library INC O.A.7.2 [888], fol. CLXXXVII^v. Hartmann Schedel, *Liber cronicarum* (Nuremberg, 1493). Coloured woodcut of men and women dancing in the churchyard. By permission of the Syndics of Cambridge University Library.

l. 4v realme, to the great honour of yt, / commaundyd through the hole Empyre Christ to be honoured, the holy crosse to be exaltyd and S. Sylvester the pope to be the head of all the bishoppes in the worlde.

I passe over how by the signe of the crosse, which he sawe in heavyn shewyd to hym by an angle, with these wordes – Constantine, in hoc signo vinces – that ys to say, 'In this signe, Constantyne, thou shalt vanquishe', he overcamme Maxentius the tiraunt, and Cristes flocke set at libertye, all idolatry began to cease, tyll that a newe bytter basilyck, the false herityck Arrian, well nere subvertyd all.[7] What harme that his heresy dyd, what bloud sheding and destructyon of kingdomes and contryes came by yt, he that ys any thing lettured knowith yt, and therfore most gracyous Lady, I overpasse yt. And it shall suffise to tell that the Grecyans, being the noblest people in the worlde, forsaking the head of the church of Rome, the popes holynes, fyll from emperour to emperour to innumerable of erronyous opynyons. Among whom Julyan the Apostata, seing the strife betwixt the Catholickes and the Arryans forsoke them both, to his perpetuall harme, for going against the Persians, he was slayne, as it is thought, by the stroke / l. 5r devyne, and dyeng sayd in the despite of Christ 'Vicisti Galileae'.

To conclude, excellent Quene, as well the emperours that folowed for the most part never ensued the Church of Rome till God, being wrothe for ther heresyes, within one hundred yeares punnished them by Machomet, the great Turke, in suche wise that he wanne the head cytie of Constantinople and all Grece, slewe ther emperour, defyled his wife in the temple of Sancta Sophia, and brought the mighty Grecyans into such misery that ther ys not at this day one

Grecyan can say that he holdeth one fote within that londe.[8] Oh Jesu, most noble Quene, what an example is this for all good Catholickes to beware to fall into suche heritycall opynions as the Grecyans dyd.

It folowith of the Egiptyans. Egypt, convertyd unto the faythe of Christ, having many notable clerkes, great bishoppes, and holye men, amonge the cheife Athanasius was one, that made that excellent psalme of 'Quicunque vult salvus esse'.[9] It was not long after his death, but that they, fol. 5v not obeyng the sea of Rome, sent unto the / pope, onles he wolde agre to ther opinyons, they wolde not take hym the head of the church. It folowed shortly after in the tyme of the emperour Eraclius, the Arrabyans, wher fyrst the lawe of Machomet began, vanquished them, and chased the bishoppes and the Cristen men away.[10] And they at this day are all Machomettes and heretyckes and ther contrey evermore called throughout the worlde stultus Egiptus. I wyll not forgett to declare unto your grace what myscheife fyll unto Eraclius, who being at his begynnyng a worthy emperour and so fortunate that he vanquished with his owne hande Cosdrus, the kinge of Persia, and brought unto Jerusalem the holy crosse with great pompe and glory, yet seyng manifestly the miracle that God ther shewid unto hym, fyll from the true catholyck relygion unto the heresy of the Moniclites and perished shortly after by such a straunge death that yt is not honest to tell it. Thus farre of the Egyptyans.

Now, excellent princesse, I wyll breifly declare how by the Arryans secte mischeife fyll amonge the Italyens and how God suffred them to be scourgyd by the Hunes, by the Vandales, and by fol. 6r the Gotes. / And among other Radagasus, who had in his army two hundred thousand Gotes, entryd Italy and beseiged Rome for no nother cause, as the aucthours wryte, but that in those dayes they were not only heretyckes, many one of them, but also they were necligent in doing devyne service.[11] Nevertheles, they crieng to God for mercy were delyveryd from this tyraunt and he by the Romaynes was slaine. After this Radagasus succedyd Alaricus to be the king of the Gotes and beseigyd Rome and toke it.[12] And albeyt that he was a paynyme he usyd this humanytie, that is he comaundyd all his men of warre, paine of death, not to hurt no Romaine that fledde to the Church of S. Peter and S. Paull.

Not long after entryd Italy Athala, the king of the Hunes, who toke Padua, Vincentia, Virona, Milayne and Papia and at the last going towarde Rome, the Romaynes being in an exceding feare, desyred Leo, then Pope of Rome, the first of that name to go to hym to appease hym.[13] And he so doing, ther chaunced a wonderous thing of yt, for the barbarous prynce only with the syghte of Leo lefte Rome untouched, and when certaine of his demaundyd of hym why he, being fol. 6v the scourge of God, wolde not enter Rome and take yt, / he aunsweryd that he sawe by this good pope two men stonding with two nakyd swordes in ther handes, threatyng hym and his armey to destroy them if they procedyd any further. Wherfore he retourned home agayne. And suerly, most excellent princesse, this is a wonderous story that he which was so fearfull and mighty a prynce, by the only sight of that holy father, pope of Rome, was glade to depart away.

And yt is for conclusyon to be remembrid that as long as the Arryans sect was in Italy they never fayled to be scourgyd, other by the Hunes, the Gotes, the Vandales or the Sarasyns. And the contrey once pacifyed from heresy yt hath prosperyd and doth prosper unto this present day. Thus farre of the Italyens.

And now I shall breifly declare the ruyne of the Affricanes. The great doctour of the Church, S. Austyne, who florished in the yeare of grace foure hundred and thirtye, being bishoppe of Iponense in the sayd contrey of Affryck, had moch to do to stablishe the contrey by his excellent lernyng and to kepe the people from heresy and specially from the sect of the Arryans. But he could not so bring the matter to passe for all his great lernyng but that the people contynued in fol. 7r many false opinions / styll, untyll that tyme that Gensericus beseigyd the citye wher as he lay syck, and shortly after his death toke the cytye and persecutyd so the Catholickes that I have horrour to tell yt.[14] And albeyt that his sonne raignyd after hym and was even lykewise of the Arryans sect and more mischevous then ever was his father, yet he prosperyd not long but dieng miserably, shortly after hym the Sarasyns conqueryd all the contrey and holde and kepe yt styll, to the great rebuke of Cristen men, unto this present day. And thus farre of the Affricans.

It folowith of the noble realme of Spayne. The Spanyardes havyng many worthy prynces and rulers, at last by succession the realme fyll to Theodoricus, that was descendyd of the bloud of the Goates, who fyll into such heresy and such pride that he utterly despised the sea of Rome and sayd that to hym appertayned only to make all the ecclesiastycall lawes, and usyd his lyffe so dissolutely that by the permissyon of God the Sarasyns, that then had gotten by sworde the gret contrey of Affryke, entryed Spayne and Theodoricus geving batayle unto them, albeyt that he was a very valiaunt prynce of his person and dyd / many notable actes with his owne hande, yet at the last his people was put to flyght and he flyeng away was drounyd in a ryver and within a lytle while after all Spaine loste, savynge one lytle contrey in the kingdome of Castyll.[15] How long yt was or the noble prynces of Castyll could recover againe the contrey of Spayne. Ther cronycle declareth that in sevyn hundred yeares they had moch worke to expulse the Sarasyns, tyll at the last Fardinando, that worthy king your grauntfather, gotte Garnado and so being lorde of all Spaine, he and his successyon unto this daye triumphantly enjoyeth yt.[16] Thus farre of Spayne.

fol. 7v

Now, most Cristen Quene, although that I can not tell yt without lamentatyon of my hart what misery the Britaynes, somtyme rulers of this realme, fyll in by heresy, yet wyll I tell yt, to that intent that I wolde wishe that your devyne prechers shuld teache the people by the example of the Brytaynes to beware how to fall to vayne argumentes and false beleife, leste that percase might fall to us that which fyll to the Brytaynes, which is this. Afore the incarnatyon of Christ and after, ther / was many a worthy Britayne, as Brenius, Belinus, Uterpendragon, Aureliambrose and the noble Arthur, with dyvers other, that raignyd triumphantly tyll the great Constantyne, in whose tyme, as Polydorus wryteth,[17] the Brytaynes being in great prosperitye, an heretyck callyd Pelladian, a monke, preched unto the Brytaynes that a man might be savyd by his owne good workes, without the grace of God, which so infectyd the Britaynes with that heresy, that although Lucius, a Britayne, was long before that kinge of this realme, cristenyd at Rome, wherby in dede the kinges of this realme, your noble progenytours, doth clayme to be the most Cristen kinges because he was the first cristened king before any king in Fraunce,[18] yt folowed, the Britaines thus fallen to heresy, the Saxons entryd this londe and by lytle and lytle expulsed quyte away the Britaynes and chaungyd the name of the realme, which was afore callyd Brytaine, unto Inglond, and the Brytaynes, which the Welch men say they be descendyd of, subjectes to your Imperiall croune for ever.[19] This example is fearfull, most noble princesse, well worthye for us Inglish men to note it well, leste that the/like perchaunce may fall to us. And thus farre of the Britaynes.

fol. 8r

fol. 8v

Now for the kingdome of Boheme, most excellent princesse, which yt is not long synce ther heresy began by Wickliff, a scoler of the Universitye of Oxforde, whose damnable heresy Luther inespecially hath folowyd, procedyd thus. About the latter dayes of the most worthy prince, King Edward the Third, this Wickliff usyd, as Randolde the monke of Chester writeth,[20] many divers straunge fashions to cloke his heresy withall, as well in his apparell as in using a fayned false dessembling holynes and drewe to his company one Jerome of the kingdome of Boheme and one Hust, two bitter poison persons, who going home into ther contrey, subvertyd all the hole regyon of Boheme. And yt is to be notyd that though this King Edward was the most famous prynce of the worlde, yet as yt is thought, bycause he dyd not sodenly suppresse this Wicklif he was nothing so fortunate in his warres at the latter ende of his dayes as he was at his begynning.[21] But, leaving that apart and retournyng againe to the kingdome of Boheme, the head cytye therof called Prage, being at that / tyme in great welth and prosperytie and one of the head universyties of Cristendome, this Jerome and this Hust so subvertyd the religyon ther that they fyll into such a discorde and sodayne batayle among themselves that the hole contrey came utterly to ruyne and specyallye by a gentilman whose name is called Johannes Ciskay, who so burnt churches, pulled downe religious houses, defyled virgins and made suche racket in that realme that it could never prosper as it dyd, unto this present day. And thus farre of the kyngdome of Boheme.[22]

fol. 9r

Now, gracyous lady, to tell the misery of the Germaynes that hath fallen unto them in these our dayes, it shulde seme superfluous to write yt. Nevertheles, yt is most true that I, beynge embassadour from your most victorious father unto the noble king of Romaynes, Fardinando, bearing to hym the Garter, Luthers secte then newly begunne, scant was I retournyd unto this your realme but that the contrey was in such a rebellion, that is to say, the vilaynes against the lordes that, or they coulde be appeasyd, yt cost of both partes above the lyves of an hundred / thousand men, and such crueltye was executyd by the vilaynes to certayne of the nobylytye that I have horrour to tell it, how many religious persons was slayne, how many churches burnt, how many virgines defyled, and harmes innumerable done and executyd, yt is impossible for me to tell.[23] One thing ys that Luther, the aucthor of all mischeife and as I do think the very antechrist for our synnes sent from God to persecute Cristendome, in his writinges is so vyle and abhomynable in certayne places that although, excellent quene, I professe I have redde Alkarom, Machomettes lawe, lately translatyd into the Italyen tonge, yet is ther nothing so spurke and detestable wordes wryten in that lawe as is writen by hym.[24] And thus farre, vertuous lady, for the Germaynes.

fol. 9ᵛ

And now to this your realme, most excellent princesse, I dare not say what that I thinke. But thus moche, with your pacyence, I may say. Wher is become all the plentye that was in your wyse grauntfathers daies, King Henry the Seventh, and my godly maistres the Lady Margaret, your great grandame, and in your worthy fathers dayes, King Henry the Eight? Wher is the plentye of corne, / the haboundaunce of cattall, the frutefulnes of all thing, as well of the water as of the londe? Wher is become the quyetnes of subjectes and obedience to ther headis? Wher is the golde and silver that in such haboundaunce was in this realme that, as sayd ys, I being embassadour sent by your worthy father to the king Fardinando, ther in reverting home being lodged in a denes house in the cytye of Mastrick in Base Almaine, he sayd unto me, when I departyd from hym, these wordes: 'God sende the, lorde embassadour, safe and sounde to thy golden contrey and most plentyfull region in the worlde'? All this, gracious lady, is past and gone: our golde is turnyd unto copper, our sylver to brasse,[25] and ne were the hope that we have in God and you swete, delycate, red rose, the very maynteyner of faythe, I thynke that we shulde be in worse case then other Grece or Boheme.

fol. 10ʳ

But, your highnes, as I have sayd at the begynnyng of myne oration, ensuing all goodnes and vertue and folowyng the wise counsell of the unculpable vertuous cardinall your cosyn, whose conversatyon and life is knowen to be through Cristendome without spotte, I say that your highnes in folowing / his counsell, and with your godly wyt together, the golden worlde shall in processe come againe and this your realme prosper in peace and in haboundaunce.[26] And if ther be any of your obedient subjectes that by false teaching of the heretyckes have had or have any ungodly opinyon in ther stomack, with Goddes mercy and your most Cristen example they shall revert home to ther mother, holy church, againe, which I pray to God, and to his blessyd mother, may in your most happy raigne come to passe and that I may se it or I die.[27]

fol. 10ᵛ

Thus hitherunto, most Cristen Quene and my most deare and gracyous soveraigne ladye and maistres, I have breifly declared the ruine, the destructyon, the hunger, the penury, the battayles and the subvertyon of realmes and empires that hath come by heresy. And suerly to write or to tell the matter how it was at lenght, it shuld fulfyll a hole volume and a worke that I were not able to bring to an ende. But this that I have breifly sayd, I do affirme yt for to be true as the greatest aucthours that hath ben synce Christ suffred his death doth declare yt, and by experience in our tyme we / have sene yt. And for that intent that divers hath taken opinion against the devine and holy sacrament of the aulter, that it shuld not be really the precious body of God that was borne of the blissyd virgin Mary and also have despised the holy masse, I have translatyd unto your highnes certayne examples what wonders God hath wrought to such as hath not belevid yt, and usyd the receyving therof unreverently, prayeng your excellent magestye to accept this my pore lytle labour well and in good part. And I shall contynually pray unto God, and to

fol. 11ʳ

his blessyd Mother, to preserve your gracious highnes and my deare soveraigne lorde and kynge, your husbande, long to lyve together in helth, glory and vyctorye. Finis. /

11v <1> A wonderfull myracle of a woman that wolde have holden the blyssed sacrament when she receyvyd it in her mouthe, and how she was punnished for it. Declaryd and tolde by the holy martir and great doctour S. Ciprian in a sermon that he made *de lapsu*.[28]

Ther was a certayne woman, saieth he, passed childes age was present among us that did the devyne service, and when she should have receyvid, as other did, the precious sacrifyce by the preistes handes she toke it into her mouthe, meanyng to hide it tyll she might otherwise use it ungodly. But she had no soner recyvid yt into her jawes but that she thought it persyd her lyke unto a sharpe sworde, and forthwith in the presence of all them that were ther assistent, trembling and quaking she fyll downe dead unto the grounde. Thus the vengeaunce of God taried not long after her offence comytted, but that she that thought to deceyve men could not deceive God, that so punished her for her abhominatyon. /

12r <2> Another example folowing declared by the sayde holy martir Ciprian.[29]

Ther was also another, sayeth he, that wolde have openyd the pyxe where the precious sacrament lay, with his polutyd handes, but ther folowyd after a wonderfull thing. For yt semyd to hym that a fyer came from that holy place, wher that the sacrament lay, and put hym in such dreade and feare that he fled away. Thus farre tellyth S. Cipryan

<3> A mervaylous saieng of S. Crisostome concernyng the reverence to be done unto the holy sacrament, with a wonderfull tale he tellith was done at the blissed masse.[30]

Consyder, saieth S. Crisostome, what cleane handes the minister shulde have, and what a pure tonge the preist shuld have withall that pronounceth the wordes of Cryst in the consecratyon of the devine sacrament. At that present tyme the angells be asystent to the preist, and the sacrifyce that is ther done in the / honour of hym, is fully replete with angels, which may be well belevid so to be, for the reverence that is ther done at that worthye sacrifyce. And I will tell you for truthe that a certayne man tolde me that he hard a holy old father tell hym that he had many revelatyons, and therby did often discusse many devine misteries. That same olde father tolde the sayde man that God shewid to him this vision: at the tyme when the preist was mynistring he sawe sodenly a multytude of angels, that mans sight could not be of power to se, cladde in shyning bright vestimentes, compassing the aulter, inclyning and bowing downe ther headis with reverence, as those that be assistent about great kinges and princes. And I can easely perswade with my self that yt was so indede, for another affyrmed to me, not this man that I spake of, but one that for his holy lyfe God vouchsafed to reveale unto hym that those persons that in ther extremes do receyve and take this holy mistery with a pure and clene conscyence, at the passing oute of this worlde the angels, after the manour / as those that have many souldiours about them, bring ther soulys to heavyn, for the receyvyng of so worthy and holy a sacrament. This is tolde by the great clerk S. Jhon Crisostome.

(margin: 12v, 13r)

<4> Saynt Austen in the 22 boke *de civitate Dei*, the 8 chapiter, tellith this that folowith.[31]

Ther is with us a tribune whose name is Hesperius. The sayd tribune had a certayne territory in Fusilens callid Cubedy, in whiche place as well he hymself as his servauntes and his cattell were often infestyd with evill spirittes. He being so vexed prayed one of our preistes, I being absent, to come thither, that by his praiers the cursyd spirittes might be dryven away. One of ours went thither, and offring ther in sacrifyce the body of Christ, prayed to Crist that the vexatyon might cease, and by Goddes mercy according to his prayer the plage ceasyd. This declareth the great doctour Saynte Austyne.

<5> This that folowith tellith the holy blessyd S. Gregory, the fyrst of that name. /[32]

13v Ther is many of you, saith S. Gregory, that knowith what folowyd of that which I wyll tell of to bring yt againe to remembraunce, for as moch as yt is not long distaunt from our tyme when it was done. Thus yt is that a certayne man taken with enemies was carried into a straung contrey and put in prison and iron bandes. His wyfe wenyng none other but that he had ben dead, made to be done and sayde for hym the holy oblatyon wekely for his absolution. And yt was not long after or that he gotte out of prison and came home to his wife, and greatly mervailing tolde his wife what happenyd unto hym, which was that every sondry weke at a certaine houre his irons fyll from hym. Which when his wife heard, marking the tyme and the houres, then she knewe that at that houre that the holy hoost was offred for hym then present he was loosed from his bondes. Remember therfore good brethren, sayeth S. Gregory, with a wise consyderatyon and call to your mynde how moche this holy sacrifice may unbynde the hardnes fol. 14r of our hartes, that being offred for another might unbinde / the bondes of his body tyed in iron.

<6> Another wonderfull tale tolde by the sayde S. Gregorye.[33]

Many of you, sayd he, knew Cassius of Narvensius, who had a custome dayly to offerre this holy sacrifyce in such wise that ther passid not one day while he lyved, but that he offred to almighty God the holy hoost of placatyon. And his life and conversatyon was well concordaunt with his sacrifyce, for he gave all that he had to the pore people. And when he came unto that houre that he offred that holy sacrifice, as one washyd all with teares with a great contrytyon of hart he sayd his masse. Whose lyfe in this world and whose passing out of this world I knewe it by a venerable deacon of his that tolde it me sayeng, upon a certaine night our lorde appearyd to a preist of his, sayeng to him 'go and tell the bishop that he do as he doth, and that he worke as he workith. Let not thy fote cease nor let not thy hande cease; upon the apostels day thou shalt fol. 14v come unto me and I shall gyve the thy reward.' / The preist arose and because the feast of the apostles was at hande, he was afrayd to tell yt to the bishop. Another night our lorde came to the preist and moche blamyd his disobedyence, charging him to say to the bishop as he hadd sayd before. The preist then arose for to go, but againe his feable weake hart made hym afrayde to go, so that he did neglect to tell the bishop as he was commaundid by God. But for bicause that a great suffraunce and pacyence of God asketh the more punishment, at the thyrd warnyng he was sore beaten in such a sharpe wise that the hardness of his hart was mollifyed with the suffring of the payne of his beating. He arose therfore and went to the bishop, and founde hym as his custome was, to be ready to do his sacrifyce at the tombe of S. Juvenall the martyr, and desyring to speke with the bishop, falling downe at his fete, weping and sobbing in such wise that he could not tell his tale tyll the bishop lifted hym up, demaunding of hym what the matter was. At the last he declaryd unto hym what he was commaundyd by God to say to hym. The bishoppe fol. 15r hearing yt, geving God thankes, and the feast / day come of the Apostells, sayd his masse, and after masse, touchyd with a lent fever layde hym downe upon his bedde, and calling his brethren togither, exhorting them to peace and concorde, even in so teaching them, sodenly with a terrible voice he cryed, 'the houre is come', and so taking a clothe, as the use is, to cover the faces of such as lye on dieng, he knellyng the sayd cloth about his face with his owne proper handes, even so departyd that blessid soull to God. And this wryteth S. Gregory.

<7> A wonderfull myracle shewyd in Almaine unto those that beyng upon a brydge dauncyng, and seing a preist passing by them with the blissed sacrament to a sycke man, they doing no reverence to it, how they were punyshed.[34]

Ther is in Germany in the lowe or base Almayne a cytye callyd Mastrick, the which stondyth upon a ryver callyd the Mase. Ther ys over the sayde ryver a fayre brydge, the which I myself fol. 15v have twise passed it.[35] Yt so / chaunced that in the emperour Radulphus tyme this straung thing happenyd ther, which is: In the sayd emperours daies yt fortuned that ther were a great nomber of men and women, dauncyng and caroling upon the sayd bridge, and as they so were, a preist with his clerk, as the custome is, caryed the blissed sacrament with hym to minister yt to one that lay sick on the other syde. They, seing the preist so goyng with the blissed sacrament, did no reverence to yt at all, but daunced and carolyd still and so let the preist passe. It folowid that the preist and his clerk were no soner gone over the bridge but that sodenly the brydge brake and more then two hundred persons of one and other that were stonding upon the sayd brydge were drownyd. This tellith all the Germaynes stories, which is suerly a fearefull tale to heare. And I pray Crist that these ungodly sacramenters may marke yt well.

<8> But this that folowith next ys a more wonderfull myracle.[36]

16r It chauncyd in the tyme of the thyrd Henry / Emperour of Rome a mervaylous thing done, not afore hard of the like. In the contrey of Saxum in the diocesse of Maydeborough ther was in a village a parysh church halowed in the honour of S. Magnus. The preist or curate of the sayd church upon the even of the natyvitye of our Saviour Jesu Christ was at his masse, and ther was in the churchyarde 18 men and 18 women dauncyng in the said churchyarde. The preist being troubled at masse with the noise that they made, sent to them, praieng them to cease ther dauncyng, and come to heare the devine service or els chargyd them to go ther waye. But they, mocking and scornynge the preist, lefte not ther pastyme but dauncyd still. The preist vexid therwith prayed to God and to S. Magnus that they might styll to daunce tyll that day twelvemoneth came agayne. A mervaylous thing, they, as he prayed, that hole yeare without ceasyng dauncyd and plaied still and ther fyll not on them neither dewe nor rayne, nor they were not weryed, neither eate nor dronke, nor ther garmentes that they had on them, nor ther shoes 16v were neither broken nor torne. The yeare passyd. Hubertus, who then was / archbishop ther, in whose diocesse this wonder chauncyd, commyng thither, assoyled them of the bonde that the preist had bound them in and reconsyled them before the high aulter. Thre or foure of them incontynent upon ther absolution departyd this worlde, certayne of them slept incontynent thre dayes and thre nightes and never dronke, and not long after dyvers of them dyed and those that lyved either they had the palsey or trembling of ther membres or such lyke diseases. This storye Hubertus, that was one of them, left in his writing for a perpetuall remembraunce.

<9> Of the grace that God gave to S. Clare to chase away by the vertue of the holy sacrament of the aulter the Sarasyns that wolde have spoyled and destroyed her monastery.[37]

Saynt Clare, a mervaylous holy virgin and borne of an honorable parentage, was disciple to 17r S. Frauncis and she lyved many yeares in relygion in a colledge of her foundation / callyd the colledge of povertye, leading continually a vertuous life, in prayers, fasting, and doing good workes. In her tyme the church was sore troubled by Frederick then emperour, by the warres that he made against the pope. And she being at Assyce wher S. Frauncys is buried, Frederick having dyvers Sarasyns to his men of warre, they came wher as thys good lady was, in purpose to have spoiled her monastery, and had spoiled yt indede, but that this blissed Clare toke the pixe in her hand wher the holy sacrament lay, and albeit that she was then very olde, she went to the place wher they wolde have entryd, sayeng, 'my God is it thy pleasure, oh good Jesu, thus to delyver thy handmayde into the infydells handes. Kepe us, oh Jhesu, and defende us and suffer them not so to do'. She had no soner this worde spoken, but that a voyce semyd to speake to her sayeng, 'I have ever kept you, and will ever defende you.' And sodenly yt folowyd that the Sarasyns that were scaling the walles for feare fledd away. This ys not only tolde in her legend in *Cronica* 17v *cronicorum* and in many places of her life,[38] but also yt is alowyd by many gret auctours / and her miracles approvid by the sea apostolyck.

10> A miracle declaryd by the Venerable holy preist S. Bede[39]

Saynt Bede, who wrote the stories *de gestis anglorum*, in whose tyme ther were dyvers kinges raignyng in this realme, as in Essex, in Norfolk, in Kent, in Northumberlande, and in Lyncolneshire, then callyd Marcia, tellith that ther was a grevous battaile foughten betwixt Etheldred king of Marcia and Elgfrydus king of Northumberlande, in which batayle Egwinus the brother of Elgfridus was slayne, a yong man deare and wel belovyd in both twaine provinces. And the battayle was fought nighe to the ryver of Trent, for whose death at the instaunce of the archbyshop Theodorus, and certayne money gyven for that yong gentilmans death ther was concludyd a peace betwixt the two princes. But in that conflyct ther was one of the saide Egwinus knightes that was forewounded and, as he wolde have savid his lyfe, was taken prisoner, which 18r being suspect to be some great gentylman, was solde / from one to another, tyll at the last he came into the handes of one of Fryselande, who kept hym very straightly in iron bandes, and threte hym if he tolde hym not what he was, he wolde sle hym. Nowe this gentylman had a cosin that was a relygious man, who being a preist sayde ofte masse of requiem for hym, as supposing none other but he had ben dead, but when this preist his cosyn so dyd, alwaies his yrons fyll from hym to the great wonder of hym that had hym prisoner, to whom at the last he confessyng what he was, and paieng his raunsome, knewe perfytely at that houre that the preist sayd masse for hym, the irons loosed from hym. This the Venerable Bede tellith.

<11> A wonderous storie of King Edwarde the Confessour and Leofricus the erle, that sawe Jesu Cryst our Savyour betwene the preistes handes at the elevation tyme.[40]

It is tolde of the good king Edwarde the Confessour that, being at his masse at Westmynster, having very neare to his person the / fol. 18v noble earle Leofricus, a lord vertuous and of gret fame, that the houre that the preist offred on the aultar the sonne unto the father almighty, the sayd earle, who knelyd not farre from the king, sawe betwixt the preistes handes our Sauiour Christ in forme of a child, blessing the kynge. The earle seyng so swete a sight, removyd from his place, thinking that the good kynge had not sene that which he dyd se. The prynce, perceyving hym, turnyd toward hym and sayde, 'stande, I bydde the stande, and suffer and abide for hym that thou visybly doest se, visybly do I honour hym and worship hym.'

<12> A mervailous miracle shewyd by the holy sacrament to the great clerk Hugo de Sancto Victore at his departing out of this worlde.

Hugo de Sancto Victore was a Frenchman borne and, as many affyrme, a chanon reguler. This sayd Hugh, which was in his flowers in the yeare of grace a thousand and a hundred, was of such erudityon and lernyng that he was countyd the greatest clerke of / fol. 19r all the universitye of Parris. And he wrote dyvers excellent workes, which the devines at this present day do greatly alowe in ther sermons, and among other his notable workes, he wrote one boke of the sevin sacramentes of the church, and dyvers godly sermons. At the last, being syck and approching very neare to his death, he desyred to have the blyssed sacrament to be brought unto hym and, for bycause that by the weaknes of his stomack he coulde not kepe nothing within hym, for the reverence of the sacrament he wolde not recyve it, but sayd these wordes folowing: 'Let my Lord', sayde he, 'and my savyour ascende up into hevin, and my spiryte go to hym that creatyd it'. And sayeng these wordes the hoost vanished away and the gret clerk and good saynt expired. This is tolde by many famous clerkes and therfore worthy to be belevyd.[41]

<13> A wonderfull tale that a gentylman that was servaunt with your gracyous great grandame, my most noble maystres, dyd oftentymes tell as well unto her grace / fol. 19v as to us that were her servauntes.[42]

This sayd gentylman was named Bygott[43] and was carver to your sayd noble gret grandame, and in that offyce I thinke he had no felowe within this realme. He had ben afore in that service with Quene Anne that was King Richardes wife and after her death servid the sayd King Richerd so truly that unethes he myght abyde that any man shulde despraise him. Which doing your sayd good great grandame toke so well that she wolde often say to us, he being absent, that Bygott was worthy to be praysed, that once having a master and sworne unto hym, as he was to King Richerd, to be ever more so true a servaunt to hym. For he was hurt with hym at the fylde and lykely to have ben slayne and if that noble prince Kynge Henry the Seventh your graunfather had taken hym in that heate he shuld have suffred for it. But God gevyng victory to the king your grauntfather, and King Richarde slayne by the verye devine punishment of God, Bigott sayd that Kyng Richard callyd in the mornyng for to have had masse sayd before hym, but when his chap- / fol. 20r pelyns had one thing ready, ever more they wanted another. When they had wyne they lacked breade, and ever one thing was myssing. In the meane season King Henry commyng on apace, King Rychard was constrayned to go to the battayle, wher God shewed his puissaunce, that the noble king your grauntfather having but a fewe vanquished hym that had thre men for one, and King Richard, layd upon a horse nakid, was caryed through the felde with shame infynyte. I tell this bycause I thinke God wolde not that same day that he shulde se the blyssed sacrament of the aulter nor heare the holy masse for his horrible offence comytted against his brothers children.[44]

<14> I will folowing this example, most excellent princesse, shewe what reverence that most noble and vertuous great grandame of yours dyd alwayes to the most devine Sacrament and what a fortunate and godlye ende she made, the preist being at masse before her at that present houre. And I humbly praye your gracyous magestie not to thinke that I do / [20v] tell this, as S. Jerome writeth to that noble lady Salvina, after that sorte that the Grekes do, to have the more grace of you in telling an untrue tale – God be my judge such kinde of speche I never usyd to that vertuous person of yours. The love and the truth that I have borne to your highnes from your childhod is a wytnes for me afore God, and your magestie, for the which I have receyvyd of you, my most gracious Lady and maistres, a rewarde more precyous then golde or stone, that is libertye to ende myne olde dayes in quyet. And albeyt that I thinke ther is unethe fyve men and women alyve at this present day that then were about her godly person at that houre, yet my chaunce was ther to be, as one that, unworthy, she so tendrid that wher and to what place her highnes went I was ever one by her speciall comaundement about her person, either in that roume to be her carver or her cuppe bearer. And I do ensure your highnes that doctour Fysher, then bishopp of Rochester, being her ghostly father, shewyd me not long before his death that he had writen her life, which I suppose is in your graces hande.[45] Then if yt so be, oh good Jhesu, how joyous / [21r] wolde yt make me to se and to reade it, writen by so good a man, and so devine a clerk as that bishop was. But breifly I shall declare, as my rude witt is, her godly maners as folowith. Thus did she use her life: her grace was every mornyng in the chapple betwixt sixe and sevyn of the clock and dayly sayde matyns of the day with one of her chaplyns. And that sayde, from sevyn tyll yt was eleven of the clocke, as sone as one preist had sayd masse in her syght, another beganne.[46] One tyme in a day she was confessyd,[47] then going to her dynner how honorably she was servyd, I think fewe kinges better. Her condityon alwaies at the begynnyng of her dyner was to be joyous and to heare those tales that were honest to make her mery, the myddes of her dynner either her amner or I redde some vertuous tale unto her of the life of Chryst or such like, the latter ende of her dinner agayne she was disposed to talk with the bishop or with her chauncelour, which satt at her bordis ende, of some godly matter. And her grace wolde often say at her table, when she heard that the Great Turke prevayled so against the Crysten men, she wolde wyshe / [21v] that she were a launder to them that shoulde go against them.[48] In Cristmas tyme she kept so honorable a house that, upon one Newe Yeares Day, I being her sewer of the age of fyftene yeares had fyve and twentye knightes folowing me, of whom myne owne father was one, and syttyng at her table the erle of Derby her husband, the Vicount Wellys, the olde Lord Hastinges, the byshoppe of Lincolne, and by her person under her clothe of estate the Lady Cecyle, King Edwardes doughter, your aunte.[49] In her hall, from nyne of the clock tyll it was sevyn of the clock at night, as fast as one table was up another was sett. No pore man was denayed at that sayde feast of Cristmas if he were of any honestye, but that he might come to the buttrye or to the cellar to drinke att his pleasure. Her liberalytie was such that ther came no man of honour or worship to her, as ther came many of the greatest of the realme, but that they were well rewardyd. I sawe myself the Duke of Buckingham came to her unto Collyweston, to whom she gave a jewell to the value of one hundred pounde.[50] Yf it were an erle his reward was no lesse then fortye poundes, yf yt were a baron and his wife his rewarde and / [22r] hers was twenty poundes. To the ladies and gentylwomen that came to do ther duetye to her, she usyd such humanitye that never princes coulde do more.[51] And although that she had in her cheker roule contynually two and twenty score of ladies, gentylmen, yeomen, and offycers, yet it ys a wonder to tell, ther was neither man nor woman, if thei were of any reputatyon, but she coulde call them by ther names.[52] In that kynde of remembraunce I thinke she might have ben comparyd unto Methridatus, kinge of Pontho. Ther were none of her sayd servauntes, but if he were syck or in perell of his life, if her phisicions did not forbydde her, she wolde in person visite hym, having no mo with her but one cheife gentylwoman, and one gentylman usher before her. And as he was in degre so she wolde rewarde

hym, geving hym good instructyons not to trust to the worlde but only to put his mynde to God, if he died she wolde herself see hym buryed.[53] She kept her chapple egall with the king her sonne. She buylt two colledges in Cambridge, that is Cristes College and S. Jones College,[54] and was of (fol. 22v) such a benygne nature that never man went from her hevy nor / sadde, wherby she might well be comparyd unto Titus Vaspasianus. Wylliam of Malmesbury, that wrote the lyves of the kinges and quenes that were before the Conquest, prayseth moch Elfleda, the noble quene, for her vertue and for her magnanymytie,[55] and Mawde, that was the wife of King Henry the Fyrst, was likewise commendid of all writers, and among all other one indited these versys in her laude:

Prospera non letam fecerunt, nec aspera tristem,
Aspera risus ei, prospera terror erat.
Nec decor effecit fragilem, nec sceptra superbam.
Sola potens humilis, sola pudica decens.[56]

So was your Grandame, for neither prosperitye made her proude, nor adversytye overthrewe her constant mynde, for albeyt that in King Richardes daies she was often in jeoperdy of her lyfe, yet she bare paciently all trouble in such wyse that it ys wonder to thinke it. And in that she was like to Seneca or Socrates. But what shuld I more say, yf I had Demosthenes eloquence or Tullius or Lactantius fayre style, I could not suffyciently laude nor commende her high vertues and her honor. But as I tolde before, and as the grete doctour S. Jerome writeth of Salvina for the death (fol. 23r) of her / husband Nebrodius,[57] this redolent floure, this precious margaryte, is past from this worlde, not as other floures be that today be fayre, and tomorowe withered and drye, but this our fayre floure as long as the sea hath fyshes, and the skye twinkling starres, untyll the sounde of the last trompet shall call all creatures to Judgment, her fame, her honour, her liberalitye, her prudence, her chastytye, and her excellent vertues shall be commendyd for ever.

Now breifly to shewe your magestye of her death, which renueth my sorowe to lose so gracyous a miastres, and to revert to shewe your highnes of her devotion to the sacrament, ther was not one day escaped her but that she offred to the sacrament, and every night or she went to her rest she sayde her prayers afore the devine sacrament[58] and upon high dayes went downe solempnely to her chapell with great honour. And to conclude, your wise prudent grauntfather King Henry the Seventh being deade, upon S. John Baptystes day she sawe the coronatyon of the worthy prynce your father in a place apointyd on the right syde of Westminster Hall. And that (fol. 23v) day I / being her cupbearer and a gentilman callyd Hyuyngham being her carver,[59] it is thought she toke her infyrmyte with eating of a cignet, and so being syck untyll S. Peters day in the mornyng, calling her ghostly father, being shryven and receyving the blyssed sacrament of the aulter, the bishop sayd masse before her and as he lifte up the precyous hoost this worthy lady expyred.[60] And so as she had honoured the blissyd sacrament, even so the laste thing that ever she sawe, as I do thinke, was God in his essence and ys now joyfull in that celestiall court of heaven wher she shall be in eternall felycytie for ever.[61]

<15> I shall breifly conclude with a wonderous tale to your hyghnes tolde by a great clerke of the order of S. Frauncis named Bernardus de Busto, of a clerke that prechyd that the blissed Virgyn Mary was borne in origynall synne, approvyd to be true by Sextus the fourth, that was pope of Rome[62]

In the tyme of Martyn the fyfth, of thatt name pope of Rome, ther was at Tholouse a doctour that preched that he durst affyrme /

NOTES

1 Philip ascended to the Spanish throne in January 1556: the Account must therefore have been completed after her marriage to Philip in 1554 but before January 1556, since Mary is 'Pryncesse' of Spain. On further details of dating see above, p. 45.

2 Claudian, *Panegyricus de quartu consulatu Honorii Augusti*, ll. 299-300: '... Componitur orbis / Regis ad exemplum' (ed. by J. B. Hall, Teubner [1985], p. 72).
3 Virgil, *Aeneid*, II.12.
4 i.e. Essenes.
5 Eusebius of Caesarea, *Historia ecclesiastica*, trans. by Rufinus: pr. *PL* 21.465-540.
6 i.e. Montanistes.
7 Hartmann Schedel, *Liber cronicarum* (Nuremberg, 1493), fol. CXXIX[r] has: 'Eam [Christian faith] ita complexus est ut iturus ad bellum: non alio quam crucis signo uteretur: quod sereno celo dum in Maxentium tyrannum copias movet: & viderat & adoraverat. Astantesque angelos audierat dicentes. Constantine: in hoc signo vinces. Quod etiam fecit & tyrannos omnes a cervicibus populi ro[mani] Christianorumque omnium depulit.'
8 Schedel, *Liber cronicarum*, fol. CCLXXIIII[v] gives a detailed account of the fall of Constantinople, but Morley may well have had another source: Schedel did not state that the conquering sultan raped the empress in Santa Sophia.
9 For Athanasius and the 'Quicunque vult salvus esse' see Schedel, *Liber cronicarum*, fol. CXXXI[r].
10 On Eraclius and his Monothelitism see Schedel, *Liber cronicarum*, fol. CLI[r].
11 On Radagasus see Schedel, *Liber cronicarum*, fol. CXXXV[v]. Morley manipulates his source here, as Schedel's report has the pagans of Rome blaming the disaster on the neglect of the traditional deities.
12 On Alaric see Schedel, *Liber cronicarum*, fol. CXXXV[v]: 'Hac tamen moderatione usus est Alaricus & clementia ut suis mandaverit: a cede & sanguine quoad fieri poterat abstinere. Utve confugientibus ad basilicas Petri & Pauli parceretur.'
13 On Attila see Schedel, *Liber cronicarum*, fol. CXXXVII[v]: 'inde movens Paduam: Vincentium: Veronam: Mediolanum: Ticinum que Papia dicitur cepit. Romani tunc & ceteri Italie populi Athilam qui se flagellum dei: terroremque populorum diceret. Ac re ipsa ostenderet: horrendo pavore expectabant. Quod cum Leo Pontifex Romanus eius nominis primus cernerit mestus compatiensque populis. Atque etiam cohortante Valentiniano legationem ad eum suscepit: quem reperit apud Minthium castra habentem. Facundus Pontifex orando mollivit: effecitque ut omissa Italia ad propria redire regna promiserit. Que res omnem execitum [i.e. exercitum] in admirationem adduxit. Sciscitantibus vero causa respondisse Athilam fama est. Non se presulis adductum oratione id fecisse: sed magis duorum qui strictos tenentes gladios astabant. Necem sibi ac exercitui comminantes. Et hi Petrus & Paulus fuisse creduntur. Igitur Athila tali modo a sua sevicia repressus: relicta Italia Pannonias repetit.'
14 Schedel, *Liber cronicarum*, fol. CXXXVII[v] provides the material on Genseric himself, but Morley must derive his material on Augustine from elsewhere.
15 The last king of the Goths was in fact Rodrigo, but he is here conflated with Theodoric II, who had ruled both Spain and Italy, vigorously promoted Arianism, and had Boethius put to death. The conflation is probably Morley's own, as he makes similar errors elsewhere in this text. One Latin form of Rodrigo was 'Rhodoricus', which is close to 'Theodoricus'. It has not proved possible to identify Morley's source. Neither Schedel nor the *Polychronicon* contains this information. The Spanish chronicle tradition, in describing Rodrigo's defeat by the Moors, usually states that his fate was unknown, but that his belongings were found abandoned beside a river. See, for example, the various accounts found in *Rerum Hispanicarum Scriptores*, ed. by R. Belus (Frankfurt, 1579).
16 Morley's words 'Ther cronycle' suggest that he is referring to a Spanish chronicle. However, there were many of them, and it has proved impossible to identify his specific source. His narrative here, though, bears certain similarities to the chronicle of Ferdinand and Isabella compiled by the Spanish humanist Antonio de Nebrija: 'Hos Roderico ultimo Gothorum rege fugarunt, atque Hispaniarum possessione spoliavere Poeni Maurique, qui totam fere aut magna ex parte per annos circiter septingenta quinquaginta tenuere, quoad nostra aetate ductu atque auspiciis optimorum Principum Ferdinandi & Elisabes pulsi sunt, atque Hispania tota sibi ipsi restituta est.' See Nebrija's *Rerum a Ferdinando et Elisabe Hispaniaru Felicissmis Regibus Gestarum, Decades Duae*, in *Rerum Hispanicarum Scriptores*, pp. 1077-8. But Nebrija's work was itself highly derivative, and there is no particular reason to think that Morley used it. He might equally easily have derived a similar idea from, for example, Raphael Volaterranus, *Commentariorum Urbanorum Raphaelis Volaterrani, Octo & Triginta Libri* (Basel, 1530), fol. 12[r], where Ferdinand is praised in the following terms: 'qui limites imperii, gloriaeque Hispaniae propagaverit, & gentem Saracenicam quae Granatae regnum, Beticae partem, annis iam prope DCC occupaverat, suis armis ac virtute anno MCCCCXCII penitus expulit'.

17 Polydore Vergil, *Anglicae Historiae* (Basel, 1534), p. 56, mentions in close proximity both Pelagius and one Palladius, a bishop sent to a Scottish king named Constantine. This seems to explain both Morley's curious form of 'Pelladian' for the name of the heretic, and his still more curious claim that Pelagius lived in the age of Emperor Constantine. As so often in this treatise, he is conflating different men of the same or similar names. On p. 58 Polydore Vergil went out of his way to distinguish the Scottish Constantine from the Emperor, so Morley is obviously not reading carefully or thoroughly. Morley's list of other British kings may also derive from Vergil, pp. 20-4 (Bren and Balin) and 55-7 (Uther Pendragon and Aurelius Ambrose).

18 The mythical story of Lucius was commonplace in the British chronicle tradition from Bede onwards, and Morley would probably not have drawn on a particular source but on his general knowledge. However, his suggestion that Lucius was christened at Rome, although admirably suited to his polemical purpose, is not, to the knowledge of either of the editors, found in the British chronicle tradition. Morley may be making it up, or else conflating Lucius with somebody else. Many chronicles anticipate Morley's description of Lucius as the first Christian king,but the editors have been unable to find earlier instances (although there probably are some) of the use of this fact by the English monarchs to dispute the French monarchs' right to the title 'Most Christian King'.

19 Morley's general idea here, that the Saxon conquest was a providential judgement on the Pelagian heresy, may well derive from the fact that the two things are mentioned in close proximity by Vergil, *Anglicae Historiae*, p. 56.

20 Ranulf Higden, *Polychronicon*. Although there is a modern edition we quote from the version with additions known to Morley: *Polycronycon* (Southwark [Peter Treueris for John Reynes], 1527). The material on Wyclif is found in Caxton's continuation, Liber ultimus (i.e. 8), cap. 8, fol. CCCXXIII^{r}: 'Aboute this tyme was that cursed heresye of Johan Wyclyfe in Engelonde. And Johan Hus in Bohemye / and Jherom of Praghe / whiche heresye enfected moche people. And under the habyte of a lambe hydynge woluysshe crueltee hadde purposed to subverte all the state of the chyrche.' The implication that Huss and Jerome studied under Wyclif at Oxford is not found in the *Polychronicon*, but may perhaps be derived from Aeneas Sylvius Piccolomini (Pope Pius II), *Bohemicae Historiae Papae Pii Libri V* (Venice, 1503), sig. gg.iii^{v}-iiii^{r}, which has Huss studying at Oxford.

21 Morley seems here to be finding precedent for the suppression of heresy that formed part of Mary's policy.

22 Piccolomini's history was probably the most widely available account of Bohemia, and is therefore the most likely source for Morley's account of John Zizka. See *Bohemicae Historiae Papae Pii Libri V*, sig. ii.1^{v}: 'Recens obierat Venceslaus: cum Johannes Cisca genere nobilis ex loco cui Trosnovia nomen est: censu tenui: in curia regis a puero enutritus: & bellis exercitatus uno carens oculo: quem strenue pugnans iampridem amiserat: infectus Hussitarum veneno & rapinarum auidus collecta perditorum hominum multitudine: in ecclesias quae restaverant impetum fecit. Simulacra sanctorum & imagines magni Dei perfregit. Monasterium Cartusiensium Pragae vicinum invasit: & direptum incendit. Monachos eius ordinis tanquam populo inutiles: qui veluti sues in claustro saginarentur: migrare alio iussit.' This account is substantially the same as Morley's, and the differences look like little more than embroidery.

23 Morley left on a mission with Edward Lee, Sir William Hussey, and Sir Thomas Wriothesley to convey the Order of the Garter to Ferdinand, Archduke of Austria late in the summer of 1523. They reached Antwerp on 20 September, were in Cologne in early October, and had arrived in Nurenberg by mid November where the Order was presented on 8 December. By 3 February 1524 the party was back at Calais. Four of Morley's letters chronicling the trip survive, one to Henry VIII and three to Wolsey; for discussion and excerpts see *Forty-six Lives*, ed. by Wright, pp. xv-xviii.

24 Presumably a reference to *L'Alcorano di Macometto* (Venice, 1547).

25 This is no doubt an allusion to the extremely debased state to which the coinage had been reduced, largely thanks to the extravagant military expenditures of Edward VI's regime. The coinage was not returned to a sound metallic basis until the early years of Queen Elizabeth's reign.

26 Reginald Pole (1500-58), created cardinal in 1536, archbishop of Canterbury in 1556.

27 The slogan of 'mother church' was particularly favoured among English Catholics in the sixteenth century, especially in the reign of Mary, when the theme of England's return to the bosom of mother church was sounded in endless variations. One of the fullest explorations is found in John Proctor's preface to his translation of Vincent of Lerins, published as *The waie home to Christ and truth leadinge from Antichrist and errour* (London, 1554). See for example sig. A.v^{r}: 'Thys waye to Christe, this meane

to truth, is by a generall name called, *Ecclesia catholica*, the catholyke Churche: which is our mother, & we her children.' His whole preface is in effect an oration in praise of mother church.

28 Cyprian, *De lapsis*, ed. by M. Bévenot, *CCSL* 3 (1972), pp. 217-42 (pp. 224-5). The Latin text on which Morley's paraphrase is based is also found in John Fisher's *De veritate corporis et sanguinis Christi in eucharistia* (Cologne: Quentell, 1527; folio edition), fol. 59v. (See also Fisher's *Opera omnia* (Würzburg, 1597), p. 921: 'Consequenter subdit & aliud miraculum, de altera quae fuerat aetate provecta, & in annis adultioribus constituta. Haec (inquit) sacrificantibus latenter obrepsit, non cibum, sed gladium sibi sumens, & velut quaedam venena lethalia intra fauces & pectus admittens angi, & anima exaestuante concludi postmodum cepit. Et pressuram non jam persecutionis, sed delicti sui passa palpitans & tremens concidit. Impunitum diu non fuit, nec occultum dissimulatae conscientiae crimen, quae fefellerat hominem, Deum sensit ultorem.')

29 Cyprian, *De lapsis*, ed. by Bévenot, p. 225. See also Fisher, *De veritate*, fol. 59v (*Opera omnia*, p. 921): 'Et quum quaedam arcam suam, in qua Domini sanctum fuerat, manibus indignis tentasset aperire, igne inde surgente deterrita est, ne auderet contingere.'

30 John Chrysostom, *De sacerdotio*, tr. by Annianus, VI.4: pr. PG 48. 668. Fisher refers to this story in *De veritate*, fol. 60v (*Opera omnia*, p. 923). However, Morley gives one sentence more from Chrysostom than does Fisher; and Fisher changes the order of the original, whereas Morley cites in the original order, and without breaks. The *Dialogi* of Chrysostom were widely printed in Latin (Cologne *c.* 1470 &c), so if Morley took Fisher's *De veritate* as his starting-point, he must also have consulted the text itself.

31 Fisher (*De veritate*, fol. 59v (*Opera omnia*, pp. 921-2) quotes directly from Augustine (*De ciuitate Dei*, ed. by B. Dombart & A. Kalb (*CCSL* 47-8; 1955), II.820) and gives the form Cubedi.

32 Gregory, *Dialogi*, IV.59, ed. by A. de Vogüe, Schr 251, 260, 265 (1978-80), III.196-200.

33 Idem. IV.58, ed. by Vogüe, III.194-6.

34 Schedel, *Liber cronicarum*, fol. CCXVIIr: 'Cum in trajecto homines utriusque sexus super pontem coreis ac vanitatibus operam darent. Contigit sacerdotem cum divinissimo sacramento eucharistie ad egrotantem deferendum pertransire. Illi immemores divine rei cultum vullum ac reverentiam adhibentes. ponte fracto in aqua Mose. ad 200. homines aquis absorpti sunt atque perierunt.'

35 i.e. during his Garter mission.

36 Schedel, *Liber cronicarum*, fol. CLXXXVIIv: 'Contigit temporibus Heinrici imperatoris mirabile prius inauditum. Cum in villa quadam saxonie in Madeburgensi diocesi. ubi erat ecclesia sancti magni quidam sacerdos missam celebraret in vigilia natiuitatis domini. decem & octo viri [sil'] cum .xv. mulieribus in cimiterio ecclesie ubi celebrabat. choreas ducendo alta voce cantarent. sacerdotemque ipsum celebrantem impediebant. Mandat illis sacerdos. ut tacerent aut inde recederent qui sacerdotis verba deridentes. desistere noluerunt. Is amaricatus imprecando inquit. Placeat Deo & sancto Magno ut ita cantantes permaneatis usque ad annum corisantes. Et ita factum est ut toto illo anno sine intermissione aliqua. corisando cantarent. Mirabile dictu toto illo tempore nec ros nec pluvia super illos cecidit. Sed nec lassitudo nec fames illos affecit. nec vestimenta nec calciamenta eorum toto illo tempore attrita sunt. Anno autem revoluto Horebertus archiepiscopus in cuius dyocesi hoc mirabile contigit ad locum veniens a nodo quo sacerdos illos ligaverat. absoluit atque ante altare dicte ecclesie reconciliavit. filia presbyteri cum duobus aliis continuo exanimata est. ceteri continuis tribus noctibus proximis dormierunt aliqui postea obierunt. Ceteri vero penam suam membrorum tremore prodierunt. Hoc scriptum reliquit Ubertus qui fuit unus ex eis.'

37 The story as Morley gives it is a very close translation of the story given in Schedel's *Liber cronicarum*, fol. CCXr: 'Cum sub imperatore Friderico quassata esset ecclesia. Et in assisium hostilis furor irrueret. Et sarracenorum gens apud Damianum Sanctum. intra claustrum virginum influerent. Clara infirma ad hostium agmen se duci iubet. Et ante hostes poni precedente ea capsula argentea in qua erat sacramentum eucharistie. & in oratione cum lacrimis ait placet mi domine inermes ancillas tuas manibus tradi paganorum? Custodi famulas tuas illico ad aures eius intonuit. Ego vos semper custodiam. Et mox qui muros ascenderant. obsidionem derelinquunt.'

38 The story is also told in the *Golden Legend* (London: Wynkyn de Worde, 1527), 'The lyfe of saynt Clare', fols CCCVIIIr-CCCXVIr, at fol. CCCIXv.

39 Bede, *Historia ecclesiastica gentis Anglorum*, IV. 21-2, ed. by B. Colgrave & R. A. B. Mynors, Oxford Medieval Texts (1969), pp. 401-5. Fisher also tells this story (*De veritate*, fol. 59v; *Opera omnia*, p. 922) though much more briefly and without giving any names, and with only a vague reference to Bede.

40 Fisher specifically refers to Edward the Confessor in a list of some saints in whose lives eucharistic

miracles were recorded (*De veritate*, fol. 60[r]; *Opera omnia*, p. 923). But the story would doubtless have been familiar to an English reader. It can be found, for example, in the *Golden Legend*, 'The lyfe of saynt Edwarde kynge', fols CCLXXI[v]-CCLXXXII[r], at fol. CCLXXVI[r], where the story of Leofric's vision is told in full. It first appears in Osbert of Clare's Life.

41 Schedel, *Liber cronicarum*, has the following passage at the end of its account of Hugh of St Victor, fol. CC[r]: 'Infirmatus ad mortem cum vicio stomachi ob vomitum laboraret ne sacramento irreverentiam faceret: ait. Ascendat filius ad patrum suum. & servus ad dominum suum qui fecit illum. Et eucharistia disparuit. Et vir sanctus deo suo spiritum reddidit.'

42 For a discussion of the Lady Margaret materials see R. M. Warnicke, 'The Lady Margaret, Countess of Richmond (d. 1509), as seen by Bishop Fisher and by Lord Morley', *Moreana*, 19 (1982), 47-55. For the account of Richard III see id. 'Lord Morley's Statements about Richard III', *Albion*, 15 (1983), 173-8.

43 Sir Ralph Bigod: see M. K. Jones & M. G. Underwood, *The King's Mother: Lady Margaret Beaufort, Countess of Richmond and Derby* (Cambridge, 1992), pp. 34, 68, 179-80.

44 Warnicke, 'Lord Morley's Statements', p. 178, considers this statement 'evidence that even those contemporaries who had daily contact with and remained friendly to the loyal servants of Richard III genuinely believed him guilty of a "horrible offence" against his nephews'. She also suggests (p. 177) that Richard's failure to hear mass on the day of his death is made to contrast rhetorically with Lady Margaret's own saintly experience at her last hour.

45 It might be thought that Morley is referring to Fisher's memorial sermon for Lady Margaret, published as *A mornynge remembraunce had at the moneth mynde of the noble prynces Margarete countesse of Rychemonde & Darbye* (London: Wynkyn de Worde, 1509), and now most conveniently available in *The English Works of John Fisher*, ed. by J. E. B. Mayor (EETS, ES 27; London, 1876), pp. 289-310. For the sermon contains a good deal of biographical material. However, Morley was serving as her cup-bearer when she fell ill and died, and so must have long known about Fisher's memorial sermon, and indeed probably owned a copy, for some of the details he gives here seem to be drawn from that source. The document about which Fisher 'not long before his death' informed Morley must therefore have been a proper biography, or, to be precise, a hagiography. There seems every reason to suppose that Fisher would have sought to promote the cause of Lady Margaret's canonisation. Even his memorial sermon has a distinctly hagiographical tone.

46 Fisher, *Mornynge remembraunce*, in *English Works*, p. 294, has Lady Margaret rising shortly after 5.00 a.m., reciting Our Lady's Matins with one of her gentlewomen, and then proceeding to Matins of the day with a chaplain, followed by four or five masses until dinner time around 10.00 a.m.

47 Fisher, *Mornynge remembraunce*, in *English Works*, p. 295, has her making her confession 'every thyrde daye'.

48 Fisher, *Mornynge remembraunce*, in *English Works*, p. 308, 'She whom I have many tymes herde saye that yf the crysten prynces wolde have warred upon the enmyes of his faith, she wold be glad yet to go folowe the hoost & helpe to wasshe theyr clothes for the love of Jhesu.'

49 Thomas Stanley, Earl of Derby, Lord John Welles, Edward, Lord Hastings, William Smith, bishop of Lichfield and Lincoln, Cecily of York. Concerning this occasion see Jones and Underwood, *The King's Mother*, pp. 158-9.

50 Edward Stafford, Duke of Buckingham (d. 1521).

51 Fisher, *Mornynge remembraunce*, in *English Works*, p. 296, observes that she entertained visitors 'accordynge to theyr degre'.

52 Fisher, *Mornynge remembraunce*, in *English Works*, p. 296, emphasizes her close concern for her household.

53 Fisher, *Mornynge remembraunce*, in *English Works*, p. 297, records that she maintained twelve poor folks in her household, and personally cared for them when they were sick.

54 Fisher, *Mornynge remembraunce*, in *English Works*, p. 308, 'she that buylded a college royall to the honour of the name of Crist Jhesu, & lefte tyll her executours another to be buylded to mayntayn his fayth & dotryne'.

55 See William of Malmesbury, *Gesta regum Anglorum*, ed. by W. Stubbs, 2 vols (Rolls Series 90; London 1887-9), I, 136.

56 *Ps.* Peter of Blois continuation of the Crowland Chronicle, ed. by William Fulman (Oxford, 1684), p. 129. The full text actually runs: 'Prospera non letam fecere, nec aspera tristem, / Aspera risus ei, prospera terror erant. / Nec decor effecit fragilem, nec sceptra superbam. / Sola potens humilis, sola

pudica decens. / Maii primo dies nostrorum nocte dierum / Raptam perpetua fecit inesse die.'

57 Jerome, *Epistola LXXIX* (*ad Saluinam*): pr. *PL* 22. 724-32.

58 Fisher, *Mornynge remembraunce*, in *English Works*, p. 295, recalls that 'at nyght before she wente to bedde she faylled not to resorte unto her chapell'.

59 George Hevenyngham is listed as a member of Lady Margaret's household receiving rewards (£5) in an undated document (probably prepared shortly after her death) found among her executors' papers: see Cambridge, St John's College, Archives D56.131. We thank Malcolm Underwood for this reference.

60 Fisher, *Mornynge remembraunce*, in *English Works*, pp. 308-9, 'dyvers here presente can recorde how hertly she answered whan the holy sacrament contaynynge the blessid Jhesu in it was holden before her, & the questyon made untyl her whether she byleved that there was verayly the Sone of God that suffred his blessyd passyon for her & for all mankynde upon the crosse. ... And so sone after that she was aneled she departed & yelded up her spyryte in to the handes of our lorde.'

61 Fisher, *Mornynge remembraunce*, in *English Works*, p. 309, 'who may not nowe take evydent lyklyhode & conjecture upon this that the soule of this noble woman ... was borne up in to the countre above with the blessyd aungelles deputed & ordeyned to that holy mystery'.

62 The little story of which only the beginning now survives was in fact the sixth reading for the fifth day of the Office of the Immaculate Conception, compiled by the Observant Franciscan Bernardino de Busti and approved by Pope Sixtus IV. This office can be found in Bernardino's *Mariale*, quoted here from the Hagenau edition of 1519. The text of the story (sig. G3^{v}) reads as follows: 'Tempore quo Martinus quintus Romane urbis pontificatum tenebat: quidam theologie magister Tolosani studii rector: determinare ausus est beatam virginem originali fuisse peccato corruptam. qua de re in furore populi de eodem expulsus civitate. Romam veniens: apud summum pontificem de illata sibi iniuria conquestus est: conclusionem suam asserens publica velle disputatione tutari. Audiens autem hoc memoratus antistes: diem fiende disputationis indixit. Collectoque maximo doctorum conventu: cum frater ille non veniret: missus est qui eum nuncius aduocaret. Fratres igitur apud quos gloriose virginis inimicus hospitatus fuerat ad eius cellam pergentes: ipsum mortuum repperiere: interiora ventris non habentem. Sicque beatissima virgo hostis sui argutias debita mulctatione confudit.'

INDEX